OPUS DEI

A HISTORY
(1928–2016)

VOLUME TWO

From the
Second
Vatican
Council
to 2016

José Luis González Gullón
and John F. Coverdale

 Scepter

Published by Scepter Publishers, Inc.
info@scepterpublishers.org
www.scepterpublishers.org
800-322-8773
New York

Text and cover design by Rose Design

Library of Congress Control Number: 2021947549
ISBN: (pbk.) 9781594174520
ISBN: (eBook) 9781594174537

CONTENTS

PART II

THE YEARS OF ESCRIVÁ'S
FIRST SUCCESSOR (1975–1994) / 143

PART III

THE THIRD GENERATION (1994–2016) / 275

PART I

International Consolidation
(1962–1975)

During the 1960s and 1970s, the world continued to be divided by the Cold War into two blocs, led by the United States and the Soviet Union. There were moments of great tension including the construction of the Berlin Wall (1961), the Cuban missile crisis (1962) and the Vietnam War (1955–1975). Despite the hostility between them, the leaders of both blocs were aware that armed conflict between them could lead to an irremediable catastrophe, and they did what was necessary to avoid it.

Important events of the 1960s included the rapid process of decolonization by which thirty-eight countries achieved independence between 1959 and 1965; greater economic integration in Western Europe; and the passage of the 1964 US Civil Rights Act, which prohibited discrimination on the basis of race, sex, or religion.

The United States led the scientific, economic, and cultural development of the West. After two decades of recovery from the Depression and World War II, millions of people had cars, home appliances, and easy access to television, home stereo systems, and tourism. Television became a powerful influence in most people's lives. Both programs and commercials introduced viewers to new modes of thinking and ways of life.

The sixties witnessed unprecedented economic and technological progress, especially in the natural and applied sciences. In 1961, the USSR put a man into space, and eight years later, the United States landed men on the moon.

The sixties were also years of crisis. Many people, especially students, rejected a regulated world that sought economic prosperity as its overriding goal. Their discontent was translated into movements that challenged authority, established ways of life, and legal and moral norms as repressive of personal freedom. Many western intellectuals embraced neo-Marxist and Freudian ideas. Countercultural and disruptive currents exploded in France with the May 1968 protests and soon spread to the United States. The youth rebellion led to widespread public abuse of alcohol and drugs, as well as promiscuous sexual activity. Excesses were justified by reference to a perceived right to self-satisfaction.

In the communist world, the Soviet Union and its allies carried out energetic campaigns of ideological and practical repression. New communist dictatorships were established in Central and South America, Asia, and Africa. Mao Zedong initiated the Cultural Revolution in 1966 to strengthen his power and preserve communism in China. The movement was transformed into a violent class struggle that led to the persecution and execution of millions of people, a massive purge of officials, and huge forced migrations. In Latin America, there was strong interference from both the Cuban Castro regime and the United States. Twelve nations, from Guatemala to Argentina, fell under the control of non-communist military dictatorships.

These years were key for the role of the Church in the modern world. In October 1958, Pius XII died and the cardinals elected John XXIII. At first, his pontificate was thought of as a transitional stage because the new Pope was seventy-six years old. Three months after his election, however, he surprised the world by calling an ecumenical council in which he invited the Church to reflect on its identity in a moment of cultural change.

The Second Vatican Ecumenical Council began in October 1962. There were 2,778 Council fathers, the great majority of whom were diocesan bishops. John XXIII asked them to open the Church to the contemporary world and to seek points of union with other Christians. As a sign of good will, he indicated that, contrary to established practice, the Council would not issue anathemas. Shortly after the opening of the Council, in June 1963, John XXIII died of a tumor. The new Pope, Paul VI, announced that the Council would continue.

The Council Fathers reflected on Revelation, the Church, the roles of bishops, priests, laity, and religious, the liturgy, the ecumenical movement, and dialogue with modern society. They reached an astonishing degree of consensus. At least 95 percent voted in favor of each of the Council documents. Between 1963 and 1965, they approved a constitution on the liturgy (*Sacrosanctum concilium*); two dogmatic constitutions, one on the Church (*Lumen gentium*) and the other on Revelation (*Dei verbum*); a pastoral constitution on the Church in the modern world (*Gaudium et spes*); nine decrees on various topics including the priesthood, the lay apostolate, and the media; and three declarations of which the most important focused on religious freedom (*Dignitatis humanae*). The Council concluded on December 8, 1965.

Daily media reports on the meetings of the Council shaped world public opinion, both Catholic and non-Catholic. Not surprisingly, the content and approach of the reports reflected the editorial policy of each publication and the opinions of individual journalists. Many divided the Council Fathers into two groups: a majority which they praised as open to innovation and dialogue with the contemporary world, and a minority which they condemned as traditional and concerned with safeguarding ecclesiastical doctrine and discipline. Some sectors of the press openly asked for changes in areas of the Church's teaching and practice not included in plans of the Council, most notably the abandonment of priestly celibacy. Both John XXIII and Paul VI sometimes lamented the confusion sown among the clergy, religious, and lay faithful not by the Council's actual decisions but by media reports and statements made by some theologians and Church officials outside the Council meetings.

CHAPTER 1

Governance of a Global Entity

On October 17, 1960, Msgr. Josemaría Escrivá celebrated Mass in the Pontifical Basilica of St. Michael in Madrid, a church that the Papal Nuncio had entrusted to priests of Opus Dei. For the first time, he looked out at a group of hundreds of members and cooperators, both men and women. In his homily he recalled his arrival in the Spanish capital thirty-three years earlier: "The Lord brought me here with inklings of our Work. I could not imagine then that I would see this church full of souls who love Jesus Christ so much. I am moved."[1]

During the previous decade, Opus Dei had grown rapidly. According to the data prepared for the third General Congress, held in Rome in 1961, there were some 6,000 members of the Work: 3,700 men—of whom 263 were numerary priests—and 2,300 women. Forty-five percent (2,700 people) were supernumeraries, that is, men and women whose vocation to Opus Dei did not include a commitment to celibacy. Most of these were married. In addition, 335 diocesan priests belonged to the Priestly Society of the Holy Cross. Half of the members of the Work belonged to the Region of Spain.[2] Numerical growth had been accompanied by geographical expansion. Opus Dei maintained at least one center in fourteen countries in the Americas, ten in Europe, one in Asia, and one in Africa.

During the 1960s, the number of women in Opus Dei became equal to the number of men, although in some regions there were still significantly more men. Also, for the first time, there began to be considerable numbers of families with members from two generations who belonged to the Work.

Escrivá had once remarked that for every numerary member he would like to see two associates and eight supernumeraries.[3] By the mid-1960s the proportion of supernumeraries to numeraries was nearly eight to one. On the other hand, there were significantly fewer associates than numeraries. In Spain in 1966, for example, for every one hundred numeraries there were 770 supernumeraries, but only thirty associates.[4]

The social composition of Opus Dei had also changed over the years. In the 1930s, the majority of the small number of members were college students or recent college graduates. Although this continued to be true in the 1940s, during that decade women from poor rural families began to join the Work as numerary assistants. The 1950s saw people from a broader range of social backgrounds joining Opus Dei as associates and especially as supernumeraries. These changes both caused and were caused by a growing variety of apostolic activities. For example, in Madrid and environs in 1965, 5 percent of the supernumeraries could be considered wealthy, 65 percent were college graduates or held professional degrees, 25 percent were craftsmen, skilled workers, clerks, and small shop owners, and the remaining 5 percent were unskilled workers and peasants. The message of the Work, which is intended for men and women of all social sectors, was beginning to reach widening circles of society, although its presence among unskilled workers was still minimal.[5]

Section 1. An Ongoing Process of Founding

Growth in the number of members, geographic expansion, and diversification of the Work's apostolates radically changed the context in which the Founder worked, but he continued to be the founder of a new path in the Church, father of the Opus Dei family and President General of the institution. His activity was informed by an awareness that it was up to him "by God's very special grace, to which I must respond in conscience, to point out what the spirit of the Work is and what it is not, and how it must be lived in different circumstances."[6]

The Founder often reminded the members that their personal lives and their activities should be rooted "in an intense inner life, in which we are all effectively and truly contemplative."[7] They were called to search for holiness through the sacraments, prayer, sanctified work and family life, knowledge of Christian doctrine, and apostolate. As he told one of the first members of the women's branch, Encarnación Ortega, he measured the development of the Work "not by the number of new cities in which we worked, or by the activities carried out there, but by the growth in interior life of each of my daughters."[8]

In the 1960s and 1970s, Escrivá wrote extensively explaining the spirit of Opus Dei, specifying the way in which the norms of the plan of life and customs were to be fulfilled, structuring the activities carried out by Opus Dei to provide formation to its members and cooperators, and reorganizing its collective apostolic activities.

As a result of his accumulated experience and the questions raised by members, he modified in minor ways a number of the devotions and practices of Christian piety that Opus Dei recommended to its members as part of their plan of life. For instance, he indicated that rather than reciting all fifteen mysteries of the Rosary each day, they could recite five mysteries and meditate very briefly on the other ten. He also suggested that as a way of increasing their devotion to the Eucharist, they should sing or recite the Eucharistic hymn *Adoro te devote* on Thursdays, the day of the week the Church dedicates specially to the Eucharist.[9]

He completed the list of saints to whom he entrusted the various apostolates of Opus Dei. At the beginning of the Work, Fr. Escrivá had named the Blessed Virgin and St. Joseph, the archangels St. Michael, St. Gabriel, and St. Raphael, and the apostles St. Peter, St. Paul, and St. John as his patrons. Later, the Founder had added some intercessors. In the 1930s, he had appointed St. Nicholas of Bari as intercessor for the financial needs of the apostolic activities of the faithful of Opus Dei, and St. John Baptist Mary Vianney as intercessor for relations with local bishops. In November 1957, he named St. Pius X as intercessor for the relations of Opus Dei and its members with the Holy See, and St. Thomas More as intercessor for relations with civil authorities. On May 13, 1964, he added St. Catherine of Siena as intercessor for the apostolate of public opinion.[10]

The founder promoted the causes of beatification and canonization of Opus Dei members as examples of men and women who had lived the call to holiness in the midst of the world. The cause of Isidoro

Zorzano, which had been opened in 1948, was joined by that of Montserrat Grases, a young woman from Barcelona who died in 1959 of bone cancer at the age of eighteen. By the end of the sixties, hundreds of thousands of information bulletins and prayer cards for private devotion about both Isidoro and Montserrat had been printed.[11]

Escrivá's priority was to spread the spirit he had received to many people, leaving theological studies and treatises on the charism to those who would come later. He wrote new texts about the spirit of the Work and how to live it and preached frequently to the members of the General Council and the Central Advisory. He preached less frequently to the students of the Roman Colleges of the Holy Cross and of Holy Mary, but often talked with them in informal get-togethers about all sorts of topics ranging from the spirit of Opus Dei to lighthearted commentaries on daily events. In addition, from the late 1950s on, the Founder met frequently with small groups of people who were visiting Rome: members of the Work, relatives and cooperators, in many cases married couples and priests.

Those who lived with the Founder took notes or recorded on tape some of his meditations and talks because they saw in them a rich foundational legacy for coming generations. Escriva used these texts as the starting point for preparing published meditations, interviews, and lengthy letters to the members of the Work. The texts were also used by others to write articles for the Work's internal publications and six volumes of *Meditations* published between 1964 and 1974 to facilitate the personal prayer of Opus Dei members. The volumes of *Meditations* comprised texts for each day of the year, usually commentaries on the readings of the day's Mass with glosses of the Founder and other spiritual authors. From 1970 onward, a number of full texts of meditations preached by the Founder were also published in *Crónica* and *Noticias*.[12]

The Founder was not only disinterested in writing theological treatises that would reflect his spirit in a systematic way. He did not even write many spiritual books, even though by 1965 *The Way* had sold more than two million copies in more than twenty languages. Instead, he concentrated on explaining Opus Dei in two types of documents which he called *Instructions* and *Letters*. All these documents summarize the founding spirit and are the fruit of Escrivá's prayer and experience. Sometimes they reaffirmed ideas from thirty years earlier, such as the summary he made in 1968 of the ideal of holiness in the Work: "Simple Christians. Dough that is fermenting. Our thing is the ordinary, [done] with naturalness. The means: professional work. Everyone a saint! Silent surrender."[13]

The *Instructions* offer concrete rules and guidelines in light of the substantial elements of the Work's message. They are intended to assist in the governance and development of Opus Dei. The founder wrote three before the Spanish Civil War: one about *The Supernatural Spirit of the Work of God*, another about the *Way to Proselytize*,* and a third about *The Work of St. Raphael*. The *Instruction on the Work of St. Gabriel* was completed in 1950. In the 1960s, he finished the *Instruction for Directors* and the *Instruction for the Work of St. Michael*. The six *Instructions* were compiled in two volumes in January 1967, with notes by Álvaro del Portillo.

The *Letters* are "documents that sometimes contain doctrinal, ascetic, or legal norms, and others offer practical apostolic guidelines."[14] Most of the letters focus on a detailed exposition of a specific theme in light of the spirit of the Work. There are a total of forty-two *Letters*. Thirty-eight were elaborated over many years, especially between the end of the 1950s and 1967. One was written in 1971 and three over the course of 1972–1973. Although the Founder used preexisting material to write the letters, he later destroyed most of it. Some of the letters bear the date on which they were finalized. Others have earlier dates because Escrivá wanted to emphasize that they reflected the foundational inspiration and his constant preaching over a period of forty years.

In December 1964, the Founder sent eight *Letters* to the regions in Latin because, in addition to expressing his appreciation for the language, he wanted to establish the founding explanation of the spirit of Opus Dei in the universal language of the Church.[15] From

---

* In Spain in the 1930s, the terms *proselytize* and *proselytism* did not have the negative connotations they acquired later. Escrivá stopped using them in the 1960s. See chapter 2, section 1, at footnote 8.

the very moment they reached the regions, the *Instructions* and the *Letters* were used in the formation of the members of the Work. It soon became apparent, however, that many members had difficulty understanding them in Latin, so a new version in Latin and Spanish, with two more *Letters*, was sent in 1965. Shortly afterward, the practice of translating the *Letters* into Latin was abandoned.

In the following years, Escrivá revised the printed *Letters* to polish the texts and correct misprints. In November 1974, he had them removed from the centers because Opus Dei was at a delicate moment in its legal itinerary. He wanted to safeguard the texts from being plagiarized by people outside the Work, presenting the contents and terminology as their own. In addition, he was preparing definitive versions of them all and preferred not to circulate previous versions. He died before completing this task, so the definitive publication of the *Letters* was left in the hands of his successors.[16]

The *Letters* set out the perennial features that define the spirit, apostolic activity, and history of Opus Dei, such as the sanctification of ordinary life, professional work and family life, friendship, the way of starting the Work in new countries, the priesthood in Opus Dei, and the formation of its members. Those which focus on the Work's legal itinerary make the Founder's mind clear, particularly in explaining secularity. The style of all the letters is straightforward and direct, appropriate to a family letter, avoiding academic and technical terms and approaches. The *Letters* are intended primarily for members of the Work, but the Founder foresaw that, in time, they would be published and made available to the general public.[17]

Certain major themes run through most of the letters. The first is divine filiation. For the Founder, the awareness of being a child of God is a "joyful truth that underlies our entire spiritual life, that fills with hope our inner struggle and our apostolic tasks."[18] Awareness of their identity as children of God should transform Opus Dei members' personal, intimate dealings with God through piety and witness to Christ in daily life.

A second leitmotif is being ordinary Christians, called to holiness in the world through professional work and family and social relationships. With the help of grace, the members of the Work should strive to become men and women of God, "godly citizens," people with a priestly soul and, at the same time, a lay mentality, who love the world passionately. These secular Christians transform the world from within and direct it to God. "There will always be this phenomenon: that there are people from all walks of life who seek holiness in their own state, in their own profession or occupation, as contemplative souls in the midst of the street."[19]

A third recurring theme is a vision of Opus Dei as "a family with supernatural links."[20] It is a part of the Church modeled on a normal Christian family. This family character essentially marks the relationships within the Work; a father and children who deal with each other and love each other as brothers and sisters.

Beginning in 1966, the Founder began to grant interviews as another way of explaining Christian doctrine and the message of the Work. Between 1966 and 1968, he was interviewed for seven publications, three from Spain (*Gaceta Universitaria, Palabra, Telva*), two from the United States (*The New York Times* and *Time*), and one each from France (*Le Figaro*), and Italy (*L'Osservatore della Domenica*). The texts of the interviews were published in book form in 1968 in Spanish, English, Italian, and Portuguese with the title *Conversations with Monsignor Escrivá.*

The interviewers asked him about the situation of the Church after the Second Vatican Council and about the nature and apostolates of Opus Dei. Escrivá discussed some fundamental aspects of the spirit of the Work, including a filial relationship with God, the divine call to secular sanctity in the professional and family spheres, and the freedom of members to act in social life. For example, he told Jacques Guilleme-Brulon, a correspondent for the newspaper *Le Figaro*: "Since 1928 my preaching has been that holiness is not something for the privileged, that all the paths of the earth can be divine because the hinge of Opus Dei's specific spirituality is the sanctification of ordinary work."[21]

He also explored Christian doctrine on marriage and gave practical advice to increase conjugal love. Most people's path to holiness involves starting and developing a family. Spouses are called to "cooperate with the creative power of God in procreation and then in the education of children. The Lord asks them to make their home and their entire family life a witness to all the Christian virtues." With regard to birth control, a topic very much in the media during those years, he recommended that spouses seek God's will and live their participation in God's power with gratitude, without "stopping up the sources of life." In accordance with Catholic doctrine, he advised that periodic continence could be used "in isolated and difficult cases,"* but rejected, as illicit, the pill and other means of contraception.

Conversations with Monsignor Escrivá de Balaguer also included a homily given by the founder of the Work in October 1967 on the campus of the University of Navarra to more than twenty thousand people. The text, of great expressive beauty and theological content, explains that secular Christian existence is a vocational sphere.

> God calls you to serve him in and from the civil, material, secular tasks of human life: in a laboratory, in a hospital operating room, in an army barracks, in a university chair, in a factory, in a workshop, in the fields, in a family home, and in the whole immense panorama of work. God awaits us every day. Know this well: there is something holy, divine, hidden in the most common situations, and it is up to each one of you to discover it. . . . Our era needs to give back to matter and to the situations that seem most commonplace their noble and original meaning, to put them at the service of the Kingdom of God, to spiritualize them, making them the means and occasion of our continuous encounter with Jesus Christ. . . . Either we know how to find the Lord in our ordinary life, or we will never find him. . . . My children, heaven and earth seem to merge on the horizon. But no, where they really meet is in your hearts, when you live your ordinary life in a holy way.[22]

---

* Josemaría Escrivá, *Conversations with Monsignor Escrivá*, no. 94. This response was part of an interview granted by the Founder in February 1968, five months before Pope Paul VI published the encyclical *Humanae Vitae*. General Note 67/63 (May 15, 1963), AGP E.1.3, 243-3, and General Note 21/69 (June 28, 1969), AGP E.1.3, 246-1, reminded the members of the Work that the magisterium indicated that periodic continence should be used "only for grave reasons."

Section 2. Central and Regional Governing Bodies

The third ordinary General Congress of Opus Dei was held in Rome in 1961. Thirty-nine men attended the first session from September 29 to October 1. Nineteen women attended the second session from October 20 to October 22. The participants reviewed the situation of the Work and established some guidelines for the next five years. They called for opening centers of studies and retreat houses in all the regions; sending students to the interregional centers of studies; developing the apostolate of public opinion; beginning the apostolic work of Opus Dei in Australia and Belgium; and encouraging the apostolic emigration of supernumeraries and cooperators to transmit the message of Opus Dei in other nations.[23] During the five years which followed, considerable progress would be made in all of these areas except for apostolic emigration.

Despite spending large amounts of time working in several commissions of the Second Vatican Council, Álvaro Del Portillo, secretary-general of the Work and *custos* of the Founder for spiritual matters, continued to be Escrivá's most important support in governing the Work and in maintaining relations with ecclesiastical authorities in Rome. For the women's branch, the central secretaries Mercedes Morado (1961–1973) and Carmen Ramos (1973–1988) played key roles. Like the other members of the General Council and the Central Advisory, they respected Escrivá's unique role and authority as founder. They consulted him on all important issues and implemented his decisions.

A member of the Central Advisory during this period describes the work of the central government of Opus Dei as focused on "laying the foundations and consolidating the institutional reality and promoting its development."[24] The General Council and the Central Advisory established and modified regions and delegations, and appointed electors and inscribed members, directors of the interregional centers, and members of the regional governments. They also decided on loans or donations of capital for corporate activities in regions with lesser resources.

In these years there was some interchange of personnel between central and regional governments, which enriched both. For example,

María José Monterde was Mexico's regional secretary from 1960 to 1966, but before and after those years she was the deputy secretary of St. Michael in the central advisory. Pedro Casciaro, who had been councilor of Mexico from 1948 to 1957 and then delegate to that region, became general procurator of the General Council and delegate of Italy in 1959. Casciaro occupied those positions during the years of the Vatican Council and in 1966 returned to Mexico as councilor. José Luis Múzquiz was central secretary priest from 1961 to 1964. Prior to that he had occupied the position of councilor in the United States for nine years and delegate for another four years.

The spirit of the Work was transmitted and essential governing guidelines were communicated from the top (the Founder, the General Council, and the Central Advisory) down to the regional organisms and thence to the local centers and the individual members. Overall, however, the Work was very decentralized. The central governing bodies respected the freedom and initiative of the regional and local bodies. Relatively important developments could be triggered by the personal decisions of an individual member. For instance, a supernumerary might move to a town where the Work had no presence, and his or her apostolate might give rise to enough vocations to make it necessary to open a center there, even though the town might not have figured in any plan for expansion. The role of the directors was to safeguard the spirit of the Work and provide overall guidance to its activities, but they did not control the members, and the central directors left the vast majority of decisions about the development of the Work in a country to the people on the ground. Playing with words, Escrivá described Opus Dei as a "disorganized organization" or an "organized disorganization."[25] "The spirit," he said, "is given primacy over the organization. The life of the members is not straitjacketed by slogans, plans, and meetings."[26]

The regional directors traveled to Rome from time to time to seek help in solving a problem or to exchange information and points of view. Starting in 1963, regular meetings in Rome of councilors and delegates of the men's branch and of regional secretaries and delegates of the women's branch, gave them an opportunity to talk with the

Founder and the central directors. The purpose of these meetings was to intensify the desire of the regional directors for personal holiness, improve their formation, and promote regional corporate activities. Escrivá usually began these meetings by recalling that the "secret" of Opus Dei lay in personal union with God.

Members of the central government had begun to visit the regions from time to time as early as 1953. This gave rise to a practice of visits to each region every five years by one or two people delegated by the Father to get to know the situation there, help find solutions to problems, and report back to Rome.[27]

Day-to-day relations between the central and regional governments were carried out by notes, notices, and letters. Over time, more and more matters were delegated to the regions.

To guide their decisions, the regional commissions and regional advisories had the *Constitutions* of Opus Dei; the *Instructions* written by the Founder (bound copies were sent in 1958 and a revised edition with extensive notes by Álvaro Del Portillo in 1966); the document *De spiritu*, which summarized the message of Opus Dei and the way of living its norms and customs; a regulation for the regional government; a pamphlet entitled *Constructions*, with practical suggestions for constructing and remodeling buildings that were the headquarters of the centers; and the *Catechism* of the Work.[28]

To ensure that all regions had the same general guidelines and to avoid having to answer the same questions repeatedly, guidance previously given on various topics was compiled between 1963 and 1972 into forty-nine documents called *Compilaciones* [Compilations]. They covered a wide range of topics: practices and procedures for central, regional, and local government, the Works of St. Michael, St. Raphael, and St. Gabriel, formation, and how to explain the Work and its activities. In addition, the central governments drafted standard practices for how to take care of oratories and liturgical objects and on the work of the Administration.

The fourth General Congress of Opus Dei was held in the spring of 1966. Thirty-four men met from May 3 to 5 at Villa Tevere, and twenty-four women from May 15 to 17 at Villa delle Rose. The conclusions of the congress were similar for the two sections of the Work. Among the topics stressed were: the responsibility of the associates, supernumeraries, and cooperators in corporate activities; the importance of having a center of studies in every region; the desirability of supernumeraries' emigrating with their families to countries where the Work was just getting started; founding and developing centers of higher education that could eventually become universities, while at the same time continuing to encourage members to work professionally at public universities; founding new personal works of apostolate in the fields of primary and secondary education;* and studying the possibility of bringing the Work to more countries in Africa and Asia.[29]

The numerical growth of Opus Dei and the increase in the number and size of collective apostolic activities required strengthening its regional and local governments. One delegate rightly pointed out that they were living through a few years of a "growth crisis."[30] (This was particularly true in Spain at the time; something similar would happen in Mexico in the 1970s). Like a teenager who had outgrown his clothes, there was the feeling that it was impossible to provide proper follow-up on so many people and projects. More people were needed in government, in the direction of corporate undertakings, and in the tasks of spiritual formation. The priests of the Work and the staff of the Administrations were overwhelmed with work. For the moment, the heroic dedication of many was the only remedy for the shortage of personnel.[31]

As early as 1957, the founder had proposed to the General Council slowing for a while the Work's expansion to new countries to be able to strengthen the "internal development of the Work in the already erected regions, especially the centers of studies and the governance of the regions."[32] In fact, the 1960–1975 period was marked more by development in the places where the Work was already established than by geographic expansion. During those

---

* For an explanation of the concept of personal works, see chapter 3, section 2, "Primary and Secondary Schools."

fifteen years, the Work began in a stable way in only six new territories: Paraguay (1962), Australia (1963), the Philippines (1964), Belgium and Nigeria (1965), and Puerto Rico (1969).

Central and regional directors concentrated on improving the
formation given in the centers of studies to ensure that the members
fully appreciated the whole vocational reality of their call to the Work
and were able to explain it in depth to others. They also sought to
ensure that there would be some numeraries giving formation full-
time in the local government of large corporate works and centers
with many people.

A particular concern of the central directors was giving personalized attention to the members of Opus Dei, especially those who had
just applied for admission. This depended primarily on the members
of the local council of each center. The local directors coordinated the
spiritual direction of the members of the Work, provided the bulk of
the collective formation, and followed the progress of their activities.
The numeraries who directed these local councils had to know and
practice the spirit and customs of Opus Dei and teach others to live
them. They had to be men and women with leadership skills, a vision
of the whole, an understanding of people, and the ability to analyze
and solve problems The delegates to the General Congress were concerned that some local councils were weak due to high turnover or
because their members were young and lacked experience.

To improve the formation and apostolates of the Work, intermediate governing bodies called *delegations* were created. These were
dependent on the regional commissions and advisories. In Spain, delegations were established in Barcelona (1957), Seville (1957), Pamplona (1960), and Madrid (1962, divided in 1971 into Madrid-East
and Madrid-West), Valladolid (1965), and Valencia (1969). In Mexico, delegations were established in Guadalajara (1967), Monterrey
(1970), and Mexico City (1975). In Italy, they were created in Rome
(1968) and Palermo (1971). In some regions which encompassed
more than one country, delegations were established for the countries where the Work was less developed. The delegations of Paraguay
(1963) and Uruguay (1973) depended on the regional commission

of Argentina. The delegation of Costa Rica (1968) depended on the regional commission for Central America, which was in San José. Finally, the delegation of Belgium (1973) depended on the regional commission of the Netherlands.[33] Having delegations that were responsible for a limited territory made it easier for the directors to get to know the members of the Work in their area more personally and follow the development of the Work's apostolic activities.

Initially, the directors of the regional commissions and delegations were mostly Spanish, but as the Work developed, more of them were natives of the country in which they served. Confining ourselves to looking at the head of the Work, the Councilor, we find Nuno Girão Santos Ferreira (Portugal, 1958), Richard Mulcahy (Ireland, 1959), James Albrecht (Washington, 1961), and Luigi Tirelli (Italy, 1964).

One experiment in structuring the intermediate-level governing organisms of the Work proved short-lived. The idea was that in countries with many members or where distances were large, quasi-regions should be established instead of delegations, with the expectation that they would become full-blown regions. Quasi-regions were established in Chicago and Washington (1957), and Barcelona (1965). After a while, however, Escrivá concluded that having more than one region in a country hampered relations and coordination among the various governing bodies, made it harder to move people from one center to another, and hindered the development of activities. In 1969, Barcelona returned to being a delegation dependent on the regional commission of Spain and the United States returned to being a single region with headquarters in New York and a delegation in Chicago.

It continued to be difficult to staff adequately the regional commissions, advisories, and delegations, especially their legal and economic offices and the office for the apostolate of public opinion. For lack of properly trained numeraries, some positions remained unfilled or the same person had to cover two or three positions. The Work's efforts to strengthen its internal structures by having more numeraries working in its offices was in tension with its desire to have more numeraries working professionally in noninstitutional settings where they could spread the message of the call to sanctity in the professional and social spheres in which most people live their ordinary lives. The problem was especially acute for the women's branch because many women numeraries had been dedicated to a large extent to training, government, and the domestic administration of centers. The 1966 General Congress called for "many more women members to exercise their profession, whatever it may be, in noninstitutional settings in order to bring the spirit of Christ to all environments, and thus be able to broaden the basis of our apostolic work."[34] Eight years later, in a report to the Founder and the central advisory about the development of the Work in Spain, an Opus Dei director noted that many women were working "in professional positions of special apostolic impact (university and high school education), media, etc."[35]

On the financial side, as the regional and local governing bodies gained greater experience and expertise, they gradually acquired greater autonomy in setting budgets and deciding on the use of funds. The more developed regions had a legal office as well as a technical office, composed of economists, engineers, and architects, which supervised the construction, remodeling, and major maintenance of the centers and corporate works. The regional administrators had technical advisors that reviewed the financial statements of the auxiliary companies, so that they did not get carried away by single-minded focus on growth to the detriment of financial stability.

The development of the apostolic undertakings of the Work generally followed a similar pattern in all countries despite some variations to accommodate local circumstances. The first undertaking in a new country was generally a student residence or some other corporate apostolate. That was usually followed by a retreat house, which was used not only for retreats but for workshops and a wide variety of other formational activities. When there was a sufficient number of members of the Work, centers of studies were opened and courses of study for associates and supernumeraries were started. Eventually, the time came to open corporate activities in the field of education—from elementary schools to high schools, as well as training centers for workers and peasants. In addition, members of Opus Dei, together with other people, were encouraged to start common works with an apostolic purpose, such as magazines, book distributors, and publishing houses.[36]

The 1960s witnessed the opening of many retreat houses in Europe and the Americas. Spain added to those that already existed La Pililla (Madrid, 1960), Solavieya (Gijón, 1965), Islabe (Bilbao, 1966) and La Lloma (Valencia, 1968). Retreat houses were founded in other regions, such as Miranda (Quito, Ecuador, 1959), Toshi (Atlacomulco, Mexico, 1960), Antullanca (Santiago de Chile, 1960), Centre International de Rencontres de Couvrelles (Soissons, France, 1964), Wickenden Manor (East Grinstead, United Kingdom, 1964), Lismullin (Navan, Ireland, 1964), Arnold Hall Conference Center (Boston, 1964), Manoir de Beaujeu (Montreal, Canada, 1964), Torre-blanca (Bogotá, Colombia, 1966), La Chacra (Buenos Aires, Argentina, 1966), Sítio da Aroeira (São Paulo, Brazil, 1967), Okuashiya Study Center (Ashiya, Japan, 1967), Tigoni Study Center (Nairobi, Kenya, 1970) and Makiling Conference Center (Manila, Philippines 1971). Country houses and other properties made available by supernumeraries or cooperators were also used for retreats and other formational activities.

The Spanish region played a unique role in Opus Dei for a number of reasons. It was there that Opus Dei had been born, and it had a more than fifteen-year head start on all the other regions. In part, perhaps, for this reason, the rate of growth was faster there than anywhere else. Although it was the region that had made the most sacrifices to send people to other countries, in the 1960s and '70s, the number of members and people attending apostolic activities in Spain was exploding. There was a flurry of building to accommodate them, with a proliferation of student residences, retreat houses, new buildings at the University of Navarra, clubs for young people, schools, and small centers. Between 1962 and 1965 activities with youth grew by 40 percent, due in good measure to the activities of high school clubs. Monthly retreats for married men and women and other activities of the Work of St. Gabriel began to be held in almost all the provincial capitals and large towns. Opus Dei in Spain had clearly moved beyond the period in which it had centers only in cities with a university. All this implied that Spain was a testing ground or model, although the Founder and the central directors insisted that many things would need to be done differently outside of Spain.[37]

In the 1960s and '70s, Spain continued to contribute the most people to the task of starting Opus Dei in new countries and to strengthening it in places where it had begun only recently. Nonetheless, growth in other regions made it possible to form multinational teams, in some cases composed entirely of people from outside of Spain. For example, in 1960, twenty numeraries—ten from Spain and ten from Latin American countries—went to live in the United States. In January 1961, the General Council decided to send more priests and lay numeraries from Spain and Portugal to Brazil to speed the Work's development there. The small group of women that moved to Asunción (Paraguay) to begin the activities of the women's branch there in 1963 had no Spanish members. It comprised two Argentineans (Ofelia Vita Lara and Rosa Clara Pinotti), one Peruvian (Elena Varillas Montenegro), and one Chilean (María Angélica Cáceres Meza). They were joined two months later by another Peruvian (Ángela Galindo).

In Italy, the sixties witnessed the beginning of major corporate works, with student residences in Rome, Milan, Bologna, Verona, Naples, Bari, Palermo and Catania, a cultural center in Genoa, and hotel schools in Rome and Palermo. The construction of the Residenza Universitaria Internazionale in Rome and the remodeling of the Castello di Urio retreat house on Lake Como were especially large projects. In 1969 a second retreat house opened in Terrasini (Sicily).[38]

In Rome, Opus Dei undertook the creation of a large center for the professional and Christian formation of young blue-collar workers in the city's working-class section of Tiburtino. It was made financially possible by a major donation from Baron Francesco Mario Oddasso to the Holy See for an international center for young workers. The Vatican Secretariat of State asked Opus Dei to take on the project, which came to encompass four distinct entities: Centro ELIS (*Educazione, Lavoro, Istruzione, Sport* [Education, Work, Training, Sports]), which offered professional training to technical designers, fitters, welders, mechanics, and electromechanics; a men's residence for two hundred students; SAFI (*Scuola Alberghiera Femminile Internazionale* [Women's International Hotel School); and a parish for the neighborhood, San Giovanni Battista in Collatino. On the day they opened, November 21, 1965, Pope Paul VI celebrated Mass in the parish and visited the ELIS center and SAFI school. As he was leaving, he embraced the Founder and said: "Here everything is Opus Dei."[39]

In countries where Catholics were a minority, an important component of Opus Dei's apostolic activities was courses on the Catholic faith for Christians who wished to enter into full communion with the Catholic Church, for people of other religious groups, and for nonbelievers. Escrivá called the Work's effort to help others approach the fullness of revealed truth the apostolate *ad fidem*. He stressed the importance of respecting their freedom. For example, he indicated that in the Work's student residences "our non-Catholic friends should always be allowed to attend acts of worship in our oratories; but without making things too easy for them. They should come only if they really want to, thereby emphasizing their personal freedom."[40]

Netherhall House, the Work's university residence for men in London, had an agreement with the British Council under which only 20 percent of the residents could be British. The majority came from Commonwealth countries, and 60 percent were non-Catholic. In 1966, the residence completed an addition that allowed it to increase the number of residents. The Queen Mother inaugurated the new building and visited the Lakefield Center for Hospitality Training, a school run by women of the Work in the part of the building dedicated to the administration of the residence. Outside London, Opus Dei had centers in Oxford and Manchester for both men and women.[41]

Escrivá visited Greece in the spring of 1966 to gather information in preparation for future apostolic activities of Opus Dei in that country. He returned to Rome disappointed, because the connection between the civil authorities and the Orthodox Church left no room for people from other countries to spread the Catholic faith. He decided that, for the time being, Opus Dei would have to focus on giving formation in its spirit to Greeks living abroad. Later, they could carry the message of sanctity in the midst of the world to their homeland. He foresaw that these men and women would probably belong to churches of the Byzantine Catholic rite.[42]

The development of the men's branch of the Work in Kenya centered on Strathmore College. In the mid-sixties, it had a boarding high school with one hundred students and an accounting program with seventy-five students. Most were not Catholic. Strathmore had an excellent reputation. It wanted, however, to avoid being considered a foreign school and so preferred not to seek publicity until more of the school's responsible positions were held by African members of the Work. Strathmore's charges for tuition and accommodation were high by East African standards, but the staff worked diligently to find scholarships from the government, foreign foundations, and private donors for the many students whose families could not afford to pay full tuition. The women of the Work concentrated on developing Kianda College, where the percentage of Catholic students was also low. It began as a secretarial school, the first such institution for African women in Kenya.[43]

Jesús Estanislao and Bernardo Villegas—Filipinos who had joined the Work as graduate students in economics at Harvard University—returned to Manila in 1964 and started Opus Dei's activities there. Soon after, they were joined by José Rivera, an engineer, and two priests, Fr. José Morales and Fr. Javier de Pedro. A year later the first women of the Work arrived: Soledad Usechi, Eulalia Sastre and María Teresa Martínez Barón. They started the Mayana School of Home and Fine Arts, which offered classes to housewives and domestic workers.[44] The beginning of Opus Dei in the Philippines delighted Escrivá. He considered the Philippines the "vanguard" for Opus Dei's apostolic activities in the East. He told the Filipino members of the Work that just as they had received the faith, they should transmit it to many countries in Southeast Asia, which was mostly non-Christian.

Naturally not everyone who joined Opus Dei persevered. The directors rarely terminated anyone's membership, and only for serious reasons. In most cases, the persons involved came personally to the conclusion that they should not continue to belong to Opus Dei. Generally, this occurred early on, before they had made the oblation. Since they were in a period of discernment and had no canonical obligations to Opus Dei, they could simply stop living as members of the Work at any time. Those who had committed themselves for a specified period of time and subsequently decided they no longer wanted to be members, would simply not renew their commitment when it expired. Those who had committed themselves for life through the fidelity had to ask for a dispensation from the president general, but this dispensation was always granted.

Some people who left the Work should perhaps never have been allowed to join in the first place. The local directors may not have invested enough time and effort into getting to know them well enough to discern accurately if God was calling them to the Work. In other cases, the local directors may have failed to provide adequate formation to a new vocation. Still other people simply discovered that they were unable or unwilling to meet all the demands of living as members of Opus Dei day after day.[45]

Whatever the reason, for someone who had made a sincere effort to answer what he or she thought was God's call to Opus Dei, leaving was often painful and sometimes traumatic. The Founder asked the directors and other members to make an effort to remain friends with those who had been in the Work, helping them in their spiritual life if they wished. At a formal level, former members who wished to do so could become cooperators as soon as they left Opus Dei. If after a considerable time they felt they had a vocation, they could again apply for admission as a supernumerary.[46]

In the period we are discussing, two cases stand out. The first involved Raimundo Pániker, who had been a numerary since 1940.

Ordained a priest in 1946, he published some studies on the relationship between nature and grace that were rejected by the bishops of Salamanca and Seville. He moved to Rome in 1953 and dedicated himself to theology. He carried on research in India, looking for points of connection between Christianity, Hinduism, and Buddhism. Increasingly, he distanced himself from pastoral tasks and from the spirit of the Work. After four canonical admonitions, he was subject to a trial that led to his resignation from Opus Dei in June 1966.[*]

A possibly even more painful departure was that of María del Carmen Tapia. After working in the central advisory for three years, she was named the regional secretary of Venezuela in November 1956. After several years, Escrivá and the central directors became concerned about reports that she was forming a dissident group within Opus Dei, one critical of its spirit and activities. It was also reported that she had had open confrontations with Fr. Roberto Salvat, the head of Opus Dei in Venezuela, and with other members of the regional advisory.

The Founder called her to Rome in October 1965, removed her from her position as head of the women's branch in Venezuela, prohibited her from returning to Venezuela or contacting members of the Work there, and asked her to amend her ways. For the next six months, Tapia lived in Villa Tevere, and was assigned menial tasks. She continued in contact by mail with her supporters in Venezuela and spoke critically about the central directors to the Venezuelan members who were studying in Rome. In an effort to prevent her from returning to Venezuela where they feared she would do serious

---

[*] He adopted the name Raimon Panikkar at the end of his life. After leaving Opus Dei, he was incardinated in the Indian diocese of Vanarasi and worked at Harvard University and the University of California Santa Barbara. He continued to have a close relationship with the founder of Opus Dei. In 1984 he contracted a civil marriage and was suspended by the Church from celebrating the sacraments. The suspension was lifted in 2008, when he had already separated from his wife. He died two years later, having reconciled with the Church. He maintained contact with people in Opus Dei until the end. See Josep-Ignasi Saranyana, "Raimon Panikkar: On the Subject of a Biography," *Studia et Documenta* 11 (2017), pp. 323–348.

damage to Opus Dei, the central directors confiscated her Venezuelan passport, although she retained at all times her Spanish passport.*
The situation continued to deteriorate. After two canonical admonitions, Escrivá told Tapia in May 1966 that she should resign from
Opus Dei, and that if she did not, she would be subject to a trial in
the Holy See which would lead to her ejection. Tapia chose to leave
and returned to her family in Spain.

Notes

1. *Obras*, December, 1960, 21. AGP Library P03.
2. See Third Ordinary General Congress (1961). AGP D.1, 457-4-5; AGP
D.1, 457-5-2.
3. See General Note 17/62 (May 9, 1962). AGP E.1.3, 243-1; Fourth Ordinary
General Congress (1966). AGP D.1, 457-5-7.
4. Calculated by the authors from data in AGP E.2.1, 204-1-2.
5. See AGP E.2.1, 204-1-2.
6. General Note 28/73 (June 20, 1973). AGP E.1.3, 246-5.
7. General Note 5/67 (February 11, 1967). AGP E.1.3, 245-3.
8. Recollections of Encarnación Ortega Pardo, Valladolid, August 21, 1975.
AGP A.5, 232-1-2.
9. See General Note 44/65 (April 26, 1965). AGP E.1.3, 244-4; General Note
5/68 (February 28, 1968). AGP E.1.3, 245-5.
10. See General Note 100/64 (June 25,1964). AGP E.1.3, 244-1.

---

* We have not found any contemporary documents referring to these events. In a book
published in 1992, Tapia depicts herself as being subject during this period to psychological and verbal abuse and virtually held captive. See María del Carmen Tapia, *Tras el
umbral: Una vida en el Opus Dei* (Barcelona: Ediciones B, 1992). The person who was
the international head of the women's branch at the time paints an entirely different
picture, depicting Escrivá as treating Tapia with great affection and describing her as
participating as just one more person in the daily life of the center made up of people
who worked in the central government of Opus Dei. See Marlies Kücking, *Horizontes
insospechados* (Madrid: Rialp, 2019), pp. 162–164. Tapia remained in occasional contact with some members of the Work. For her attitude toward Escrivá around the time
of her beatification and canonization, see infra chapter 12, section 2.

11. See AGP D.1, 457-5-2.

12. See Josemaría Escivá de Balaguer, *En diálogo con el Señor* (edición crítico-histórica) (Madrid: Rialp, 2017), pp. 34–55.

13. This is a 1968 addition to *Intimate Notes*, no. 35.

14. General note 131/64 (October 26,1964). AGP E.1.3, 244-2.

15. Perhaps this decision was influenced by the fact that the Apostolic Constitution *Veterum Sapientia*, published by Pope John XXIII in February 1962, affirmed that the Latin language was a precise language that facilitated an unchangeable interpretation and required its use in the teaching of ecclesiastical subjects. This requirement fell into disuse soon afterward because many young professors in the pontifical universities no longer had sufficient mastery of Latin to be able to teach in it.

16. See Josemaría Escrivá de Balaguer, *Cartas. Edición critico-histórica preparada por Luis Cano*, vol. 1 (Madrid: Rialp, 2020). We follow the approach of this critical edition in quoting the *Cartas*.

17. As of April, 2022, two volumes of Escrivá's letters have been published in Spanish, under the title *Cartas. Edición critico-histórica preparada por Luis Cano*, vols. 1 and 2 (Madrid: Rialp, 2020 and 2022). The first volume has been published in English under the title *The Collected Letters* (Strongsville, Ohio: Scepter, 2022).

18. Letter 6, no. 2. AGP A.3, 91-6-1.

19. Letter 3, no. 92. AGP A.3, 91-3-1. Work as a means of sanctity is one of the essential elements of the spirit spread by the founder of the Work: "The particular character of the spirituality of Opus Dei is that each person must sanctify his own profession or office, his ordinary work; sanctify himself, precisely in his professional task; and, through that task, sanctify others." Letter 31, no. 10. AGP A.3, 94-2-2.

20. Letter 27, no. 76. AGP A.3, 94-1-3.

21. Letter 27, no. 34. AGP A.3, 94-1-3.

22. Josemaría Escrivá, *Conversations with Josemaría Escrivá* (New York: Scepter, 2002), nos. 114 and 116.

23. See Conclusions of the III Ordinary General Congress (October 1, 1961 for men; October 22, 1961 for women). AGP D.1, 457-4-4 and AGP D.1, 457-4-8, respectively.

24. Marlies Kücking, *Horizontes insospechados. Mis recuerdos de san Josemaría* (Madrid: Rialp, 2019), p. 112.

25. *Intimate Notes*, No. 956 (III-1933). See Escrivá, *Conversations* nos. 35 and 63; and Letter 29, no. 11. AGP A.3, 94-1-5.

26. Escrivá, *Conversations*, no. 63.

27. See Kücking, *Horizontes*, pp. 115–121. Kücking summarizes her own assignments in various countries of Europe and America during the years 1968–1975 when she was secretary of the Central Advisory.

28. The first printed edition of the *Catechism* dates from 1947. The second edition (1951), the third (1959), and the fourth (1966) improved the explanation of some ideas about the nature and work of Opus Dei. AGP E.1.1, 181-1 and 181-2. The first edition of *De spiritu is* dated October 24, 1963. AGP L.1.1, 14-3-6.

29. See Conclusions of the IV Ordinary General Congress (May 5, 1966 for men; May 17, 1966 for women). AGP D.1, 457-5-4 and AGP D.1, 457-5-8, respectively.

30. Report of Service Commission to Mexico, Octobder 31, 1967. AGP Q.2.1, 4-122.

31. See AGP E.2.1, 204-1-2.

32. Minutes of the General Council, November 30,1957, 22. AGP E.1.2.

33. See AGP G.1.1.1, 55-1-4.

34. Fourth Ordinary General Congress (May 17, 1966). AGP D.1, 457-5-8.

35. Service commission to Spain, January 3, 1974. AGP Q.2.1, 6-176; see General Note 511 (April 13, 1962). AGP E.1.3, 242-4. This issue affected numeraries almost exclusively. The vast majority of the supernumeraries and associates worked in the same places where they would have worked if they had not joined Opus Dei.

36. See General Note 101/65 (December 31, 1965). AGP E.1.3, 244-4.

37. See AGP Q.2.1, 2-79.

38. See AGP E.2.1, 203-3-17.

39. See Cosimo di Fazio, "*Centros ELIS y SAFI*," in José Luis Illanes (coord.), *Diccionario de san Josemaría Escrivá de Balaguer* (Burgos: Monte Carmelo - Instituto Histórico San Josemaría Escrivá, 2013), pp. 30–231.

40. Letter 3, no. 77. AGP A.3, 91-3-1.

41. See Maureen Mullins, "Gran Bretaña," in Illanes, *Diccionario de san Josemaría*, pp. 585–589; James Pereiro, "Netherhall House, London (1960–1984): The Commonwealth Dimension," *Studia et Documenta* 5 (2011), pp. 13–51.

42. See Note from Josemaría Escrivá to Angelo Dell'Acqua, April, 1966. AGP H.1, 166-3.

43. See ae-Kf 2/67 (January 16, 1967). AGP R.3.1, 1-1.

44. See Ana Labrada Rubio, *La vanguardia del Oriente. Recuerdos sobre la expansión del Opus Dei en Filipinas* (Madrid: Rialp, 2015).

45. See AGP R.1.3.3, 1-3.

46. See General Note 15 (November 12, 1955). AGP E.1.3, 242-1; and AGP R.1.1.4, 1-1.

CHAPTER 2

Formation

rom the beginning, Escrivá had insisted that the three "dominant passions" of the members of the Work were teaching doctrine, providing spiritual direction, and strengthening the unity of the Work. Both the members and the people they were in contact with needed doctrine to find their own ways of living the gospel in the world and help others do the same. This reality was reflected in the activities of St. Raphael, St. Gabriel, and St. Michael, which the Founder described as the "backbone of the Work."[1] All three offered opportunities for both individual and group formation. As we have seen, personal formation was given primarily through confession, spiritual accompaniment, and fraternal correction. The principal vehicles of group formation were classes and circles, meditations, informal get-togethers, days of recollection, and retreats.

Until the late 1940s, the people responsible for giving formation were celibate men and women, mostly in Spain. The men were all college students or recent graduates and much of their apostolate was carried out at universities. By the 1960s, the people giving formation had come to include a significant group of priests and large numbers of lay men and women, single and married, college-educated or not. They came from various walks of life and a growing number of countries. Similarly, the people receiving formation from the Work were becoming increasingly diverse.

Escrivá stressed that, despite their diverse circumstances, the members of the Work all had the same vocation. That vocation was to sanctify themselves by living the spirit of Opus Dei in their work and the rest of their ordinary life and to strive to bring their friends, colleagues, relatives, and neighbors closer to God by communicating to them the teaching of Christ and specifically the spirit of Opus

Dei. In this sense, he repeated frequently, they formed a single class within Opus Dei. Nonetheless, the Work's apostolic activities and the means of formation it employed had to be adapted to people's diverse circumstances.

Section 1. St. Raphael's Work

St. Raphael's Work was aimed at "bringing young people closer to Opus Dei and giving them spiritual and human formation," with the goal of helping them "know and love Jesus Christ, who is the reason for all our work."[2] It began with Spanish college students in the 1930s, especially through the activities of the DYA Residence. DYA focused on encouraging them to study well, develop a personal relationship with God, and be open to others. These three goals would lie permanently at the heart of the St. Raphael Work.

Whenever Opus Dei began in a new country, the initial members tried to get to know a few students who could, in their turn, introduce them to other students. As soon as possible, they opened centers and university residences, for both women and men, which provided a stable base for a wide range of activities including cultural gatherings, courses on study methods and professional orientation, film and press clubs, language classes, sports tournaments, get-togethers, social gatherings, excursions, and summer camps.[3] Many of the students who took part in these activities were also interested in receiving spiritual formation.

The most important means of personal formation in the Work of St. Raphael was the spiritual accompaniment of each young person. Group spiritual formation was offered in circles and other classes, meditations, days of recollection, and retreats. The students who participated in these activities were encouraged to deepen their own faith by teaching catechism to children preparing for their First Communion, especially in poor areas, visiting needy people, giving alms, and making pilgrimages to a shrine of the Virgin Mary.[4]

The formation classes called circles were a central part of St. Raphael's work. They were organized in two cycles. They began with a one-year preparatory course. It was markedly practical in character, designed to help the students develop an interior life of prayer and sacrifice based on personal friendship with Jesus Christ. That was followed by a course which offered guidance on moral dilemmas or current doctrinal questions.

Although until at least the late 1940s most of the Work's youth activities were aimed at college students, some young people in their final years of high school also took part in activities at the centers or attended retreats preached by Opus Dei priests. During the 1950s, the Founder promoted formation classes specifically for high school students, including for those who were too young to attend the St. Raphael circles. The goal was to help young people to understand Christian principles from an early age and to see an example of Christian coherence in their mentors. This, he thought, would help counter the advance of secularism among adolescents.[5]

In 1956, the central offices of the Work asked all the regions to organize cultural, academic, and sports entities and associations for youth, in accordance with the civil legislation of each country. The first clubs for high school boys were the Gurkhas Club (Guatemala City, 1957), Daumar (Barcelona, 1958), Jara Club and Argüelles (Madrid, 1958). The first clubs for girls were at the Verapaz residence (Guatemala City, 1958) and the Roca Club (Madrid, 1963). Each club created a board of trustees composed primarily of parents. These boards established monthly dues for members and sought other sources of income. In some cases, they were able to obtain state aid as nonprofit organizations. The day-to-day operations of the clubs were coordinated by a handful of numeraries. The parents of the young people helped organize sports, camps, and other activities.

Clubs for young people soon sprang up all over the world. Initially they focused on fourteen- to eighteen-year-olds, but soon they reached out to ten- to thirteen-year-olds as well. The clubs were designed to promote character development and the progressive use of freedom in adolescents, with times for study, sport, and recreation combined with times for meeting with mentors and formational activities. Clubs offered the younger students sports, hobby activities, and excursions but also short periods of group study and spiritual formation adapted to their age. The appeal of different activities varied with age group and country. For example, high school seniors in Spain—where the university system forced incoming students to choose immediately what they wanted to study (law, medicine, architecture, chemistry, history, physics, etc.)—were enthusiastic about orientation courses on university careers. By contrast, in the United States, leadership programs were highly successful.[6]

During the 1960s, the Work began to open small centers for young numerary members with space for fewer than fifteen residents, rather than concentrating exclusively on relatively large university residences. The new centers offered seminars and conferences, study skills courses, and sports, in addition to formational activities. Each center focused on a certain social group: office workers, college students, clerks, or young professionals. The reduced number of residents made it easier to achieve a family atmosphere. On the other hand, they tended to operate at a deficit because they lacked economies of scale and because the residents were mostly students who could not afford to pay much. They attempted with varying degrees of success to solve the problem through donations.[7]

All these efforts to spread the gospel among young people led some to find their Christian path in Opus Dei. Escrivá called the proposal made to a person to answer the call of Jesus Christ in the Work "proselytism." He summarized this call in the phrases, "may you seek Christ; may you find Christ; may you love Christ." At the time, the term *proselytism* did not bear the negative connotation of coercion that it does today. For the Founder, the invitation to be part of the Work "is not like a material push, but an abundance of light, of doctrine. It is the spiritual stimulus of your prayer and your work, which is an authentic witness to the teaching of Christ. It is the sum of the sacrifices, which you know how to offer as well as the smile, which comes to your mouth because you are children of God," as well as "your attractive personality and likeability." Escrivá stressed the importance of freedom in responding to God's call while underlining both the beauty and the demands of a vocation which allows a person to "fall in love with Christ and to serve him fully according to the spirit of the Work."[8]

The late 1960s witnessed the beginning of what would grow to be an important international meeting of students in Rome at Easter time. In April 1966, a group of German university students from the Müngersdorf residence in Cologne went to Rome for Holy Week, to see the Pope and visit the city's monuments. The Founder of the Work had an informal get-together with them. Two years later, a larger group from several countries came to Rome during Holy Week and met with the Holy Father and the Founder. The organizers called the week the Roman Meeting (*Incontro Romano*). In later years, this informal student gathering was supplemented with a university congress organized by the *Istituto per la Cooperazione Universitaria* (ICU), a nonprofit organization created by Umberto Farri and other members of Opus Dei to promote social development projects. In 1974 more than a thousand students from five continents took part in the *Incontro Romano*; it was the last one in which Escrivá took part.[9]

Section 2. Philosophical and Theological Education of Numeraries

The publication of the first edition of the *Syllabus of Initial Formation* in 1960 systematized for the first time the formation given all over the world to everyone who joined Opus Dei. It provided for thirty-two classes on the spirit of the Work in the first six months after anyone applied for admission and another fifty during the next year. It also called for forty refresher classes on the fundamentals of Christian faith and morals to be given during the same eighteen-month period leading up to the person's admission, whether as a numerary, associate, or supernumerary.[10]

To prepare them to explain the spirit of the Work to others, numeraries normally received more intensive formation at the center of studies for two years (until 1967, women usually spent only one year there). In most cases, they attended the center of studies while studying at the university. The academic program consisted of the philosophical training that the Church required of candidates for the priesthood.

The women's branch opened centers of studies in Argentina and the United States (1960), Chile (1961), Germany and Portugal (1962), Colombia and Venezuela (1964), Peru (1965), Ireland and England (1966), Central America and Italy (1967), Brazil and France (1969), and the Philippines (1974). In Spain, the Los Rosales study center moved to Pamplona in 1960, taking the name Izarbide, and in 1967, it became an interregional center and moved to to a new building called Goroabe College. In 1957, the women's branch had started a second center of studies in Spain, El Pedroso, in Santiago de Compostela. It moved in 1963 to the Alcor university residence in Madrid, and four years later to the residence called Zurbarán College, also in the capital. Five more centers of studies for women were subsequently opened in different parts of Spain: Dársena (Barcelona, 1965), Alborán (Seville, 1969), Saomar (Valencia, 1972), Los Arces (Valladolid, 1974), and again Alcor (Madrid, 1975).[11]

At the beginning of the 1960s the men's branch had three centers of studies in Spain: Diego de León (Madrid), Monterols (Barcelona) and Aralar (Pamplona). To these were added centers in Valencia, Valladolid, Seville, and Granada (in this case, for a short time). In addition a second one was opened in both Madrid and Barcelona, the latter short-lived. Outside of Spain, the men's branch opened centers of studies in Ireland (1956), Colombia (1959), Venezuela (1965), Argentina (1966), Peru (1967), Guatemala (1967), Germany (1970), Chile (1970), and Brazil (1971).[12]

Numeraries who had completed the center of studies went on to study in the *Studium Generale* of their region. By 1961, nineteen regions had organized a *Studium Generale*. The coursework was modeled on the four years of theology required of candidates for the priesthood. The implementation of the curricula, however, proved difficult and often extended over many years. Once they graduated from college, most numeraries were working full time in addition to being involved in apostolic activities, so they had very little time for classes and study. Usually, they were able to take one or two courses during a three-week annual program that also served as their vacation, and perhaps one or two more courses during the rest of the year.

The interregional study centers, which were in Madrid, Washington, and Rome, underwent some changes. In 1958, the Diego de Leon interregional center for men was transferred to Pamplona, where it was called Colegio Mayor Aralar, and in 1967 an interregional center for women (Colegio Mayor Goroabe) was established. This made it possible for both men and women from different regions to complete higher studies in ecclesiastical subjects at the University of Navarra. This was the case, for example, of Ursula Okondo, the first woman numerary from Kenya. On the other hand, the interregional center for men in Washington—which had originally been intended as the embryo of a future school of journalism for English speakers—was short-lived. After two years in the nation's capital, it moved to Boston in 1960. Because of a shortage of students, however, it was transformed into a regional center of studies and the incipient journalism school closed months later.

During the 1960s the student bodies of the Roman Colleges of the Holy Cross and of Holy Mary grew more geographically diverse. By 1961, 491 men had studied in the Roman College of the Holy Cross, including 313 Spaniards, 59 Americans, and 32 Mexicans.[13] Among those who enrolled during the 1960s were Soichiro Nitta and Koichi Yamamoto (1967) from Japan, Rom Josko (1968) from Australia, and Fernand Cruz (1969) from the Philippines. The Roman College of Holy Mary saw the arrival of Kikuko Yoshizu and Yoko Ando (1963) from Japan, Maria Lourdes Ygoa (1970) from the Philippines, Christine Gichure (1972) from Kenya, and Graziella Montano from Australia (1974).

During the 1960s, some of the members of the Work who came to Rome to study were young people who had not yet earned a college degree. To facilitate their pursuing civil as well as ecclesiastical degrees in Rome, the International Institute of Pedagogy began to offer degrees in 1963. Its students were women numeraries attending the Roman College of Holy Mary in its new campus called *Villa delle Rose.* Many of them would become professors at the *Studium Generale* of the various regions of the Work or teachers at high schools or centers of professional education for women. A year later, the Holy See authorized the transformation of the International Institute of

Pedagogy into a special section of the School of Philosophy and Letters of the University of Navarra with headquarters in Rome[14] It was renamed the International Institute of Educational Sciences in 1968 and had about fifty students from various countries. The four-year course of study focused on education but included theology as well. After obtaining their degree, most of the students went on to complete a doctorate in pedagogy.[15]

In 1964, a separate section for men was added to the International Pedagogical Institute. In this way, students at the Roman College of the Holy Cross could also obtain a master's degree or doctorate in Educational Sciences from the University of Navarra. This program ended after a decade of operation, however, since by that time most of the numeraries arriving at the Roman College already had a college degree.

A pioneer in women's access to higher studies in ecclesiastical studies, Escrivá was delighted to see several women numeraries enroll in the School of Theology at the University of Navarra. In the spring of 1973, Mercedes Otero Tomé and Isabel Sánchez obtained doctorates in theology. Otero served as a faculty member at the Roman College of Holy Mary for the next ten years.[16]

In the mid-1960s, students who entered the Roman College without having finished the basic four-year course of theology (*quadrienium*) delayed going to one of the pontifical universities until they finished the *quadrienium* in the Roman College. Only after they had completed it did they enroll in the doctoral program in philosophy or theology at the Pontifical Lateran University, or in canon law at the University of Navarra. In 1969, Escrivá established the Institute of Theology in Rome as a section of the School of Theology of the University of Navarra. The students at the Roman College pursued their doctoral degrees in theology from the University of Navarra, with a markedly Thomistic orientation. Three years later, in 1972, the Institute of Philosophy in Rome was founded. It depended on the *Studium Generale* of the Work, and granted doctorates in philosophy.[17]

Between twenty and thirty numeraries were ordained each year during the 1960s. As a general rule, they returned to their regions of origin, where they devoted themselves fully to the pastoral needs of Opus Dei. In response to the growth of the Work and its apostolic activities, the number increased sharply in the early 1970s. From 1973 through 1975, a total of 149 numeraries were ordained. During his lifetime, the Founder called 692 members of the Work to the priesthood.

Until 1966, the summer activities of the Roman College of the Holy Cross continued to be held at Salto di Fondi on the Mediterranean shore between Rome and Naples. Because growing numbers of people at the beach and nearby developments had gradually deprived the area of its tranquil character, the summer campus was moved in 1967 to the Apennine Mountains, near the city of L'Aquila. The new house was called Tor d'Aveia.

Section 3. Professional and Family Care of Persons

Throughout the twentieth century, women's self-understanding and the opportunities open to them changed radically. In the 1960s women's role in public life and participation in the labor market in Spain expanded significantly, although it continued to lag more economically developed countries. The founder of Opus Dei occasionally commented on these developments. For example, in response to a question about the role of women in society and, more specifically, in Spanish politics, he replied: "The presence of women in social life as a whole is a logical and totally positive phenomenon. . . . A modern, democratic society must recognize women's right to take an active part in political life, and must create favorable conditions for the exercise of that right by all those who wish to do so."[18]

Not content with commenting on the situation, he introduced important changes in the training Opus Dei offered and the activities it carried our in many fields, but especially with regard to work in the home.* These changes were reflected in the evolving terminology. In

---

* As we have seen, from the very beginning of the Work, Escrivá encouraged the women who followed him to reach high professional goals and proposed intellectual and educational undertakings, such as the creation of a publishing house or the establishment of university residences, which were not usually led by women at the time.

1964, the training centers which had been called Sunday schools were renamed home and cultural schools.[19] A year later, Escrivá indicated that the term "numerary assistant" should be used instead of "numerary servant" because the word servant had acquired a pejorative character that it had not had before.*

In a 1965 pastoral letter on the sanctification of domestic work, he addressed "what today is called the process of women's emancipation." He expressed joy at the fact that "on the social level, important conquests have been made to achieve a just equality of rights with men because women have in common with men their personal dignity and responsibility." "In the supernatural order," he continued, "we all have the same adoptive divine filiation," an identity which, "far from suppressing differences, demands and ennobles diversity" and which is different from "a misunderstood equality with men." Among the characteristic aspects of women, he underlined "careful delicacy, great generosity, sharp wit, tenacity, constancy, and religious piety."† Women had a special characteristic contribution to make in all areas of society as well as in the full gamut of jobs and professions.

The Founder recalled that men as well as women should take care of the family home. He considered men's paternal contribution to family life to be as essential and valuable as women's maternal contribution. He urged all the married members to contribute their abilities in the home through dialogue and complementary collaboration, and to teach their children to contribute as they grew up. He

---

* See General Note 65/65 (June 9, 1965). AGP Q.1.3, 6-29. Numerary Assistants do not constitute a separate class among the members of the Work, nor are they considered inferior to other members. "They are called *Assistants* because they help the other numeraries in all kinds of apostolic works; especially in the Administration of our houses, which is the apostolate of the apostolates; but, in fact, the other numeraries are also auxiliaries of the Auxiliaries" (Collection on the Administration, 1969. AGP Q.1.3, 21-142).

† Letter 36, nos. 3 and 4. AGP A.3, 95-1-1. The Founder's words reflect the vocabulary and understanding of his time. As time went by, the vision of women in society and in the Church evolved, as did many other ways of understanding life and the human condition.

also stressed that in the centers of the Work of both branches, care of the house was the responsibility of everyone in different ways and forms. This aspect of life in the Work would naturally reflect the fact that the centers were normally the home of a larger number of people than the average family. Their management, therefore, demanded a high degree of professional dedication and skills. At the same time, as we have seen, Escrivá considered it a foundational element of Opus Dei that the apostolic and formative work involved in the Administration of the centers of the Work was specific to women and led by them.

As time went by, society began to demand greater professionalism in the care of homes, in the hotel and catering industry, and in the care of persons generally. Social change and advances in technology, equipment, and organization also drove the development of training and education in these fields. In less economically developed countries, a high school diploma became a requirement, while in the economically developed world college-level training was increasingly demanded.[20]

In keeping with the spirit of Opus Dei, the Founder wanted the members of Opus Dei to be in the vanguard of the promotion of women and the elevation of the dignity of their work. Rather than merely reacting to social transformations, the spirit of Opus Dei moved its members to the frontlines of social development. The Founder asked the directors of the women's branch to make it possible for the numeraries who worked as administrators of centers to earn college degrees in home economics, hotel management, dietetics, or similar fields. He urged them to make sure that all the women who worked in the Administrations of the centers were well remunerated and had good working conditions, medical insurance, and other benefits.

Changing social norms and conditions also led to a gradual elimination of distinctions in the way of life of the administrators and others who worked in the Administration. In countries whose languages have formal and informal modes of address (like the Spanish *Usted* and *Tú*), the distinction was eliminated among the people who worked in the Administration. A higher level of education contributed to the professional and personal development of the numerary assistants and helped make it clearer that being a numerary assistant was not a vocation only for those with little education. In the 1970s, the Founder observed that "there will be college graduates and PhDs who will be numerary assistants of Opus Dei."[21]

Escrivá stressed that housework and related occupations involving the direct care of people were not only important professions that required professional training but also vocations. Professional work in one of these fields, he believed, should not be a last resort dictated by the lack of other options, but a freely considered choice based on the desire to care for other people and contribute to their happiness. Embraced in this way, these professions were a path to holiness, a way of encountering Christ through ordinary work. To dedicate oneself principally to domestic tasks was in some cases—for example, that of the numerary assistants—a specific call that gave meaning to life. Those who aspired to holiness through lovingly caring for others were invited by God to make their entire life a continuous prayer. This point of view offered a new perspective on domestic work, one which made clear that its value does not depend on the level assigned to it by society but on the human and spiritual character of the person who undertakes it.

In the 1960s, the rising standard of living in Western society might have suggested that housework would disappear or become meaningless. In some ways, this was occurring in economically and culturally developed areas. The regional advisories in the United States, Italy, and Ireland reported to the central government of the Work that they were having difficulty finding young women who wanted to attend their schools for domestic workers. Girls in their countries were not attracted to those jobs because the society at large suggested they should seek occupations outside the home. Domestic work enjoyed little social esteem and was even criticized as an offense to women's dignity. Girls thought of domestic work as something to do only until they could find a better job. Little by little, the tradition of service in the home was disappearing.

The Founder praised women's desire to work in all professions, something he had encouraged for years. Nonetheless, he thought domestic work was just as valuable and worthwhile as other types of work, with the added bonus that it directly nurtured the growth of individuals. He thought that this profession would continue to exist because the harmonious development of a person is achieved first and foremost in a family environment. He continued to see the home as a unique space where each members feels valued and loved for what he or she is, develops a balanced way of life, and learns the exercise of virtue.

The Founder defined the work of Administration in Opus Dei's centers as the "apostolate of apostolates" because it made it possible for everyone who visited them or lived there to experience an atmosphere of a Christian family, where God is at the center and a common mission is shared. Escrivá saw the work of the Administration as a way of developing a sense of responsibility in caring for family members and of offering society a luminous example of the value of housework and the care of people. In this way, it became a rich professional model of how to place individual persons at the heart of every service provided.

To professionalize these tasks, Escrivá suggested that the women of Opus Dei create schools that would raise home economics and related subjects to the university level. If, as he put it graphically, the kitchen was to be a laboratory and the pantry a school of art, then specific training was needed in subjects like dietetics and food science, organization of tasks, and accounting. In 1964, a pilot activity began in the staff area of the Colegio Mayor Alcor, a center of studies for numeraries of the women's branch near the campus of the University of Madrid. The one-year program was called Escuela de Administración (EDA) and combined practical classes with theory. In each of the following four years, between twelve and fifteen students enrolled in EDA.[22]

Building on this experience and on what was being done in programs of home economics in US colleges and universities, an academic program was developed for numeraries who were thinking of becoming administrators. In May 1968, Escrivá established the School of Domestic Sciences as part of the *Studium Generale* of the Spanish region. Ana Sastre, a physician, coordinated the team that established the curriculum. The course awarded a diploma after three years and a college degree after four. Some students went on to pursue a doctorate. The school had departments of nutrition, physics, and chemistry, business management, and the organization of work. It also offered courses in physiology, interior decorating, and equipment maintenance.[23]

Six months later, in November 1968, the school opened its doors at the Colegio Mayor Zurbarán in Madrid. In 1971 a foundation gave it three large apartments in a building located on Ríos Rosas Street. When it changed its location, it also changed its name to *Centro de Estudios e Investigación de Ciencias Domésticas* (CEICID). The new space included classrooms, teachers' offices, a library, a teaching kitchen, and food, textile, cleaning, and machinery maintenance laboratories. CEICID graduated about thirty students a year. They received a private degree, but not one that was recognized by the Spanish government.

The CEICID model was followed with local variations in other regions: Mexico (1968), Peru (1972), Colombia (1975), and Central America (1975). In Mexico, the *Escuela Superior de Administración de Instituciones* (ESDAI) offered government-recognized classes in hospitality management.[24] In Colombia, the *Instituto Superior de Ciencias Sociales y Económico-Familiares* began a technical level program in administration with government recognition. In Peru, future administrators attended the *Instituto Técnico Superior Montemar*.

The centers of studies for numerary assistants offered one-year courses that included professional training as well as in-depth formation in the spirit of the Work and philosophical and theological studies adapted to their circumstances. In Spain, the center of studies for numerary assistants at the Molinoviejo conference center was joined by new ventures in El Pedroso (Santiago de Compostela, 1963), El Vallés (San Cugat del Vallés, 1969), and Los Rosales (Villaviciosa de

Odón, 1969). These four centers could accommodate a total of one hundred fifty students.[25]

Other regions also opened centers of studies for numerary assistants: Chicago (1961), Chile (1962), Portugal (1964), Italy (1965), Guatemala (1967), Peru (1968), Colombia (1969), Venezuela (1974), and Kenya (1975). These were professional training centers, located in the Administration of a retreat house with adequate facilities. The small number of students was a challenge for some. In Portugal, it forced the center to close.[26]

Most of these centers granted a diploma of some sort. As time went by, a number of them won accreditation of their diplomas in hotel management, catering, and home economics. The first was El Vallés in Spain, which was accredited by the government as a vocational training center in the hotel and catering industry. It also received a small subsidy from the Ministry of Education and Science.

Some numerary assistants and administrators went to Rome to work in the centers there. While in Rome, they earned diplomas and certificates that complemented the ones they had earned in their home countries. In addition, they had the opportunity of getting to know the Founder and deepened their knowledge of the spirit of the Work by interacting with him. Some numerary assistants from regions where there were many vocations went to work in other regions, like the United States, where vocations of numerary assistants were few or nonexistent.

The women responsible for planning and overseeing the domestic care of the Work's centers in Spain soon extended the idea of buying food at wholesale for a number of centers to the purchase of furniture and decorative items. In 1971, at a time of rapid growth in the number of residences and centers in Spain, a group of Opus Dei women set up the company *Instalaciones Comerciales y Decoraciones, S.A.* (Incodesa). It had a workshop for cabinet making, decoration, upholstery, furniture repair, gilding, and the creation of tapestries. Incodesa received commissions for the decoration of centers of the Work, family homes, hotels, and large spaces, such as the Torreciudad shrine or the Cavabianca interregional center in Rome.[27]

Section 4. Associates and Supernumeraries

The legal developments which created the categories of supernumerary (1947), associate (1950), and diocesan members of the Priestly Society of the Holy Cross (1950) made it possible for people to belong to Opus Dei no matter what their personal circumstances. Escrivá stressed that the existence of these various categories did not mean that there were different vocations. There was only one vocation: all members of Opus Dei had the same call to holiness in the midst of the world and the same responsibility to maintain and develop its spirit and apostolates. The various categories simply reflected broad differences in the concrete way of living out that single vocation in people's varying personal circumstances.

The first associates, Francisco Navarro and Rafael Poveda, joined Opus Dei in Madrid in 1950 at a center called Bravo Murillo. Four years later, there were seventy associates living in different parts of Spain as well as some in Italy, Mexico, and Colombia.

The first women associates were Elena Blesa, who joined the Work in Valencia, and María Luisa Udaondo, who joined in Bilbao. Soon women outside of Spain began to join the Work as associates. In 1953, María Teresa Pequich became the first associate in Argentina. A year later, Isaura Santamaría Carrasco applied for admission in Mexico. By 1956 there were already more than one hundred fifty associates in the women's branch. Some of them would go on to have brilliant professional careers. Pilar de la Cierva earned a PhD in chemistry, something quite unusual for a Spanish woman at the time. Lourdes Díaz Trechuelo, who held a PhD in American history, became a pioneer in studies of the Philippines during the colonial period.

The associates gave themselves to God in secular apostolic celibacy in all types of social settings and geographical locations. Some asked for admission when they were young, others as mature adults, still others as elderly men and women. By the early 1960s there were associates who were research scientists, tradesmen, clerks, university professors, administrative workers, laborers, village teachers, farmers, miners, nurses, social workers, domestic servants, and porters.

Half the women associates had completed higher or technical studies, such as teaching or nursing. Many worked as civil servants and employees. The other half had only completed primary or secondary education. At this time, women associates in Spain had to cope with a culture that frowned on women seeking higher education or working outside the home unless their families were experiencing economic difficulties.

Unlike the numeraries, many of whom moved from place to place with some frequency to support the growing apostolates of Opus Dei, most of the associates spent their lives in the place where they joined the Work. They spread its message among people they knew in their professional and family environments. Some associates worked in the corporate apostolates of Opus Dei, especially in the field of education, such as the University of Navarra, the Tajamar school in Madrid, Brafa in Barcelona, the boys' and girls' farm schools in Montefalco (Mexico), and the ELIS center and the SAFI hotel school in Rome.

The centers where associates received formation and gathered for informal get-togethers and other family activities were usually based in apartments rented for that purpose or in centers where numeraries lived. As early as 1952, there were centers of associates in Madrid, Valencia, Barcelona, Tarrasa and Zaragoza, and small groups of associates in many Spanish provinces. Many associates lived with their parents or siblings. Others chose student or professional residences, while still others preferred to live alone in their own apartment or house. They provided for possible periods of unemployment, sickness, and retirement through government-sponsored programs in addition to private insurance and savings plans.[28]

Normally, associates did not live in centers of the Work, but they attended days of recollection, retreats, and annual courses in retreat houses and residences. Formative activities were organized for relatively homogenous groups, taking into account age, education, and background. The annual courses gave them a chance to get to know each other better while deepening their understanding of the spirit of the Work.

The General Council and the Central Advisory adapted the plan of formation which had been devised for the numeraries to the life situations of the associates. They encouraged the numeraries who were more closely involved with groups of associates to make a special effort to understand their often very different circumstances and to keep in mind that those circumstances were part of their journey toward holiness. They asked the directors to take an interest in the housing situation of the associates, especially of those who lived alone, and to make sure that those who were ill were properly cared for. The regional commissions of countries where there were a large number of associates often had a director charged with overseeing the apostolate and formation of the associates.

In the 1960s, Opus Dei devised a course of studies for the associates who had already been incorporated into Opus Dei through the oblation. The classes focused on the doctrinal foundations of Christian life as well as on a detailed explanation of the spirit, norms, and customs of the Work and how to live them in daily life. The two-year course was comprised of two sixty-day semesters with four hours of classes each day. An effort was made to devise schedules that were compatible with normal working hours.[29]

The vocation to Opus Dei as an associate made it possible for men and women who felt called by God to live celibacy in the midst of the world to dedicate themselves full time to all kinds of professional work, without being called to spend time on the internal tasks of government which fell to the numeraries. On the other hand, the associates did collaborate in giving formation to the extent that doing so was compatible with their family and work circumstances. Some oversaw groups of supernumeraries and were responsible for organizing their formation. Others were coordinators and gave spiritual direction to other members of Opus Dei.[30]

In 1974, some college-educated associates who had completed the two-year course of studies raised the possibility of studying the philosophical biennium and the theological quadrennium in the *Studium Generale* of Opus Dei. The Founder liked this idea, although he stressed that it was completely optional and had to be compatible with their family and professional duties.

Since the 1930s, Escrivá had given spiritual direction and formation to married people and people likely to marry. In 1947, he was finally able to allow married people to join the Work as supernumerary members. The first supernumeraries of the men's branch were Tomás Alvira, Mariano Navarro Rubio, and Víctor García Hoz. The first women supernumeraries were Aurora Nieto and Ramona Sanjurjo.

In 1950, the Founder finished writing the *Instruction on the Work of St. Gabriel*, in which he presented the vast panorama of a "vocational call to a multitude of men and women." The St. Gabriel Work would be a "general mobilization of souls, dedicated to the service of God in the midst of all the noble and clean activities of this world, with their exemplary conduct and doctrine." The supernumeraries, like the other members, were called to divinize temporal affairs, "knowing that they were chosen by God to achieve personal holiness in the midst of the world, precisely in the place they occupy in the world, with a solid and enlightened piety, through the willing fulfillment of the duty of each moment, even though it may be difficult." At the same time, they transmit the gospel through an apostolate "that embraces all human activity including doctrine, interior life, and work. It influences individual and collective life in all its aspects: family, professional, social, economic, political, etc."[31]

A small and flexible organizational structure was needed so that institutional aspects did not reduce the spontaneity of personal undertakings and the spread of Opus Dei's spirit in all kinds of environments, each in his own place in society. Friendship, the trusting relationship of friend to friend, was the key element in spreading the spirit of Opus Dei. In addition, however, supernumeraries and cooperators contributed actively to the corporate activities of Opus Dei by serving on boards, establishing supporting organizations, and running educational and recreational programs in clubs and other centers for boys and girls.

The supernumeraries received formation in classes called study circles, which were held two or three times a month, a monthly day of recollection which typically lasted two or three hours, a three-day annual retreat, and a weeklong annual workshop. The retreats and workshops were normally held at the Work's retreat houses. The days of recollection were generally organized in centers of the Work or local churches. The study circles took place in centers of the Work, or in the homes of individual supernumeraries or other locales.[32]

St. Gabriel centers were established to take care of the formation of the supernumeraries and cooperators and to coordinate and encourage their apostolates. Each supernumerary was assigned to a specific center. As the number of supernumeraries in a center grew, they would be divided into groups of no more than twenty persons. As far as possible, these "small Christian communities,"[33] as the Founder liked to call them, were more or less homogenous, taking into account age, educational background, and profession. A numerary or associate would lead each group. Two senior supernumeraries, normally married and with children, would be appointed coordinators. From time to time they would teach the weekly formation class, but their primary responsibility was promoting the unity and cohesion of the group and maintaining close contact with its members. Sometimes they also gave individual spiritual direction to other supernumeraries. A married man or woman's being responsible for this type of spiritual accompaniment was quite new in the tradition of the Church.

The directors of the Work reminded the supernumeraries that their apostolate began at home, with the love between husband and wife, and the friendship and good example given to their children. Many supernumeraries found time to collaborate in corporate works that offered formation to young people. For example, some young supernumeraries lived in the Work's university residences; others participated in activities for young people and collaborated in the financial support of the centers for students and other young people.

The first "courses of studies" for supernumeraries who had completed the program of initial formation and made the oblation was held in 1972 in Madrid. It consisted of a two-year program of classes in philosophy, theology, and the spirit of the Work aimed at improving the supernumeraries' knowledge of the Christian faith and the spirit of Opus Dei. Although the classes were scheduled to accommodate family and work schedules, it was understood that not all supernumeraries would be able to find the time to attend the course of studies. The in-depth formation supernumeraries acquired in the course of studies led them to grow in their sense of responsibility and, in some cases, they became coordinators or collaborated more directly in corporate undertakings.[34]

The number of cooperators continued to grow, reaching some ten thousand men and women by the late 1960s. Catholics, Christians, members of other religions and even nonbelievers who wished to receive formation and collaborate with the various apostolates of Opus Dei joined the association of cooperators. Technically, it was an association of the faithful "proper to and inseparable from the Work."[35] They helped the Work with their prayer, donations, and collaboration in various activities. Some already had a long association with Opus Dei because they had known it in their youth through the Work of St. Raphael. Others first learned about the Work as adults. The centers of St. Gabriel organized days of recollection, retreats, classes, and workshops for cooperators. In addition, some regions created a nonprofit organization called the Association of Cooperators of Opus Dei to support the undertakings of the Work and to collaborate with diocesan activities.[36]

The growth in the number of supernumeraries and cooperators and the increasing diversity of their backgrounds led to a proliferation of projects aimed at meeting social needs and spreading Christian values in society. Perhaps the most significant examples were the spread of Family Orientation courses and the multiplication of schools connected with Opus Dei.*

Family Orientation courses began in the mid-1960s due to the efforts of a number of supernumeraries and cooperators in Barcelona to improve their own parenting skills and help their friends do the same. Rafael Pich-Aguilera, a Catalan businessman who taught at the IESE business school, proposed applying to parenting the case study method used at the business school. Together with José Manuel Fontes

---

* On schools, see chapter 3, section 2.

de Albornoz, he launched a Family Orientation course at the Daumar boys club. The beginnings were modest, a total of eight couples who met to study and discuss cases that posed issues commonly faced by families in raising their children. The idea was not to offer concrete solutions or ready-made formulas, but to learn to think clearly about the challenges that families encounter in helping their children grow and develop. Guided by a moderator, the couples learned to identify the facts and problems described in the case and to think about the pluses and minuses of various approaches. By 1973, the courses had grown enough to justify the creation of the FERT Family Association in Barcelona and the Family Classroom in Madrid.[37] Their activities benefited from materials developed at the Institute of Educational Sciences of the University of Navarra.

In the early 1970s, Family Orientation spread throughout Spain and to other European countries. The directors of the Work did not direct Family Orientation, but they urged supernumeraries to get involved and spread this activity among friends and acquaintances. Supernumeraries from Italy, France, Belgium, and Germany began organizing courses. They found the courses helped to improve the participant's family relationships as well as facilitating friendships. Through the courses, some people encountered the means of Christian formation of the St. Gabriel Work.[38]

Section 5. The Diocesan Clergy

For the first seven years after its foundation in 1943, the Priestly Society of the Holy Cross was made up entirely of numerary priests and other numerary members of the Work who were candidates for ordination to the priesthood. The priests of the Work spread the message of personal sanctification in the exercise of their ministry among diocesan clergy. They helped their priest friends improve their doctrinal and ascetical formation, provided spiritual direction to some of them, and participated in informal meetings with other secular priests. Until 1950, however, it was not possible for diocesan priests to become members of the Priestly Society.

The Holy See's definitive approval of the Work in 1950 made it possible for diocesan priests to join the Priestly Society. It began to organize formative meetings for diocesan priests, including retreats, monthly days of recollection, circles for cooperators and members, and a wide range of informal get-togethers as well as meetings that combined formation and relaxation. These activities were preceded and maintained by personal contact and friendship among priests.

Diocesan priests were attracted both by a practical way of seeking holiness in their daily lives as secular priests and by the Christian family spirit of the Work. They appreciated being encouraged to have a spiritual plan of life and to meet every week or two to receive ongoing formation and strengthen their friendships. They were also excited to know that from their own place in the parish and other pastoral assignments they were helping Opus Dei by praying and explaining its message of holiness in ordinary life.

Some diocesan priests who attended activities of the Priestly Society but did not feel called by God to join it became cooperators. Some of them were appointed ecclesiastical assistants because they spiritually accompanied the members of Opus Dei. To make them better acquainted with the vocation of lay supernumeraries, the priests in charge of their formation read and commented on the *Instruction on the Work of St. Gabriel* at the meetings of the ecclesiastical assistants.

Other diocesan priests joined the Priestly Society as oblates or as supernumeraries. As the Founder explained to the numerary priests responsible for giving formation to oblates and supernumeraries of the Priestly Society, for a priest to join Opus Dei he had to understand it as a divine vocation that increased his desire to be a saint. The means for attaining Christian perfection were the same as those of the other members of the Work: a plan of life, study of doctrine, work well done, and apostolate. A priest's work was the exercise of his ministry, that is, preaching the Word of God, celebrating the sacraments, and caring for the people entrusted to him. An essential element of the vocation to the Priestly Society was summed up in the motto *nihil sine episcopo* (nothing without the bishop), which translated into affection for their own diocesan bishop and obedience to him.

Moreover, they were asked to pour their enthusiasm into the parish and the seminary, united with their brother priests, without forming a separate group within the priests of the diocese.[39]

Escrivá pointed out that, in time, the priests of the Priestly Society would develop other activities such as apostolic emigration or collaboration in corporate works of the Work with the approval of their bishop, the opening of a residence for priests in Rome, and discreet fraternal help to those who had abandoned the priesthood.

To underline the importance of the expression *nihil sine episcopo*, the Founder established several practices not mentioned in the Constitutions. Diocesan priests could join the Priestly Society only with the permission of their bishop, and they would strengthen their diocesan spirit by taking a vow of obedience to the local ordinary at the moment they became part of the Priestly Society.* In addition, he asked Amadeo de Fuenmayor, the Counselor of the Spanish Region between 1952 and 1956, to visit the local bishop whenever the first priest in a diocese decided to join the Priestly Society to explain the Priestly Society to the bishop and to give him a copy of the Constitutions. He suggested stressing to the bishops a number of points: that the spiritual accompaniment offered by the Work did not interfere with the ministerial activity of the members who depended exclusively on his bishop; that membership in a priestly association that sought the holiness of the priest should unite its members to the rest of the priests of the diocese; and that the Holy See encouraged these associations, whether or not promoted by the hierarchy.

The Priestly Society of the Holy Cross spread rapidly, beginning in Spain and Portugal. In September 1952, fifteen diocesan priests participated at Molinoviejo in the first meeting for diocesan members of the Priestly Society of the Holy Cross. Three years later, there were 177 members of the Priestly Society in Spain from more than thirty

---

* The requirement of requesting the permission of the ordinary—and also the vow of obedience—"was suppressed in 1963, because they were no longer in conformity with the praxis of the Holy See in similar cases of priestly associations" Amadeo de Fuenmayor, Valentin Gómez-Iglesias, and José Luis Llanes Maestre, *The Canonical Path of Opus Dei: This History and Defense of a Charism* (Princeton, NJ: Scepter, 1994), p. 349, nt. 150).

different dioceses, mostly young parochial vicars. In 1957, forty-one Portuguese members of the Priestly Society belonged to seven different dioceses. The first Portuguese priest to apply for admission had been Alberto Cosme do Amaral, who became a bishop years later.[40]

Most of the bishops gave their approval for the Priestly Society of the Holy Cross to spread the message of priestly holiness among the diocesan clergy of their diocese. By 1953, thirty-eight Spanish bishops had authorized meetings of the clergy organized by Opus Dei and the incorporation of priests of their diocese into the Priestly Society. Six prelates, on the other hand, raised some objections. The reasons were fear of loss of authority (based on the mistaken belief that a member of the Priestly Society had two superiors and, therefore, was obliged to double obedience) and fear that the priests of the Priestly Society would stop being friends and brothers to the rest of the diocesan priests.

At the end of the 1950s, the Priestly Society of the Holy Cross began to collaborate in the Founder's dream of working in a territory in need of clergy. The Holy See had drawn up a plan of evangelization in some areas of Peru through the establishment of prelatures (some *nullius* and some territorial) that would be entrusted to various institutions of the Church. Bishop Antonio Samorè, secretary of the first section of the Secretariat of State, informed Escrivá that Pope Pius XII wished to entrust one of these prelatures to Opus Dei. The Founder replied that it was proper for priests of the Work to work in the dioceses where they were incardinated or where there were Opus Dei activities. But, he added, they would gladly accept this assignment because it came from the Pope. Rather than choosing one prelature or another, he said they would take the one that no one else wanted.

On April 12, 1957, the Holy See established the prelature of Yauyos and named the numerary priest Ignacio de Orbegozo its prelate. The prelature covered 15,000 square kilometers (about 6,000 square miles) located between 2,500 and 6,000 meters (8,000–20,000 feet) above sea level. Its 175,000 inhabitants were scattered in often inaccessible small villages throughout the mountains. Orbegozo began his pastoral ministry with five associate priests of the Priestly Society of the Holy Cross from various Spanish dioceses. With the permission of their bishops, they accompanied him in the adventure of spreading the faith among the indigenous peoples of the Andes. The first years were spent in the hard work of traveling and administering the sacraments in an extremely poor territory with many villages accessible only by horse or mule.

In 1962, the Holy See added the territory of the civil province of Cañete to the Prelature of Yauyos. Located on the Pacific coast, Cañete had more resources that could be used to improve the rest of the prelature. In January 1964, Orbegozo was ordained titular bishop for the prelature and that same year opened the doors of a minor seminary. In 1968, Luis Sanchez-Moreno replaced Orbegozo as prelate.[41]

During the 1960s and 1970s, the Priestly Society of the Holy Cross grew especially in Spain, Portugal, Mexico, and Italy. The 300 associates and 35 supernumeraries of 1961 became 904 and 170, respectively, in 1975. In addition, there were 817 cooperator priests. The priests of the Priestly Society collaborated in the spiritual care of the supernumeraries and cooperators of Opus Dei and of young people living in residences and schools run by members of the Work. They fomented vocations among their parishioners for the diocesan priesthood and for various institutions of the Church, including Opus Dei.[42]

To facilitate imparting formation and to provide a setting where priests could socialize with each other, the Priestly Society gradually opened centers. For example, in Spain during the mid-1960s it had apartments in Madrid, Pamplona, Barcelona, Zaragoza, Oviedo and Santiago de Compostela. In Italy there were centers in Milan, Verona, Rome, and Palermo. In Portugal centers were located in Porto, Coimbra, and Lisbon. Mexico had centers in the capital and in Guadalajara. Ten years later, the number of centers of the Priestly Society had grown to sixty-five, half in Spain and the rest in eighteen other regions. Associates of the Priestly Society who served as coordinators played a vital role in establishing and operating these centers, which offered a range of formational activities. Among the best known were the pastoral theology courses held in Spain in the Pontifical Basilica of San Miguel (Madrid), Pozoalbero Conference Center (Jerez de

Frontera), Castelldaura Conference Center (Barcelona), and the University of Navarra (Pamplona). Similar courses were held in Italy at Castello di Urio Conference Center on Lake Como.[43]

In 1959 Escrivá set up a center of the Priestly Society in Rome to serve members and cooperators who were studying for their licentiate or doctorate in the pontifical universities. To meet and offer formation to more secular priests, Joaquín Alonso and other numerary priests created the *Centro Romano di Incontri Sacerdotali* (CRIS) [Roman Center for Priestly Meetings] in 1968. It offered spiritual retreats, study groups, conferences on current religious topics, and formation circles. Some of its activities attracted considerable attention because they were given by prominent lecturers including the Viennese psychiatrist Viktor Frankl and the Cardinal Archbishop of Krakow, Karol Wojtyła.

At the end of 1959, the Holy See entrusted to Opus Dei the pastoral care of the Pontifical Basilica of San Miguel (Madrid) which belonged to the apostolic nunciature. This was the first time that numerary priests took charge of a public church. In a short time, Escrivá realized that having a church facilitated the pastoral care of supernumeraries and cooperators and was a visible and appropriate way of making the presence of Opus Dei in a city a reality. He encouraged the regions to ask the bishop in cities where there were many members of the Work to entrust to priests of the Work a church, preferably one that was not a parish.

A decade later, the priests of the Work were running eight other churches in Spain, Mexico, Italy, and Austria: San Giovanni Battista in Collatino (Rome, 1964), Santa Vera Cruz (Mexico City, 1965), San Alberto Magno (Madrid, 1965), Señor San José (Seville, 1965), San Juan del Hospital (Valencia, 1966), Santa María de Montalegre (Barcelona, 1967), Santa Cruz (Zaragoza, 1967), and Peterskirche (Vienna, 1970). In addition, in 1968 the Congregation for the Propagation of the Faith and the Pontifical Commission for Sacred Archaeology entrusted to the Priestly Society of the Holy Cross the basilica and catacomb of Sant'Alessandro, located on the Via Nomentana, on the outskirts of Rome.[44]

Most of these churches continued to be owned by the diocese. Exceptionally, the Priestly Society acquired the church of Señor San José in Seville at the request of the bishop. Opus Dei and the diocese signed an agreement for pastoral care. The agreements established that the corresponding church was entrusted to Opus Dei *ad nutum Sanctae Sedis*, that is, as long as the Holy See did not order otherwise.

The bishop appointed particular priests of Opus Dei designated by the Work to provide pastoral services in the churches entrusted to the Priestly Society. The Founder reminded them that they should follow the pastoral instructions, liturgical norms, and schedules "the diocesan Ordinary prescribes for other churches served by secular priests."[45] They organized traditional associations of the faithful, helped to spread the Work's message, and offered monthly retreats for cooperators and supernumeraries. In some cases, the rectory premises were converted into a center of the Work, after suitable remodeling.

Notes

1. Quoted in *Meditaciones*, vol. 3, 527. AGP Biblioteca, P06; Handwritten note, April 23,1964. AGP K.1, 186-2.

2. "Labor de San Rafael," in AGP Q.1.3, 19-152; General note 118 (May 25,1958), no. 6. AGP Q.1.3, 2-13.

3. See General Note 36/63 (March 27, 1963). AGP E.1.3, 243-2.

4. See General Note 451 (January 4, 1962), General Note 465 January 24, 1962), and General Note 467 (February 2, 1962). AGP E.1.3, 242-3.

5. See General Note 75 (December 8, 1956). AGP E.1.3, 242-1.

6. See General Note 434 (November 30,1961). AGP E.1.3, 242-3; and General Note 481 (February 24, 1962). AGP E.1.3, 242-4.

7. See Hf 221/66 (June 1, 1966). AGP R3.2.2, 2-14.

8. Escivá, *The Way*, no. 382; Letter 7, no. 9. AGP A.3, 91-7-1; General Note 118 (May 25, 1958). AGP Q.1.3, 2-13.

9. See Kücking, *Horizontes insospechados*, pp. 184–186.

10. See AGP E.1.1, 133-4-3; and AGP Q.1.7, 1-4.

11. See AGP R4.2.3, 2-21. The *colegios mayores* in Spain—which date back to the late Middle Ages when they offered academic training as well as lodging—are equivalent to residences in other countries.

12. See AGP G4.2.3.

13. See *Informe de Prefectura de Estudios* (September 24, 1961). AGP D.1, 457-4-2.

14. Office of the Congregation of Seminaries and University Studies, Rome, October 2, 1964. AGP G4.4.1, 51-3-5.

15. See AGP R4.2.2, 5-41.

16. See César Izquierdo and José Ramón Villar, *Notas para un aniversario. 50 años de la Facultad de Teología de la Universidad de Navarra (1967–2017)* (Pamplona: Servicio de Publicaciones de la Universidad de Navarra, 2017), p. 16.

17. See General Note 20/68 (June 7, 1968). AGP E.1.3, 245-5.

18. Escrivá, *Conversations*, n. 90. This response on the vision of women is found in the interview "Women in the Life of the World and the Church," conducted by the journalist Pilar Salcedo in 1968 (*Conversations*, nn. 87–112).

19. See General Note 90/64 (July 9, 1964). AGP Q.1.3, 6-29. In earlier years, some Sunday schools were already called "home schools."

20. In 1966 an international congress of domestic workers was held in Barcelona, organized by Catholic institutions. Some women from the home and cultural schools of Barcelona participated. Later they informed the central advisory that, during the debates, "the numerary assistants spoke at length about the professional meaning of their work, about the preparation and improvement it demands, about the importance it has in society." Hf 261/66 (14-VI-1966). AGP R6.3, 1-2.

21. Quoted in General Note 17/82 (April 5,1982). AGP E.1.3, 1141.

22. See Ana Sastre, *Con las alas del viento* (Madrid: Rialp, 2013), pp. 147–151.

23. See AGP R4.2.4, 1-8.

24. See AGP R4.2.4, 1-8, and AGP R4.2.4, 2-12.

25. See AGP R6.2.2, 1-8.

26. See AGP R6.1, 1-1.

27. See Remembrance of Salud Fernández-Castañeda Álvarez-Ossorio, Madrid, August 21, 1975. AGP A.5, 323-2-6.

28. See AGP G1.4, 230-1-1.

29. See AGP R1.4, 2-47.

30. See General Note 77 (December 8, 1956). AGP E.1.3, 242-1; and General Note 408 (June 22, 1961). AGP E.1.3, 242-3.

31. *Instruction on the Work of St. Gabriel*, nos. 1, 5, 8 and 9. AGP A.3, 90-3-1.

32. The first meeting for supernumeraries of the men's branch took place in September 1948, and the first for supernumeraries of the women's branch in June 1955, both at the Molinoviejo retreat house.

33. *Instruction of San Gabriel*, no. 85. AGP A.3, 90-3-1.

34. See AGP R4.2.3, 6-731, and AGP R2.3, 1-3.

35. *Instruction of San Gabriel*, no. 148. AGP A.3, 90-3-1.

36. See General Note 29/62 (June 5,1962). AGP E.1.3, 243-1; General Note 103/63 (December 5, 1963). AGP E.1.3, 243-3.

37. See Daniel Arasa, *Rafael Pich, pasión por la familia. La Orientación Familiar, un sueño hecho realidad* (Barcelona: Styria, 2010).

38. See AGP R2.4.2, 1-11.

39. See AGP I.4, 278-1-1.

40. See AGP I.4, 279-1.

41. See Federico Prieto Celi, *Don Ignacio. Por las montañas a las estrellas* (Madrid: Palabra, 2018); Esteban Puig Tarrats, "Los inicios de la Prelatura de Yauyos (Perú) 1957–1968," *Studia et Documenta* 4 (2010), pp. 295–338.

42. See AGPI.4, 278-2-1; Des 392 (March 18,1961). AGPI.4, 278-1-3.

43. See AGP I.4, 278-2-1; AGP I.4, 278-4-1.

44. See AGP G1.5, 57-3-1; AGP G1.5, 58-4-1; AGP G1.5, 58-4-3; AGP G1.5, 58-4-5; and AGP E.41, 88-3-1.

45. General Note 13/67 (March 29, 1967). AGP E.1.3, 245-3. See General Note 115/63 (November28, 1963). AGP E.1.3, 243-3; and General Note 37/64 (March 11,1964). AGP E.1.3, 243-4.

CHAPTER 3

~⟋⟍~

Institutional Activities

Since Opus Dei's foundation, friendship has been the basic element in spreading its spirit. As the number of members grew, corporate activities increased, but the message continued to spread primarily through the individual Christian witness of the Work's faithful. For this reason, the Founder urged the regions of the Work to be careful not to allow corporate activities to stifle "what is essential: the formation of numeraries, associates and supernumeraries; and the personal apostolate that they carry out through their professional work in all human activities."[1] He also stressed that corporate activities should not be limited to any specific field whether educational, social, cultural, or health-related.

In the 1950s, Opus Dei's collective apostolates included corporate works (the University of Navarra, residences, high schools, and vocational training schools) and common works in the field of communication and culture. In both cases, Escrivá insisted that the fundamental element in spreading the message of holiness in the midst of the world was the witness of each person, avoiding giving priority to structures over people.

The 1960s witnessed three major changes in Opus Dei's collective presence in society: the opening of more universities, high schools, and technical schools aimed at the various strata of society; the appearance of the so-called personal works; and the end of the common apostolic works. The corporate works concentrated on education, health care, and social development, especially training centers for workers and for the development of women. Escrivá strongly encouraged this formula because it completed the founding mission. The practice of the first decades of starting with intellectuals as a method of reaching all social strata was now bearing fruit in institutional activities.

Escrivá did not want many corporate-work high schools or grade schools, but he encouraged supernumeraries and cooperators to create schools in response to families' demand for well-oriented schools, a demand increased by the doctrinal confusion of the 1960s. Supernumeraries and cooperators wanted their childen to receive at school a coherent explanation of the faith and Christian life so that they would have an intellectual foundation and a practical experience of Christian living before reaching adulthood. The directors of Opus Dei began to encourage and offer formative and doctrinal support to members of the Work and cooperators who wanted to start schools which were not corporate apostolates of Opus Dei. They soon began to call them "personal works."

Section 1. Higher Education

As we have seen, from the beginning Escrivá stressed apostolate with educated people because he was convinced that through them the whole society could be improved. (He referred to them as "intellectuals," but he had in mind a much broader group of people than that word suggests in English.) "Intellectuals have an overall vision and animate every important cultural, technical and artistic movement in human society."[2] He wanted to spread the spirit of Opus Dei to people from all walks of life and social groups, but he viewed apostolate with the educated as the way to later extend the Work's evangelizing action to other groups

Opus Dei's principal corporate work in the field of higher education, the University of Navarra, grew vigorously during the 1960s. New buildings were built and new academic centers opened: the School of Social Assistants (1963), the Higher Institute of Secretarial Studies and Administration (1963), the Institute of Philosophy (1964), the School of Architecture (1964), the Department of Biology (1964), the School of Pharmacy (1964), the Department of Physical Sciences (1965), the International Institute of Educational Sciences (1965), and the School of Theology (1969). By the end of the decade, the university had students from thirty-nine countries.

Thirty-two percent of its students were children of workers and peasants, and Navarra was the Spanish university that granted the most scholarships.[3]

Escrivá asked that the members of the faculty be told that he respected those who had a clerical or one-party mentality, but that he did not share it. Opus Dei did not corporately follow a particular theological, philosophical, educational, or cultural school of thought.[4] Faculty members were free to hold the views they considered most convincing among the positions compatible with Catholic doctrine. He also encouraged the university to make an advisor available to all students and encourage the students to express their opinions freely.

In Pamplona, the University of Navarra abandoned the prevalent Spanish urban university model and moved to the campus-based model common in English-speaking countries. This meant a campus with a large open spaces between the buildings despite the disadvantage of being somewhat removed from the social life of the city. Large residential colleges were built: Belagua for men, with a total of four hundred places, and Goroabe and Goimendi for women, with a total of two hundred places. They strove to offer a welcoming environment and a host of social and intellectual opportunities open not only to residents but to all students.[5]

In the mid-sixties, the Founder urged Opus Dei's members in other countries to study the possibility of creating corporate works in the field of higher education. He reminded them that corporate dedication to private education was not an end of the Work, but pointed out that the growing secularization of modern society made it important to create academic institutions which would show the compatibility of the gospel with all fields of knowledge. These corporate works would be few. They would exist only in regions where there was a significant number of members of the Work, and even in those countries there might be only one. They would try to offer a model of competent professional work and Christian life open to people of all beliefs.

Opus Dei's second corporate university began in Piura, Peru, at the urging of the local bishop. It opened in April 1969 with a strong emphasis on social development and programs that would contribute to the much-needed economic development of the area.

Several regions began activities in various fields of higher education with the hope that they would eventually develop into universities. In Guatemala City, the *Instituto Femenino de Estudios Superiores* (1964) began, with schools of social work, interior design, and secretarial and administrative studies, all of which granted government-recognized degrees or diplomas. In Mexico, some members and cooperators of Opus Dei, including both academics and businessmen, launched the Pan-American Institute of Business Management in 1967 and the Pan-American Institute of Humanities and the Institute for the Training and Education of Middle Managers in 1968. In Manila, the Center for Research and Communication opened its doors in 1967 and soon developed a master's program in business economics. The *Instituto Superior de Educación* (1971) began in Colombia and the *Centro de Extensión Universitaria* (1972) in Brazil.[6]

In the United States, the failure of an attempt to start a college in Washington and the existence of a large number of prestigious colleges and universities led the Work to concentrate on student residences near the best universities, including Harvard, the Massachusetts Institute of Technology, the University of Wisconsin, Notre Dame, Columbia, and the University of Chicago.

Vicente Rodríguez Casado, in his personal capacity as professor of world and modern history at the University of Seville, started what he called called the Hispano-American University of Santa María, which operated from 1943 to 1974. It was not really a university but a specialized summer school that brought together some fifty students and professors to study and discuss Ibero-American history and culture as well as current affairs in an informal atmosphere not to be found in Spanish universities.[7]

Rodríguez Casado also founded what he called *Ateneos Populares* [Popular Atheneums] in industrial areas throughout Spain. They organized conferences, colloquia, and cultural debates between workers and university students. He hoped they would help promote open dialogue between workers and university students, breaking down class barriers and lessening the resentment of many young workers at being treated with paternalism or used for political purposes. Annual meetings of the Ateneos in La Rábida gave workers and students an opportunity to live together and interact on an equal footing. Among the topics they debated were the causes of working-class anticlericalism in Spain. The Ateneos met with opposition from both the Falangists and the Communists, but at the end of the 1960s there were twenty-six scattered around Spain.[8]

Section 2. Primary and Secondary Schools

In the summer of 1963, the founder of Opus Dei spent a few weeks in a country house located in the northern part of Navarra. One day, Florencio Sanchez Bella, the Counselor of the Spanish region, mentioned that supernumeraries and cooperators from various cities had asked the Work to open more schools, both because of the quality of teaching in the existing ones and because, in some cases, the religious education in their children's schools was at best confused.[9]

After thinking about the question, Escrivá said that he understood the parents' concern and wanted to help them but didn't see how the Work could create a network of schools that would be corporate works. That would require many trained people and might bring with it a danger that teaching would become the main institutional activity of Opus Dei. He suggested a different possible solution— what would be called, starting in 1966, personal work schools. The name was chosen to emphasize that they were not institutionally promoted by Opus Dei. If parents started schools and took responsibility for their management, hiring competent teachers, devising the curriculum, and ensuring their economic viability, Opus Dei would provide chaplains and make certain that there were trained religion teachers. As he had done with respect to the existing corporate work schools, the Founder suggested that attention should be focused first on the parents, then on the teachers, and finally on the students.[10]

In a short time, a group of supernumeraries including Tomás Alvira and Víctor García Hoz (both specialists in pedagogy) as well as Antonio García de Gúdal, Félix Falcón, and Vicente Picó, started a company called *Fomento de Centros de Enseñanza* to promote new schools, appoint their management teams, and provide a legal structure to ensure the continuity of the schools' initial orientation. *Fomento* hoped to offer high-quality education with a stress on the humanities and culture in single-sex schools that would emphasize personal tutoring and character development based on the virtues and Christian doctrine. The first *Fomento* school, Ahlzahir (Córdoba), started in 1963 with 108 students. It was supported by a group of three local couples with the support of other families. The following year, El Prado and Montealto began in Madrid, and Canigó in Barcelona.

In 1965, the headquarters of Opus Dei encouraged the regions to start many personal work schools, although corporate work schools would continue to be few.[11] The subsequent rapid growth in the number of personal work schools was due to the professionalism and prestige of the directors and teachers and in many places to high demand for more good schools caused by postwar baby booms. In Spain, where the largest number were located, government policy on private schools facilitated approval, made land available at low cost, and provided monetary credits for school construction. By the mid-1970s, there were a total of twenty *Fomento* schools in Barcelona, Córdoba, Gijón-Oviedo, La Coruña, Madrid, Murcia, Pamplona, Seville, Valencia, Vigo, and Zaragoza. In addition, three other educational companies had been founded: the Cefasa group, with schools in Granada, Jaén, Málaga, and El Puerto de Santa María; *Institució Familiar d'Educació*, with schools in Barcelona, Tarragona and Igualada; and the Coas educational group with schools in Bilbao and San Sebastián.

Personal work schools were established in many regions, especially in Latin America. Frequently, the supernumeraries and cooperators most directly involved created not-for-profit corporations that sponsored a school for boys and another for girls to which they sent their own children: Gimnasio de Los Cerros (1965) and Gimnasio Iragua (1969) in Bogotá; Cedros (1966) and Yaocalli (1970) in Mexico City; Intisana (1966) and Los Pinos (1968) in Quito; Los Arcos (1967) and

Caniguá (1974) in Caracas; Los Molinos (1970) and El Buen Ayre (1968) in Buenos Aires; Tabancura (1970) and Los Andes (1969) in Santiago de Chile; El Roble (1971) and Campoalegre (1972) in Guatemala City; Argonne and Monforte in Milan (both in 1974).

The number of corporate schools in Spain also increased, although at a slower pace. Viaró (Barcelona, 1963) and Retamar (Madrid, 1966) were located in prosperous new neighborhoods. Other schools were begun in working-class neighborhoods: Irabia began in 1964 on the outskirts of Pamplona; Xaloc (1964) and Pineda (1968), in Hospitalet de Llobregat (Barcelona); and Altair (1967) in the Cerro-Amate district of Seville.

Many corporate and personal work schools offered classes in the late afternoons and evenings to working-class students who had to work during the day to help support their families. Gaztelueta (Bilbao) had some 500 students during the day and and 300 in the evening section. Los Cerros (Bogotá) had 450 during the day and 110 in the evening.

The multiplication of corporate and personal work schools gave Opus Dei a presence in the world of education it had not had before. The schools also helped to spread the Work's message of holiness in the midst of the world to thousands of students and their families. They contributed to the apostolates of the works of St. Raphael and St. Gabriel. Frequently centers were established close to the schools to provide young people and their parents with access to the means of formation outside school hours. The proliferation of educational centers and the number of members of the Work involved in them also had a downside in that it tended to obscure to some degree an essential feature of the spirit of Opus Dei: work in all kinds of places and entities, especially in public institutions

Shortly before the birth of the first personal work schools, Escrivá had stressed the importance of trying to spread the spirit of Opus Dei "among primary and secondary public school teachers, in university schools of education, and in teacher training colleges."[12] This continued to be an important emphasis. Frequently teachers trained in schools connected to the Work later moved to public schools and vice versa.

Section 3. Technical and Vocational Training Centers

The spirit of Opus Dei echoes Catholic Social Doctrine's stress on the need for Christians to educate and contribute to the professional and social development of those in vulnerable situations, so that they can live with greater dignity. In the 1960s, members of Opus Dei in increasing numbers worked professionally in a wide variety of technical, trade, and professional training schools that made it possible for students from underprivileged backgrounds to improve their economic and social position. These included secretarial schools, hotel management training centers, and agricultural and trade schools. In some cases, schools and other centers started by individual members and cooperators eventually became corporate activities of Opus Dei, but most never had any official connection with the Work. These undertakings relied for their effectiveness on technical competence, adaptation to social demand, and the conviction that professional work can and should be a way to raise people's standard of living and, at the same time, a way to spread in different professions and jobs the teaching of Christ and Opus Dei's message of the call to sanctity in daily work. The ones that were corporate apostolates of the Work, in addition to providing professional training and skills, offered religious formation, and made known the activities of the Works of St. Raphael and St. Gabriel.

Secretarial schools became popular in the 1960s because they offered women a way to have a well-paid job that would give them greater autonomy. Spanish women of Opus Dei created the *Instituto Superior de Secretariado y Administración* (ISSA) [Higher Institute of Secretarial Services and Administration] of the University of Navarra in San Sebastian in 1963. It offered theoretical and practical training, classes in foreign languages, and internships. That same year, they inaugurated the Instituto Superior Zalima in Córdoba, with courses in secretarial skills, household techniques, cooking and interior decoration. They opened the Escuela de Secretariado Aloya in Vigo in 1967.[13] There were also short-lived secretarial schools in Italy (Palermo and Naples) and in Nigeria (Lagos).

As the 1970s progressed, interest in secretarial schools waned because many young women opted for other studies. The secretarial schools run by women of Opus Dei adapted to this new reality in various ways. Aloya became a technical school offering a broad range of programs. Albaydar evolved into a vocational training and high school. Kianda College in Nairobi became a secondary school.

Until the 1950s, most middle-class and upper-class families in Spain had one or more maids, cooks, or the like. Often the woman of the house played a very limited role in running it. In the 1950s and '60s, in response to changing social conditions, many middle- and upper-class mothers began to take a more active role in homemaking and the education of their children. In many cases, they found themselves with little or no domestic help and soon began to recognize that they needed to learn more about home economics. In response to this demand, women of Opus Dei started several "home and art schools" which taught the elements of home economics as well as art and interior decoration: Almenara (Zaragoza, 1951), Llar (Barcelona, 1952), Montelar (Madrid, 1956), Albaydar (Seville, 1956), Alsajara (Granada, 1958), Montealegre (Oviedo, 1964), and Leku-Eder (Neguri), among others.[14]

These schools gave classes in various subjects including cooking, interior decoration, gardening, and ceramics. In addition, they offered Christian formation courses and organized volunteer activities. For example, Montelar had a social aid department which prepared food baskets that were distributed to the poor. Some women who learned to sew or embroider made vestments for oratories. In the following decade, as more women began to attend college, many of these schools closed or were transformed into educational centers offering state-recognized intermediate careers.

In Spain and some Latin American countries, significant numbers of girls from rural villages and other working-class backgrounds sought work as maids and cooks in private home or in the hotel and tourism industries. Women of Opus Dei made a major effort to improve their professional, economic, and social situation. At first, they focused primarily on training centers and residential schools and relied mostly on on-the-job training. This was combined with basic general education, including in many cases, basic literacy. In 1966, there were twenty Spanish home and culture schools attended by some 1200 students, mostly domestic workers in private homes. In Mexico City, the Alhucema School of Home, Culture, and Handicrafts had 190 students; in San José, Costa Rica, the Pavas School for the training of women had 110. In Santiago de Chile, the domestic workers' section of the Fontanar Academy of Studies had 120. An estimated 2,900 girls and young students attended these centers worldwide.[15]

As improving social and economic conditions gradually brought with them greater educational opportunities for women from underprivileged backgrounds and rising expectations on the part of employers, the schools and residential programs began to offer more theoretical training and placed less emphasis on on-the-job training. The level of general education offered also improved, because the students had received more education before enrolling. Different schools took different paths. Some became specialized institutes of home economics. Others focused on training for the hotel and tourism sector. Still others became high schools that offered training in home economics. Wherever possible, they took steps to have their diplomas and degrees accredited by the government, since this would open doors in the labor market.[16] In Spain, some home schools were transformed into vocational training centers which offered training programs in kindergarten education, family economics, and hotel management, with internships in restaurants, hotels, and private homes. Something similar happened with Kibondeni School of Catering (Nairobi), which received government authorization to issue its own certificates because the curriculum followed the state guidelines for secondary schools and the requirements for British diplomas in administration and services.[17]

Members of the Work began a number of schools to teach trades to young people people from disadvantaged districts of large cities. For example, the Kinal educational center for workers (Guatemala City, 1961), established in a depressed area next to the municipal dump, offered boys and young men courses in carpentry, gardening, warehouse work, and electricity. A similar school for women was started near Kinal, called Junkabal (1962), with studies in secretarial service, home economics, retail services, and fashion design. The Morro Velho Social Center (São Paulo, 1963), in an impoverished area on the edge of the city, taught craft skills and typing.

From the very beginnings of the Work, Escrivá's *Apuntes íntimos* showed a concern for helping the rural poor, especially women. He hoped that with sufficient training they could achieve a better standard of living, without being forced to emigrate to the cities, where at the time and for many decades thereafter they often faced very harsh conditions.

In the early 1960s, several agricultural schools were started in Spain and America. For men, the experimental agricultural center El Peñón (Montefalco, Mexico, 1961); the school for middle managers in agriculture Las Garzas (Chimbarongo, Chile, 1963); the Valle Grande school for farmers (San Vicente de Cañete, Peru, 1966); and the *Instituto Técnico Agrario Bell-lloc del Pla* (Gerona, Spain, 1965), which offered a high school program with classes in agriculture and livestock raising. The women of Opus Dei began the Montefalco farm-school, which became a girls' high school in 1968; the school for peasant women at Hacienda Toshi (Mexico), which from 1960 on had a medical dispensary and an adult literacy center; and the Condoray vocational training center (San Vicente de Cañete, Peru 1963), which offered various programs to women in impoverished rural areas. In addition, in Peru, three laypeople of the Work took charge in 1964 of Radio ERPA (*Escuelas Radiofónicas Populares Andinas*) to transmit agricultural, human, and spiritual education programs to schools and individual indigenous people.[18] Similarly, beginning in 1968, secondary education courses via radio were held in Montefalco.

In the late 1960s, several Spanish members of the Work began what would soon become a substantial chain of specialized rural schools called *Escuelas Familiares Agrarias* (EFAs) [Family Farming Schools]. Joaquín Herreros Robles, Felipe González de Canales, and Teresa María Pérez-Payán took their inspiration from the *Maison Familiale Rurale* (France) and the *Federazione Coltivatori Diretti* (Italy). The

EFAs offered a Christian vision of life and gave the sons and daughters of small farmers the general and professional education they needed to become successful rural entrepreneurs. During three years, the students alternated one-week periods living at the school and taking theoretical classes with two-week periods of work on their parents' farms. They learned to make their families' small farms economically viable, and the religious education they were offered contributed to maintaining vibrant Catholic life in the small towns where they lived. At the end of their studies, they received a government-recognized diploma.[19]

The first two EFAs for boys were Molino Azul and Casablanquilla (1967), northeast of Seville. The first for girls were called Elcható (Seville, 1968) and Yucatal (Cordoba, 1970). In the early 1970s, there were sixteen EFAs in Spain, with eight hundred students. Five years later, the number of schools had doubled. Most of the young people were the children of small farmers who cultivated less than ten hectares (25 acres).

The EFAs were owned by a corporation. Day-to-day management of each school was in the hands of a management committee, made up of the school's directors and the students' parents. The EFAs relied on tuition, subsidies from the Ministry of Education, and grants from local sponsoring entities including savings banks, cooperatives, and municipalities. Each EFA had an association of families that participated in the governance of the school. The local associations formed a nationwide federation. In 1975, it participated in the birth of the *Association Internationale des Maisons Familiales Rurales* [International Association of Rural Family Homes].[20]

Section 4. Development and Demise of Common Works

As we have seen, common works in the field of communication had taken shape in the 1950s.* They included several cultural and university magazines, the publisher Ediciones Rialp and the Europa Press agency, which began distributing feature articles and later became a

---

* See volume 1, chapter 11, section 2, "Common Apostolic Works."

news agency. The founder of the Work saw in all of them a secular and modern channel through which Christian and human values could be disseminated in a capillary way.

In 1962, the General Council of Opus Dei proposed to all the regions that some members of the Work try to start in their countries a wide-circulation news magazine "as a way of forming the conscience and the sense of responsibility of Catholic laymen."[21] It suggested that the magazines might include letters to the editor, current events, news of the life and activities of Catholics, as well as reviews of books, movies, television, and art. Shortly thereafter, in February 1963, the first issue of *Mundo Cristiano*, of the SARPE group, appeared in Spain. It was a graphic and current affairs magazine, with general information for the family from a Christian point of view. It was very well received. Two years after its inception, it had a circulation of more than 200,000 copies, a level that it maintained until the early seventies. The same publishing group began publishing in 1964 *Tria: A Magazine for the Countryside*, but its circulation was always small.

Pilar Salcedo, Covadonga O'Shea, and a few other women started in 1964 a woman's magazine called *Telva*, also published by the SARPE group. The magazine focused heavily on fashion and attempted to influence fashion professionals ranging from haute couture designers to dressmakers. It promoted styles that combined elegance and attractive appearance with dignity and decorum. "The *Telva* girl was a classy, dynamic woman, committed to her time and of firm convictions."[22] *Telva* also focused on women's rights and equal access to the full range of professions as well as motherhood. Its graphic design was modern and attractive. It soon became a leader among women's publications, with a monthly press run of 75,000.

Although it was not a common apostolic work, another important women's magazine, *Ama*, was started by three women of the Work in 1959. It was a biweekly magazine subsidized by the government and aimed at housewives. It had print runs of more than 175,000 copies.

The publications started outside of Spain mostly had very modest circulation and survived for only a few years. This was the case of the magazine *Report: The News of the Month in Perspective*, published by Carl Schmitt and three other members of the Work in New York (1963–1967); *Gaceta Social in Mexico* (1963–1969); *Analyse* (Vienna, 1965–1969); *Cuadernos del Sur* in Buenos Aires (1964–1970); *Catholic Position Papers* in Ashiya, Japan (from 1972); and *Position Papers* in Dublin (from 1974).[23]

As an institution, Opus Dei put considerable effort into the French literary and cultural magazine *La Table Ronde*, which had existed since the end of World War II. In 1958, some members of the Work who lived in Paris became part of a group of Catholic professors and intellectuals who wrote on contemporary political, economic, and artistic topics. Later, they created a corporation that bought the magazine in order to maintain its Catholic orientation. In the following years, *La Table Ronde* developed an impressive stable of writers and contributors whose articles enriched the French cultural debate. On the other hand, it always lost money. To solve the problem, the General Council asked all the regions of the Work to convince supernumeraries and cooperators as well as libraries and universities to subscribe. This effort had limited results. In 1969, the last issue of the magazine was printed.[24]

The DELSA bookstore network prospered in the mid-sixties. It had thirteen stores in Spanish cities and worked closely with three more belonging to the LINESA group. In addition to selling books during regular business hours, the bookstores also held cultural and educational events after business hours.[25] In some large towns where it did not have a bookstore, DELSA had representatives who stocked some books and facilitated ordering others. In Madrid, DELSA's Neblí art gallery sponsored exhibitions and colloquia.

DELSA had a bibliographic studies department at its headquarters in Madrid. The people who worked in OBISA (*Orientación Bibliográfica, S.A.*) reviewed the most important new Spanish publications, discussing not only their content and literary merit but also their moral character and suitability for different groups. The reviews were intended to help bookstore employees make recommendations to clients, but other people could also subscribe to the review service. Outside of Spain, attempts to establish bookstores proved short-lived.[26]

In February 1964, a meeting was held at Villa Tevere for numeraries working in activities related to the apostolate of public opinion. Among the participants were José Luis Cebrián, editor of the daily *El Alcázar*; Enrique Cavanna, editor of *La Table Ronde*; Manuel Fernández Areal, editor of *Diario Regional*; and Alfonso Nieto, from the regional office of the apostolate of public opinion in Spain. In addition to noting the effectiveness of some publications such as *La Actualidad Española* or *Mundo Cristiano*, they discussed the challenge of using television as a means of making Christian doctrine known. They also studied how to explain the exclusively spiritual purpose of Opus Dei, with the corresponding freedom of thought and action of its members, and how the values of the gospel could be more widely disseminated in the media.[27]

It gradually became clear that the common works of the apostolate had serious problems. In the first place, they involved an inherent and irresolvable tension between the professional independence of their directors and staff and the action of the directors of the Work. They were professional undertakings of the members of the Work who directed them or worked on them individually. Each had its own management team and was financially accountable to the financial company that supported it. But the directors of Opus Dei oversaw them to ensure both that they served an apostolic purpose and that they were economically viable. Specifically, the office of the regional commission responsible for the Work's economic affairs reviewed the balance sheets of the companies that owned the common works, and the general president of Opus Dei confirmed the appointment of the director of each common work and appointed the doctrinal advisor of the publications. These interventions were based on trust without written agreements, but they were inevitably in tension with the full professional autonomy of the journalists.

Perhaps even more important, the existence of common apostolates also made it unnecessarily difficult to explain convincingly Opus Dei's exclusively spiritual and apostolic aims, and that it did not hold corporately any particular social, political, or economic positions. Given the cultural environment of the time and the prevailing concept of the Catholic press, it was very difficult for many people to understand how Opus Dei could try to disassociate itself from the editorial line of the publications.

In many countries, and concretely in Spain, the Catholic press was an established reality. It publicly defended the faith, was recognized as Catholic by Church authorities, and was owned by dioceses or religious institutions. The common works were quite different from the publications that made up the "Catholic press." Although inspired by Catholic teaching, they were nondenominational and were owned by secular companies. The journalists who directed them or wrote for them did so in their personal capacity. The authorities of the Work did not dictate an editorial line and therefore did not take responsibility for their content.

Many people, however, inevitably thought of the common works as Catholic publications and believed that Opus Dei as an institution was responsible for their editorial policy and content. When the leaders of Opus Dei denied that, they were accused of secrecy and of controlling the media from the shadows. Even some members of the Work complained to the regional directors about the points of view expressed in publications run by members of the Work. These complaints were to some extent understandable, since the directors of the Work had encouraged members to subscribe to the cultural magazines that were common works.

In Spain, these problems were complicated by a strong cultural traditionalism, a single-party mentality, and the lack of freedom of association. Many Spanish Catholics could not conceive how publications promoting Christian values were not confessional or that they judged political events with freedom of thought, often different from the positions of the Franco regime.

Two other problems were due to particular circumstances rather than to anything inherent in the nature of the common apostolates, but they were nonetheless real and important. Some of the publications were staffed by quite young people with little professional experience. In addition, the cultural magazines published outside Spain, such as *Studi Cattolici, La Table Ronde, Rumo, Report* or *Gaceta Social de México*, found it impossible to attract advertising. It gradually became apparent that they would never turn a profit or even break even. They kept going only thanks to donations, solicited in many cases by the regional commission from members of the Work and cooperators.[28]

After considering these problems, on December 5, 1966, Escrivá put an end to the experiment of common works. From then on, the collective apostolic tasks of Opus Dei would be divided "*only into two groups*: corporate works and personal works."[29] No new common works would be created, and the regional directors would stop making suggestions to the publications that till then had been common works. The people who had been appointed technical and doctrinal advisors to the publications ceased to hold those positions, and the office in charge of the Work's finances stopped overseeing their finances. A year later, the General Council noted that, with respect to the media, "the Work, neither officially nor informally, nor through fiduciaries, will ordinarily participate in promoting" media. Such "activities must be personal undertakings of individuals in the use of their professional freedom, whether working individually or in association with others. They have full moral and legal responsibility for what they do."[30]

The companies and media that had been common works evolved in different ways. Some of them closed due to economic problems. *La Actualidad Española* experienced a few successful years until the crisis of graphic magazines due to television; *Studi Cattolici* and the publishing house Ares passed into the hands of the journalist Cesare Cavalleri; *Telva* created its own company. The businessman Francisco Martín Fernández de Heredia bought the Europa Press agency. The Mexican magazine *Istmo* became a publication of the Universidad Panamericana. The publishing house SARPE was dismembered and disappeared a decade later. The ESFINA group remained in the hands of the financiers Pablo Bofill and José Ferrer and retained its name but shifted focus toward banking, purchasing Banco Atlántico and creating Bankunión and the Fundación General Mediterránea.

In the following years, members of the Work continued to found and develop cultural and journalistic ventures, but they did so on a strictly personal basis. The collective apostolates of Opus Dei, whether corporate works or personal works, were limited to educational, welfare, and formative activities.

Section 5. Financial Support of Apostolic Activities

From the very beginning of Opus Dei, the Founder explained that all members of the Work should live the virtue of poverty in keeping with their secular state and condition in life. They should act, he stressed, with the mentality of a father or mother of a large, needy family. They should avoid having superfluous things, complaining when they lacked something necessary, or treating what they did have as something exclusively for their personal use. They should also seek advice before incurring extraordinary expenses. The members should support themselves through their professional work and contribute to the support and development of the Work's apostolates. Every apostolic activity and every center should be financially self-supporting.

What this would mean in practice for numeraries and associates would be different from what it would mean for supernumeraries. Numeraries and associates would use their earnings first to cover their personal expenses, but they should use any additional earnings to support the apostolates of the Work. As regards inherited goods, they could retain ownership and pass them on at their death to whomever they preferred. They should, however, generally hand over the administration of those goods, their use, and the income they might produce to family members or to someone else, including, if they wished, the apostolic activities of the Work.[31] Supernumeraries, on the other hand, were asked to make a monthly contribution according to their abilities. The majority, who are middle-class or poor, and the minority, who are wealthy, are all asked to be generous, but there are no fixed quotas. These contributions are earmarked for the institutional needs of Opus Dei, above all the operating expenses of the central and regional government offices, the interregional and regional formation centers, and the support of the clergy. In addition, the contributions of supernumeraries and cooperators are used to help support corporate works of apostolate through donations or capital contributions to the entities that own and manage these educational and apostolic activities.

Of course, the individual schools, residences, and welfare centers sought direct contributions from their supporters as well as aid from foundations and the government. In the 1960s, many corporate and personal works had a sponsoring group and a board of patrons. At the beginning of each project, a small sponsoring group of five or six families would be formed to launch the undertaking. Its members established a not-for-profit corporation or similar entity which sought contributions and ensured the autonomy and continuity of the project. It acquired the necessary property, undertook the construction of buildings, applied for bank loans, drew up financial plans and sought the active participation of more people, especially the parents of students.

Once the project was underway, a board of patrons, whose members might be the same people who formed the sponsoring group, was asked to take responsibility for raising money on an ongoing basis. The board set annual goals, looked for donors, and sought government subsidies. In some cases, the supernumeraries in a particular center might be asked to cooperate with the board of patrons to support an apostolic activity like a youth club.[32]

The goal was for each apostolic activity to be self-supporting. Many schools, student residences, and retreat houses, however, could not do so, both because they kept their fees low or granted large amounts of financial aid to be accessible to everyone, and because mortgage repayment was a heavy burden.[33] To help solve this problem, members of the Work formed a wide variety of institutions which for a time were referred to within Opus Dei as "Auxiliary Societies." Many of them built or acquired properties that they leased on favorable terms to schools, residences, and other apostolic activities.

Some auxiliary societies were not-for-profit corporations or foundations. Others were for-profit entities that paid their investors a modest but relatively secure rate of return or ran businesses whose profits they donated to apostolic activities. In 1966 the women's branch had 21 auxiliary societies and the men's branch 117 (29 in Spain, 14 each in the United States and Mexico, 6 in Italy, and smaller numbers in the remaining regions). Half of the properties which housed corporate apostolic activities were owned by auxiliary societies and the other half were rented from third parties.[34]

During the General Congress held in September 1969, the electors pointed out that many people outside the Work thought that Opus Dei owned large amounts of property and managed businesses. It was not easy to convince them that the entities that owned the properties used for apostolic activities were completely distinct from the Work. In response to this problem, the Founder decided to eliminate the category of auxiliary societies in the hope this would help people to understand "that the material instruments used in the apostolic work are really the property of the citizens [or entities who are their legal owners] and that the Work does not administer the societies that they may establish to help carry out apostolic works."*

Terminating the category "auxiliary societies" within Opus Dei did not dissolve the entities that had made up the category, change their assets, or alter the persons who owned or otherwise controlled them. The relationship between the Work and the auxiliary societies that had been involved in media had already ended when the common works were eliminated. The relations of the Work with the auxiliary societies that supported schools and other corporate or personal work apostolates, however, did not immediately change when the category was abolished. They continued to send their financial statements to the regional commissions and to receive suggestions from them.[35] Even cosmetically the change was not very effective, since most people who thought of the Work as having a lot of property were not even aware of the category of auxiliary societies.

---

* Minutes of the Special General Congress, 12-IX-1970, in AGP, D.3. The proposal was put forward by Escrivá in the first part of the congress, in September 1969, and ratified a year later, in the second part of the congress. We will speak in detail about this congress in the following chapter.

Institutionally, Opus Dei owned very little property: only its headquarters (the Villa Tevere complex), the Torreciudad shrine, the churches of Señor San José (Seville) and Santa María de Montalegre (Barcelona), and the burial places of the numeraries and associates.

Almost nothing in Opus Dei fell into the canonical category of ecclesiastical goods. As early as 1950, the Founder had decreed that the only ecclesiastical goods in Opus Dei would be: "1) The amounts of money necessary for the formation and support of our priests; and 2) the alms given each year by the President General, with the deliberative vote of the general council or the central advisory."[36] A decade later he added the assets necessary for the support of members who could not support themselves, primarily the sick and elderly.[37]

The regions sent to Rome an annual contribution of ten percent of the amounts that the members had made available for apostolic activities and other donations received. This money supported what was called the Work of St. Nicholas, Opus Dei's intercessor for economic needs. With the favorable vote of the General Council and the Central Advisory, the President General allocated part of the accumulated resources to the support of the Roman Colleges and the headquarters of the Work, as well as to apostolic projects in the regions that were just beginning and were not yet self-supporting.

Most of the help provided to the regions took the form of low or no-interest, long-term loans, although non-repayable grants were also given when necessary. In the period 1961–1966, the Work of St. Nicholas gave forty-eight loans and six grants totalling $2,360,000 on the part of the men and another $470,000 on the part of the women to promote or support residences, retreat houses, schools, and training centers in twenty-one regions.[38]

Two numerary members of the Work started significant foundations. Luis Valls-Taberner, vice-president and later president of *Banco Popular Español* between 1957 and 2004, convinced the members of the bank's board of directors to include in its bylaws a provision that the share of the bank's profits to which they were entitled by law would instead be contributed to the Fundación Hispanica. These contributions were used to support guarantees and loans on favorable terms to civil and ecclesiastical institutions. The beneficiaries included training and education centers that helped young people prepare to make a living, many cloistered convents, several parishes, theology students at the University of Navarra, and some residences and retreat houses promoted by Opus Dei.[39]

Antonio Zweifel, a Swiss member of the Work, founded the Limmat Foundation in Zurich to support social undertakings throughout the world. Limmat supported projects proposed and implemented by private local institutions. It focused on the promotion of women and vocational training in rural areas. It insisted that the local communities be deeply involved in projects to improve their standard of living and that local institutions should finance at least one-third of the total costs of each undertaking. Some of the projects Limmat supported had been created by Opus Dei members, among them Condoray vocational training school for women (San Vicente de Cañete, Peru) and El Alto vocational training center for peasant women (south of Medellín, Colombia). Others, including ORT schools for Jewish refugees and several orphanages for children of the Buddhist minority in Bangladesh, had no connection to Opus Dei.[40] By the 1980s, other members of Opus Dei had created similar organizations that support charitable activities worldwide.[41]

Notes

1. General Note 101/65 (December 31, 1965). AGP E.1.3, 244-4.

2. *Catechism* (1966, 4th ed.). AGP E.1.9, 208-1-2.

3. See General Note 26/64 (February 28, 1964). AGP E.1.3, 243-4.

4. Javier Echevarría, *Memoria de San Josemaría*, 6th ed. (Madrid: Rialp, 2016), p. 304.

5. See AGP E.2.1, 204-1-2.

6. See AGP R4.5, 2-34.

7. See Fernando Fernández Rodríguez (ed.), *El Espíritu de la Rábida* (Madrid: Unión Editorial,1995).

8. See AGP G3.2.4, 1673.

9. Authors' interview with César Ortiz de Echagüe, Madrid, March 30, 2017. In 1963, Ortiz de Echagüe held the position of Defender in the Regional Commission of Spain.

10. See Remembrance of Florencio Sánchez Bella, Madrid, August 15, 1978. AGP A.5, 244-1-1.

11. See General Note 25/65 (March 13, 1965). AGP E.1.3, 244-3.

12. See General Note 482 (March 2, 1962). AGP E.1.3, 242-4. See General Note 408 (June 22, 1961). AGP E.1.3, 242-3.

13. See AGP R4.5, 1-24.

14. Remembrance of Gloria Toranzo, Madrid, April 10, 2014. AGP U.1.2, 4-75. There were similar schools in other parts of the world, such as Kianda College (Nairobi, Kenya, 1961) and the *Colegio de Arte y Hogar Ogarapé* (Asunción, Paraguay, 1964).

15. See AGP R3.2.5, 1-4.c

16. See AGP R6.3, 1-2. f. Ana Maria Sanguineti, "*El Instituto de Capacitación Integral en Estudios Domésticos* (ICIED): *génesis y evolución de una escuela dirigida a promover la dignidad de la mujer y el valor del servicio,*" Studia et Documenta 13 (2019), pp. 127–173.

17. See AGP R6.3, 2-9 and AGP R6.3, 1-2.

18. See Samuel Valero, *Yauyos: una aventura evangelizadora en los Andes peruanos* (Madrid: Rialp, 1990).

19. See AGP R4.5, 1-18.

20. See Felipe González de Canales and Jesús Carnicero, *Roturar y sembrar. Así nacieron las Escuelas Familiares Agrarias (EFA)* (Madrid: Rialp, 2005).

21. General Note 507, no. 4 (June 13, 1962). AGP E.1.3, 242-4.

22. Authors' interview with Covadonga O'Shea y Artiñano, Madrid, November 1, 2019. See Roberta Bueso and Mónica Codina, *La democratización de la moda en España. Telva, 1963–1975* (Pamplona: EUNSA, 2020).

23. See AGP M.2.5, 45.

24. See General Note 168 (September 5, 1958). AGP E.1.3, 242-1; and General Note 509 (April 13, 1962). AGP E.1.3, 242-4.

25. See AGP T.7, 1-2.

26. See AGP T.7, 1-5.

27. See AGP K.1, 186-4.

28. See General Note 12/65, no. 1 (January 14, 1965). AGP E.1.3, 244-3.

29. General Note 80/66 (December 5, 1966). AGP E.1.3, 245-2.

30. General Note 80/67 (December 2, 1967). AGP E.1.3, 245-4.

31. Opus Dei supports the parents of numeraries and associates when they are in serious need. In 1966, for example, this assistance amounted to 43 million Italian lire per year.

32. For the organization of promoter groups and boards of patrons in Spain, see Hf 32/79 (March29, 1979). AGP R2.4.1, 1-5.

33. See General Note 6/66 (January 20, 1966). AGP E.1.3, 244-5.

34. See AGP D.1, 457-5-2.

35. See sac 469/84 Annex I, 2, j. AGP Q.1.3, 55-9.

36. Manuscript, Rome, December 8, 1950. AGP D.1, 457-1-3. He also maintained the custom that Opus Dei priests did not receive stipends—money given by the faithful to the priest to say Mass for a specific intention—and only dispensed from this practice in places where the members were especially short of money. This happened for longer or shorter periods in El Salvador, Costa Rica, Belgium, Holland, Italy, Japan, Nigeria, and Paraguay.

37. General Note 366 (February1, 1961). AGP E.1.3, 242-2.

38. See AGP D.1, 457-5-2.

39. For Valls-Taberner's performance in this bank, see Gabriel Tortella, José María Ortiz-Villajos and José Luis García Ruiz, *Historia del Banco Popular. La lucha por la independencia* (Barcelona - Madrid - Buenos Aires: Marcial Pons, 2011).

40. Agustín López Kindler, *Toni Zweifel. Huellas de una historia de amor* (Madrid: Rialp, 2016), p. 73.

41. Kindler, p. 82.

CHAPTER 4

─❦─

Theological-Legal Developments

After the 1947 publication of *Provida Mater Ecclesia*, the apostolic constitution which created secular institutes, and the almost simultaneous approval of Opus Dei, the Congregation for Religious gradually erected other secular institutes of pontifical right. At the same time, other institutes of diocesan right were born throughout the Church. Although *Provida Mater Ecclesia* emphasized the secular character of these institutes, the congregation often viewed them as very similar to religious congregations and applied to them norms derived from the law of religious orders and congregations. It approved, for example, secular institutes whose members took public vows, lived canonical common life, wore a habit, or used terminology proper to religious. The Congregation of the Council prohibited members of secular institutes from engaging professionally in commerce and finance, and representatives of secular institutes were invited to join federations of religious orders and congregations and to attend meetings of religious superiors.[1]

Escrivá protested to the Holy See against this cutting back on secularity, which threatened to distort the spirit of Opus Dei which was aimed at ordinary laypeople and diocesan priests. If the members of the Work were considered religious, they would not be seen as what they were: people equal to others in their work and social relations. When he asked for clarifications or requested minor changes in the Constitutions of Opus Dei, the Congregation for Religious granted his requests in ways that seemed to involve privileges. Opus Dei's position became more ambiguous and anomalous as the congregation approved more secular institutes with elements taken from the law of religious. Cardinal Arcadio Larraona commented to Álvaro del Portillo that, after the approval of Opus Dei, "the mold was broken." Since then, no other institution with the secular characteristics of the Work had been approved.[2] For the next three decades, treating the members of secular institutes as members of religious orders and congregations would be a serious institutional problem for Opus Dei.

Section 1. An Anomalous Situation

The changes in the concept of secular institute and its application moved Escrivá adopted some measures to reinforce the secularity in Opus Dei. With the approval of the Holy See, he instructed the counselors and regional secretaries of the Work not to attend the meetings of religious superiors or federations of religious. Around 1955, he asked three specialists in canon law, Álvaro del Portillo, Salvador Canals, and Julian Herranz, to publish studies on the doctrine, legislation, and historical development of secular institutes.[3]

By the early 1960s, in addition to Opus Dei, there were four male and nine female secular institutes of pontifical right. Two of the male institutes carried out activities similar to those of the religious orders and congregations, and two asked their members to keep their membership secret as an apostolic tactic in order to be able to work unhindered in environments considered hostile to Catholicism. Five of the female institutes were very similar to religious congregations and four were secret. All these institutes were happy with their legal situation and the rules the congregation required them to abide by.[4]

By contrast the foundational charism of Opus Dei was incompatible with secrecy and with a way of life or status in the Church like that of the religious. Opus Dei could not accept the characterization of its members as living in "a state of perfection," because that category was identified with the perfection acquired in the religious state, incompatible with dedicating oneself to God in the midst of the world as an ordinary lay man or woman, or a secular priest.

Escrivá venerated the way in which members of religious orders and congregations dedicated themselves to God but was convinced it was not the only way of living fully and radically the Christian vocation. Full dedication to God did not necessarily require living the evangelical counsels of poverty, chastity, and obedience the way religious did. Simple faithful could give themselves fully to God in the ordinary circumstances of secular life. There they could reach the summit of holiness, living in a way suitable to ordinary Christians all the virtues, including, of course, obedience, chastity, and poverty.*

Because all the other secular institutes seemed content with the legislation applied to them and the way it was interpreted by the congregation, after 1959 Opus Dei stopped petitioning the Congregation for Religious to maintain the original law of secular institutes. The move away from the original concept of secular institute was harmful to Opus Dei but beneficial to other groups in the Church, so Escrivá concluded Opus Dei would have to look for some other legal status.[5]

On March 5, 1960, Escrivá had his first audience with Pope John XXIII. The Founder gave him brochures and printed material on some of the corporate works of Opus Dei. For his part, the Pope recalled that during a trip to Spain when he was Cardinal of Venice, he had visited two residences run by Opus Dei. During the meeting, which was very cordial, they briefly discussed the legal situation of the Work.[6]

A few weeks later, Escrivá informally consulted Cardinal Domenico Tardini, Secretary of State and Cardinal Protector of Opus Dei, about the possibility of the Work's ceasing to be a secular institute and becoming dependent on the Consistorial Congregation because "the members of Opus Dei were not, and could not be equated with, religious."[7] As a possible juridical solution, which would not involve privileges, Escrivá suggested that Opus Dei might be reclassified as a prelature *nullius* or as a territorial prelature with a minimal territory, perhaps a single church. Either solution would allow priests to be incardinated in Opus Dei. As a concrete example of what he had in mind, he pointed to the Mission de France, a secular interdiocesan entity dependent on the Consistorial Congregation. Nothing came of

---

* In the 1960s, the Founder rejected the use of the term "state of perfection" and similar terms to refer to the canonical situation of the members of the Work. See José Luis Illanes, "Apuntes para una reflexión teológica sobre el itinerario jurídico del Opus Dei," *Studia et Documenta* 10 (2016), p. 357.

this proposal because in June Cardinal Tardini informed Escrivá that it would not be opportune to present a formal request.[8]

Cardinal Tardini died in 1961, and Cardinal Pietro Ciriaci took his place as Cardinal Protector. Ciriaci suggested Opus Dei formally request a new canonical framework. The founder was hesitant because Tardini had advised that the time was not ripe and because the Second Vatican Council was about to begin. At Ciriaci's insistence that the request would be well received, however, Escrivá officially proposed on January 7, 1962, that Opus Dei be transformed into a prelature *nullius* or, at least, that the president of Opus Dei be entrusted with a prelature in which he could incardinate the priests of the institute. To the request he added a note, also written at the suggestion of Cardinal Ciriaci, in which he mentioned institutions with prelates that had territorial and personal jurisdiction, such as those in charge of spiritual assistance to the emigrants of various Eastern rites, the military vicariates, and the Mission de France.[9]

During the following weeks, Cardinal Carlo Confalonieri, secretary of the Consistorial Congregation, commented that diocesan bishops were uneasy about institutions not under their jurisdiction. Cardinal Valerio Valeri, prefect of the Congregation for Religious, expressed his fears that Opus Dei's change would be followed by other secular institutes. Bishop Antonio Samorè of the Congregation for Extraordinary Ecclesiastical affairs also expressed some concerns.

On May 20, 1962, the Secretary of State, Cardinal Amleto Cicognani, informed Escrivá that, "since it was a new and delicate matter," several dicasteries had opposed the proposal to erect Opus Dei as a prelature *nullius*. Taking these reports into account, the Holy See had decided not to accept a request that raised "almost insurmountable legal and practical difficulties."[10] The Founder immediately replied that he fully accepted the decision and that, at the same time, he reserved the right to return to the matter, since he considered it a duty of conscience. Taking into account the refusal of the Holy See, Escrivá decided to wait a long time before taking any further official steps. For the moment, he asked the members of the Work to pray and offer their work to God for his intentions.

A month later, on June 27, 1962, John XXIII again received Escrivá in audience. The Founder briefly alluded to the legal problem of Opus Dei. He mentioned that it was a problem for the Work to depend on the Congregation for Religious but assured the Pope that he would not make a new formal request any time soon. He also explained that Opus Dei's activities were exclusively apostolic, since articles in the international press had attributed political and economic activities to the Work. He then spoke with the Holy Father about ecumenism, specifically about Opus Dei's having non-Catholic and non-Christian cooperators.[11]

Over the previous decade, Escrivá had used the authority given him by the Holy See to introduce a number of changes in Opus Dei's Constitutions, almost all aimed at safeguarding the secularity of the members. In October 1963, he incorporated them into a new edition of the Constitutions, which was approved by the Congregation for Religious. In addition, in the mid-1960s, he revised the Work's nomenclature, adopting categories more in keeping with its secular nature and activity, avoiding anything that might seem to suggest religious consecration. Thus he changed secular institute to *association of the faithful*, constitutions to *particular law* [*ius peculiare*], Christian perfection to *sanctity*, state of perfection to *perfection in one's own state*, superiors to *directors*, *missus* to *regional delegate*, oblates to *associates*, regional seminary to *Studium Generale* of the region, visit to a region to *service commission*, house to *center*, minor silence and major silence to *afternoon work time* and *evening time*, spiritual exercises to *retreat*. Starting about this time, the Founder began to say orally and in writing that Opus Dei was no longer in fact a secular institute, even though that was still its legal classification.[12]

On January 24, 1964, Josemaría Escrivá had his first audience with Pope Paul VI. The Founder assured him of his own prayers and those of his children for the success of the Vatican Council. He also referred to the problems Opus Dei was encountering because the legal category of secular institute had lost its original character. Weeks later, he sent the Pope a thank-you letter, enclosing the particular law of Opus Dei and a long note in which he expressed his desire that, when the time was right, the Work would be put into a legal category appropriate to its specific charism.[13]

In July, Escrivá, who was in northern Spain, was surprised to learn that the Vatican curia was examining the note sent to the Pope with a view to changing the legal status of Opus Dei. Concerned, he asked Cardinal Antoniutti, prefect of the Congregation for Religious, to wait for his return to Rome since the letter did not offer all the data necessary for a canonical study of the Work. He added that a possible solution appeared in the section on priests and personal prelatures of the conciliar schema *De sacerdotibus*. He also wrote to Bishop Dell'Acqua, substitute for the Secretary of State, insisting that the pastoral phenomenon of Opus Dei could not "be judged, nor understood, with the mentality of one who is used to studying problems of clerical or religious life, but is not well versed in the problems of the laity"[14] Cardinal Antoniutti replied that nothing would be done before the conclusion of the Vatican Council.[15]

On October 10, 1964, Pope Paul VI granted Escrivá a new audience. The Pope urged him not to worry about Opus Dei's legal category, because it would be resolved later. He also added that he understood the freedom enjoyed by the members of the Work in their professional, economic, and political activities. He gave him a handwritten letter in which he praised Opus Dei, "born in our time as a lively expression of the perennial youthfulness of the Church." He expressed his satisfaction with Opus Dei's apostolate and sent words of encouragement to its members as they exercise the "apostolate of presence and witness in all sectors of contemporary life." He encouraged them to be "in mutual agreement with the old and new religious works and institutions."[16]

In November 1963, the priest and theologian Hans Urs von Balthasar published in the Swiss newspaper *Neue Zürcher Nachrichten* two articles under the title "Integralismus." A month later they were republished in the Austrian magazine *Wort und Wahrheit*. The articles described Opus Dei as the most important fundamentalist power in the Church; criticized the political, economic, and social strength they claimed the Work had in Spain, and accused it of giving priority to temporal power over evangelical values. Von Balthasar also criticized *The Way* for offering a spirituality lacking theological substance. Immediately, Pedro Turull and Juan Bautista Torelló, who lived in Switzerland and Austria respectively, contacted the author. Von Balthasar, who had founded a small secular institute called the Community of St. John, said that he could not find theological or spiritual reasons to explain the spread of Opus Dei. He acknowledged, however, that he had been influenced by some Jesuits in Zurich who criticized the residence promoted by the Work.[17]

Section 2. The Message of Opus Dei at Vatican Council II

Of the almost 2,800 council fathers who participated in the ecumenical council, three were from Opus Dei. Ignacio de Orbegozo, prelate of the prelature *nullius* of Yauyos (Peru), and Luis Sanchez-Moreno, auxiliary bishop of Chiclayo (Peru), were numeraries. Alberto Cosme do Amaral, auxiliary bishop of Porto (Portugal), was an associate of the Priestly Society of the Holy Cross. None of them played a large role in the Council.

Three members of the Work served as experts: Álvaro del Portillo, secretary general of Opus Dei; José María Albareda, rector of the University of Navarra; and Salvador Canals, a judge of the Roman Rota tribunal. In addition, another priest of the Work, Julián Herranz, acted as an official of two commissions. Del Portillo served as president of the ante-preparatory commission on the laity before the Council opened. During the Council, he was secretary of the commission on the discipline of the clergy and the Christian people, and a consultant to the commissions on bishops and the governance of dioceses, on religious, on associations of the faithful, on the discipline of the faith and on the revision of the Code of Canon Law. His contributions can be seen in the conciliar texts on the sanctification of the laity and the mission of the priest, which clearly reflect aspects of the spirit of Opus Dei that make explicit what was already part of the common patrimony of the Church.[18]

The Founder did not participate in the sessions or commissions of the Council. He did not want to be named a Council father because he would have been placed among the religious superiors, giving rise to further confusion about the secular nature of Opus Dei. When Bishop Capovilla, personal secretary of Pope John XXIII, suggested that he might be appointed a conciliar expert, Escrivá declined the offer, since it would be strange for some members of the Work to be council fathers and the Founder an expert.[19]

Escrivá prayed fervently for the work of the Council and followed it attentively. During the four years of the Council, he met more than two hundred times at Villa Tevere with a total of fifty-three council fathers and various theologians and canonists. Most of those who came to see him were Spanish diocesan bishops or Italian members of the Vatican curia. He also went to visit them in the houses where they were staying in Rome.

The Founder took advantage of these conversations to explain the spirit of Opus Dei. On one occasion, for example, Archbishop François Marty of Rheims commented that the laity should transform the structures of the temporal order. Escrivá replied with a smile: "Only if they have a contemplative soul, Your Excellency. Because, if not, they will not Christianize anything. Worse still, it will be they who will allow themselves to be transformed; and instead of Christianizing the world, Christians will become worldly."[20]

Several conciliar documents proclaimed central aspects of the spirit of Opus Dei. The Dogmatic Constitution on the Church, *Lumen gentium*, confirmed the universal vocation to holiness: "Fortified by so many and such powerful means of salvation, all the faithful, whatever their condition or state, are called by the Lord, each in his own way, to that perfect holiness whereby the Father Himself is perfect."[21] The Council's teaching in its decree on the apostolate of the laity is reminiscent of Escrivá's approach: "Since the laity, in accordance with their state of life, live in the midst of the world and its concerns, they are called by God to exercise their apostolate in the world like leaven, with the ardor of the spirit of Christ."[22] The Pastoral Constitution on the Church in the Modern World, *Gaudium et spes*, explained that human work "accords with God's will"[23] and is a means of elevating man and everything he accomplishes to the Creator. The same decree recognized the freedom of the faithful in temporal matters. The decree on priests, *Presbyterorum ordinis*, stressed the ideas often repeated by the Founder that the Mass is the center and root of the spiritual life and that secular clerics enjoy the right of association. The Council documents on the liturgy, the media, ecumenism, and religious freedom included other points that coincided with important elements of the spirit of Opus Dei.

The Council's texts contained approaches Escrivá had preached since the foundation of the Work and expressions that reflect currents of thought and Christian life that enhance the vocation of secular men and women. By making these points part of the Church's official teaching, the Second Vatican Council confirmed and theologically strengthened the spirit of Opus Dei. In 1967, the Founder wrote in the prologue to the fourth edition of the *Catechism* of the Work: "In that great Ecumenical Assembly and in subsequent documents of the Roman Pontiff, the fundamental principles Opus Dei has preached and practiced since 1928 have been ratified in a most solemn way: the universal call to holiness, sanctified and sanctifying professional work, and divine filiation which make us contemplative souls in the midst of the street, each one seeking Christian perfection, in the fulfillment of his personal duties of state and in the midst of his ordinary work. Help me to give thanks to God."[24]

The Council called for the creation of flexible ecclesiastical organizations to respond to pastoral needs. Concretely, it suggested that, although territorial divisions (dioceses) would remain central in the organization of the Church, units ("ecclesiastical circumscriptions") might also be formed on the basis of personal circumstances. This approach made it easier to systematize some of the phenomena that had arisen in previous decades. Specifically, section 10 of the decree *Presbyterorum ordinis* contemplated the possibility of having personal prelatures and particular dioceses for the service and attention of some pastoral activities. From the moment the document was promulgated, the Founder said that one of these legal categories based on personal circumstances could be an appropriate solution for Opus Dei.[25]

Section 3. The Special General Congress

On January 25, 1966, a few weeks after the conclusion of the Second Vatican Council, Pope Paul VI received Escrivá in audience. The Founder presented him with a special edition of *The Way* commemorating the publication of two million copies. They spoke again about the legal situation of Opus Dei, and Escrivá reminded the Holy Father that he preferred to wait before beginning another study on the canonical solution of the Work. A year and a half later, on July 15, 1967, the Pope granted him another audience. The Founder spoke to him about many topics: vocations to Opus Dei in various parts of the world; the people who found the Catholic faith through contact with the apostolates of the Work; the growth of corporate social activities and projects for new universities. He stressed that Opus Dei taught people to seek sanctity through ordinary professional activity united to doctrinal formation. On the other hand, in that audience, he did not refer to the legal framework of Opus Dei.[26]

In August 1966, Paul VI published *Ecclesiae Sanctae* with norms for the application of certain decrees of the Council, including the renewal and updating (*aggiornamento*) of religious institutions and secular institutes. Opus Dei had just celebrated a general congress and Escrivá did not see any immediate need for another. In spring 1969, however, several cardinals told the Founder that criticisms against the Work were circulating in the Vatican. At the proposal of the prefect of the Congregation for Religious, Cardinal Antoniutti, a special commission had been created to study the canonical situation of Opus Dei and to modify its Constitutions. The commission was composed of five people, three of whom—Fr. Ramón Bidagor and Monsignors Sotero Sanz Villalba and Achille Glorieux—were notoriously opposed to Opus Dei.*

---

* Bishop Sotero Sanz, advisor to the Roman Curia, later changed his mind. In 1974, when he was nuncio in Chile, he met with Escrivá and asked his forgiveness for his behavior five years earlier (see Andres Vazquez de Prada, *The Founder of Opus Dei*, vol. 3, *The Divine Ways of the Earth* (New York: Scepter, 2005), p. 626, nt. 91).

On May 20, 1969, Escrivá asked the Holy See for permission to hold a general assembly of Opus Dei to review its particular law in accordance with the orientations of the Council and the founding spirit. After receiving the Vatican's approval, he called a Special General Congress. The first meeting was held from September 1 to 15, 1969, for men and from September 4 to 16 for women. A total of 192 congress members from all the regions studied the spirit, praxis, and law of Opus Dei. In their conclusions, they expressed their union with the Pope, the diocesan bishops, and the founder of the Work, and their adherence to the teachings of the Second Vatican Council. They indicated that "a conceptual and terminological revision of our particular law" should be carried out.[27] As part of that process, they called for consulting all the members of Opus Dei and holding a second meeting a year later.

The Founder informed Cardinal Antoniutti about the progress of the congress. He also sent Paul VI a long report. He lamented the unilateral creation of a secret commission to revise Opus Dei's constitutions without seeking its input. The Vatican was aware that Opus Dei was not happy with its existing constitutions and was holding a congress to study the issue. Why then would it not wait to learn the outcome of that study before moving ahead on its own? He also pointed out that three members of the commission were known to be hostile to the Work and therefore should not have been appointed.[28]

Weeks later, Cardinal Jean Villot, Secretary of State, replied that there was a special commission, but only for the study of the constitutions of priestly secular institutes, not Opus Dei. He added that some expressions in Escrivá's letter had displeased the Roman Pontiff. The Founder immediately wrote again to the Pope to ask his forgiveness for any displeasure he might have felt and to express his complete filial attachment to him.[29] Shortly afterward he learned that the commission for the study of Opus Dei had been dissolved.

The Founder suffered because some highly placed people in the Holy See showed little openness and little trust in him and in Opus Dei. In this rarefied climate, the Work was viewed with a certain coldness and distance. He was told from time to time that the Work was accused of being detached from the Pope, or even opposed to him. In order not to fuel the controversy, he preferred to remain silent publicly and, at the same time, to hold meetings with the Roman Curia to clear up misunderstandings.

Escrivá encountered great difficulties in dealing with Bishop Giovanni Benelli, who became Deputy Secretary of State in 1967. In part, this was due to their contrasting views on the political activity of Catholics. The Secretariat of State was backing, with the Pope's approval, a program that included the distancing of the Spanish hierarchy from the Franco regime, the progressive withdrawal of well-known Catholics from the government, and the formation of a Spanish political party similar to the officially Catholic Italian *Democrazia Cristiana*. Benelli had asked Escrivá to instruct the members of the Work, and especially those who held political office, to support this plan. The Founder believed he could not do so because political freedom was an essential element of the spirit of the Work. Moreover, he argued that if in a given country the Church felt it needed to adopt specific political positions, it was up to the bishops of the country to give concrete guidance to Catholics, something that the Spanish hierarchy had not done up to that point.

With such divergent positions, there was no hope for an understanding. Benelli felt that Escrivá was obliged to help him disassociate the Church from the Franco regime by instructing Opus Dei members to withdraw from the government. For his part, the Founder insisted that the Work could not intervene in the political decisions of its members, however well-founded Benelli's desire to disassociate the Church from the Franco regime.[30]

Opus Dei's insistence on changing its legal status and its refusal to collaborate institutionally in the Vatican's political plans for Spain took their toll. Between 1968 and 1973, Escrivá was not able to obtain a single audience with the Pope. During the first two years, he requested an audience ten times, both by letter and by word of mouth, almost always through Bishop Benelli, who controlled the Pope's appointments. Since he received no reply, in 1970 he decided to stop asking for an audience and wait for circumstances to change.[31]

During this period, Escrivá met a number of times with the head of the Jesuits. After the difficulties that had arisen in 1951–1952, when some Italian students from Jesuit schools joined Opus Dei, Escrivá had advised the members of the Work to avoid close dealings with members of the Society of Jesus. The years passed and the waters calmed down to a certain extent. In May 1965, a Spanish Jesuit, Fr. Pedro Arrupe, was elected Superior General of the Society of Jesus. At that time, the Jesuits were going through a period of *aggiornamento* in the light of the Council, including a search for forms of popular piety and pastoral and social action. It was a difficult period in which they were experiencing a decline in the number of vocations, a certain doctrinal confusion, and a lack of religious discipline.[32]

In July 1965, Arrupe asked to meet with Escrivá. They had lunch at Villa Tevere on September 12. Over the next five years, they met eleven times, sometimes at the Jesuit general curia and others at Opus Dei headquarters. Their meetings were cordial. Often, they discussed spiritual topics, such as the need to strengthen Catholic doctrine and to promote the traditional means of Christian practice. From the beginning, Escrivá asked Arrupe to put an end to the animosity of some priests of the Society of Jesus toward Opus Dei. He added that he did not want to criticize anyone for events that now lay in the past, but only sought to clear the air by discussing the source of tension between the two groups.

For his part, Arrupe suggested the possibility that the Jesuits and the members of the Work carry out some joint apostolic activity. Escrivá replied that it did not seem appropriate to him because they were two such different institutions. The Jesuits were consecrated religious while the members of the Work were secular faithful. In addition, their charisms were different. The Jesuits focused primarily on a number of specific types of apostolate: schools and universities, Marian congregations, missions, and the press, where devotion to the Sacred Heart was propagated. Opus Dei did not have specific areas of concentration. Because its aposolate was carried out by its membedrs primarily in their different professions, it was "a sea without shores." Escrivá realized that Arrupe was interested in the Work's lay and secular way of forming the laity and directing the apostolates, and that he appreciated the development of the Work. But he considered it better for each institution to seek in its own spirit the way to orient its apostolates. Moreover, some Jesuits continued to criticize Opus Dei, publicly alleging that it controlled the government, universities, and banks in Spain. Others used terminology or imitated external forms of the apostolates of the Work. For these reasons, in March 1970 he decided to stop meeting with Fr. Arrupe.[33]

In the early 1970s, the Founder intensified his prayer for the Church and for the legal development of Opus Dei. In April 1970, he traveled to Spain and Portugal to pray before Our Lady of the Pillar and Our Lady of Fatima. He also visited the shrine of Torreciudad, near Barbastro. On May 8, he heard interiorly, without the sound of words, the phrase *Si Deus nobiscum, quis contra nos*? (If God is with us, who is against us: Rom 8:31). Three months later, on August 6, he heard another locution: *Clama, ne cesses!* (Cry out, do not cease: Is 58:1). Both served to strengthen his confidence in God and moved him to continue praying.

From May 15 to June 23, 1970, the Founder visited Mexico. It was the first time he left Europe. He began his stay with a novena to Our Lady of Guadalupe. Through the intercession of Our Lady, he prayed intensely to God for the situation of the Church and for the "special intention," that is the legal solution that would safeguard the genuine nature of Opus Dei. Later, he held meetings with people of the Work from all social groups, from intellectuals living in Mexico City to peasants participating in activities in Montefalco or Jaltepec, a retreat house near Guadalajara.[34]

On August 30, 1970, the second part of the Special General Congress of Opus Dei began. During the previous months, members of the Work all over the world had sent more than 54,000 observations and proposals to Rome. During the congress, several commissions studied the main proposals. The men's and women's plenary sessions concluded on September 14. Their conclusions emphasized the validity of the norms of piety and the spiritual and doctrinal formation given in the Work and the need for "a legal

category different from that of a Secular Institute" that would eliminate "the elements proper to the Institutes of Perfection, that is, the
profession of the three evangelical counsels."[35] The spirit of Opus
Dei, the Congress stressed, does not lead to the acquisition of a different canonical state, the state of Christian perfection. Rather it
leads each person to seek perfection in his or her own state (clerical, lay, single, married, widowed, etc.). The Congress members also
decided that the Congress would not close. Instead, it would continue its work through a twelve-member technical commission with
two subcommissions, one juridical-canonical and the other theological, to propose solutions to the institutional problem of Opus
Dei under the presidency of Álvaro del Portillo.

As the technical commission began its work, new difficulties
arose in the Vatican. Anonymous rumors accused Opus Dei members
working in the Holy See of double obedience. They were obliged, it
was said, to obey not only their Vatican superior but also the directors
of the Work, whom, it was claimed, they consulted on professional
matters, thus failing to maintain secrecy in reserved matters. It was
even said that several Opus Dei members had secretly infiltrated the
Roman congregations.[*] In January 1971, Cardinal Villot, the Vatican
Secretary of State, asked Escrivá for a list of Opus Dei members working in the Vatican. The Founder promptly sent the requested information but expressed his perplexity at the request because the Vatican
already had the information. Not only had the individual members
involved "never concealed their membership in our Association,"[36]
they had been hired precisely because they belonged to Opus Dei.

---

[*] At the time of definitive incorporation, the numeraries undertook to consult the
directors on questions of particular professional or social importance: see *Constitutio-
nes Societatis Sacerdotalis Sanctae Crucis et Operis Dei* (1950), no. 58, §3. The Founder
explained that the request for advice was made by the interested party "only insofar as
it related to his interior life and apostolic task." The members were free to consult with
whomever they wished and to decide in conscience, and they were obliged not to speak
about confidential information known for professional reasons (professional secrets).
General Note 81/66 (December 9, 1966), in AGP, series E.1.3, 245-2; and General
Note 11/73 (February 21, 1973). AGP, series E.1.3, 246-5.

At that time only five members of Opus Dei were working in the offices of the Holy See: four priests (Salvador Canals, Julian Herranz, Julio Atienza, and Justo Mullor), and one layman, a lawyer named Antonio Fraile. The only one who held a position of some prominence was Canals, a judge of the Roman Rota. The rest were midlevel employees of the congregations. In addition to these Vatican employees, there were five members of the Work who were consultants to different congregations. Only one of them, Álvaro del Portillo, resided in Rome.

Escrivá concentrated his energies on prayer, God, the expansion of the Work, and the formation of the members and of the people who participated in the apostolic activities of Opus Dei. On May 30, 1971, he consecrated the Work to the Holy Spirit. The Founder asked the divine Spirit to grant his children firmness in the faith and to assist the "Church, and in particular the Roman Pontiff, that he may guide us by his word and example, and that he may attain eternal life together with the flock entrusted to him." He prayed "that good shepherds may never be lacking and that all the faithful may serve you with holiness of life and integrity of faith, so we may reach the glory of Heaven."[37] Three months later, on August 23, he heard another locution that confirmed the need to have continual recourse to the intercession of the Virgin Mary: *Adeamus cum fiducia ad thronum gloriae ut misericordiam consequamur* (Let us go confidently to the throne of glory to obtain mercy).[38]

Six years after the previous audience, Pope Paul VI received Escrivá on June 25, 1973. The Founder told him about the growth of the corporate apostolic work in democratic countries and the personal apostolate carried out in those behind the Iron Curtain. He informed him about the increase of vocations in Opus Dei and about how he asked his children to love the Pope and the magisterium of the Church more and more each day. He stressed the political freedom of the members of the Work, which was challenged in Spain by those who had a monopolistic and single-party mentality. Paul VI praised Escrivá, commenting, "You are a saint."[39] The Pope referred to the rumors about the presence of members of the Work in the Vatican Curia and the claim that they consulted the directors of Opus Dei about their work there. The Founder replied that those comments were slanderous, coming from politicians and clerics opposed to freedom of opinion in temporal matters.

In the meantime, the technical commission appointed by the Special General Congress examined the individual communications and suggestions from the plenary sessions. The task stretched out over four years because of the volume of material to be studied and because difficult relations with some Vatican authorities made a certain delay prudent. On October 1, 1974, the Founder finally approved the draft of the *Codex Iuris Particularis Operis Dei* (Code of Particular Law of Opus Dei) prepared by the technical commission.[40] The document was based on the supposition that Opus Dei would become a personal prelature and eliminated all terms taken from the terminology proper to the state of religious or secular perfection. Escrivá approved the draft but decided to wait before asking for the Holy See to transform Opus Dei into a personal prelature.

Notes

1. Decree "Pluribus ex documentis," March 22, 1950, in AAS 42 (1950) 330-331.

2. *Relación de una conversación entre Arcadio Larraona y Álvaro del Portillo*, July 12, 1963. AGP series L.1.1, 14-2-19.

3. Among other studies, see Álvaro del Portillo, "*El estado actual de los Institutos Seculares,*" *Nuestro Tiempo* VIII (May,1958), pp. 515–530; Salvador Canals, *Institutos seculares y estado de perfección* (Madrid: Rialp, 1954.); Slavador Canals, *Los Institutos Seculares* (Madrid: Rialp, 1960); Julián Herranz, "Natura dell'Opus Dei ed attività temporali dei suoi membri," *Studi Cattolici*, VI/31 (1962), pp. 73–90.

4. See Julian Herranz, "The Evolution of Secular Institutes," *Ius Canonicum* IV/8 (1964), p. 329.

5. See AGP E.4.1, 89-1-1.

6. See AGP E.4.1, 227-2.

7. *Appunto*, no. 2, April 9,1960. AGP L.1.1, 14-1-1. Eight days later, the Founder sent a supplementary note in which he pointed out that he proposed

the change because Opus Dei was going against the current among other secular institutes. AGP L.1.1, 14-1-7.

8. Valentín Gómez-Iglesias, *"El proyecto de prelatura personal para el Opus Dei en los primeros años sesenta,"* in Eduardo Baura (coord.), *Estudios sobre la Prelatura del Opus Dei. A los veinticinco años de la Constitución apostólica "Ut sit"* (Pamplona: EUNSA, 2009), pp. 149–158.

9. See AGP L.1.1, 14-2-5. The prelature *nullius* was equivalent to the territorial prelature of current canon law.

10. Dispatch from Amleto Cicognani to Josemaría Escrivá, May 20, 1962. AGP L.1.1, 2-14-18.

11. See AGP E.4.1, 227-2.

12. Letter of Josemaría Escrivá to Ildebrando Antoniutti, Rome, October 31, 1963. AGP L.1.1, 14-3-4; and General Note 27/64 (April 29, 1964). AGP E.1.3, 243-4.

13. See AGP E.4.1, 227-4-1; Letter of Josemaría Escrivá to Paul VI, Rome, February 14, 1964. AGP L.1.1, 17-3-2.

14. Letter from Josemaría Escrivá to Angelo Dell'Acqua, Paris, August 15, 1964. AGP E.4.1, 227-3-1.

15. See Manuscript of Álvaro del Portillo, 27-IX-1964. AGP L.1.1, 17-3-8.

16. Chirograph, 1-X-1964. AGP L.1.1, 17-3-8.

17. A decade later, Von Balthasar affirmed that the message of Opus Dei was a synthesis of the gospel. For the whole affair concerning Von Balthasar, see AGP M.2.4, 128-1 and 128-2.

18. See Manuel Valdés Mas, "Algunos aspectos del trabajo de Álvaro del Portillo como secretario de la Comisión conciliar *De Disciplina Cleri et Populi Christiani,"* *Studia et Documenta* 9 (2015), pp. 57–100.

19. See Álvaro del Portillo, *Entrevista sobre el Fundador del Opus Dei* 10.ª ed. (Madrid: Rialp, Madrid 2014) 21–22.

20. Cited in Julián Herranz, *En las afueras de Jericó. Recuerdos de los años con san Josemaría y Juan Pablo II*, 4th ed. (Madrid: Rialp, 2007), p. 111. See Carlo Pioppi, *"Alcuni incontri di san Josemaría Escrivá con personalità ecclesiastiche durante gli anni del Concilio Vaticano II,"* *Studia et Documenta* 5 (2011), pp. 165–228; Barbara Schellenberger, *"Begegnungen des hl. Josemaría mit deutschen Bischöfen 1949–1975,"* *Studia et Documenta* 10 (2016), pp. 261–292.

21. Second Vatican Council, Dogmatic Constitution *Lumen gentium*, no. 11.

22. Second Vatican Council, Decree *Apostolicam actuositatem*, no. 2.

23. Second Vatican Council, Pastoral Constitution *Gaudium et spes*, no. 34.

24. Manuscript, March 25, 1967. AGP E.1.1, 182-2-1. The text was published in the new edition of the *Catechism* see AGP E.1.1, 182-2-3.

25. See General Note 59/66 (October 22, 1966). AGP E.1.3, 245-1.

26. See AGP E.4.1, 227-4-3; and AGP E.4.1, 227-4-4-4.

27. Conclusions of the Special General Congress, September 15, 1969 (men) and September 16, 1969 (women). AGP D.3.

28. Letter of Josemaría Escrivá to Paul VI, Rome, September 16, 1969. AGP A.3.4, 294-4, 690916-2.

29. Letter of Josemaría Escrivá to Paul VI, Rome, October 11, 1969. AGP A.3.4, 294-4, 691011-2.

30. See Herranz, *En las afueras*, pp. 234–240.

31. See AGP E.4.1, 227-4-5.

32. See Teófanes Egido (coord.), *Los jesuitas en España y en el mundo hispánico* (Madrid: Fundación Carolina, 2004), pp. 399–430.

33. See AGP E.4.3, 104-1-2.

34. See AGP A.4, 72-2-1.

35. Conclusions of the Special General Congress, September 14, 1969. AGP D.3.

36. Letter from Josemaría Escrivá to Jean Villot, Rome, February 2, 1971. AGP A.3.4, 298-4, 710202-1.

37. Cited in Andrés Vázquez de Prada, *The Founder of Opus Dei*, vol. 3 (New York: Scepter, 2005), p. 611. See AGP A.1, 52-5-1.

38. The phrase is a variant of the text of the Epistle to the Hebrews 4:16, which says "throne of grace," instead of "throne of glory." For Escrivá, this new understanding of the phrase indicated that, in order to appeal to God's mercy, he had to go through the mediation of Mary (see Vazquez de Prada, *The Founder of Opus Dei*, vol. 3, p. 609, nt. 56.

39. AGP E.4.1, 227-4-5.

40. See AGP L.1.1, 115.

CHAPTER 5

◦⁓◦

A Post-Conciliar Legacy

When the Second Vatican Council closed in December 1965, Paul VI and the synod fathers expressed great joy and confidence in the future of the Church. The conciliar assembly had fulfilled its mission. The People of God was a human and divine reality that appeared to have found its place in the modern world, with a message rich in doctrine and open to dialogue with contemporary humanism, including its agnostic and atheist varieties.

It fell to Paul VI to put into practice the provisions approved by the Council. He undertook reforms in many areas: modernization of the Vatican curia, giving a preeminent role to the Secretariat of State; creation of the Synod of Bishops, an advisory body that reflected the principle of collegiality; ecumenical dialogue through meetings with representatives of various confessions in different countries, in particular with Athenagoras I, Patriarch of Constantinople; and establishment of national episcopal conferences. He was particularly interested in liturgical reform, because he wanted the faithful to participate more actively in the celebration of the Eucharist. Following the lead of the Council, he approved the use of the vernacular in the liturgy as well as altars facing the people.

Despite the optimism of the immediate post-conciliar period, the Church soon suffered an acute crisis. Reform and updating were frequently replaced by discontinuity and rupture with the past. These circumstances within the Church were compounded by increasing secularization and the countercultural movements that challenged the legitimacy of authority in the wider society. Some churchmen advocated abandoning the Church's hierarchal structure in favor of one based on principles of contemporary liberal democracy. The Church faced a crisis of faith and Christian lifestyles beginning with the younger clergy and confessional organizations and later spreading to the ordinary laity.

The most serious phenomenon involved the rejection of key parts of Christian dogma and morals, including the Real Presence of Jesus Christ in the sacrament of the Eucharist, the actualization of Christ's sacrifice in the Mass, the virginity of Mary, and the need for the sacrament of Penance. Some influential theologians gave scant importance to the substantive text of Vatican II's documents, invoking instead a supposed "spirit" of the Council that distorted the provisions of the ecumenical assembly, the pontifical magisterium, and the sacred tradition of the Church. An immanentist vision of life which largely ignored God, the dissolution of moral principles, and the departure from previous forms of religious practice left many Catholics perplexed and unsure about the meaning of their Christian vocation and the ways of living it. All this led to a loss of a sense of identity in the Church and especially among the clergy.

Another result of the crisis was the erosion of unity, first among the clergy and later also among the laity, expressed in a repudiation of authority, disobedience to the hierarchy, and rejection of doctrine as well as sacramental, liturgical, and moral practices. The Dutch Catechism for Adults (1966), which questioned essential aspects of Catholic faith, had wide resonance. At the opposite extreme, traditionalists like Archbishop Marcel Lefebvre, creator of the Priestly Fraternity of St. Pius X, rejected aspects of the teaching of Vatican Council II.

Liturgical reform was accompanied by many abuses, to the point that it seemed to many that the only valid criterion for renewal was novelty. Some priests celebrated Mass guided by their own "creativity" and in complete disregard for established rituals and rubrics. Worship of the Eucharist outside the Mass was often treated with contempt. Individual confession was replaced in many parishes, and even in entire dioceses, by collective absolutions. Disorientation also manifested itself in the relaxation of ecclesiastical discipline, criticism of authority, and the abandonment of clerical dress by many priests and religious.

Paul VI frequently sought to strengthen the faithful in the face of a loss of faith in God and his action in the Church. He published rich doctrinal encyclicals such as *Ecclesiam suam* (1964), on the nature and mission of the Church in the contemporary world, *Mysterium fidei* (1965), on the presence of Jesus Christ in the Eucharist, and *Populorum progressio* (1967), on cooperation between economically well-off nations and developing countries. In 1968, he solemnly reaffirmed the truth of Christian revelation in a profession of faith entitled "Creed of the People of God."

The Pope struggled with two controversial issues that he had reserved to himself during the Council. The first concerned the celibacy of priests. In June 1967 he published the encyclical *Sacerdotalis caelibatus* on the pastoral and theological desirability of priestly celibacy. Four years later, the synod of bishops reiterated the obligation of celibacy in the Latin Church. But, by then, controversy over celibacy had taken its toll on vocations and on the perseverance of priests and religious. Seminaries in Europe and North America lost 75 percent of their students, leaving a difficult legacy for the Church in Western nations. Some 5 percent of both the regular and the diocesan clergy were laicized in the decade after the Council. The worst years were 1973 and 1974. During those two years, more than 8,000 priests were laicized.

The second topic of debate was the family. Some sectors of public opinion criticized traditional family structures, arguing that they led to the oppression of women and that sexual intimacy should be separated from procreation. Divorce was accepted in the legislation of many countries, including those of long Catholic tradition. The United States Supreme Court held in 1965 that contraception was a constitutional right. Other Western countries soon followed suit. This was followed by the legalization of abortion, sometimes seen as the necessary remedy for failed contraception.

In this environment, the Church needed to address the morality of birth control. Paul VI published in July 1968 the encyclical *Humanae vitae* on the transmission of life and conjugal morality. The Pope explained that conjugal love required a union of its unitive and procreative aspects, and that births should be regulated only by natural methods and only for just reasons. No action was licit, he said, which, "either in anticipation of the conjugal act or in its performance, or in the development of its natural consequences, proposes, as an end or as a means, to make procreation impossible."[1] The publication of this document marked a turning point in the pontificate of Paul VI. Some bishops, priests, and professors of moral theology rejected the encyclical and publicly supported the pill and other artificial means of contraception. The Dutch hierarchy, for example, criticized the condemnation of the use of contraceptives as unjust.

Section 1. Doctrinal and Liturgical Measures

Since the 1950s, Escrivá had warned about some doctrinal errors that were gradually infiltrating the Church. In a 1964 letter to the Pope, he expressed his conviction that "the Holy Spirit will draw from the present Ecumenical Council abundant fruits for the Holy Church." Nonetheless, he also expressed his concern that because of "the propaganda being spread, no doubt in good faith, by many of those who participate directly or indirectly in the work of the great Assembly . . . the Council has so far been the occasion for a state of grave uneasiness, I would dare say confusion, in the souls of the Pastors and their sheep: priests, seminarians and faithful. Many of them find themselves, as it were, lost."[2]

After Vatican II, Josemaría Escrivá quoted the conciliar documents in his writings, but he did not carry out a theological reflection on the texts because he saw that as a task for professional theologians. What he did try to do was respond to the confusion being created in the wake of the Council. Although the pontifical magisterium had pointed out abuses and deviations, the positions of some theologians and liturgists were producing disorientation in the Chuch. It was natural and desirable that there be an evolution after the Council, but what was occurring seemed to be not a development of the Church's teaching but a clean break with central dogmatic and moral elements of the Catholic faith.

Interviewed about the process of updating the Church (*aggiorna-mento*), Escrivá responded that it represented a hopeful but also worrisome stage. The Council's message was a call to safeguard Christian revelation and the intangible essence of the Church. On the other hand, the Council wanted the Church to be present in today's world and to speak in ways contemporary people could understand. In its way of acting and speaking, it needed to combine progress and tradition, reform and continuity

As part of the Church, Opus Dei also needed to progress in time, with the peculiarity that the Founder was alive and therefore able to clarify what were the permanent elements of its spirit and apostolic activities. Escrivá saw in the message of the Council not a call to modify elements of Opus Dei's spirit but an endorsement of what the Work had been doing and preaching. "Without boasting," he said, "I must say that, as far as our spirit is concerned, the Council has not been an invitation to change. On the contrary, it has confirmed what—by the grace of God—we have been living and teaching for so many years."[3]

Escrivá personally prayed a lot for the Church and asked his sons and daughters, especially the members of the General Council and the Central Advisory, to accompany him in his prayer. He once described the historical moment as a hard period of trial. He suffered when he learned about the problems the Church was facing, failures to transmit the doctrine of Jesus Christ intact, opposition to the Pope and the bishops, and silence on the part of some members of the hierarchy who failed to distinguish the wheat from the tares. He was pained by priests leaving the priesthood and the defenseless position of so many faithful who lacked adequate guidance. At the same time, he remained hopeful and optimistic. He repeated that faith in God was a source of security and confidence in the future. In time, he felt, the waters would return to their course.

As pastor, the Founder felt he had a grave responsibility to care for and defend the people entrusted to him by the Holy Spirit. He could not remain mute or hesitant when Christian doctrine and practices were called into question. He had to strengthen his children's faith in

God, in the Church, in the magisterium of the Pope, and in the divine origin of the Work. At the same time, he had to take prudent steps, both to know what was really happening and to adopt the appropriate general and specific measures without falling into unbridled haste or paralyzing immobility.[4]

In addition to Álvaro del Portillo, Josemaría Escrivá relied on the priest and philosopher Carlos Cardona, who was the central spiritual director of the Work from 1961 to 1976.[5] Neither Cardona nor the regional spiritual directors had a governing function. Their mission was to ensure that authentic Christian doctrine reached the members of the Work and the Priestly Society of the Holy Cross in its entirety. They were in charge of preparing lists of topics and outlines for preaching, assigning priests, and preparing schedules for Masses, confessions, meditations, retreats, and other priestly activities. They gave advice to authors and publishers on articles and books that dealt with faith and morals. They also approved books on these topics that were made available in the centers of the Work, and provided moral guidance on movies.[6] The contribution of the spiritual directors in giving formation and doctrinal guidance was decisive in the late sixties and early seventies. They assembled abundant material to provide guidance to the members of the Work and cooperators in matters of faith and morals, especially outlines of catechetical talks and syllabi for courses on current doctrinal and moral questions.[7] They also prepared lists of topics and outlines for meditations and retreats, reviews of theological books, doctrinal essays and articles in the internal magazines *Crónica* and *Noticias*, and a series of books entitled "Notebooks," with chapters on faith and morals as well as on the spirit and apostolate of Opus Dei.[8]

In April 1967, Escrivá sent a note to all Opus Dei members in which he warned that vast sectors of ecclesiastical life had become mired in doctrinal confusion. He outlined several guidelines for those trying to follow safe doctrinal explanations: leaving the study of new theological opinions to specialists, maintaining a serene vigilance so as not to be influenced by possible errors, and asking for advice on reading material. The note concluded: "It is not a matter of being alarmists: it is a matter of facing reality serenely, with love of God and with zeal for souls."[9]

Acting with the General Council, during the sixties the founder of Opus Dei approved a series of doctrinal and liturgical measures. In the doctrinal area he focused on books and articles that could impact faith and morals. He asked members of the Work who needed to read a book included on the Holy See's *Index* of prohibited books or Marxist books to ask the directors for permission, with an explanation of the reasons for the request and the time they were going to spend reading it.* The authorization would be accompanied by suggestions of books that offered sound doctrine in the same area as a sort of "antidote." The member who received the authorization was asked to write a review of the book which could prove helpful to others and to discuss in spiritual accompaniment the book he was reading in order to receive advice. Because of their restrictive nature, and because they mostly involved matters for specialists, requests for this type of authorization were relatively few.

The regional spiritual directors were given the mission of ensuring that all the books in the centers of Opus Dei were in accordance with the faith and Christian morals, and also that doctrines inspired by Marxism or a theological progressivism hostile to Catholic tradition (widespread in various areas of Catholic thought at the time), did not affect the members of the Work.[10]

In 1966, the Holy See abolished the *Index* of prohibited books, although it insisted on the moral obligation to abstain from readings contrary to faith and morals. The ecclesiastical *imprimatur* continued to be given, but in some places, it was no longer a guarantee of orthodoxy. Escrivá decided that Opus Dei members should continue to request permission to read works on the recently

---

* Since the sixteenth century, the Holy Office had published an *Index* of books that Catholics were forbidden to read because they were contrary to Catholic dogma and morals. The Church understood this measure as an act of prudence to prevent the spread of doctrinal and practical errors. By the middle of the twentieth century, the list of books exceeded four thousand titles. If a Catholic needed to read any of these works for professional reasons, he was supposed to request permission from diocesan authorities.

suppressed *Index* or of a Marxist tendency. The office of central spiritual direction coordinated the preparation of bibliographies of authors in vogue, accompanied by commentaries on the doctrines they held and a doctrinal classification.[11] In addition, it prepared "detailed critical notes on current works whose content has a direct bearing on faith or morals."[12] These notes were especially useful to high school and university students who were recommended or required to study Marxist works.

The Founder also established a number of provisional prudential measures: permission should be requested to read the works of current theologians whose works had not yet been reviewed by the office of spiritual direction; translations of Sacred Scripture at least ten years old should be used; and the participants in all annual courses and workshops should review the Catechism of St. Pius X (which presents the principal elements of the Christian faith briefly, in question and answer form).[13] He also warned the members to be careful in choosing catechetical programs for their children since they often contained doctrinal errors or silenced fundamental truths of the Catholic faith.[14]

The General Council stressed that it did not wish to restrict the freedom of individuals or to reject new theological contributions made in the light of faith and in conformity with the magisterium of the Church but that these prudential measures were required by the circumstances of the moment. "Everyone should understand that it is not a question of limiting or restricting intelligence in any way, but of the grave duty, common to every Christian, not to endanger the faith," explained a general note of 1967.[15]

Escrivá was very interested in having priests and laypeople dedicated to theological research and the dissemination of Christian doctrine and spirituality. The spirit of Opus Dei could contribute to dogmatic, moral, pastoral, and spiritual studies on topics such as "the spirit of service, divine filiation, freedom in all temporal and theological matters, and sanctification of work."[16] Until 1966, the books written by priests of Opus Dei and inspired by its spirit were all books of spirituality directed to the general reader. The most important among them were: Jesús Urteaga, *El Valor Divino de lo Humano* (1948) [published in English in 1959 as *Man the Saint*]; Federico Suárez, *La Virgen Nuestra Señora* (1956) [published in English in 1960 as *Our Lady the Virgin*]; and Salvador Canals, *Ascética Meditada* (1962) [published in English in 1970 as *Jesus as Friend.*] The first theological analysis of an aspect of Opus Dei's spirit was José Luis Illanes's short book, *La Santificación del Trabajo. Tema de Nuestro Tiempo* (1966) [published in English in 1967 under the title *On the Theology of Work*].

In the mid-1960s, Escrivá suggested that Ediciones Rialp publish a multivolume Catholic encyclopedia. After a preliminary study, the publisher decided on something more ambitious, "a university-level work of a global character but centered on the Hispanic world, with a pluralistic approach." It would summarize current thought in the different areas of knowledge, particularly the humanities.[17] The sixteen thousand entries of the *Gran Enciclopedia Rialp* (GER) were published in twenty-four volumes between 1970 and 1977.

In 1967, the University of Navarra opened a Theological Institute, which was canonically erected as a School of Theology by the Holy See two years later. Alfredo García, José María Casciaro, and Pedro Rodríguez comprised the initial faculty. They focused their research on ecclesiology and biblical studies. The Founder encouraged them to develop new knowledge and opinions in their publications while confirming the faith and doctrine of the Church. In their teaching, he encouraged them to follow the common opinion of theologians, in accordance with the fundamental principles of St. Thomas Aquinas.[18]

In 1972, Escrivá commissioned the faculty of the School of Theology to prepare a new Spanish translation of the Bible in language accessible to the general public and accompiend by extensive introductions and notes. The biblical scholar José María Casciaro coordinated the team of professors who took on the *Navarra Bible* project. Between 1976 and 1989 they published the New Testament in twelve volumes.[19] The final volume of the Old Testament appeared in 2004.

The television programs of two Spanish numerary priests appealed to very wide audiences, bringing the Church's teachings into many homes. Jesús Urteaga was a pioneer of religious programming on Spanish television. Hired in 1960 to participate in *El Día del Señor*, a year later he created a program for teenagers *Solo Para Menores de 16 Años* [Only for Those Under Sixteen]. The program's motto, *"Siempre alegres para hacer felices a los demás"* [Always be happy to make others happy], soon became famous. Later, between 1967 and 1970, he produced the program *Habla Contigo Jesús Urteaga* [Jesús Urteaga Speaks to You]. During these same years, Ángel García Dorronsoro hosted a religious program on the second Spanish television channel called *Tiempo para Creer* [*Time to Believe*].

Escrivá also focused on the liturgy. Throughout his life, he had been inspired by the liturgical movement. In the 1930s, for instance, he encouraged dialogue Masses in which the congregation participated actively. Before the Vatican Council, he created altars facing the people in churches and large oratories.[20] In the period following the Second Vatican Council, Opus Dei implemented in its centers the liturgical reforms required by the Council and the decrees of the Holy See. The changes especially affected how Mass was celebrated, and would culminate in the new Roman Missal (with two editions, one in 1970 and the other in 1975). New Eucharistic Prayers and Prefaces were introduced; provision was made for Prayers of the Faithful; rites for the reception of Holy Communion under two species were established; rituals for concelebrated Masses were prepared; and the use of the vernacular became widespread. In the churches entrusted to Opus Dei, priests followed the norms given by the diocesan bishop.[21]

Most of the reforms called for by the Holy See left a wide margin of freedom in the concrete way of implementing them. The Founder decided to apply in the centers of the Work the options he considered most suitable for the spiritual life of its members and its apostolates.[22] Moreover, he echoed the repeated appeals of the Holy See for prudence in choosing the concrete ways of implementing the general norms. In the face of widespread abuse and what often seemed to be change for change's sake,[23] he indicated as a general criterion that in the liturgical acts celebrated in the centers of the Work, only the modifications required by the new rubrics would be made.[24]

The liturgical measures he adopted for the centers of Opus Dei were aimed at fostering love for the liturgy, the active participation and recollection of the celebrant and the faithful, and unity in the manner of celebration. He established that Mass should be celebrated in Latin when only members of the Work were present. He encouraged the lay members to follow the Mass with a missal of the faithful. He asked that Mass not be concelebrated in centers of Opus Dei except during workshops for priests. As a way of expressing the reverence that the Church gives to the presence of Jesus Christ in the Eucharist, he indicated that Communion be received kneeling and on the tongue, except in public churches run by priests of the Work in places where the bishop had required that it be received standing or in the hand.[25]

Escrivá realized that some of the doctrinal and liturgical measures he took reduced the capacity for research, hindered contacts with theological and philosophical avant-garde circles, restricted certain legitimate liturgical choices, and limited initiative. He was aware that they could give the impression that Opus Dei favored isolationism, uniformity, and an anti-intellectual attitude. The grave situation of the Church, which Pope Paul VI repeatedly described in somber tones, convinced him, however, that they were not only justified but necessary temporary steps.[*] Seeing them as positive measures, he commented that his conscience was clear because he had warned his children about the difficult period the Church was going through. He said he did not wish to foster an exaggerated alarmism but to encourage vigilance.[26] For love of the truth and the good of the spirit and unity of Opus Dei, he felt compelled to strengthen the members in key matters: "I have put all the means in place so that my children not fall into errors. If someone does, we will tell him so. If he does not rectify very sincerely, we will tell him to leave."[27]

---

[*] "My children, you too feel the weight of this responsibility, being vigilant. Accept with gratitude and docility the indications of prudence that I have been giving you, as a prudent person observes the sanitary measures that public health authorities impose in an epidemic that is causing havoc in the country." (Letter 40, no. 16, in AGP, series A.3, 190-2-2).

Thirty years earlier, Escrivá and Opus Dei had been labeled progressive and heretical. Now they were called reactionary and opposed to change, but this did not trouble the Founder.[28] "No one can truthfully say, because I have warned you to prevent the current environment from corroding your faith, that I am fundamentalist or progressive, that I am a reformer or reactionary. Any of these qualifications would be unjust and false. I am a priest of Jesus Christ, who loves clear doctrine."*

By and large, the members of the Work received Escrivá's doctrinal and liturgical directives in the spirit in which they were given, although three priests chose not to accept them and left the Work.[29] In contrast to what happened to many Catholic institutions, in the decade following the Council, the Work and its apostolates grew. The 11,900 members of Opus Dei in 1966 became 32,800 in 1975. Many people saw in the members of the Work an example of faithfulness to Catholic teaching and life that helped them to maintain their faith and religious practice. And the members of Opus Dei faithfully followed the measures indicated by the Founder.

On March 19, 1967, Escrivá wrote a long letter in which he once again responded to the prevailing doctrinal confusion denounced by Paul VI. The letter began: "*Fortes in fide* [strong in the faith], that is how I see you, my dear daughters and sons: strong in the faith, bearing witness to your beliefs with divine fortitude all over the world." In an effort to strengthen the faith of Opus Dei's members and of those who took part in its apostolic activities, he reviewed the principal truths of the Christian faith and the way to practice them and make them known. The letter concluded with a call to prayer: "What we need to do is to be faithful and to pray, my daughters and sons. We need to pray much. Personal prayer has been, is and always will

---

* Letter 38, no. 3, in AGP, series A.3, 190-1. With respect to the truths of faith, the Founder explained, "there is no room for ambiguity or compromise. If, for example, you were called reactionaries because you hold to the principle of the indissolubility of marriage, would you, for that reason, refrain from proclaiming the doctrine of Jesus Christ on this subject? Would you not continue to affirm that divorce is a grave error, a heresy?" (Letter 41, no. 14, in AGP, series A.3, 190-2-3).

be our great weapon. Let us pray, give glory to the Lord, and work with right intention." He urged them to have a hopeful song in their hearts, because the bad times would pass: "Optimistic, joyful! God is with us! Therefore, every day I am filled with hope. The virtue of hope makes us see life as it is: beautiful, God's."[30]

Section 2. Activity of Members in Spanish Politics and Other Settings

From the very beginning of Opus Dei, the Founder foresaw that its members would work professionally and give witness to Jesus Christ in all fields and social environments. He often described the apostolate of the Work as "an open sea without shores, open to the initiative and responsibility of all."[31] He stressed that "the most important apostolate was carried out by individual members with the witness of their life and words, in their daily dealings with their friends and professional colleagues."[32] He urged the members and cooperators to fan out to all areas of civil society, to intervene in public life, "to *be present* in social activities that influence directly or indirectly how people live together in society, including professional associations, trade unions, municipal and regional life, artistic and literary associations and competitions, and public associations of citizens of all sorts."[33]

The growth of the Work gradually made this vision a reality. Among the developments that attracted most attention was the presence of some members of the Work in important positions in the Franco regime. It shaped the perception of Opus Dei in world public opinion and led many people to think of the Work in political terms.

The Stabilization Plan of 1959 and the Development Plans of 1964, 1968, and 1972 contributed to the growth of the Spanish economy in the sixties and seventies and thereby helped the Franco regime survive. There were dramatic improvements in trade and distribution networks, the service and tourism sectors, and foreign investment. Per capita income doubled during the 1960s. Many Spaniards increased their disposable income and consumption, as could be seen in the dramatic increase in the number of automobiles. On the other hand, there were serious problems, including inflation, structural weaknesses, a deficit in the foreign trade balance, and a largely non-competitive environment.[34] The number of people living in poverty remained high especially in the agricultural south and in the slums surrounding the large cities.

From the political point of view, the authoritarian regime sought ways to survive the death of General Franco. The Organic Law of the State (1966) provided that Franco would govern until his death and be succeeded by a king. The system remained authoritarian, but gradually became somewhat more tolerant. The Press and Publication Law (1966) and the Religious Freedom Law (1967) reduced institutional censorship and restrictions on non-Catholic confessions but did not abolish them.

From the beginning of the sixties until his death in 1975, Franco reshuffled his cabinet eight times. Eight of the ministers who served during this period belonged to Opus Dei: Mariano Navarro Rubio (1957–1965), Alberto Ullastres (1957–1965), Gregorio López-Bravo (1962–1973), Laureano López Rodó (1965–1974), Juan José Espinosa (1965–1969), Faustino García Moncó (1965–1969), Vicente Mortes (1969–1973), and Fernando Herrero Tejedor (1975). These ministers, like all their cabinet colleagues, were loyal to Franco, who had chosen them. They belonged to the various political groups represented in the regime, often referred to in Spain as political families: Carlists, Falangists, supporters of Juan de Borbón or his son Juan Carlos, and "independents" not affiliated with any of these groups. They disagreed on some political strategies. For example, Navarro Rubio wanted the Ministry of Finance, which he headed, to control the Development Plan. When Franco gave control of it in 1965 to a newly created Ministry of Development headed by López Rodó, Navarro Rubio resigned. Similarly, García Moncó criticized López-Bravo's policies in the official magazine of his ministry.

The Falangist press opposed López Rodó's development policies and frequently attacked Opus Dei as part of its effort to force his resignation. Other publications depicted all the members of the Work as linked to the regime in Spain. Until 1962, Opus Dei generally ignored media criticism and attacks except in extreme cases of clearly false statements. Even in those cases, it limited itself to brief official clarifications issued by its general secretariat. In 1962, Escrivá changed policy. He decided that Opus Dei needed to regularly inform the media and other people who shaped public opinion. The Work began providing more information on its legal structure and the secularity of its members, and it explained insistently that the political actions of its members on different parts of the political spectrum were not corporate nor official positions in any respect. It also started to rectify erroneous statements about its nature and activities more frequently. The Founder saw this as part of a larger effort to help spread news about the Second Vatican Council and to combat the clerical attitude that led to thinking that all Spanish Catholics should join forces in a single party that would somewhat officially represent "the Catholic position" and the interests of the Church.[35]

In June 1962, Escrivá sent a note to the members of the Work: "Once again we recall what we have always known and lived: that corporately we are not subject or united to any person, to any regime, or to any earthly thing."[36] The general secretariat of the Work sent a note to the media stating that "the members of Opus Dei are free in their thoughts and public actions, the same as any other Catholic citizen. Within the Association, therefore, there is room for, and in fact there are, people of different and even opposing political ideas."[37]

That summer, Escrivá told Pope John XXIII's secretary, Msgr. Loris Francesco Capovilla, about some criticism coming from Spain: "It has become fashionable to say that we are fundamentalists, that we attack freedom, that we do not allow the slightest possibility of innovation and that, for this reason, in Spain we support the current political regime, which we have taken over."[38] He mentioned a concrete counterexample. Ignacio de Orbegozo, prelate of the *nullius* prelature of Yauyos, had been a Basque nationalist in his youth and had lived with people of different points of view in the Work.

It had long been a practice in Opus Dei to have a monthly intention which all the members were asked to pray for and try to implement in whatever ways they could. In December 1963, the Founder announced that until further notice the monthly intention would be to pray "that it be well understood that the few members of Opus Dei who act in the public life of Spain and other countries do so in the use of their freedom as Catholics and under their exclusive personal responsibility."[39] A few months later, he urged the members of the Work to publish and to encourage people not connected with the Work to publish information about Opus Dei, its activities, and the political freedom of its members. He stressed that it seemed fine to him that historically many upright Catholic institutions had sought governmental support for their activities, but that Opus Dei had relied on God's grace, the efforts of its members and their good humor, without government money or backing. He ended the note by expressing his opinion that whatever the circumstances of the past, it was no longer appropriate for Church institutions to rely on governments.[40]

Escrivá recommended opening Opus Dei information offices in the capitals of the countries where the Work had a significant presence. This would make it easy for journalists, foreign correspondents, news agencies, writers, embassy press attachés, and any other interested parties to contact Opus Dei and receive information about its activities. Listing of the information office in the telephone directory would also contribute to giving the Work a corporate public presence. Information offices would free the secretariats of the regional commissions from the need to send official communiqués to the press and allow their offices of the apostolate of public opinion to dedicate themselves to encouraging members' efforts to spread Christian doctrine through the media.

The first information office opened in Madrid in 1964. Its director, Javier Ayesta, would have liked to concentrate on publicizing Opus Dei's corporate activities, especially those with a marked social role. He was forced, however, to spend much of his time sending letters to the editor and clarifications to Spanish journalists and foreign correspondents, trying to explain that the Work's message was exclusively spiritual and that its members acted with personal freedom and responsibility. His task was complicated by the fact that most journalists were interested primarily in politics and that Opus Dei at the time gave out few statistics and little information about its internal organization.[41]

In May 1964, Cardinal Angelo Dell'Acqua asked Escrivá to write an extensive report on the Spanish situation to provide the Pope with "concrete orientations to speak with each of the Spanish bishops."[42] The cardinal asked him to point out in his proposal that it should be "the bishops who give the criteria and unite Catholics to prepare for the change in the current political situation."

Escrivá prepared a long report, dated June 14, 1964. This note of conscience was intended for Paul VI's knowledge, but not for publication. It began with an overview of Spanish political life in the twentieth century, emphasizing the Communist terror during the Civil War, which the Founder had suffered through. Turning to Franco, Escrivá conceded that he was a man of sober and modest private life. On the other hand, as a ruler he considered himself the guarantor of both Spanish unity and the Church, an idea that the hierarchy had praised excessively. The result, in Escrivá's opinion, was a dearth of "effective thinking about the future and the fact that in Spain everything depends on the life of a man who, in good faith, is persuaded he is 'providential.'"*

Escrivá was concerned about the danger of a new Marxist revolution in Spain and favored a progressive change in the regime: He warned that "given Franco's age, the circumstances are beginning to be serious," and believed that measures needed to be taken to insure "a rather rapid evolution." Otherwise, he feared, Spain might fall "into

---

* Between 1944 and 1953 Escrivá met General Franco eight times. In the following twenty-two years, he saw him a total of five other times: in 1960 and 1961, on the occasion of the civil recognition of the University of Navarra, and then in 1967, 1968, and 1970. (We thank Onésimo Díaz for this information, who has consulted AGP, the Francisco Franco Foundation Archives, and the Royal Palace Archives.) The Founder limited his contacts and tried to avoid receiving recognition from the government, as he explained to the Pope. "Franco has granted me several Grand Crosses. I have, however, always avoided having them imposed on me. I have not been able to refuse them because I have always received the news through the press. Besides, if I had refused them, it would have been interpreted as a political act, even more so when the bishops of my land accept them, and in many cases actively seek them."

a new revolution, which would give rise to new religious persecutions." In this he shared the opinion of Álvaro del Portillo, who had expressed "the desirability of the Generalissimo abandoning power." Looking back twenty years, Escrivá told the Pope that before moving definitively to Rome in 1946, on various occasions he had told common friends in a way that would come to Franco's knowledge that he thought he should resign.

The Founder discussed two ways in which he thought the evolution of the Spanish regime could take place. The first reflected the common doctrine that, if in a country special circumstances made it necessary to give political and social orientations to Catholics, it was up to the ecclesiastical hierarchy to do so. Without compromising the Holy See, the Spanish bishops could unite the laity, giving them clear doctrinal criteria on "the fundamental questions for the Church: the sanctity of marriage, Christian education, social justice, respect for a minimum of private property, the right to have children, to work, to help in sickness and old age, to rest, to entertainment, etc." He did not favor, however, creating a single Catholic political party. That, he argued, "would be very dangerous in Spain, because it could begin by serving the Church and easily end up making use of the Church."

The second path consisted in encouraging the laity to "personally assume political responsibility" as citizens. The laity had to receive a thorough training that would help them to work honestly for the common good, since "there are many who aspire to share the remains of the Franco regime." A broad outlook was also necessary in order to avoid the possibility that the desire for revenge could take over after the regime had ended.

Escrivá took advantage of the note to emphasize the political freedom of the people of Opus Dei. Those who collaborated

> with Franco in positions of government and administration, do so freely, under their personal responsibility. They act not as technicians, but as politicians, in the same way as the more numerous other citizens who form part of the regime and belong to Catholic Action, to the National Catholic Association of Propagandists, etc.

He stressed that the members of the Work "carry out their tasks as citizens, with the maximum freedom, the same freedom with which many other sons of mine, like Prof. Calvo Serer, oppose the Franco regime, sometimes in print." He further emphasized that in a personal capacity he had repeated to Franco twenty years earlier "in every possible way, that I was not a Francoist, nor an anti-Francoist, but a priest for all." Franco, he added, "understood it."[43]

In short, the Founder—who had had no qualms in writing to Franco in 1958 to congratulate him on the promulgation Principles of the National Movement—expressed to the Pope in 1964 his desire for a peaceful evolution of the regime toward a nonrevolutionary political form and underlined the political freedom enjoyed by his spiritual children.

Opus Dei's efforts to convince the public that it did not dictate its members' political activities and that they formed their own political opinions met with little success during the final decade of the Franco regime. A major source of ongoing criticism was the Falange and its publications. José Solís, Minister Secretary of the Movement (the highest-ranking official of the Falange), and Manuel Fraga, Minister of Information, resented the fact that influential Franco officials associated with Opus Dei did not share their views. Furthermore, they assumed that Opus Dei must be, like the Falange, a top-down structure which controlled the political activities of its members. For example, Solís wrote to López Rodó that it was inconceivable to him that a minister belonging to Opus Dei could not give instructions to a media outlet run by another person of the Work: "I will never understand, and I believe that my attitude will be widely shared, that the most preeminent men of Opus Dei declare yourselves strangers to whatever is proclaimed by those publications and newspapers that happen to be governed or directed by members of the Work."[44]

In 1966, Falangist publications launched a new press campaign against the Work to coerce some of its members to withdraw from public life. Specifically, the campaign began in response to calls for more representative and democratic unions in several publications directed by members of Opus Dei, most importantly the newspaper *El Alcázar*, directed by José Luis Cebrián.

Other attacks against Opus Dei came after Rafael Calvo Serer was named president of the board of directors of the *Madrid* evening paper, in July 1966. His long stays in Western countries with representative systems had convinced him that the opposition between a traditional authoritarian right and a revolutionary left had been overcome. Moreover, the Second Vatican Council had proclaimed autonomy in political and temporal matters. Against this background, Calvo proposed gradual changes in the regime that would lead to a democratic system with political parties and free elections. Immediately, the Falangist press launched a campaign against Calvo and Opus Dei for attacking the actions of the executive and the continuity of the National Movement.

At Escrivá's direction, the counselor of Opus Dei in Spain, Florencio Sánchez Bella, visited Solís and other leaders of the Falange to protest against their attributing Calvo Serrer's activities to Opus Dei. Since the Falangist leaders refused to desist, Escrivá wrote to Solís on October 28 asking him to put an end to the attacks on Opus Dei. The letter underlined the spiritual goals of Opus Dei and stressed that its members enjoyed freedom of thought and action in public life:

> I repeat that in all temporal and theological matters that are not of faith, which the Church leaves to the free debate of men, the members of the Work—each one of them—are personally free, as if they did not belong to Opus Dei. Therefore, it makes no sense to bring up the membership of a certain person of the Work, when it is a question of political, professional, social, etc. matters, just as it would be unreasonable to mention your wife and children or other members of Your Excellency's family when speaking of your political activities.[45]

In interviews with various journalists between March 1966 and June 1968, Escrivá responded to questions related to the Franco regime:

> take this opportunity to declare once again that Opus Dei is not linked to any country, to any regime, to any political tendency, to any ideology. Its members always act, in temporal matters, with complete freedom, knowing how to assume their own responsibilities, and they abhor any attempt to use religion for the benefit of political positions and party interests. . . . The Work's aims, I

repeat, are exclusively spiritual and apostolic. It asks its members only to live as Christians who strive to put into practice the ideals of the Gospel.

He explicitly rejected the idea that Catholics should all have the same point of view on political matters: "Those who have this mentality and claim that everyone should have the same opinion as they do, find it difficult to believe that there are people capable of respecting the freedom of others. They thus attribute to the Work the monolithic character that their own groups have."[46]

In a homily delivered on the campus of the University of Navarra in October 1967, the Founder again emphasized his approach to autonomous action in society. The freedom of Christians carries with it "a call to exercise your rights every day, and not just in times of emergency. A call to fulfill honorably your commitments as citizens in all fields— in politics and in financial affairs, in university life and in your job— accepting with courage all the consequences of your free decisions, and shouldering the personal independence that is yours." In a tone that denoted weariness of the need to repeat the same thing over and over again, he asked, "Must I affirm once again that the men and women who want to serve Jesus Christ in the Work of God are simply *citizens the same as everyone else*, who strive to live their Christian vocation to its ultimate consequences with a deep sense of responsibility?"[47]

The controversies continued. The pressure against Calvo Serer grew when the Spanish government suspended publication of the *Madrid* newspaper from June to September 1968. A year later, in July 1969, Franco appointed Juan Carlos de Borbón as his successor. Calvo Serer, who preferred Juan Carlos's father, Juan de Borbón, for future king, criticized Franco's decision. Luis Valls-Taberner, a member of Opus Dei and the banker who had set up the company that owned the paper, asked Calvo to step down as president. With no room for maneuver, Calvo Serer accused Carrero Blanco and several ministers of curtailing freedom of speech in Spain. In November 1971, the government closed *Madrid* permanently. Calvo Serer went to Paris, where he joined Spanish opposition groups that proposed the establishment of democracy in Spain.[48]

Some international media presented the struggle between Calvo and Valls and between Calvo Serer and the ministers who belonged to the Work as internal divisions in Opus Dei. Once again, the actions of individual members were confused with institutional actions. Calvo Serer reacted with a letter to the agency *France Press*:

> I have never been nor could I be the ideologue of Opus Dei. If I am an ideologue of anything, I am the ideologue of my intellectual convictions, of my personal cultural, political, and professional ideas. They have nothing to do with the doctrine of Opus Dei, which is confined to the spiritual realm. The only depositary of the spirit of Opus Dei is its founder. [I had] never been a member of any governing body of the Work at any level, even though I have been a member of Opus Dei since before the Spanish Civil War, in 1936. Therefore, it makes no sense to speak of an internal fracture in the hierarchy of Opus Dei, based on the fact that I disagree with other members of the Work in political and professional matters.[49]

In 1969, a financial scandal exploded in Spanish politics. The regime's press and radio reported that the textile machinery company Matesa was selling to its own subsidiaries the looms it had built with government export credits. Official media falsely claimed that the company's management positions were held by members of Opus Dei. They then called for the resignation of the ministers belonging to the Work, accusing them of giving public money to their own people. The Falangists hoped this accusation would pressure Franco to withdraw support for the development plans and change his mind about making Juan Carlos de Borbón, who was sponsored by López Rodó, his successor. The scandal was widely reported both inside and outside Spain. In response, Franco replaced the Falangist ministers Solís and Fraga as well as two members of Opus Dei, García Moncó and Espinosa. On the other hand, he kept López Rodó as Minister Commissioner of the Development Plan.[50]

These and other disputes of the time in which Opus Dei was involved were motivated by the struggle for political power in Spain. Escrivá often tried to explain why it was unfair to mention the Work in this context: Opus Dei and its goals, he stressed, were of a strictly religious nature; it was established in more than twenty-five countries with different political systems; it spread thanks to the personal activity of its members in all social spheres; its corporate activities were confined to education and healthcare; and finally, its members came from different social backgrounds and held different and often opposed political views.

Nonetheless, Falangist leaders and some other publicists insisted on depicting Opus Dei as a political group (or as people said at the time in Spain, a political family.) They turned political disputes into politico-religious issues. For them, the fact that prominent ministers belonged to Opus Dei showed that the Work corporately sought to control political and economic power in Spain. At a minimum, they contended, it showed that those in high positions formed a political group with a common program for the modernization of Spain within the authoritarian framework of Franco's dictatorship.*

López Rodó's ongoing political power and influence led some commentators to categorize the members of the Work who were activie in political life as comprising a political-religious group they called "technocrats of Opus Dei," marked by Catholicism, professional competence, and a pragmatic approach based on economic efficiency. This characterization was artificial and ignored important facts. López Rodó himself was more of a politician than a technocrat, and rather than forming a group around himself, he belonged to the group around Franco's second-in-command, Admiral Carrero Blanco. As we have seen, on more than one occasion the members of Opus Dei in the Franco government were at odds with each other on important issues. Nonetheless, the press's treatment of López Rodó contributed decisively to forming the public image of Opus Dei in the collective imagination of the media and, ultimately, in the historiography of Francoism. The Work came to be considered a conservative

---

* These circumstances were complicated by the fact that the ministers who were members of Opus Dei, like their ministerial colleagues, were not good communicators. They avoided taking sides in public debates and had a conception of society ordered from above, with approaches typical of Catholic corporativism.

institution, which strengthened an authoritarian regime but whose members were as liberal in economic matters as they were reactionary in doctrinal ones.[51] Only decades later did historians begin to draw distinctions between the political actions of a few prominent people during the Franco regime and the activity of the international religious institution to which they belonged.

Discussions of Opus Dei and politics tend to focus almost entirely on Spain. A number of ministers in democratic nations belonged to Opus Dei, such as Jorge Rossi Chavarría, in Costa Rica; Ruth Kelly, in the United Kingdom; Roberto Pedro Echarte, in Argentina; or João Bosco Mota Amaral, president of the regional government of the Azores and of the Assembly of the Republic of Portugal during the democratic period. In these cases, the press did not generally present Opus Dei as a group seeking political control of the country.

It does not seem that the presence of Opus Dei members in Franco's cabinets contributed significantly to the Work's numerical growth, its geographic expansion, or the financing of its institutional activities. If anything, it became an obstacle. Instead of being known for its spiritual message or its educational and social activities, Opus Dei came to be connected in many peoples' minds with Franco's government. Nonetheless, Escrivá resisted the temptation to suggest that the Franco ministers consider resigning. On one occasion, he commented to César Ortiz-Echagüe, a member of the Spanish Commission, "It would make my life much easier if those brothers of yours were not ministers, but if I suggested that I would not respect their freedom and I would destroy the Work."[52]

Two issues unrelated to politics captured the attention of Spanish public opinion during the final decade of the Founder's life. The first concerns the [Founder's] family. From the very beginning of the Work, Escrivá felt indebted to his family. He saw that his role as founder of Opus Dei had required them to sacrifice their own family life in order to take care of the members and undertakings of Opus Dei. Since his parents and his sister Carmen had passed away, he could repay the debt only by doing something for his brother Santiago.

Álvaro del Portillo learned that the Escrivá family was entitled to two noble titles, one of them the Marquisate of Peralta. The Founder could arrange for his brother to have the title, but only if he personally requested that it be reinstated, thereby making him Marqués, and then renounced it in favor of his brother. At first Escrivá rejected the possibility because it meant the Work would be criticized for having a founder who wanted a noble title. At Del Portillo's insistence, he consulted with several prominent members of the Vatican curia. Cardinal Larraona told him that it was not only a right but an obligation of justice and an example of secularity for his spiritual sons and daughters.

On July 24, 1968, the Spanish government reinstated the title of Marquis of Peralta in favor of Josemaría Escrivá. As he had expected, he was criticized for eagerness for public recognition. In reality, during the four years he held the title, he never made use of it or employed it on his letterhead or calling cards. After waiting the required time, he ceded the title to his brother.[53]

The second issue has as its context the complex relationship between the Franco regime and the Spanish hierarchy after the Second Vatican Council, particularly after the 1965 declaration *Dignitatis humanae* on religious freedom. Despite his declining health and the changing cultural and political climate which made his authoritarian regime increasingly unpopular, Franco refused to reform its ideological basis and legal structure. The post-conciliar Spanish Church, on the other hand, began to disassociate itself from Franco's political institutions in the midst of numerous tensions within the ecclesial community. These were years of manifestos, surveys, weakening of episcopal authority, haste in updating seminaries, novitiates, and convents, and doctrinal disorientation. Part of Catholic social action was oriented toward the improvement of living and working conditions, without proposing structural political changes. Another part, however, promoted critical awareness, social commitment, and political change.

Political parties and free trade unions were forbidden. Catholic Action groups were the most important organizations not sponsored by the government that were legally tolerated. They were increasingly used as platforms for expressing political opinions critical of the established order. Despite their avowed religious and spiritual aims, they became increasingly politicized, generating a major identity crisis within Catholic Action. In the working-class world, some leaders and young people of Catholic Action as well as members of religious orders embraced Marxist positions, accepting the revolutionary class struggle as a means to achieve the just distribution of wealth. Several Christian workers' movements participated, together with other political forces, in the beginning of the communist trade union *Comisiones Obreras.*

In this complex Spanish ecclesial context, a Joint Assembly of bishops and priests took place in September 1971 to facilitate dialogue, elaborate a program for post-conciliar renewal of the clergy, and study the adaptation of the Church to a future free and pluralistic society, disengaged from the Franco regime. Five months later, a document signed by the president and secretary of the Vatican Congregation for the Clergy, Cardinal John Wright and Archbishop Pietro Palazzini, disavowed a paper of the Assembly for distorting the nature and purpose of the Church and the priestly ministry in favor of socio-political action. The Congregation's document expressed doctrinal and disciplinary reservations about some aspects of the Assembly's positions.

Cardinal Enrique Tarancón, president of the Spanish Episcopal Conference, was deeply upset by the Congregation's document, which he said he had not officially received. He met in the Vatican with the Secretary of State, who said that the Vatican document had no legal force, and with Pope Paul VI, who expressed his confidence in the Spanish cardinal.

Several Spanish ecclesiastical publications accused Álvaro del Portillo, a consultant for the Congregation for the Clergy, of being the author of the Roman document. Althoiugh he denied it, the accusation convinced some Spanish Catholics that Opus Dei opposed the application of the Second Vatican Council in Spain. In addition, it strengthened the idea of the Work as a political family of the Franco regime. Although the Roman document was suspended, and the controversy died down over time, important sectors of public opinion remained suspicious about the actions of Del Portillo.[54]

Press controversies involving Opus Dei were not confined to Spain. In February 1964, Princess Irene of the Netherlands, second in the line of succession to the crown, made public that she had converted to Catholicism and would marry Prince Carlos Hugo de Borbón-Parma, a Carlist pretender to the Spanish throne. The Dutch press protested because the monarchy was traditionally Protestant and, in addition, the princess resided in a country with a dictatorial regime. The Work became involved because one of the people who had contributed to her conversion was a member of Opus Dei. After Princess Irene renounced her rights to the throne, the controversy died out, but people did not immediately forget the image they had formed of Opus Dei.

Another incident involved a corporate work in Sydney, Australia, Warrane College. The residencial college had begun in 1970 as a partner institution of the University of New South Wales. Under agreements with the university, Warrane provided accommodation for two hundred male students, an unusually large number for an Opus Dei student residence. In order to help so many students, Warrane created a system of tutors, some academic and some to help the students adjust to life in the university and the residence, rather like the resident advisors at many American colleges. From the beginning, Warrane welcomed young people from all over the world, including many from Southeast Asia. Only half the residents were Catholic. Both cultural and sports activities and Warrane's atmosphere of serious study produced good results. For example, in 1973, 82 percent of the residents passed all their exams, an unusually high percentage at the University of New South Wales.

A radical minority of students wanted the University of New South Wales to champion the social and political changes being demanded by student protesters in Europe and North America. They identified Warrane as an easy target for their demands, although few if any of them were residents of Warrane. The magazine sponsored by the student union published articles against

Opus Dei, accusing it of being authoritarian, a supporter of Franco's regime, and contrary to university principles, since it did not allow female students to go to the bedrooms or to the dining hall of the residence. In August 1971 and again in June 1974, hundreds of students demonstrated in front of Warrane and demanded its closure. University officials spoke out in favor of a pluralism of ideas and the autonomy of the college. As it became clear that the protest movement would not succeed in its final objective of unseating the university authorities, the attacks on Warrane died out, but they left behind an unpleasant memory.[55]

Section 3. The Founder's Final Projects, Writings, and Travels

In the mid-1960s, the Founder promoted two major construction projects: a Marian shrine and the definitive headquarters of the Roman College of the Holy Cross. Given the size of these undertakings and the special difficulties created by the challenges the Church faced in the decade after the Council, he called them his "last follies." He added jokingly that he hoped to add a third folly, "dying on time," that is, leaving this world when he could no longer work, without causing any inconvenience to those around him.

Escrivá had commented on many occasions that he wanted to build a large church in honor of the Blessed Virgin Mary, in gratitude for her maternal protection of Opus Dei. In 1968 he expressed his desire that the people of the Work in the United States would promote a shrine dedicated to the Mother of Fair Love, to pray for the sanctity of families. That did not prove possible during his lifetime and has not happened yet, but he was able to go ahead with a shrine in his homeland, the Somontano region of Aragon.

On the brow of a cliff in the municipality of Bolturina (Huesca), the ancient shrine of Our Lady of Torreciudad was home to an eleventh-century Romanesque statue of Our Lady to which the people of the region had great devotion. In 1956, at Escrivá's suggestion, some members of the Work visited it. Although the place was remote and difficult to reach, they proposed restoring the shrine and building a retreat house nearby. In September 1962, the bishop of Barbastro ceded it to Inmobiliaria General Castellana, a corporation established by members of the Work to maintain the cult of the Virgin of Torreciudad and restore the ancient shrine.

The architect Heliodoro Dols designed a project that included not only restoration of the small existing chapel and the statue of Our Lady, but also construction of a large shrine to accommodate eight hundred people with a mammoth esplanade with enough space for twenty thousand to attend outdoor Masses, a retreat house, and a rural training center to promote social work in the region. A board of trustees was set up to manage the project and raise funds. Donations were received from thousands of Opus Dei members and cooperators from all over the world

Construction lasted from 1969 to 1975. Members of more than six hundred local families found work on the project, slowing the incipient depopulation of the area. Dols used a modern style reminiscent of traditional local architecture, combining stone and brickwork. The sculptor Joan Mayné carved a polychrome alabaster altarpiece, with eight large scenes from the life of the Virgin. For the chapel of the Blessed Sacrament, the Italian sculptor Pasquale Sciancalepore created a bronze statue of Christ still alive on the Cross. Forty confessionals were installed in the crypt, since the Founder envisioned Torreciudad as a place of conversion, a place of encounter with God through the Virgin.

The second major project was the construction of the definitive campus of the Roman College of the Holy Cross. After unsuccessful efforts to find a suitable existing building in downtown Rome, the directors of the Work decided to purchase land on the outskirts of Rome and construct new buildings. At the end of 1969, a site was acquired near Via Flaminia, in northern Rome. Construction of classrooms, residential accommodations, and sports facilities for 150 students began in 1971 under the direction of the architect Jesús Álvarez Gazapo. The project, called Cavabianca, was completed in 1975. Sciancalepore cast a copy of the bronze crucifix he had created for Torreciudad for the chapel of the Holy Cross.

During the period 1968–1973, Escriva shifted his attention from completing his *Instructions* and *Letters* to the members of the Work and press interviews to publishing some of his homilies to help ordinary Christians seek holiness and bear witness to Christ. Starting with transcriptions of homilies he had preached at various times, he polished the texts, adding biblical references and quotations from the magisterium and spiritual authors, but retaining the oral style of personal conversation with God and with the listeners and readers. The individual homilies were first published separately in magazines and newspapers. In 1973, he brought eighteen of them together in a book he entitled *Christ Is Passing By*. The book follows the liturgical seasons and the principal feasts of the Church's calendar and reviews the great mysteries of Christian revelation.

Encouraged by the success of *Christ is Passing By*, he began preparing another volume composed of homilies focused on the Christian virtues. By the time of his death, he had finished revising the text of fourteen homilies. Four others, which were still in preparation, were finished by his successor. All these homilies appeared posthumously in 1977 under the title *Friends of God*. Both volumes were translated into numerous languages.[56]

Between March 1973 and February 1974, he wrote what would prove to be his last three *Letters* to the members of Opus Dei. Recalling the Spanish parish custom of ringing the bells three times to warn the faithful that Mass was about to begin, he referred to the three letters as the "three bells," intended to warn the members of the Work about the difficult situation the Church was going through and to confirm them in the faith.

The overall tone of these pastoral letters was clear and hopeful, although he stressed that the contemporary world was undergoing a crisis of values: "An entire civilization is tottering, impotent and without moral resources."[57] He warned that criticism of Catholic doctrine and the abandonment of religious practice had led to the loss of a sense of sin and to materialistic approaches to life. There was "a total subversion: eternity is replaced by history, the supernatural by nature, the spiritual by matter, divine grace by human effort."[58]

Confusion and slippage were patent in many areas: delay or omission of the baptism of children; catechisms with statements contrary to the Catholic faith; mistaken moral principles; manipulation of the texts of Sacred Scripture; denial that the Mass is a sacrifice: and loss of the sense of the real and substantial Presence of Jesus Christ in the Eucharist. Escrivá pointed out that the Pope had "spoken clearly of the *self-destruction* of the Church, and returns periodically to lament what is happening."[59]

Despite these problems, the Founder asked his sons and daughter to avoid falling into discouragement or isolating themselves in a fortress. The solutions were, in the first place, the personal search for holiness, being very demanding in the spiritual struggle, and remaining loyal to revelation and to the commitments they had made. He urged them to pray with a humble heart, to adore Christ in the Eucharist, and to trust in the power of divine grace. They should also sow Christian doctrine by explaining the truth about God and man in contemporary culture, being modern without slipping into modernism. And all of this, with hope and optimism. He recalled the example of his daughters and sons who had spread the Christian message of the Work throughout the world with joy and optimism. As a result, God had "poured out his sanctifying efficacy: conversions, vocations, fidelity to the Church in every corner of the world. This is how the supernatural fruit of unconditional dedication comes about."[60]

In the 1960s, the Founder had occassionally met with large groups of people in Spain in theaters, in residences of the Work, and in the open. Most of these events had been organized in Pamplona by the University of Navarra. [61]

After a novena at the shrine of Our Lady of Guadalupe in Mexico in 1970, he met with people of the Work in Mexico City and Guadalajara. He called the voyage a catechetical trip to stress that his goal was to expound Christian doctrine and the spirit of Opus Dei in a colloquial way. These meetings were a new way of conveying the Church's teaching and the spirit of the Work to large numbers of people.

In 1972 he decided to make a two-month tour of Spain and Portugal to reaffirm the faith of his spiritual children, cooperators, and other people who wanted to listen to him. From October 4 to November 30, he visited Pamplona, Bilbao, Madrid, Porto, Lisbon, Seville, Valencia, and Barcelona. He met with many groups, often in Opus Dei's corporate centers. In total, he saw more than one hundred thousand people. Escrivá called the meetings *"tertulias"* (get-togethers), even though they were attended by thousands of people. Most began with Escrivá speaking briefly about some aspect of Christian life. The bulk of the time was devoted to questions from the audience. The topics were varied, generally related to the joys and difficulties of life, the meaning of pain, the compatibility between professional work and family, dealing with adolescent children, and cultivating a personal relationship with God.[62] Some of the gatherings were professionally filmed

In 1974, Escrivá decided to make another catechetical trip to Latin America. From May 22 to August 31, 1974, he visited Brazil, Argentina, Chile, Peru, Ecuador, and Venezuela. With the experience acquired in the previous trips, things were organized to make it possible for most of the members to see the Founder. For many, it was the first time they had seen him in person.[63]

The schedule of meetings and visits to centers, residences, home schools, and corporate activities was intense. In Brazil and Argentina, he also held gatherings in public theaters with up to five thousand people. Because Chile was governed by a military junta under General Pinochet, he preferred to confine himself there to smaller meetings in Opus Dei's corporate works.

As his trip through Latin America proceeded, his health deteriorated. In addition to ongoing chronic kidney and heart failure, he suffered from bronchitis which made him stay in bed for five days in Lima, Peru. Quito, Ecuador's altitude of 9,000 feet above sea level complicated his breathing problems and forced him to meet with only a few people. In his final stop in Caracas, Venezulea, he suffered a new bout of bronchitis but was able to hold several meetings before returning to Europe.[64]

His last catechetical trip was to Venezuela and Guatemala, from February 4 to 25, 1975. Increasing kidney failure and anemia compelled him to shorten his stay and restrict himself to meeting only with relatively small groups of members of the Work and cooperators. Despite ill health, his direct and positive style turned all these encounters into pleasant, sometimes humorous, family gatherings.

During his 1974 and 1975 trips, Escrivá saw firsthand the formative, educational, and welfare work carried out by members of the Work. He explained the spirit of Opus Dei to people of all social and cultural backgrounds, adapting his responses to each person's situation. He dealt with all the topics that were put to him, many of which involved the fundamental truths of the Christian faith. He recalled that Christian life is rooted in union with Jesus Christ and stressed that every Catholic should find time to pray during the day, receive the sacraments of penance and Eucharist frequently, and carry out of works of charity and mercy. He emphasized the Church's doctrine on chastity and sexual morality, and encouraged the practice of ascetic means of proven usefulness such as the practice of modesty, guarding the heart and the senses, fleeing from close occasions of sin, sincerity in personal spiritual direction, and seeking advice when choosing readings and other entertainment.[65]

When asked about the situation of the Church, he reminded his listeners that the treasure of Catholic faith and morals had not changed with the Second Vatican Council. On the contrary, they were living in an era in which men and women were called to give bold public witness to Jesus Christ in social life. He also insisted on unity and love for the Pope, the bishops, and priests and religious. He commented that there was not a hierarchical Church and a charismatic Church, but only one Church that united the two realities. When he was told about an abuse or disorder, he used to say that he did not know any bad priests, although some were "sick" from the doctrinal point of view. Prayer was the first and best way to help them.

From May 23 to 26, 1975, he was in Spain to receive the gold medal of his hometown, Barbastro. He also visited the Torreciudad shrine, whose construction was far advanced. During the visit, he consecrated the main altar.

Back in Rome, Escrivá focused on matters that needed to be resolved before the summer. On June 26, he offered Mass for the Church and for the Pope.* Afterward, he went to Villa delle Rose to spend some time with his daughters in the Roman College of Santa Maria. After a short time, he felt ill and returned to Villa Tevere. As soon as he entered Don Álvaro's office, he collapsed, probably due to ventricular fibrillation. Despite medical care and artificial respiration, he died within a few minutes.

On one occasion, he had noted: "This is our destiny on earth: to fight for love until the last moment. *Deo gratias*!"[66] At the age of seventy-three, Josemaría Escrivá suddenly ended his earthly journey. The foundation of Opus Dei was over.

Notes

1. Paul VI, encyclical *Humanae vitae*, no. 14, in AAS 60 (1968) 490.

2. Letter of Josemaría Escrivá to Paul VI, Rome, April 23, 1964. AGP E.4.1, 227-3-1.

3. Josemaría Escrivá, 349–350.

4. See General Note 9/70 (May 12, 1970). AGP E.1.3, 246.

5. Cardona analyzed in his studies the particular link between the act of personal being, freedom, and love: God—personal Being and Love by essence—creates man for love and endows him with freedom to love (see Carlos Cardona, *Metafísica de la opción intellectual* (Madrid: Rialp, 1973). Among others, he maintained academic contact with the philosopher Cornelio Fabro, who sought a renewal of Thomism as a way to confront the immanentism established in Western culture, as well as with Augusto Del Noce, an analyst of the evolution of Marxism and its influence on society.

---

* Since the end of the 1960s, and in the face of the doctrinal and disciplinary crisis of the post-conciliar period, the Founder asked for prayers for the successor of Paul VI, who would be responsible for restoring unity: "The Church hurts me: everything is confusion and lack of authority. We should pray—and pray a lot—for the next Pope, because he will have to be an unpopular martyr, if he picks up the reins and puts everyone in his place. Pray, I repeat. Later that new Pontiff who has authority and makes it felt (he is the Vicar of Christ) will be adored and loved by the whole earth" (Letter of Josemaría Escrivá to Florencio Sánchez Bella, Rome, June 17, 1968, in AGP, series A.3.4, 291-2, 680617-1).

6. See General Note 108/64 (July 14, 1964). AGP E.1.3, 244-2; and General Note 44/66 (June 6, 1966). AGP E.1.3, 245-1.

7. Of special importance were the short studies sent from 1970 onwards, which explained Christian doctrine in the light of the changing circumstances of the life of the Church (see General Note 26/70, dated December 4, 1970. AGP E.1.3, 246-2).

8. See General Note 8/72 (April 1, 1972). AGP E.1.3, 246-4. Through 1975, three volumes of *Notebooks* were prepared, dealing with faith, morals, and ascetical themes.

9. General note 18/67, no. 8 (April 20, 1967). AGP E.1.3, 245-3.

10. See General Note 212, no. 6 (March 18, 1959). AGP E.1.3, 242-2.

11. See General Note 89/64 (June 6,1964). AGP E.1.3, 244-1.

12. General Note 10/69 (March 6, 1969). AGP E.1.3, 246-1; and General Note 23/70 (November 27, 1970). AGP E.1.3, 246-2 (prohibiting reading the works of Marxist authors). See list of 1,852 books on topics of faith and morals approved for the libraries of the centers of the Work, in "Apunte a la Nota general 17/72 (June 24, 19721972). AGP E.1.3, 246-4.

13. See General Note 2/69 (January 22, 1969). AGP E.1.3, 246-1. The Catechism had two grades or levels: the "minor," for children, and the "major," for adults.

14. See General Note 9/72 (April 1, 1972). AGP E.1.3, 246-4.

15. General note 20/67 (April 20, 1967). AGP E.1.3, 245-3. See General Note 1/70, no. 6 (January 10, 1970). AGP E.1.3, 246-2.

16. General Note 33/67, no. 5, b (June 24, 1967). AGP E.1.3, 245-3. See General Note 81/65 (June 18, 1965). AGP E.1.3, 244-4.

17. Mercedes Montero, *Historia de Ediciones Rialp. Orígenes y contexto, aciertos y errores.* (Madrid: Rialp, 2020) 231.

18. See General Note 20/71 (September 15, 1971). AGP E.1.3, 246-3.

19. They then added the Old Testament in four volumes and grouped the New Testament volumes into a single volume. The project was completed in 2004. This work has been published in many languages. See César Izquierdo and José Ramón Villar, *Notas para un aniversario. 50 años de la Facultad de Teología de la Universidad de Navarra (1967–2017)* (Pamplona: Servicio de Publicaciones de la Universidad de Navarra, 2017), p. 28.

20. See General Note 67/65 (May 28, 1965). AGP E.1.3, 244-4.

21. See General Note 44/64 (March 30, 1964). AGP E.1.3, 243-4.

22. See *Cronica* April 1974, 14. AGP Library, P01.

23. See General Note 76/65 (June 10, 1965). AGP E.1.3, 244-4.

24. See General Note 24/69 (September 23, 1969). AGP E.1.3, 246-1.

25. General Note 29/70 (December 23, 1970). AGP E.1.3, 246-2. See General Note 97/65 (November 11, 1965). AGP E.1.3, 244-4; General Note 45/66 (June 24, 1966). AGP E.1.3, 245-1; General Note 7/70 (Marcrh 27, 1970). AGP E.1.3, 246-2; and General Note 18/73 (March 27, 1973). AGP E.1.3, 246-5.

26. See General Note 8/71 (12-II-1971). AGP E.1.3, 246-3.

27. Recollections of Covadonga O'Shea y Artiñano, Madrid, 15-IX-1975. AGP A.5, 235-1-2.

28. During these years, he referred frequently to freedom using a classic term from the teaching of Pius XI: the "freedom of conscience," Letter 3, nos. 66 and 72, in Escrivá, *Cartas*, vol. 1. All persons, he stressed, had the right to be respected, defended, and helped to act in conscience, without suffering physical or moral coercion. In this way, each person could make the decisions that seemed most appropriate to him and be responsible for his actions. Also, in this way, the life of others was not constrained nor were second-class citizens and faithful created in civil society or in the Church. He also insisted on freedom within the Church, as opposed to clericalism that tried to govern all activities or that interfered in temporal matters that were the responsibility of the laity. For example, he was against the so-called *pastoral de ensemble* which imposed single criteria on the diocese "under the guise of *coordination* of energies, unification of efforts, *exchange of* methods of apostolate and experiences." Such an attitude stifled other particular methods of doing apostolate and the freedom of individuals to have recourse to the associations, priests, and means of formation of their choice. See General Note 69/67, no. 6 (November 7, 1967). AGP E.1.3, 245-4.

29. Authors' interview with Fernando Valenciano Polack, Rome, January 24, 2020. Valenciano was vice-secretary of the Work of St. Michael of the General Council from 1961 to 1994.

30. Letter 38, no. 1, 149 and 150. AGP A.3, 190-1. Paul VI proclaimed a "Year of Faith" from July 1967 to June 1968.

31. Letter from Josemaría Escrivá to Florencio Sánchez Bella, Rome, February 29, 1964. AGP A.4, 280-2, 640229-2.

32. Josemaría Escrivá, *Conversaciones con Mons. Escrivá de Balaguer, edición crítico-histórica* (Madrid: Rialp, 2012), 230. See Julián Herranz, "Opus Dei," *Nuestro Tiempo*, 97–98 (1962) 3–28.

33. General Note 31/65 (March 24, 1965). AGP E.1.3, 244-3.

34. See Jaume Aurell Cardona, "La formación de un gran relato sobre el Opus De," *Studia et Documenta* 6 (2012), pp. 242–250; Onésimo Díaz and Fernando de Meer, *Rafael Calvo Serer. La búsqueda de la libertad (1954–1988)* (Madrid: Rialp, 2010); Pablo Hispán Iglesias de Ussel, *La política en el régimen de Franco entre 1957 y 1969. Proyectos, conflictos y luchas por el poder* (Madrid: Centro de Estudios Políticos y Constitucionales) 2006); Laureano López Rodó, *Memorias* (four volumes) (Barcelona: Plaza & Janés, 1990–1993).

35. Handwritten note, April 23, 1964. AGP K.1, 186-2; and General Note 20/64, no. 4 (February 27,1964). AGP E.1.3, 243-4.

36. General Note 25/62 (May, 1962). AGP E.1.3, 243-1.

37. *ABC*, June 12, 1962, 37.

38. Report on the interview between Josemaría Escrivá and Loris Francesco Capovilla, Rome, July 6, 1962. AGP E.4.1, 227-2.

39. Monthly intention, December, 1963. AGP K.1, 186-1.

40. Handwritten note, April 23, 1964. AGP K.1, 186-2; and General Note 20/64, no. 4 (February 27,1964). AGP E.1.3, 243-4.

41. Authors' interview with Javier Fernández del Moral, July 6, 2020. Fernández del Moral worked in the information office of Opus Dei in Spain between 1969 and 1975.

42. Report of the interview between Josemaría Escrivá and Angelo Dell'Acqua, Rome, May 19, 1964. AGP E.4.1, 227-3-1.

43. Note from Josemaría Escrivá to Paul VI, Rome, June 14, 1964. AGP E.4.1, 227-3-1.

44. Letter from José Solís to Laureano López Rodó, Madrid, April 27, 1966, quoted in Jordi Rodríguez Virgili, *El Alcázar y Nuevo Diario. Del asedio al expolio (1936–1970)* (Madrid: CIE Dossat, 2005), p. 285.

45. Letter from Josemaría Escrivá to José Solís Ruiz, Rome, October 28, 1966. AGP A.3.4, 285-4, 661028-1.

46. Josemaría Escrivá, *Conversaciones*, pp. 275–6 and 322–4.

47. Josemaría Escrivá, *Conversaciones*, pp. 496–7.

48. On this particular issue, see Carlos Barrera, *"El Opus Dei y la prensa en el tardofranquismo,"* *Historia y Política* 28 (2012), pp. 139–165; Onésimo Díaz and Fernando de Meer, *Rafael Calvo Serer. La búsqueda de la libertad (1954–1988)* (Madrid: Rialp, 2010).

49. Rafael Calvo Serer, *La dictadura de los franquistas. I. El affaire del "Madrid" y el futuro político* (Alençon:Impr. Alançonnaise, 1973), p. 196.

50. See Juan Vilá Reyes, *El atropello MATESA* (Barcelona: Plaza & Janes, 1992); Mariano Navarro Rubio, *Mis memorias. Testimonio de una vida política truncada por el "Caso Matesa"* (Barcelona: Plaza y Janés, 1991).

51. See Antonio Argandoña, "El papel de los *tecnócratas* en la política y en la economía española, 1957–1964," in Paulino Castañeda and Manuel J. Cociña (eds.), *Iglesia y Poder Público. Actas del VII Simposio de Historia de la Iglesia en España y América* (Córdoba: Obra Social y Cultural Cajasur, 1997, 221–235); Jesús María Zarategui Labiano, *La tecnocracia y su introducción en España*, (Valladolid:Universidad de Valladolid 2019); Anna Catharina Hofman, *Francos Moderne. Technokratie und Diktatur in Spanien 1956–1973* (Göttingen: Wallstein, 2019).

Among the books that most contributed to creating an image of Opus Dei as a pressure group with great political and economic power in Spain were: Daniel Artigues (pseudonym of Jean Bécarud), *El Opus Dei en España. Su evolución ideológica y política* (Paris: Ruedo Ibérico, 1971); Jesús Yfante, *La prodigiosa aventura del Opus Dei. Genesisy desarrollo de la y desarrollo Santa Mafia* (Paris: Ruedo Iberico, 1970); and Yvon Le Vaillant, *Sainte Maffia. Le Dossier de l'Opus Dei* (Paris: Mercure de France, 1971). All three authors relied on press reports. In addition, Ynfante had access to papers taken from the Commission of Opus Dei in Spain, which he presented in a distorted way. Bécarud and Ynfante published in Ruedo Ibérico, a Spanish anti-Francoist publishing house based in Paris.

52. Cited in Aurell Cardona, "La formación," p. 285. Escrivá may have thought at the time—although he did not publicly talk about the issue—that the presence of competent Catholics and professionals in the Francoist government would favor a future peaceful transition to a democratic regime, avoiding a revolution against the Church (Authors' interview with Bishop Julián Herranz, Rome, February 25, 2020). In agreement with the Founder, the directors of Opus Dei frequently explained that the relationship of fraternity among the members of the Work "must not have any manifestation in social life (see *De spiritu*, no. 109). No member should offer a job to another member, if he knows him exclusively because he belongs to the Work": General Notice 141/75, no. 2 (May 9, 1975). AGP E.1.3, 255-3.

The accusation that Opus Dei supported authoritarian regimes appeared years later in the media of other countries—specifically, in Argentina during the civil-military dictatorship of 1976–1983 and in Chile during the military regime of General Pinochet (1973–1990). Although the accusations made were similar to those in Spain in connection with the Franco regime, the controversies were shorter-lived because in those countries there were no members of the Work who were government ministers. According to Stefan Moszoro, regional vicar of Opus Dei in Poland, in the case of Eastern European countries "the sources of information under the influence of Soviet propaganda criticized the Work, at various times, well into the 1990s. With greater or lesser emphasis, they presented Opus Dei as a Catholic anti-communist force. To some extent—this is something that will have to be studied with archival documentation—when they rejected Opus Dei, they were ultimately aiming at the thought and teachings of John Paul II." (Authors' interview, January 3, 2011).

53. See Constantino Ánchel, "Nombramientos y distinciones Appointments and Distinctions of St. Josemaría," in *Diccionario de San Josemaría Escrivá*, 888–892.

54. See Fernando De Meer Lecha-Marzo, *Antonio Garrigues embajador ante Pablo VI. Un hombre de concordia en la tormenta (1964–1972)* (Cizur Menor: Thomson-Aranzadi, 2007), p. 342, nt. 52; Yolanda Cagigas Ocejo, *La revista Vida Nueva (1967–1976). Un proyecto de renovación en tiempos de crisis* (Pamplona: EUNSA, 2007), pp. 203–204.

55. See José Manuel de la Cerda, "Like a Bridge over Troubled Water in Sydney: Warrane College and the Student Protests of the 1970s," *Studia et Documenta* 4 (2010), pp. 147–181.

56. See Josemaría Escrivá, *Es Cristo que pasa* (2nd ed., critical-historical edition) (Madrid: Rialp, 2013).; Josemaría Escrivá, *Amigos de Dios* (critical-historical edition) (Madrid: Rialp, 2019).

57. Letter 42, no. 10. AGP A.3, 190-2-4.

58. Letter 41, no. 12. AGP A.3, 190-2-3. In another letter, Escrivá went into detail to indicate that the evil had its origin in clerics "who have lost hope with their faith: priests who hardly pray, unbelieving and arrogant theologians—so they call themselves, although they contradict even the most elementary truths of revelation—professors of religion who teach garbage, mute pastors, agitators in sacristies and convents, who infect consciences with their pathological tendencies, writers of heretical catechisms, political activists," Letter 42, no. 13. AGP A.3, 190-2-4).

59. Letter 41, no. 20. AGP A.3, 190-2-3.

60. Letter 42, no. 5. AGP A.3, 190-2-4.

61. In 1960, he received an honorary doctorate from the University of Zaragoza and the title of adopted son of the city of Pamplona; in 1966, the title of adopted son of Barcelona. In 1964, 1967, 1972, and 1974 he presided as grand chancellor over the honorary doctorate ceremonies at the University of Navarra at which a total of thirteen people, including the canonist Willy Onclin, the medical geneticist Jérôme Lejeune, and the biochemist Jean Roche received honorary degrees. In these cases, he gave public or academic speeches and met with many people.

62. See José Antonio Loarte, "Catequesis, Labor y viajes de," in *Diccionario de San Josemaría*, pp. 219–223.

63. See Carlo Pioppi, "*I viaggi di catechesi in America Latina di Josemaría Escrivá. Uno sguardo d'insieme (1974–1975)*," *Studia et Documenta* 11 (2017), pp. 49–64; Alexandre Antosz Filho, "*Com os braços abertos a todos. A visita de São Josemaria Escrivá ao Brasil*," Studia *et Documenta* 11 (2017), pp. 65–100; Antonio Ducay Vela, *San Josemaría en el Perú. Crónica de viaje: 9 de julio a 1 de agosto de 1974* (Lima: Centro de Estudios y Comunicación, 2017); María Eugenia Ossandón Widow, "*Josemaría Escrivá en Santiago de Chile (1974)*," *Studia et Documenta* 11 (2017), pp. 101–150.

64. See Diego Martínez Caro and Alejandro Cantero Fariña, "¡Sanctificado sea el dolor! Aspectos medicos de la biografía del Beato Josemaría Escrivá de Balaguer" *Scripta Theologica*, 34/2 (2002), pp. 605–621.

65. These ideas on chastity and Christian purity appeared several times in the notes sent to the members of the Work. See General Note 5/70 (March 17, 1970). AGP E.1.3, 246-2.

66. Words of December 31, 1971, quoted in Vázquez de Prada, *The Founder of Opus Dei*, vol. 3, p. 639.

PART II

The Years of Escrivá's
First Successor
(1975–1994)

The 1978 election of Cardinal Wojtyła as the first non-Italian Pope in 450 years strongly marked the next quarter century of the Catholic Church's life. Pope John Paul II worked to implement Vatican II in continuity with the Church's tradition and from the Christocentric perspective of his first encyclical, *Redemptor hominis* (1979). He struggled to guide the Church down a path which avoided both the exaggerated traditionalism of Archbishop Lefebvre and his followers and the philo-Marxism of large parts of Liberation Theology. He reached out to young people, especially through World Youth Days, which began in 1986. At the one held in Manila in 1995, an estimated five million attended the closing Mass. The *Catechism of the Catholic Church* (1992) presented a detailed overview of the Church's perennial teaching in the light of Vatican II and of John Paul II's numerous encyclicals and other publications. The revised Code of Canon Law (1983) both modernized the Church's law and reflected the theological developments of Vatican II.

Institutions like Mother Teresa's Missionaries of Charity gave new vibrancy to the life of the Church. Many of them, like the Neocatechumenal Way, Communion and Liberation, the Focolare Movement, Charismatic Renewal, and the Community of Sant'Egidio, stressed the role of lay men and women in bringing Christ's message to the world.

Rapid technological development in the burgeoning information age transformed not only business but also people's personal lives.

Personal computers were introduced in the late 1970s. Although initially expensive and hard to use, by the mid-1990s they were widespread and their use no longer required specialized knowledge. Email made communication faster, cheaper, and easier. Video games began to occupy many people's free time, and music became the continuous background of their lives.

Concern for the environment, centered at first on air and water, found expression in the legislation of many countries. Among young people, environmentalism became a defining concern. In the 1990s, major environmental organizations began to focus on climate.

The effects of the sexual revolution of the 1960s made themselves felt increasingly in subsequent decades. Contraception, divorce, and extramarital sex spread rapidly. Pornography became widespread and, in some circles, socially acceptable. Public schools offered sex education programs beginning as early as kindergarten. Growing numbers of men and women disclosed that they were homosexual" and by the mid-1980s the Democratic Party in the United States had officially rejected discrimination based on sexual orientation.

More women began working outside the home and in increasingly diverse areas including politics. Indira Gandhi served as prime minister of India from 1966 to 1977 and again from 1980 until her assassination in October 1984. Margaret Thatcher became Chair of the UK's Conservative Party in 1975 and served as Prime Minister of Great Britain from 1979 to 1990.

Western Europe took great strides toward toward unification. The Schengen agreement in 1983 led to the opening of borders and the elimination of passport control in most of Western Europe. In 1992, the Maastricht Treaty created the European Union, greatly expanding the competencies of the European Communities and eventually leading to the creation of the Euro. The Maastricht Treaty was also a major step toward the development of a common European foreign and security policy. Increasing numbers of young Europeans began to study outside their own countries. This led to much closer contacts among them across Europe and greatly facilitated cooperation among Opus Dei centers throughout Europe.

The political transformation of Russia and central and eastern Europe began in the mid-1980s when Mikhail Gorbachev, General Secretary of the Communist Party of the Soviet Union, initiated policies of *perestroika* (reforms to restructure society and the economy) and *glasnost* (openness). He rejected the Brezhnev doctrine of supporting Communist regimes in client states and withdrew Soviet troops from central and eastern Europe. In 1989, elections in most of the Marxist-Leninist states of central and eastern Europe resulted in multi-party regimes with elements of market economies. The East German government allowed its citizens to cross into West Germany and the Berlin Wall was torn down, leading to German reunification. In 1991, the Union of Soviet Socialist Republics dissolved and was replaced by a relatively loose Commonwealth of Independent States, including Russia headed by Boris Yeltsin. The Communist Party was banned.

The death of Mao in 1976 and the policies of Deng Xiaoping marked the beginning of China's movement toward market socialism. Many people hoped this meant greater political openness, but the brutal 1989 suppression of protest in Tiananmen Square and throughout the rest of the country demonstrated that political reform had sharply marked limits.

Francisco Franco died in 1975, opening the way for a peaceful transition to a parliamentary democracy under King Juan Carlos. The Union of the Democratic Center, led by Adolfo Suarez, won the first free elections in four decades, and governed until the victory of the Socialist Party in the 1986 elections. The Socialist government under Felipe González created an extended welfare state, legalized abortion, expanded divorce (which had been legalized in 1981, but with many restrictions), and led Spain into NATO and the European Communities. The radical Basque separatist movement ETA carried out a campaign of bombings, assassinations, and kidnappings that claimed more than eight hundred lives between 1968 and 2010. In 1979, it set off a bomb at the shrine of Our Lady of Torreciudad which did extensive damage but caused no serious injuries.

Italy, where Opus Dei was headquartered, suffered economic crisis and terrorist attacks in the 1970s and early 1980s. The economy recovered in the mid 1980s, and Italy joined the G7, but government spending drove the national debt above 100 percent of GDP. The Christian Democratic Party retained its dominant position until 1992 when public disgust with political paralysis and corruption led to further fragmentation of the political spectrum.

The end of the Soviet Union marked the end of the Cold War. Many other stresses, however, continued. The Ayatollah Khomeini's overthrow of the Shah of Iran in 1979 signaled the entrance of Islamic fundamentalism onto the world stage. International terrorism, whether supported by states or non-state actors, became a major factor in international relations. Ethnic cleansing and genocide horrified the world repeatedly, especially in Rwanda and in the former Yugoslavia.

CHAPTER 6

A New Hand at the Helm

O nly a handful of people had been aware that Escrivá was suffering from chronic renal and cardiac insufficiency in addition to the pneumonia and upper respiratory illnesses that had forced him to abbreviate his trips to South America in 1974 and 1975. During a visit to Spain in May 1975, he experienced two episodes of labored breathing and rapid heart rate, but he recovered quickly each time.[1] No one thought he was likely to die soon. Even Del Portillo was caught unprepared by his sudden death on June 26, 1975, and for the vast majority of Opus Dei members, it came as a complete shock.[2]

Perhaps for this reason, even amid preparations for Escrivá's funeral, Del Portillo found the time to write a lengthy letter to the members dated June 29, 1975.[3] He related in loving detail the last days of the Founder's life, and his death and funeral, even describing carefully the vestments in which he was dressed during the wake, funeral Mass, and burial. Toward the end of the narrative part of the letter, Del Portillo revealed that in 1957, Escrivá had suggested that the inscription on his tombstone say in Latin, "Josemaría Escrivá de Balaguer y Albas. A Sinner. He Engendered Sons and Daughters." Del Portillo described this as "one more great lesson in humility," but since Escrivá had said it was only a suggestion, he decided to put instead "The Father" and the dates of Escrivá's birth and death.[4]

In the second part of his letter, Del Portillo shifted from narrative to spiritual exhortation. He insisted that, "The Father lives. He lives in God. Participating in the divine life, he will continue to guide us. He will continue directing the Work." Del Portillo described the moment as one for a "decided conversion of our life to a fuller, more refined, more sincere, more loving, more generous fidelity to the spiritual inheritance that the Father has transmitted to us." In addition to fidelity, he called for unity and for greater generosity in fulfilling the norms of Opus Dei members' plan of life as a way of living continuously in the presence of God. Finally, he called for greater humility and asked all the members of the Work to implore the Lord to grant them "a holy hunger to disappear, to be the last, to obey with greater finesse than ever."[5]

During the two and half months between Escrivá's death and his election as Escrivá's successor, Del Portillo governed Opus Dei in his capacity as Secretary General. He convened an electoral General Congress for September 14, the Feast of the Exaltation of the Holy Cross.

Section 1. A New "Father" in Opus Dei

On September 14, 1975, the central advisory, made up of eight women residing in Rome and the twenty-three delegates of the President General to the regions of the women's branch, met to propose candidates. In his introductory remarks, Del Portillo, who presided over the meeting, asked them to make the resolution of "being faithful, being very united to the spirit [of the Father], and of continuing to be very united among ourselves."[6] He urged them to make their choice in light of the good of the women's branch, with the assurance that the priest who would be best for the women's branch would be best for the entire Work.[7] Each member of the central advisory wrote her choice on a slip of paper.

The following day, the 124 electors of the men's branch met. The votes of the members of the central advisory were read out. They had unanimously proposed Del Portillo.[8] He was unanimously elected on the first ballot by the electors of the men's branch.[9]

The next day, Del Portillo began by asking the electors of the men's branch for their prayers.[10] He spoke at length about the life of Escrivá and reminded the electors, "We have received the spirit of the Work as an inheritance, and we have to pass on that inheritance whole and entire to those who come after us."[11] He proposed a number of motions, expressing gratitude to Escrivá, calling for beginning as soon as possible his process of beatification and canonization, ratifying the *Codex Iuris Particularis* which Escrivá had approved in 1974, and moving forward with the search for an adequate legal framework for Opus Dei. These motions were approved by acclamation.[12] Finally, in secret ballots the electors approved unanimously (with one exception) Del Portillo's proposals for the General Council and the Central Advisory. The new General Council was made up of: General Secretary Javier Echevarría; Central Priest Secretary Francisco Vives Unzué; Under Secretary of St. Michael Fernando Valenciano Polack; Under Secretary of St. Gabriel César Ortiz de Echagüe; Under Secretary of St. Raphael Umberto Farri; Prefect of Studies Rolf Thomas; General Administrator Giuseppe Molteni; Spiritual Director Carlos Cardona; and General Procurator Daniel Cummings. The new central advisory comprised: Central Secretary Carmen Ramos; Secretary of the central advisory Marlies Kücking; Under Secretary of St. Michael Carmen Pérez-Colomer Cerredo; Under Secretary of St. Gabriel Maria Ivanna Lobay; Under Secretary of St. Raphael Alison Birkett; Prefect of Studies María Luisa Vaquero Monedero; Prefect of numerary assistants Maria Podgornik; and Central Procurator María Rosario Esteve Balzola.

The election of Del Portillo and even the unanimity of the electors in choosing him were not surprising. Escrivá had repeatedly made clear his preference for Del Portillo as his successor.[13] Only two days before his death, pointing to Del Portillo, he had said to Msgr. Alonso, "My son, if you aren't fools, when I die you will follow that brother of yours."[14] All of the electors of both branches must have been aware of Escrivá's preference and of the fact that for some thirty-five years he had been training Del Portillo to succeed him. Their unanimous approval of all Del Portillo's proposals may seem more striking, although it seems probable that they thought of voting for Del Portillo's proposals as a way of manifesting the unity of the Work and their adherence to the legacy of the Founder.[15]

Escrivá's death caused deep sorrow even to the members who had never met him.[16] He was much more than the President General, and in some ways more even than the founder. Although only a small fraction of the members had dealt with him personally and many had never seen him, they had warm affection for him as "the Father." This was due to their appreciation of his role as founder and as head of Opus Dei, but it was also due to his personality. He had a deep interior life and lived in the presence of God, but he was also an ebullient extrovert with a great capacity to love and to manifest his affection. He had won the adherence and affection of the members of Opus Dei through his spiritual message, but also through the warmth and affection which he poured out on them. The Spanish saying "Love is repaid with love" was manifestly verified in Opus Dei during Escrivá's lifetime. He obviously loved his sons and daughters, and they responded in kind. Their ties to him had been an important element of unity in Opus Dei.

Escrivá's death could have been a severe challenge for Opus Dei. Escrivá had, however, foreseen this challenge and prepared Opus Dei for it. Time and again he had urged the members not only to be united to his successor but to love him wholeheartedly.[17] Aware that Escrivá had wanted Del Portillo to succeed him, the members responded enthusiastically to the news of his selection as the new President General. One person wrote: "This is marvelous! I realize now, although I always knew it, that the Father, the President General, is always the Father. I don't know how to distinguish in my affection or in my desire to be a good son, between the Father who is with God in heaven, and the Father we now have on earth."[18] Another wrote to Del Portillo, "If our Father has won for you the grace to love us as he loved us, I can assure you that he has obtained for us the grace to love you as we loved him. And even more, because he told us we should love you more . . . "[19] Another wrote, "You can be sure, Father, that we accompany you from afar with our prayer, and we ask our common Father, who is already in heaven, to illuminate you and to obtain from the Lord the gifts of wisdom, knowledge, and fortitude necessary to guide us all."[20]

For his part, Del Portillo said, "I live only to think about our Father, about how to be more faithful to him, and about you, how to help you be saints."[21] His affection and concern manifested themselves in all sorts of ways, big and small: in generous prayer and penance, in tiny gestures, and in the effort to transmit the spirit of the Work.

To the very end of his life, Del Portillo worked at transmitting to his sons and daughters the spirit of the Founder. He frequently preached to the members of the General Council during the half hour they dedicated each morning to mental prayer. Every week he gave them a practical class on the spirit of the Work without giving in to the increasing tiredness that age brought with it.[22] His concern to form the members of the Work was not limited to those who were closest to him. He traveled frequently to establish personal contact with the people of Opus Dei throughout the world,[23] and he wrote frequent letters to stay in touch with them.[24]

Escrivá had been very much "the Father" and his fatherhood had marked to an extraordinary degree the life of Opus Dei and of its individual members. But he had also been the Founder. During his lifetime, there was no difference between the two roles. The Father was the Founder, and the Founder was the Father. Del Portillo faced the challenge of being the Father without being the founder. One of his close collaborators, Cardinal Herranz, described his way of responding as "dynamic fidelity."[25] Del Portillo recognized that he could not limit himself to repeating in a rote fashion what Escrivá had said and done, but he needed to preserve and transmit the spirit which God had given to Escrivá. Dynamic fidelity required distinguishing between a spirit which should be respected and preserved and concrete ways of living that spirit which needed to be changed to accommodate new situations.

This was especially important and difficult because the world and the Church were experiencing rapid and profound changes, especially in the wake of the sexual revolution and the rapid spread of relativism, skepticism, and the rejection of authority. The general doctrinal situation in the Church in the years until the 1990s suggested a need for caution. Under Del Portillo's leadership, the Founder's decision to require members to avoid reading books which were doctrinally questionable and to ask permission before doing so continued to resonate strongly. This helped Opus Dei avoid the hemorrhaging suffered by so many Catholic institutions, but it tended to some degree to create a climate of mistrust and suspicion toward new developments in philosophy and theology. Similarly, the Founder's caution in implementing liturgical changes in the 1960s and '70s continued under Del Portillo to create an environment in which priests of Opus Dei generally chose among the liturgical options offered by the new liturgical guidelines the ones most similar to the earlier liturgy.

Del Portillo would govern Opus Dei till 1994. From March 14 to 22, 1994, he made a pilgrimage to the Holy Land, praying in all the principal places visited by Jesus Christ. On the 22nd, he celebrated Mass in the Church of the Cenacle and flew back to Rome. Early in the morning of the 23rd, he died of a heart attack after receiving the anointing of the sick. That afternoon Pope John Paul II came to pray at his wake, and the next day, he was buried in the crypt of Opus Dei's prelatic church.

Section 2. Governing Opus Dei

First as Opus Dei's President General and then as its Prelate, Del Portillo was the head of "a small part of the Church," as Escrivá liked to describe it. Because it was also a large international organization, this involved many different tasks. Among the most important were: setting overall direction and goals within the broad framework of Opus Dei's spirit; transmitting that spirit to the members; interpreting and applying it in changing circumstances; maintaining and building the sense of family with its twin components of fraternity among the members and filiation between the members and himself as Father. It also involved making decisions about concrete issues like providing human and financial resources for specific apostolic tasks or deciding which of the members to call to the priesthood.

The Founder had established that decision-making in Opus Dei should always involve several persons. Del Portillo applied this to himself, regularly seeking the input of others before making decisions. He practiced and asked those who worked with him to practice "a demandingness that is full of affection, full of the respect and gentleness that our Father asked of us in our treatment of others—but at the same time really demanding. We have to call a spade a spade. If we don't, we're not fulfilling our obligations."[26]

Escrivá established a tradition in Opus Dei of studying and resolving most matters in writing, with only a few brief meetings. Following that tradition, Del Portillo spent many hours at his desk reviewing the issues raised in dossiers that typically contained a statement of an issue, an initial proposed solution or approach from one of the members of the General Council or the Central Advisory, written comments by other members of the General Council or the Central Advisory and their staff, and a final recommended solution.

He tried to see the persons, the souls, who would be affected by his decisions. That made him focus on each question as if it were the only thing he had to do. He commented on one occasion, "Every day I receive piles of dossiers. We don't skim them. We study everything slowly in the presence of God, doing everything possible to make the right decision, because we know very well what our Father taught us so often, that behind the papers there are souls."[27]

Over time, the governing bodies of Opus Dei in Rome developed different ways of transmitting to the Regions indications about how to govern the Work and to carry out its apostolic and pastoral activities. Toward the end of the 1960s, they had assembled the content of the notes and announcements that had been sent to the Regions in *Compilacines* ("Compilations") dedicated to various subjects. In 1980, the Compilations were summarized in a single volume entitled *Praxis* ("Praxis"), with one version for the regional governments and another for the local governments. Later the General Council and the Central Advisory decided to return to separate volumes on different subjects. Between 1987 and 1990 they published fifteen *Vademecums* and *Glosas* ("Handbooks" and "Glosses") on subjects including regional government, local government, the Works of St. Raphael, St. Michael, and St. Gabriel, priests, liturgical ceremonies, studies and formation, the apostolate of public opinion, doctrinal orientation, and the building of centers.[28]

General Congresses play a fundamental role in the governance of Opus Dei. The statutes call for both the men's and the women's branch to hold a General Congress every eight years.[29] The Congress members, who are numerary members of the prelature named for life by the Prelate, meet to assess the status of the prelature and to suggest directions for its future development.[30]

Two General Congresses were held during Del Portillo's tenure as Prelate, the first in 1984 and the second in 1992. In both cases, the Congress members arrived in Rome sometime before the formal meetings to be able to talk with one another and to make suggestions for conclusions to be voted on at the meetings. The formal meetings were spread out over four days, but there were few sessions, and each session was short. At those meetings there was no debate. Del Portillo gave a report on progress made during the years since the previous Congress. He commented that "the many fruits obtained should move us to give thanks to God with the certainty that He is the one who produces them." He also asked the members of the Congress to "ask the Lord's pardon for [their] personal lack of correspondence and omissions." Del Portillo presented a set of proposed conclusions which both the male and female electors approved unanimously.

The conclusions of both the 1984 and 1992 Congresses were generally similar and unsurprising. They both began with an expression of thanks to the Holy Trinity for the graces received during the period since the previous Congress, particularly the erection of the Work as a prelature and the beatification of the founder. Both expressed the Work's unity with the Pope and its appreciation of his teaching. The 1992 Congress added an expression of the Work's gratitude for the Pope's "repeated manifestations of affection for and confidence in the Prelature and the Father." In addition to unity with the Pope, the Congresses underlined unity with the local bishops and service to the local churches.

The conclusions did not focus on problems or difficulties. Their tone is hopeful, forward-looking, and aimed at bringing the members and many other people closer to God. The 1984 Congress proposed opening centers for the first time in Taiwan, Korea, New Zealand,

and Malaysia and in so far as possible Panama, Nicaragua, Indonesia, India, Sri Lanka, Santo Domingo, and other islands of the Caribbean. In 1992 the list included India, Korea, Indonesia, Angola, Uganda, Togo, Lithuania, Slovenia, Croatia, Israel, Panama, and, when the situation permited, Cuba.

Both Congresses called for expanding and making more effective the apostolic activities of Opus Dei with married people and young people, particularly students, stressing in particular efforts to increase the numbers of vocations to Opus Dei. With astounding optimism, the 1984 Congress urged the members to pray that their number might triple by 1992 so that the Work could better serve the Church.

Both insisted on apostolate with media professionals and on encouraging members of the Work to consider working professionally in the media. They also pointed out that it would be desirable if more young members of the Work were to choose theology or other ecclesiastical subjects as their profession. The 1984 Congress suggested encouraging young members to study humanities to give a Christian sense to the world of thought and letters.

In the report he presented to the 1992 Congress, Del Portillo pointed out that the growth in number of members had been smaller in the period 1984 to 1992 than in the 1975 to 1984 period.[31] He did not offer any explanation of this decline, but said that because of the generalized lack of formation of young people in most countries, it would be necessary to be very careful in deciding who was apt to join Opus Dei and in giving formation to new members. Perhaps for these reasons, the 1992 Congress dwelt at some length on the need for ongoing formation for all members. This formation should lead them to be constantly aware that

> they have not come to Tabor [where Christ was transfigured in glory] but to Calvary, and that since 'sanctification is the work of a lifetime' they must continually renew their total self giving to God, falling more and more in love with the Lord: This, the Congress concluded, is the 'secret of perseverance,' not a purely human, voluntarist vision.[32]

Section 3. Activities of the Prelate

Part 1. Pastoral Letters

In the weeks immediately following his election as President General, Del Portillo directed to all the members a relatively short letter and another much longer one stressing fidelity to the inheritance of the Founder and asking for prayers. From then on, he frequently wrote letters that reached all the members. Some were quite short. By contrast, his letter announcing Escrivá's beatification runs to almost one hundred printed pages and offers a detailed program of fidelity to his spirit built around a meditation on the mysteries of the Rosary. The letter he wrote for the fiftieth anniversary of the founding of the Priestly Society of the Holy Cross is even longer and examines in detail two essential characteristics of the vocation to Opus Dei, priestly soul and lay mentality.

During the first decade following Escrivá's death, Del Portillo's letters to the members were normally triggered by some specific event. In February 1984, he began to send a letter on the first of each month. These monthly letters were usually four single-spaced pages. Their goal was to help the members of the Work deepen their interior life and improve their apostolic activities. They reflect a keen awareness of the difficulties and challenges facing people who want to take their Christian vocation seriously in a world in which consumerism, hedonism, and relativism are constant threats. Between 1975 and his death in 1994, Del Portillo wrote 176 pastoral letters. In print, they run to almost 1500 pages.

Unlike those of his successors, Del Portillo's letters are not available on the Internet. Many of them were published internally between 1989 and 1994 in a three-volume set. They were translated into English and published internally between 2006 and 2015. These volumes are available in Opus Dei centers. A topically arranged anthology of short selections taken from his letters and homilies was published in 2013.[33] A second selection of texts from his letters organized around the feasts of the liturgical year appeared in 2014.[34]

Part 2. Pastoral Trips

At first, Del Portillo did not think that he could continue Escrivá's practice of meeting informally with large crowds of people and dialoguing with them. Although friendly, warm, and caring, he was shy and retiring. He spoke clearly and well, but he did not have the Founder's literary and poetic gifts, much less his sense of timing and dramatic flair. Nonetheless, at the urging of the members of the General Council and the Central Advisory, he agreed to have informal get-togethers with the several thousand students from Opus Dei centers around the world who came to Rome for Easter 1976 to see the Holy Father and participate in UNIV, an international conference for young people held annually in Rome.

Though different in style and tone from Escrivá's, Del Portillo's meetings with the students were a success. The young people sensed his genuine interest and affection and responded in kind. Members of Opus Dei came away from the get-togethers with a stronger sense of the Work as a family, while non-members often made resolutions to improve their lives as Christians, and some discovered their vocation to Opus Dei or other forms of apostolic service.

After the UNIV meeting, Don Álvaro decided that he should travel to different countries to meet with as many people as possible in question and answer sessions he liked to call *tertulias*.* Naturally he traveled more frequently in Europe than in more distant places. Some of the European visits were prolonged and gave him an opportunity to meet with many large groups, but most were short trips in which he focused primarily on get-togethers with members in the Opus Dei centers, with perhaps one or two larger meetings at some other venue. His trips outside of Europe involved prolonged stays and many get-togethers with large groups of people.

He undertook several long trips to America. The first, in 1983, centered on visiting the sanctuary of Our Lady of Guadalupe to give thanks to the Virgin for the granting of the status of prelature to Opus Dei. On the way, he stopped for two days in Canada, but the main focus of

---

* For an explanation of the term *tertulias* [get togethers] see volume I, chapter 8, section 1.

the trip was Mexico, where he stayed from April 27 to May 23. After a novena of Thanksgiving, Del Portillo had numerous get-togethers with thousands of people in Mexico City and in other parts of the country. He also found time to meet personally with members of Opus Dei who had special needs. The first was Manuel García, a middle-aged numerary who had been left paralyzed and unable to speak by a brain tumor. As he entered the room, Del Portillo greeted him saying, "You are the first person, after our Lady, whom I have come to see. Your eyes express that you love God, that you love the Work, that you love the Father, that you love your brothers. . . . I remember you every day. I pray for you every day. We need each other mutually. I need you and you need me." At the end of the visit, he asked him to be very cheerful and serene. "I realize what you are. I read in your eyes your love for God, your love for the vocation, your love of the Father." As he was leaving, he kissed him on the forehead, saying that he was kissing the Holy Cross.[35]

In Toshi, a conference center near Mexico City, Del Portillo had a get-together with members of local indigenous communities. Since many of them knew little Spanish, he spoke slowly in a very simple style. He told them that he prayed to the founder of Opus Dei that the Lord "would mitigate their sufferings, grant them the good desires they harbored in their hearts and make them better, since we all need to be better Christians, better disciples of a Master who is as great as our Lord Jesus Christ."[36]

After leaving Mexico, he visited Guatemala and Colombia, and finally New York. There he met with Cardinal Cooke, prayed in the Cathedral of St. Patrick, and spoke with members and friends of Opus Dei, encouraging them to carry out a great work of evangelization with an awareness that the United States exercises enormous influence for good and for evil in the rest of the world.[37] During this first trip to Mexico and other countries of the Americas, he spoke with more than 150 groups of people, some of them very large.

In 1987, Del Portillo spent more than a month visiting Singapore, Hong Kong, Taiwan, Korea, and Japan. Many of the participants in the get-togethers were not Christians. He spoke to them with affection and warmth, and often expressed his admiration for their virtues. In Taipei, for instance, he mentioned the industriousness which had produced an economic miracle, as well as the hospitality and other virtues he had observed in his short stay. But he also expressed his hope that "the light of Christ—which is the only true light—will reach all the people of this great country." "In saying this," he went on,

> I don't wish to offend anyone, but I have to speak as who I am: a Catholic priest who firmly believes in Almighty God, the creator of heaven and earth; and in Jesus Christ, his only son our Lord, who came to this earth to die for us, making satisfaction for our sins, and opening to us the gates of heaven.[38]

Del Portillo's longest catechetical journey took him to Canada, the United States, and Puerto Rico, with a brief side trip to Mexico to visit the shrine of Our Lady of Guadalupe. He landed in New York on January 17, 1988, and returned from there to Rome on March 11. He visited virtually every city in the United States where Opus Dei had a center: Boston, New York, Washington, Miami, Houston, Los Angeles, San Francico, Chicago, St. Louis, Milwaukee, and Pittsburgh.[39]

In Boston, Del Portillo mentioned that, seeing the campuses of Harvard and MIT he had been tempted to ask himself what Opus Dei, with its very limited means, could possibly do in such an environment. He recalled that in 1958, seeing the wealth and power of the great banks and international businesses of London, Escrivá had found himself thinking, "I just can't." On that occasion, Our Lord had responded, "You can't, but I can." "What are we going to do?" Del Portillo asked his Boston listeners. "We have to make an effort to be salt and leaven so that those who make up these powerful institutions can draw closer to God and have a more Christian spirit. In that way, we will do a great service to this nation and to the entire world."[40]

A recurrent topic was family and openness to children. In Los Angeles he addressed the question of putting off the birth of children because of economic challenges:

> This problem only comes up in rich countries where there are abundant means. Each child is a gift of God, a proof of the confidence God has in the parents, because at the moment of conception God

creates an immortal soul. Each human being is destined to enjoy eternally the Most Holy Trinity. But before that moment arrives, the Lord entrusts the new child to its father and mother to be raised and formed. Those who lack a vibrant faith and those who let themselves be carried away by egotism cannot understand this. Love children a great deal! Do not stop up the wellsprings of life! It is not true that children are a burden.[41]

Perhaps because of the size of the country and because of its influence in the world, he seems to have insisted even more than usual on the need for many vocations. Asked in Chicago what his favorite aspiration was he responded, "Seeing this immense city and this immense country, a very good aspiration is what our Father wrote in The Way: 'Jesus, souls! Apostolic souls! They are for you, for your glory.'"[42]

Del Portillo's last major trips were to Africa, where he spent more than thirty days during 1989. Because of his precarious health and the difficulties involved in getting directly from one country to another, he made four separate trips, returning to Rome between each of them: Kenya from April 1 to April 10; Zaire and Cameroon from August 22 to August 30; Ivory Coast from October 14 to October 19; and Nigeria from November 9 to November 20.

In Nairobi his reception was particularly colorful, with gifts of baskets full of vegetables and other typical food products. His induction as an elder included the presentation of a goat, a shield and lance symbolic of the elder's role of protecting his people, and a fly whisk representing the elder's obligation to open a path for those who come after him.[43]

In Kenya and the other African countries he visited, Del Portillo insisted on the need to overcome divisions among races and tribes and to work to alleviate poverty. "We have to understand and love everyone. If we have received more goods from God, we have to use them to help our brothers who are in need."[44] He said,

> It's logical from a human point of   view that people have a special affection for those who belong to the same tribal community or the same nation, but on this human reality, we must build a supernatural one. Belonging to a specific tribe should not separate us

from others. Belonging to a tribe is a reality, but over and above it we have to place Christ. Then our heart will expand and all tribes will fit within it. . . . You have a great heart, and moved by the love of God, you are capable of loving the others.[45]

By the end of his last African trip, Del Portillo was seventy-five years old and in delicate health. Virtually to the end of his life, he would continue to travel extensively in Europe, but after 1989 he was no longer strong enough to undertake major intercontinental trips. During the two decades during which he was the head of Opus Dei, he visited more than three dozen countries and spoke with hundreds of thousands of people of different cultures and social conditions, from students to peasants, from manual workers to research scientists, from wealthy to poor, and from young to old.[46]

Del Portillo met frequently with bishops from all over the world, both at Opus Dei's headquarters in Rome and during his pastoral trips. In the face of accusations that Opus Dei wanted to be independent of diocesan authorities, a sort of "parallel church," he explained that its new status as a personal prelature did not change its relationship with diocesan bishops in any way. Opus Dei does not, he explained, act as a group in ecclesiastical or civil life except for its corporate activities. Each of its members collaborates individually in his or her own name in the capillary diffusion of the Church's doctrine in each diocese. They take part in the life of their parish and encourage other members of the faithful to receive the sacraments frequently. The institutional activity of Opus Dei "fundamentally comes down to giving its members the spiritual assistance they need in their life of piety as well as appropriate spiritual, doctrinal-religious, and human formation."[47]

Del Portillo supported the causes of beatification of several members of religious orders and helped two institutions which wanted to preserve their own original charism in the face of attempts by some members of their congregation to change it. These were the Congregation of the Daughters of Holy Mary of the Heart of Jesus, which Don Álvaro helped to win approval as an institution of pontifical right in 1988, and the Carmelites of Mother Mary Joseph of the Heart of Jesus, whose constitutions were approved in 1990.[48]

Del Portillo declared several "Marian Years" of thanksgiving in Opus Dei: 1978–1980 for the fiftieth anniversary of the foundation of the Work and the fiftieth anniversary of the beginning of its activities with women; 1982 for the erection of Opus Dei as a personal prelature; and 1992–1993 for the beatification of the Founder and the fiftieth anniversary of the Priestly Society of the Holy Cross.[49]

Section 4. Relations with John Paul II

Del Portillo's relations with Paul VI went back to 1946 when he was a thirty-three-year-old priest and Msgr. Montini was a fifty-year-old old high-ranking official in the Vatican State Department. From that time on, the two men were united by mutual esteem, but they were not close and did not meet frequently. Del Portillo's friendship with John Paul II was much closer and more intimate. Because it had important repercussions in the life of Opus Dei, we will explore it in some detail here.

A mutual friend, Father Andrzej Deskur (later a cardinal archbishop and President of the Pontifical Council for Social Communications) introduced them during one of the sessions of the Second Vatican Council. In the following years, Del Portillo and Wojtyła had little contact, although Wojtyła did give a lecture at the Roman Center for Priestly Encounters, invited by one of Del Portillo's closet collaborators, and had dinner twice at Villa Tevere. More importantly, both men continued to be close friends of Deskur.

A few days before the 1978 conclave which would elect Pope John Paul I, Cardinal Wojtyła and Bishop Deskur had lunch with Del Portillo at Opus Dei's headquarters. The day following the election of John Paul II, Del Portillo went to the hospital to visit Bishop Deskur, who had just suffered a stroke. As he left Deskur's room he encountered the Pope, who gave him a warm embrace. Two days later, to repay the Pope's manifestation of affection with prayer, he visited a shrine outside of Rome, Our Lady of Mentorella, which he knew Cardinal Wojtyła had often visited. From there he sent a postcard to the Pope, assuring him that he could count on the thousands of Masses that the faithful of Opus Dei daily offered for the intentions of the head of Opus Dei and that he directed to the Vicar of Christ. John Paul II called personally to express his thanks. The next day, he received Del Portillo in an informal meeting which he characterized as "a family reunion, not an audience."[50] A few weeks later, John Paul II again invited Del Portillo to meet informally.

As Christmas drew near, Del Portillo learned that it was customary in Poland to send oranges to friends and relatives on the feast of Saint Nicholas. He personally brought the Pope some oranges as well as a crozier with an image of Our Lady of Czestochowa, some chocolate Santa Claus figures, and several books by Escrivá. John Paul II responded in kind. On December 18 he sent Del Portillo a basket of fruit together with a photograph and a handwritten blessing. On December 20, he sent some Christmas cards with his signature printed on them for distribution to the faithful of Opus Dei, and one day later, a *panettone*, a traditional Italian Christmas cake. On New Year's Day, John Paul II invited Msgr. Alonso, Del Portillo's secretary, for dinner. During the meal the Pope offered a toast to the Work and added a petition that God might give Opus Dei everything that it might need during the new year.[51]

John Paul II quickly realized that he could count on Opus Dei to support him not only with prayer and sacrifice but also with its contributions to the life of the Church, especially in family apostolate, intellectual and cultural affairs, and the presence of Catholics in professional life. As Bishop of Rome, he wanted to organize a special Mass for college students. The university chaplains told him they thought very few students would come, but Del Portillo promised Opus Dei's wholehearted support. He also offered the services of priests of Opus Dei to hear confessions in St. Peter's for several hours before the Mass.[52] Shortly thereafter, the Pope would say that the members of Opus Dei had "the charism of Confession." The first university Mass was a complete success. From then on, John Paul II celebrated Mass twice a year for ever-growing numbers of students in Rome.

The Pope also wanted to organize a Corpus Christi procession through the streets of Rome after a hiatus of more than one hundred years. Once again, many people were skeptical. They doubted that the city would give permission, and even if it did, they thought few people would attend. Del Portillo, however, lent his enthusiastic support, not only urging members and friends of Opus Dei to attend but personally participating in the procession, which became an annual event in Rome.[53]

During his pontificate, John Paul II made 147 foreign trips. Del Portillo supported them with ardent prayer and encouraged the members of Opus Dei in the countries the Pope visited not only to pray but to do all they could to ensure that the Pope received a warm reception and that his words were heard by many people. Especially in cases where it appeared that the Holy Father might not be well received, Del Portillo suggested that the members of the Work and their friends show him their affection in palpable ways like serenading him in the evening.

When the Pope found himself subject to criticism or attacks, Del Portillo took pains to assure him of Opus Dei's support. When the 1991 encyclical *Veritatis splendor* met with criticism, for instance, he personally published several articles explaining it and urged the members of Opus Dei to support it. A short time later he sent a letter to the Pope thanking him for the encyclical and attaching a number of positive articles that had been published in various countries.

The friendship between Del Portillo and John Paul II grew deeper and broader during the long years of the pontificate. The two met frequently in formal audiences and even more frequently informally. John Paul invited Del Portillo to concelebrate Mass and to join him for meals. He celebrated with him special days in the life of Opus Dei. In 1989 for instance, he invited him for dinner on Escrivá's birthday. A student of the relationship between John Paul II and Del Portillo has catalogued sixty-three meetings between the two without counting Del Portillo's participation in ceremonies or group meetings in which he greeted the Holy Father but could not speak with him at length.[54]

John Paul II habitually sent Del Portillo some small gift for his birthday.[55] For his part, Don Álvaro sent the Pope greetings on his birthday and on anniversaries. From time to time, he also sent small presents, especially books. After the attempt on the Pope's life in May 1981, Del Portillo went to St. Peter's every day to pray for him.[56] On

July 15, 1981, he was able to visit him in the clinic, although he still had a high fever. The character of their friendship is apparent in Del Portillo's saying to the ailing Pontiff that his sufferings were a caress from the Blessed Virgin because they brought him closer to God. He added that if illness is always a treasure, the illness of the Pope implies even greater riches for him and for the whole Church. The Pope responded simply, "That's exactly what I think."[57]

There were also lighthearted moments in their relations. When Don Álvaro told the Holy Father about how Escrivá used to imagine himself wrapped in his cloak saying the Rosary with the Pope, John Paul asked him, "Does his successor do the same?" To which Del Portillo responded, "His successor does the same, but without the cloak." On another occasion when Don Álvaro, Mother Teresa, and the Pope were together, the Holy Father asked jokingly, "Why does the press always talk well about Mother Teresa, but not about Opus Dei or me?"[58]

Del Portillo responded to the Pope's desires even when doing so involved significant changes in Opus Dei's plans. He was, for instance, anxious to see Opus Dei expand its presence in Asia, with an eye on beginning activities in China as soon as possible. When he mentioned this to John Paul II in December 1982, however, the Pope responded that he was particularly concerned about Scandinavia. Del Portillo immediately switched focus to Scandinavia. A few days later in his Christmas greetings to members of the Work, he asked them to pray particularly for the future apostolate of Opus Dei there. Shortly thereafter he traveled to Norway, Finland, Sweden, and Denmark to explore possibilities and to pray for the future apostolic activities of the Work there. He was fully aware of the difficulties of beginning in those countries where Catholics were so few, but the obstacles were far outweighed by the Pope's desires.[59]

Opus Dei's apostolic efforts in northern Europe formed part of a larger response to John Paul II's call for a new evangelization of Europe and North America. When the Pope requested Opus Dei's collaboration in this task, Del Portillo immediately asked the members of Opus Dei's international governing bodies to pray for this intention. In December 1985, he wrote a long pastoral letter urging

Opus Dei's members and cooperators to take very seriously this desire of the Holy Father and to redouble their apostolic efforts. Del Portillo personally traveled repeatedly throughout Europe in order to stimulate Opus Dei's apostolate there. He organized two week-long meetings in Rome and two similar meetings in Spain to plan new apostolic activities in Europe and America.

In 1994, shortly before his death, Del Portillo learned that John Paul II would like Opus Dei to begin its apostolic activities in Kazakhstan. Located in central Asia, Kazakhstan is geographically remote, and its population is largely Muslim. Catholics make up less than 2 percent of the population. It is unlikely that Del Portillo or any of his collaborators had ever thought about beginning activities there; as soon as he learned of the Pope's interest, however, he initiated studies of how to begin there as soon as possible.[60] Opus Dei opened its first center there in 1997.[61]

John Paul II clearly appreciated both the message and activities of Opus Dei and its fidelity to the Pope and the magisterium. In 1984, he made a numerary member, Joaquín Navarro-Vals, the Vatican's spokesman. His personal affection for Del Portillo led to his decision to attend his wake. He played a fundamental role in the erection of Opus Dei as a personal prelature and in the beatification of the founder. Nonetheless, taking into account his magnanimity toward other Church institutions, he cannot be accused of discriminating in favor of Opus Dei.

In some circles, Opus Dei's unwavering fidelity to the Pope was criticized, but that simply did not matter to Del Portillo. On one occasion he commented, "Maybe people will say that this is worshiping the Pope. . . . We don't care what they say. We have the pride of knowing that we are children of God and children of the Pope as well, since he is the common father of all Christians."[62]

St. John Paul II responded fully to Opus Dei's support and affection, not only with personal friendship but also with his support, especially in the beatification of the Founder and the transformation of Opus Dei into a personal prelature.*

---

* See chapters 18 and 23.

Notes

1. Vázquez de Prada, *The Founder of Opus Dei*, vol. 3, p. 555.

2. Álvaro del Portillo, Pastoral Letter, June 29, 1975, n. 16. AGP Biblioteca, 17.

3. Del Portillo, Pastoral Letter, June 29, 1975, n. 16.

4. Del Portillo, Pastoral Letter, June 29, 1975, n. 12.

5. Del Portillo, Pastoral Letter, June 29, 1975, nos. 17, 18, and 23.

6. Álvaro del Portillo, Address to the Full Central Advisory, September 14, 1975. AGP D.1, 458-1-1 (10).

7. Del Portillo, Address to the Full Central Advisory, September 14,1975, pp. 10–11.

8. Minutes of the meeting of the Electoral General Congress, First Session, September 15, 1975. AGP D.1, 458-1-5 (8).

9. Minutes of the meeting of the Electoral General Congress, First Session, September 15, 1975, p. 9.

10. Minutes of the meeting of the Electoral General Congress, Second Session, September 16, 1975. AGP D.1, 458-2-2 (1-3). The date of this session is incorrectly given as September 15, 1975 in *Itinerario*, 422.

11. Minutes of the meeting of the Electoral General Congress, Second Session, September 16, 1975, p. 12.

12. Minutes of the meeting of the Electoral General Congress, Second Session, September 16, 1975, pp. 16–20.

13. Testimony of Joaquín Alonso Pachecho. AGP APD T-19548, 96. Quoted in Javier Medina Bayo, *Álvaro del Portillo. Un hombre fiel* (Madrid: Rialp, 2013), pp. 450–451.

14. Testimony of Joaquín Alonso Pachecho. AGP APD T-19548, 97. Quoted in Medina Bayo, 2013), p. 451.

15. Minutes of the meeting of the Electoral General Congress, Second Session, September 15, 1975. AGP D.1, 458-2-2 (29).

16. *Crónica*, July 1975, pp. 241–276. AGP Biblioteca, P01.

17. See *Crónica*, September 1975, pp. 24–25. AGP Biblioteca, P01.

18. Letter from an unidentified member of Opus Dei, quoted in *Crónica*, September 1975, p. 58. AGP Biblioteca, P01.

19. Letter from an unidentified member of Opus Dei, quoted in *Crónica*, September 1975, p. 59. AGP Biblioteca, P01.

20. Letter from an unidentified member of Opus Dei, quoted in *Crónica*, September 1975, p. 63. AGP Biblioteca, P01.

21. Álvaro del Portillo, Pastoral Letter, January 9, 1980, n. 286. AGP Biblioteca,17.

22. John F. Coverdale, *Saxum: The Life of Álvaro del Portillo* (New York: Scepter, 2014), p. 160.

23. See chapter 6, section 3, part 1.

24. See chapter 6, section 3, part 2.

25. Julián Herranz, *Nei dintorni di Gerico. Ricordi degli anni con san Josemaría & con Giovanni Paolo II* (Milan: Ares, 2005), pp. 224–225.

26. Salvador Bernal, *Recuerdo de Álvaro del Portillo* (Madrid: Rialp, 1996), p. 218.

27. Medina Bayo, pp. 629–630.

28. These documents are found in AGP E.1.9 and AGP Q 1.7. An explanation of nature of the Handbooks and Glosses is found in General announcement 110/91 (June 3, 1991). AGP Q.1.2, 13-92.

29. *Codex Iuris Paticularis Operis Dei*, 1982, 133.

30. *Codex Iuris Paticularis Operis Dei*, 1982, 133.

31. See Conclusions of the 5th Ordinary General Congress of Opus Dei. AGP D 2.

32. See Conclusions of the 5th Ordinary General Congress of Opus Dei,. AGP D 2.

33. Álvaro del Portillo, *Orar: Como sal y como luz*, edited by Jose Antonio Loarte (Madrid: Planeta, 2013). English version: Álvaro del Portillo, *Like Salt and Like Light* (New York: Scepter, 2014).

34. Álvaro del Portillo, *Caminar con Jesús al compás del año litúrgico. Textos tomados de las cartas pastorales*, edited by José Antonio Loarte (Madrid: Ediciones Cristiandad, 2014.) English version: Álvaro del Portilllo, *Journey with Jesus through the Liturgical Year*, edited by José Antonio Loarte (New York: Scepter, 2014).

35. *Catequesis del Padre*, 1983, pp. 110–111. AGP Biblioteca,04.

36. *Catequesis del Padre*, 1983, p. 290.

37. *Catequesis del Padre*, 1983, p. 586.

38. *Catequesis del Padre*, 1987, p. 342. AGP Biblioteca,04.

39. *Catequesis del Padre*, 1988. AGP Biblioteca,04.

40. *Catequesis del Padre*, 1988, p. 539.

41. *Catequesis del Padre*, 1988, pp. 294–295.

42. *Catequesis del Padre*, 1988, p. 375.

43. *Catequesis del Padre*, 1989, p. 38. AGP Biblioteca,04.

44. *Catequesis del Padre*, 1989, p. 42. AGP Biblioteca,04.

45. *Catequesis del Padre*, 1989, p. 342.

46. Medina Bayo, p. 584.

47. Note 34/80. AGP Q 1.3,8-51.

48. Medina Bayo, *Álvaro del Portillo*, pp. 550–553.

49. Medina Bayo, *Álvaro del Portillo*, pp. 475–476.

50. María Eugenia Ossandón Widow, "Un calendario de encuentros entre Álvaro del Portillo y Juan Pablo II," *Studia et Documenta* 9 (2015), pp. 145–201, note 23.

51. Medina Bayo, p. 483.

52. Medina Bayo, *Álvaro del Portillo*, p. 525.

53. Medina Bayo, *Álvaro del Portillo*, pp. 525–526.

54. Ossandón Widow, "Un calendario," p. 201.

55. Ossandón Widow, "Un calendario," pp. 145–201.

56. Bernal, *Recuerdo*, 267.

57. Medina Bayo, p. 493.

58. Quoted in Medina Bayo, *Álvaro del Portillo*, p. 493.

59. Javier Echevarría, Address at the Conference for the Centennial of Bishop Álvaro del Portillo, Pontifical University of the Holy Cross, Rome, March 12, 2014, *Romana* 58 (January–June 2014), pp. 110–130.

60. Medina Bayo, p. 672.

61. *https://opusdei.org/en/article/historical-overview/*. Last visited August 7, 2018.

62. Bernal, *Recuerdo*, pp. 255–256.

CHAPTER 7

The Legal Solution

s we have seen, Opus Dei had long been dissatisfied with being classified as a secular institute.[1] Despite its name, this category failed to reflect adequately the secular character of Opus Dei members.[2] Secular institutes were widely considered one more step in the evolution of religious orders;[3] they were governed by the Sacred Congregation for Religious; and their members were required to take vows.[4] The vow of obedience required of members of secular institutes made it difficult for people to understand the freedom of Opus Dei members in their professional and political lives.[5] This problem was particularly severe in Spain in the 1960s and 1970s, where many people did not understand the freedom of Opus Dei members in politics and therefore insisted on treating Opus Dei as a political group.

The category of a personal prelature to carry out specific pastoral tasks created by the Second Vatican Council offered an appropriate niche for Opus Dei.[6] Personal prelatures were clearly secular in character.[7] Transformation into a personal prelature would permit Opus Dei to carry out its apostolic mission unhindered by legal requirements foreign to its secular character and foundational charism while retaining its essential structure.

Section 1. The Process

Part 1. Early Steps

In Del Portillo's first audience with Pope Paul VI as head of Opus Dei in March 1976, the Pope said that Opus Dei's legal classification was still an open question. Del Portillo explained that he wanted to avoid the impression of making radical changes as soon as he took control, and the Pope agreed that this was wise.[8] In an audience in June 1978, the Pope again encouraged Del Portillo to request the legal transformation of Opus Dei. This time Del Portillo promised to do so immediately, but Paul VI died on August 6 before the request could be presented.[9]

Shortly after his election, John Paul I let Del Portillo know that he felt it would be imprudent to continue to put off the legal question.[10] The new Pope also informed the Congregation for Religious that he wanted to resolve the question.[11] Before anything could be done, John Paul I died, only thirty-three days into his papacy. In November 1978, the Secretary of State told Del Portillo that the recently elected John Paul II considered "resolution of the question of the legal status of Opus Dei a necessity that cannot be postponed."[12] It must have seemed that the long-sought legal solution was imminent, but in fact it still lay four years in the future.

In January 1979, Opus Dei received permission from the Congregation for Religious and Secular Institutes to seek a legal status outside the framework of secular institutes. In a letter to Pope John Paul II on February 2, Del Portillo formally requested the transformation of Opus Dei into a personal prelature.[13] A few weeks later, the Holy Father asked the Congregation for Bishops to study the question.[14]

On April 23, 1979, Opus Dei presented a study explaining why it could and should be transformed into a personal prelature. [15] It begins stressing briefly the full personal commitment of members to live and spread the spiritual and apostolic demands of baptism. They do so with a clearly secular spirituality and are not "consecrated by the profession of the evangelical counsels."[16] Opus Dei as an institution is not a society, a movement, or an association. It is a hierarchically structured portion of the people of God. The second part of the study briefly traces Opus Dei's historical efforts to find an appropriate niche in the legal structure of the Church.[17]

The heart of the study is the third part, which argues that the appropriate legal category for Opus Dei is a prelature for carrying out specific apostolic tasks. The study stresses that personal prelatures are, like Opus Dei, clearly secular in character.[18] Furthermore, Opus Dei possesses all the characteristic features of personal prelatures.[19] Transformation into a personal prelature would not, therefore, require any stretching of the category. It would permit Opus Dei to carry out its apostolic mission unhindered by legal requirements foreign to its secular character and foundational charism while retaining its essential structure. Becoming a personal prelature would also reinforce the service of Opus Dei to the local churches and would make it easier for the Holy See to make use of a group of priests and well-trained laymen for the apostolate.[20]

In the study we have just summarized, Opus Dei requested its transformation into a personal prelature "*cum proprio populo*," that is, with its own faithful. It did this to indicate that the prelature would consist not only of the Prelate and his clergy, but also of the lay men and women who constitute its vast majority. In a letter to the Prefect of the Congregation for Bishops dated June 2, 1979, Del Portillo stressed, however, that the lay faithful of the prelature would continue to be under the authority of the local bishop like any other faithful of his diocese. The authority of the Prelate would, so to speak, begin where the authority of the local bishop ends with respect to all the faithful of his diocese.[21] Transformation into a personal prelature, therefore, would neither affect the rights of the local bishops nor change the existing regulations regarding Opus Dei's relations with them. Concretely, the Work would continue to need the permission of the bishop to open a center.[22]

Part 2. *Dilata*

The question of Opus Dei's transformation into a personal prelature was submitted by the Congregation for Bishops to a group of seven experts. Six of them were favorable. The seventh was opposed because he took issue with the development of personal jurisdictions in the Church.[23] Despite this favorable report from the experts, the cardinals and bishops who were members of the Congregation decided almost unanimously on June 28, 1979, "that there were not sufficient motives to proceed to the erection of Opus Dei as a personal prelature."[24] Their decision took the polite form of "*Dilata et compleantur acta ad Mentem*," (Defer and study further according to the mind [of the Holy Father]).[25] In this bland formula, however, the operative instruction was to "defer," and it brought with it the prospect of the question being shelved indefinitely.

On July 3, 1979, before he had learned about the Congregation's decision, Del Portillo wrote to the Holy Father expressing in words of Msgr. Escrivá his confidence that "from the Roman Pontiff only good things can come to me."[26] He asked that the Holy Father hear him before making any decision if, for whatever reason, it seemed that his April 23, 1979, proposal should be modified.[27]

Cardinal Sebastiano Baggio, Prefect of the Congregation for Bishops, informed Del Portillo orally on July 9 about the decision of the Congregation and told him that the Holy Father had approved it subject to instructions he would give later.[28] On July 12, John Paul II met with Del Portillo's secretary, Msgr. Joaquín Alonso. The Pope asked him to assure Del Portillo that he had done well in asking the Holy See to grant the legal status desired by the Founder and to tell him that the material sent to the Congregation for Bishops in April had been well presented.[29]

The next day, Del Portillo wrote a two-page letter to the Pope thanking him for his encouragement and support. He suggested that the Congregation's instruction to defer should be interpreted not as shelving but as continuing to study the matter based on what had been done so far. He requested that Opus Dei be asked to continue to work on its new statutes as a prelature as well as any other points about which the Congregation might wish more information.[30]

In the meantime, Del Portillo and his closest collaborators worked diligently to convince members of the Congregation to continue moving forward. Bishop Echevarría describes Del Portillo's efforts as involving "interviews, trips to various countries, clarification of the issues for the people who had to study the matter . . . and, above all, much prayer and expiation, carried out with constant joy."[31] Eventually, Del Portillo would succeed in converting both Cardinal Baggio and the archbishop of Vienna, Cardinal König, into firm supporters of the transformation. König later wrote,

At first, I had thought that it was merely a caprice, and that there was no need to open up a new legal path in the Church. Nonetheless, thanks to his explanations, I realized that Opus Dei was such a new phenomenon that it needed a new legal suit. I came to be an advocate of Del Portillo's intention among my fellow Cardinals.[32]

It is not clear whether Baggio, König, and other key members of the Congregation had already come around by the middle of July, but on July 18 Baggio wrote to Del Portillo to inform him about the instructions received from the Holy Father. He did not explicitly say that he had been instructed to move forward promptly, but that was implicit in the letter. It began by saying that need for further study was due to the "novelty and complexity of the problem and to the importance of the precedent that would be set in the structure of the Church." It was not due, he said, to any "reservations about Opus Dei which, as is known, enjoys the frequently expressed high esteem and sincere affection of the Supreme Pontiff."[33]

He told Del Portillo that before considering the future statutes of Opus Dei, the Holy Father wanted the Congregation for Bishops, with the help of the Congregation for Religious and Secular Institutes, to complete its general study to eliminate any reservations.[34] Baggio requested a wide range of materials and specified three particular areas to be clarified: 1) how and why the secularity of Opus Dei distinguishes it from secular institutes and differentiates its members from other faithful; 2) the submission to the Prelate of the lay and clerical members, whether men or women, according to their various degrees of membership; and 3) the concrete measures proposed to avoid establishing a "parallel Church" within the territorial jurisdictions in which Opus Dei operates all over the world.[35] It seems safe to assume these three areas for special study reflect the reservations that had led the members of the Congregation to vote to defer the matter, although some of them may also have been opposed generally to creating personal jurisdictions in the Church.

In an effort to derail the process and before Opus Dei could prepare the requested material, a priest of the Legionaries of Christ circulated an anonymous pamphlet entitled *The New Face of Opus Dei: A Personal Prelacy?** The pamphlet was mailed to many bishops and to the press in some countries. It contained Italian and English versions of Del Portillo's letters to Baggio of April 23 and June 2 and the lengthy appendix to the April 23 letter. It purported to come from "Andreas, "Bishop of X," who claimed that he was one of twelve bishops who had been asked to give their opinion by the Congregation for Bishops. The introduction asserted that the transformation of Opus Dei into a personal prelature would be the beginning of "a hierarchical bicephaly in every diocese." It would create "a parallel Church, a Church within a Church or a Superchurch." It would mean "a new diocese within your diocese, with full autonomy, setting aside the apostolic authority which was received, the same as that of Peter, from Christ [sic] hands."[36] The documents reproduced in the pamphlet made clear that these accusations were not true, but the introduction was all the recipients were likely to read.

Opus Dei issued a brief communiqué in which it denounced the falsity of the pamphlet and stressed its desire to work in close communion with the local bishops.[37] Del Portillo informed the Prefect of the Congregation for Bishops of what was happening and asked him to intervene urgently.[38] He also wrote directly to John Paul II explaining the situation, concluding, "I know that the Holy

---

* See "Relación del 6-X-79 al 12-V-80 sobre el folleto ¿El nuevo rostro del Opus Dei Prelatura Personal?," in AGP, series L1.2, 1411. In 2021, the authors of this book contacted through a third party the Legionary who sent the pamphlet to the bishops around the world. He substantially confirmed what had happened but asked that his name not be given. We have respected his request. We do not know who took the documents from the Congregation for Bishops.

In 1980, Echevarría reminded Francisco Ugarte, at the time a recently ordained Mexican priest of Opus Dei, "that we should know how to pardon from the very first moment" (Interview with Francisco Ugarte, January 19, 2021). Because of this event and several subsequent ones, the authorities of Opus Dei decided to maintain a respectful but distant relationship with the leaders of the Legionaries of Christ while its founder remained its superior general. This did not prevent individual members of the Work and Legionaries who were relatives or had other relationships from continuing to be friends. Today the relations between the two institutions have been normalized.

Father will defend his sons and daughters of Opus Dei."[39] Del Portillo also asked the regional heads of Opus Dei to visit the diocesan bishops in their regions to explain the facts to them to head off misunderstandings.

Part 3. One Step Back, Two Steps Forward

John Paul II did indeed protect Opus Dei, instructing the Congregation for Bishops to complete its study.[40] He directed the Congregation to form a mixed commission with representatives of the Congregation and of Opus Dei.[41] The representatives of the Holy See were Marcello Costalunga, Undersecretary of the Congregation for Bishops, Mario Pompedda, Judge of the Tribunal of the Holy Rota, and Marian Oleś, official of the Congregation for Bishops. Opus Dei was represented by Amadeo de Fuenmayor, Dean of the School of Canon Law of the University of Navarra, Xavier de Ayala, Councilor of Opus Dei in Brazil, and Julian Herranz, official of the General Council of Opus Dei.[42]

The commission met for the first time on February 27, 1980. Over the course of a year, it requested ample documentation from Opus Dei and held twenty-five sessions, each three hours in duration. In one of Opus Dei's submissions to the Joint Commission, it clarified that in requesting to be treated as a personal prelature "*cum proprio populo*" [with its own people] it did not mean that the portion of the people of God entrusted to the Prelate would be totally exempt with respect to other ecclesiastical jurisdictions. The lay members of Opus Dei would remain under the jurisdiction of the local bishop in everything that the law prescribes for the ordinary lay faithful. The relations of Opus Dei as an organization with the local bishops would remain substantially unchanged.[43]

The final session took place on February 19, 1981. The commission voted unanimously in favor of the transformation of Opus Dei into a personal prelature. Its six- hundred-page report comprised a first volume containing a technical legal study and a second volume of documents. The commission concluded: "The characteristics of Opus Dei, an actually existing pastoral phenomenon, meet the requirements of established law for being transformed into a personal prelature without prejudice of any sort to the local ordinaries."[44] Cardinal Baggio presented the commission's study and conclusions together with a draft of the statutes of the possible prelature to the Pope on April 4. John Paul promised to study the material and answer on May 16.[45]

On May 13, John Paul II was shot in St. Peter's Square. Del Portillo immediately asked all the members of Opus Dei to intensify their prayer for the Pope and to offer their Mass and Communion for him. The Pope's recovery was slow and difficult, complicated by a serious viral infection. From his hospital bed, he told the Prefect of the Congregation for Bishops on July 20 that he wanted the report of the mixed commission to be studied by a committee of cardinals.[46]

Before anything further could be done, another anonymous attempt to derail the process took place. In August 1981, bishops all over the world received a pamphlet that claimed to be from a member of Opus Dei who felt the need to unburden his conscience over the Work's effort to become a sort of "universal diocese" or "parallel Church." The pamphlet claimed that Opus Dei would be outside the control of the bishops and that "The Vatican itself would be submitted" to it.[47] the author went on to say that creating a worldwide personal prelature would be "contrary to the will of Christ himself," and would create in "every diocese a two-headed ecclesiastical regime."[48] The similarity in content and style between this new attack and the previous one, the use of the same methods of distribution, and the presence of the same types of errors in the Italian and English translations of the Spanish original, all strongly suggested that the two came from the same source. Opus Dei issued an official statement denouncing the falsity of the report and specifically stating that Opus Dei did not desire to change in any way its relations with the bishops of the diocese. It refrained from identifying the author of the two pamphlets.[49]

This second attack was also unsuccessful. The special committee of cardinals gave a favorable report on September 26, 1981, and on November 7, 1981, the Holy Father informed Cardinal Baggio that he had decided to transform Opus Dei into a personal prelature and to approve its statutes.[50]

Part 4. Final Steps

Before formalizing his decision and making it public, the Pope wanted information to be sent to the bishops of all the dioceses in which Opus Dei was carrying out its apostolates. This would give them an opportunity to ask questions or register objections. Some two thousand bishops in thirty-nine countries received a note on the characteristics of the prelature the Holy See planned to create. It stressed that the Opus Dei Prelature would not be completely independent of the diocese and would not displace the parishes in providing the sacraments and the other elements of what is technically called the ordinary care of souls.[51] Specifically, it stated that Opus Dei would not be a Prelature *nullius diocesis* nor a "personal diocese," and would not have complete autonomy with respect to the local churches and their bishops.[52] Of the almost five hundred bishops who responded over the course of the next six months, more than four hundred expressed their satisfaction. Sixty-eight had some reservations or perplexity, and seventy-six asked for a clarification or expressed criticism. The Holy Father asked the Congregation for Bishops to respond individually to each of the bishops who had expressed reservations or asked for clarifications.[53]

Spain represented a special case because of Opus Dei's large presence there. According to information sent by the Congregation for Bishops to the Spanish Episcopal Conference, some twenty Spanish bishops responded to the Note from the Congregation expressing their pleasure with the proposed transformation of Opus Dei into a personal prelature. Some bishops, however, including the leaders of Spain's episcopal conference, opposed it.[54]

According to the nuncio, the bishops recognized "the zeal and the effectiveness of the people and the undertakings" of Opus Dei. Some were, however, put off by what they perceived as its "desire for independence from the local Ordinaries and from the heads of the episcopal conference." They felt this attitude was particularly evident in the lay members of the Work. Some bishops felt they should control the political, financial, and other activities of Opus Dei's lay members to keep them from "compromising" the Church. Another cause of friction according to the nuncio was the bishops' perception that "the diocesan priests who were sympathetic to Opus Dei . . . separate themselves from the rest of the clergy and follow the indications of the directors of Opus Dei even when they are in contrast to those of the diocesan ordinary (Parallel Church)."[55]

Without consulting the full membership, in February 1982 the president of the Spanish Episcopal Conference, Archbishop Díaz Merchán, sent to the Congregation for Bishops two letters expressing reservations.[56] At the June plenary meeting of the episcopal conference a large majority of the bishops voted in favor of a motion that opposed the transformation of Opus Dei into a personal prelature, but according to the papal nuncio, the vote was less an expression of their opinion about the legal status of Opus Dei than a sign of annoyance with the Vatican over not having consulted them. It was also a show of support for the president of the conference, who had been criticized for having sent letters to the Holy See about the question without consulting the full membership.[57]

In a report dated July 15, the nuncio concluded:

> Even taking into account the situation existing in Spain, I think that the measure contemplated by the Holy See can go forward. It will displease some of the bishops, but once even the most prejudiced read the Statutes directly, they will . . . appreciate the benefits that legal clarity in their relations with the Work will bring to diocesan pastoral activities.[58]

Archbishop Suquía, president of the Spanish Bishops' Commission for Relations between the Bishops and the Major Superiors of Religious Orders, suggested that the Vatican act promptly to implement the plan sent to the bishops with whatever changes or corrections seemed appropriate. "To delay it would do harm to the Church in Spain, to the Work, and to the Holy Father himself," he said.[59]

John Paul II approved on August 5, 1982, the plan to transform Opus Dei into a personal prelature and the text of the declaration prepared by the Congregation for Bishops explaining the decision's background and consequences.[60] The Congregation for Bishops set the date for publishing the decision and the declaration for August 23.[61] On August 19, the Congregation for Bishops officially informed

Del Portillo that "the Holy Father has erected the Prelature of the Holy Cross and Opus Dei."[62]

The president and the secretary of Spain's episcopal conference traveled to Rome in a final attempt to stop the procedure. After a long but fruitless meeting with Cardinal Baggio, they demanded a meeting with the Holy Father. According to Bishop Sebastián, the secretary of the episcopal conference, the Pope responded after listening to their concerns:

> Opus Dei has an institutional problem which needs to be considered in light of its presence in the universal church. We have studied a solution that is foreseen in Church law. They are happy with it. After careful study, it has been seen to be compatible with already approved legal structures. In the Church, we must favor things that are growing. Everyone should feel welcome. If they like the solution that is foreseen, they will be content and will work better. That will be good for everyone. With the passage of time, it will be clear that it is good for the Church.[63]

On August 23, the Vatican Press Office issued a brief statement: "The Holy Father has decided on the erection of Opus Dei as a personal prelature. The publication of the document has been delayed for technical reasons."[64] The "technical reasons" for delaying the publication seem to have been the desire to placate those Spanish bishops who opposed the step by putting off publication until after the Pope's planned trip to Spain in November.[65]

The public announcement of the Pope's decision was a cause of rejoicing for the members and friends of Opus Dei. The Vatican member of the Joint Commission who had initially seemed most skeptical about transforming Opus Dei into a personal prelature sent a telegram to Del Portillo: *Haec est dies quam fecit Dominus* ["This is the day which the Lord has made."][66] Del Portillo wrote to Cardinal Baggio, who had worked hard to overcome opposition: "I know full well that we owe this all to your goodness and nobility and to the kindness of the Holy Father."[67]

Nonetheless, the delay in publishing the documents was a cause of suffering and anxiety. Del Portillo confided to Cardinal Baggio:

In these moments I experience the reality that the Lord blesses with the Cross. I feel inclined to write to you because the burden becomes more bearable when I think of the affection, the understanding, the help, and the sincere love of souls and of the Church that I have seen shine forth in a special way in all your interventions.[68]

During the fall of 1982, a campaign against Opus Dei in parts of the Italian press seemed aimed at reversing the papal decision at the last moment. A number of newspapers attempted to link Opus Dei to two scandals that occupied the front pages of the Italian press at the time. One involved a Masonic lodge known as P2, and the other the death of the president of a large bank who was found murdered after the bank failed. Although the charge that Opus Dei was linked to either of these two scandals lacked any basis in fact, the allegations were widely repeated, not only in Italy but in several other European countries. They did not, however, sway John Paul II.

The November 28, 1982, edition of *L'Osservatore Romano* announced that the Pope had erected Opus Dei as a personal prelature and had named Del Portillo its Prelate. The official announcement was accompanied by a document of the Congregation for Bishops explaining the nature of the newly created prelature, its structure, the authority of its Prelate and the prelature's relations with the local bishops.[69] As prefect of the Congregation for Bishops, Cardinal Baggio wrote a separate article entitled "*Un bene per tutta la Chiesa*" ["A Good for the Entire Church"]. He summarized the spiritual and ecclesial reasons which motivated the Pope's decision to transform Opus Dei into a personal prelature. He also stressed that the erection of Opus Dei as a personal prelature was important for the Church because it converted "into a living and operative reality a new ecclesiastical structure called for by the Council that until now had been a mere theoretical possibility."[70] In the same issue of *L'Osservatore Romano*, the Under Secretary of the Congregation for Bishops, Bishop Marcello Costalunga, who had served as a member of the Joint Commission, described the erection of Opus Dei as "a milestone in the doctrinal and legal development promoted by the Council." He stressed that "the new legal configuration of

Opus Dei not only maintains unchanged but defines even more sharply the norms that have regulated until now its relations with the diocesan Bishops and the Particular Churches."[71]

Del Portillo wrote to John Paul II:

> Thank you, Holy Father, for having in this way made safer our path to sanctity and our service to the universal Church and to the local churches and their pastors. We will try to pay this debt of gratitude with even more abundant prayer for Your Holiness. And as time goes by, all the souls that the Lord may wish to send to his Opus Dei will continue to do the same.[72]

Part 5. Reaching the Goal

The last remaining step was the execution of the papal bull with the definitive text of the Apostolic Constitution *Ut Sit*. During the months between the announcement of the Pope's decision and the ceremony in which the papal bull was executed, a final potential difficulty arose. A new Code of Canon Law was in the final stages of preparation. The four canons related to personal prelatures formed part of Book 2 (The People of God) Title 2 (The Hierarchical Constitution of the Church), Section 2 (Particular Churches and Personal Prelatures). At the suggestion of Cardinal Ratzinger, the commission of cardinals charged with a final review of the proposed text of the code began to consider moving the canons on personal prelatures to another location to avoid suggesting that they were particular churches. Opus Dei had no problem admitting that a personal prelature is not a particular church. It insisted, however, that personal prelatures do form part of the hierarchical structure of the Church.[73] For that reason, it preferred leaving the canons on personal prelatures in the title on the hierarchical structure of the Church. In early January, however, the Commission of Cardinals decided to move them to a newly created separate section within Book 2 on "The People of God."[74]

Cardinal Baggio immediately reassured Del Portillo that the change of position did not imply any change in the content of the canons or in the content of the documents that erected the Work as a personal prelature.[75] In an audience a few days later, the Holy Father personally reiterated to Del Portillo that the change of location in no way affected the documents by which the prelature was erected.[76] On January 17, Cardinal Baggio wrote to Del Portillo to tell him that the Holy Father had repeated that moving the canons in no way affected the nature of personal prelatures as "secular jurisdictional structures, erected by the Holy See to carry out particular pastoral works as determined by the Second Vatican Council." More specifically, the change did not affect the documents by which the Holy See erected Opus Dei as a personal prelature nor its dependence on the Congregation for Bishops.[77] Though welcome, these assurances were private, and a number of Vatican officials interpreted the new location outside the section on the hierarchy as a sign that personal prelatures do not form part of the hierarchical structure of the Church.

Another problem arose from a last-minute change to the text of Canon 296, which addresses laypeople's relationship with personal prelatures. Whereas the prior version had spoken of the "incorporation" of lay men and women into personal prelatures, the amended version spoke of their "organic cooperation" in prelatures' apostolic work. Several canonists interpreted the new language to mean that lay men and women do not fully belong to personal prelatures but are simply auxiliaries or associates.[78] According to this reading, a prelature is comprised exclusively of a Prelate and his priests. Laypeople may be associated with it, but do not form part of it.

There was a real danger that this reading of the revised canon would appear in the final version of the papal bull erecting Opus Dei. In early February, in fact, Herranz learned that the definitive Latin text being prepared in the Secretary of State's office provided that the Prelate would have no jurisdiction over the laity of Opus Dei. They would not be full members of Opus Dei, but simply associates. Had this interpretation been reflected in the final version, it would have undermined Opus Dei's entire structure.

Del Portillo reacted vigorously, writing to the Deputy Secretary of State:

> It would be a shame to send a Bull with inaccurate expressions. That would oblige me to have recourse to the Holy Father to rectify them because they would subvert the organic reality of the Work. In addition, it would be bad for the authority of the Holy Father himself if the Bull did not agree with the recent Declaration [on personal prelatures] . . . which clearly indicates that it was approved by the Pope.[79]

Cardinal Baggio also protested to the Secretary of State's office about the proposed change and spoke directly with the Pope about it. He pointed out to the Holy Father that the canons apply to personal prelatures in general. For that reason, they use the broader term "organic cooperation" of the laity to accommodate potential future personal prelatures in which the laity might have different forms of incorporation. That was perfectly compatible, he said, with the fact that in the specific case of Opus Dei "organic cooperation" took the form of true incorporation. The Pope told him he fully agreed.

The bull with the text of the Apostolic Constitution *Ut Sit* was finalized in early March. It did not contain any of the inaccurate expressions Del Portillo had feared. It described Opus Dei as "made up of priests and laymen" with a "unity of spirit, of goals, of government and of spiritual formation." It specified that the jurisdiction of the prelature extends not only to "the clerics incardinated in it [but also] to the lay men and women . . . who have dedicated themselves to apostolates of the Prelature." The bull was promulgated by the nuncio of the Holy See in Italy, Archbishop Romolo Carboni, in a solemn ceremony on March 19, 1983.

Section 2. Advantages of the New Legal Status

In a lengthy letter to the members, Del Portillo highlighted two advantages of the new legal status. Until then, the legal unity of Opus Dei as an entity made up of priests and layman, and of men and women, was based on a privilege granted by the Holy See which could be subject to attack, as it had in fact been in 1951–1952.* The erection of Opus Dei as a personal prelature and the Holy Father's approval of Opus Dei's new statutes confirmed and reinforced its legal unity not as a privilege but by applying to it provisions of the Code of Cannon Law.[80]

The new status would also protect Opus Dei's "clearly secular spirit and asceticism, and [its] specific proper ways of doing apostolate."[81] Del Portillo stressed that for the members of Opus Dei the secularity which the new legal status recognizes was not merely a legal classification, nor an apostolic tactic. The world, he wrote, is "where the Lord has placed us. We are located deep within his Heart, to carry out his Work, and to sanctify the world. There we share the joys and sorrows, the work and play, the hopes and the daily tasks of our fellow citizens, who are our equals." Secularity in Opus Dei, he underlined, implies "a connatural participation in the most serious aspects of life: in working well, in fulfilling well our family and social obligations, in participating in the sorrows of men and in their efforts to build peace and the earthly city in peace and before God."[82]

In his letter, he told the members of the Work that the long and difficult process itself had also been a great good for Opus Dei, "The Work, 'firm, compact, and secure,' closely united to our Father in the same intention, has prayed, has suffered, has hoped, and has worked. And this has been an immense good for Opus Dei and for the entire Church. . . ."[83]

Summarizing long years of hope and suffering, Del Portillo wrote:

Everything, everything that the Lord has done or has permitted to be done to the Work, led to this: to make from our poor clay good friends of his. Look: he has planned everything with a wise strategy for our sanctification. As you well know, in the entire task of sanctification the initiative belongs to the Holy Spirit who pours out on men his merciful Love. Don't ever forget it: the Work is principally

---

* See volume 1, chapter 7, "Pontifical Approvals." Escrivá wanted Opus Dei's legal status to be part of generally applicable church law rather than a privilege.

the Work of God, Opus Dei. For that reason, its history is the "history of divine mercy." . . . Everything has been carried out or permitted by God so that we may be good sons of his.[84]

Del Portillo went on to specify in more detail the benefits Opus Dei had derived from the painful process:

> We have learned to work looking only to God, without hoping for any recompense on earth. We have learned to love those who did not understand, or did not want to understand, our way, for whatever reason. We have learned to have patience and to pardon easily when some people—moved by the devil or ingenuously mistaken—carried out tenacious campaigns of calumny against us. Our Lord has confirmed us in a great love for all those who work for him, understanding and appreciating truly the generosity and the sacrifice of so many good souls—priests, religious, laypeople— who serve the Church. The Lord has urged us to love the Pope more each day. How many long hours our Father spent praying for the Roman Pontiff and what an "injection of Romanness" he gave the entire Work! We have felt the urgency and the duty of praying more intensely for all the bishops, and we have given ourselves, with greater desire for unity, in service of the dioceses where we work.[85]

Section 3. Protecting the Prelature

After the erection of Opus Dei as a personal prelature, Del Portillo explained some practical consequences of the new legal status. For example, he clarified that both temporary and permanent incorporation in Opus Dei would take place through a contractual declaration and that Opus Dei's relations with the local bishops remained unchanged.

He also stressed that the Opus Dei prelature is not a diocese or other type of particular church for at least two reasons: 1) the lay members belong not only to the prelature but also to the diocese in which they live, and 2) only those with a specific vocation can belong to Opus Dei, unlike a diocese which requires no special conditions of membership. The Opus Dei prelature is like a diocese, however, he said, because it is a hierarchical pastoral structure, a living reality in the life of the Church which presupposes and implies both lay and priestly activity in mutual organic relation.

For many years, Escrivá had urged the members of Opus Dei to pray for an appropriate legal home for the Work with the aspiration "Most sweet heart of Mary, prepare a safe way." Now that it had been erected as a personal prelature, Del Portillo urged them to pray "Most sweet heart of Mary, keep the way safe." Over the next few years, it became painfully clear that prayer to keep the Work safe was needed.

Shortly after Pope John Paul II erected Opus Dei as a personal prelature, rumors began to circulate in the Vatican that Del Portillo would be ordained a bishop very soon.* As soon as Del Portillo heard of this, he requested an audience with the Holy Father. He explained that for years he had asked people to pray that God might give Opus Dei an appropriate legal status. "If now I am named a bishop, the devil can make some people think that I have asked for so many prayers in order to become a bishop. That is not true, but I do not want to scandalize anyone. I cannot therefore, Holy Father, accept." He went even further to say that if in the judgment of the Holy See it was essential

---

* It is not necessary that the prelate be ordained a bishop, but his role is similar to that of a diocesan bishop in many ways. When he names him prelate, the Pope confers on him proper, not vicarious, jurisdiction of an episcopal nature. Episcopal ordination is theologically and juridically fitting to the mission he carries out with the help of his presbyterium for the benefit of the portion of the people of God entrusted to him. The basis of this authority is the organic relation between priests and the lay members of Opus Dei, which is typical of the hierarchical constitution of the Church that is structured by the sacraments of baptism and orders. For that reason, many canonists and theologians hold it desirable for the prelate of Opus Dei to be a bishop. See Javier Echevarría, "El ejercicio de la potestad de gobierno en las prelaturas personales," *Romana* 40 (2005), pp. 93–94; Fernando Ocáriz, "Reflexiones teológicas sobre la ordenación episcopal del Prelado del Opus Dei, *Palabra* 310 (1991/II), pp. 92–95; Velasio De Paolis, "Nota sul titolo di consacrazione episcopale," *Ius Ecclesiae* 14 (2002), pp. 59–79; Juan Fornés, "Prelado del Opus Dei," in José Luis Illanes (ed.), *Diccionario de san Josemaría Escrivá de Balaguer* (Burgos: Monte Carmelo—Instituto Histórico San Josemaría Escrivá de Balaguer, 2013), pp. 1007–1012; Valentín Gómez Iglesias, "La ordenación episcopal del Prelado del Opus Dei," *Romana* 12 (1991/1), pp. 183–192.

that the prelate be a bishop, "I from this moment put my position in your hands. I resign."[86] John Paul II understood and told him not to be concerned.

Del Portillo agreed in theory that there were powerful theological and legal reasons for the prelate of Opus Dei to be a bishop and prayed that his successor might in fact be ordained bishop. He thought, however, that he would never become a bishop himself. In late 1990, however, he was informed that the Holy Father wanted to ordain him a bishop and asked that he accept.[87] His vicar general underlined that it was not a question of personal recognition but rather something that would make the prelature more effective in the service of God. He also pointed out that the first prelate's being a bishop would make it easier for his successors to be bishops.[88] Moved by these considerations and by his deeply-rooted desire to do whatever the Pope wanted, Del Portillo wrote to the Holy Father accepting the nomination.

When he communicated the news to the members of the Work who lived in its Rome headquarters, Del Portillo said:

> The Prelate will receive the Sacrament of Orders in its fullness. There will be a new outpouring of the Holy Spirit on the head of the Work, and because of the Communion of the Saints, in some way on all of Opus Dei. It will move the Work forward all over the world. It will be a great gift of God, because in this way the Prelate will form part of the College of Bishops and will be a successor of the Apostles.[89]

John Paul II ordained Del Portillo and eleven other priests as bishops in St. Peter's Basilica on January 6, 1991. This did not change Opus Dei nor its relations with the bishops of the over three hundred dioceses in which it was present. The theologian who would eventually become Del Portillo's second successor commented: "The relation of the Prelature with the Particular Churches is necessarily one of service. All the activity of Opus Dei is directed toward collaborating in the intensification of the Christian life of the faithful of the Particular Churches, whether they belong to Opus Dei or not."[90]

Only a few weeks after his ordination as bishop, the Prelate ordained a group of Opus Dei faithful as deacons. The following

September, he ordained a group of priests. From then on, he regularly ordained members of Opus Dei and occasionally administered confirmation. As a bishop, he also participated in several synods.

The publication of the constitution *Ut Sit* helped people to understand the spiritual nature of Opus Dei and dampened some preexisting polemics. Nonetheless, personal prelatures were a significant novelty in the Church, and certain scholars and church officials understood them in ways that were incompatible with Opus Dei's essence and structure. They saw the Church almost exclusively in terms of territorial organization based on particular churches. In their minds, a personal prelature could only be an association of priests gathered round a prelate to serve in different dioceses. Laymen might associate themselves with this group of priests, but only to join in their work for the diocese. This vision of the Church left no room for a factory worker, nurse, or banker to be a full-fledged member of a prelature and to undertake an apostolate primarily in their own professional milieu. This view, whose principal exponent was Professor Winfried Aymans of the University of Munich, was initially shared to some degree by Cardinal Josef Ratzinger, as well as by some high-ranking officials in the Secretary of State's office.[91]

Many members of religious orders welcomed the potential importance of personal prelatures and understood that laypeople could be fully incorporated in them.[92] Others, however, perhaps because of the novelty of Opus Dei and more generally of personal prelatures, seem to have viewed them as threats to the consecrated life in the Church. Like the theologians and canonists who viewed the Church primarily in geographic terms, they characterized personal prelatures as associations rather than as part of the hierarchical structure of the Church and denied that laypeople incorporated in them. This, despite the fact that the overwhelming majority of the members of Opus Dei, the first personal prelature approved by the Holy See, were lay men and women. The most influential proponent of this view was a professor of canon law at the Gregorian University, Gianfranco Ghirlanda, SJ.[93] Another prominent critic was the Pauline priest Giancarlo Rocca, SSP. In 1985, he published a book in which he argued that laymen could not be true members of a prelature. He presented the history of Opus Dei as a confused quest for identity and contended that Opus Dei's transformation into a personal prelature was contrary to the Founder's intentions.[94] The book was given considerable publicity by the Italian anticlerical magazine *Panorama*.[95]

These views found an echo in the Vatican Secretary of State's office. On February 1986, Del Portillo wrote a lengthy letter to Cardinal Casaroli, the Secretary of State, about the "tenacious opposition that some religious have been carrying on for years against the legal figure of the personal prelature."[96] Without mentioning their influence in the Secretary of State's office, he asked Casaroli to do what he could to prevent the campaigns against Opus Dei from going further.[97]

A different source of concern was the position of Cardinal Ratzinger.[98] Influenced by the views of Aymans, whose theory of the structure of the Church gave such importance to territory and particular churches, he did not see any place in its hierarchical structure of the Church for personal prelatures which were neither territorial nor particular churches.

The state of affairs in April 1985 was sufficiently unclear for Del Portillo to describe the situation of the Work to Pope John Paul II as "legally unstable."[99] Opus Dei worked on two fronts to protect the position of personal prelatures as hierarchical structures made up of laymen as well as priests by trying to influence the views of Vatican officials and diocesan bishops and by working to gain acceptance for that view in the world of professional theologians and canonists.[100]

Its efforts met with limited success. In 1985 and 1986 there were several opportunities for the Vatican to apply the category of personal prelature to other institutions, but it did not do so. One involved Catholic members of the armed forces and their families. Their circumstances demanded special pastoral attention. After careful study over a period of several years, the Holy See seemed poised to approve military prelatures. Nonetheless, on April 21, 1985, the apostolic constitution *Spirituali militum curae* created military *ordinariates* rather than prelatures to provide pastoral care to members of the armed forces and other persons related to them. These personal ecclesiastical circumscriptions, which are legally assimilated to dioceses, can be thought of as a specific type of personal prelature. Like a personal prelature, they have an ordinary whose authority is cumulative with that of the diocesan bishop. They have both their own clergy and faithful who belong to them and to the local diocese. The Vatican decided, however, to call them ordinariates rather than prelatures.[101]

In 1989, three members of the Work, Amadeo de Fuenmayor, Valentín Gómez-Iglesias, and José Luis Illanes, published a detailed history of the legal development of Opus Dei from its foundation to its erection as a personal prelature under the title *El Itinerario Jurídico del Opus Dei: Historia y Defensa de un Carisma*.[102] The book explores in detail the spirit of Opus Dei and its efforts to find an appropriate niche in the Church's canonical structure, explaining its various approvals first by the Diocese of Madrid and later by the Holy See. Key documents are reproduced in a lengthy appendix. It does not mention Rocca or other authors who maintain that lay men and women cannot be full members of a prelature. It does, however, take pains to refute both this assertion and the contention that Opus Dei lacked a clear concept of itself.[103]

In 1986, Opus Dei began publishing an official bulletin under the name *Romana: Bollettino della Prelatura della Santa Croce e Opus Dei*. Most of the content was in Italian or Spanish.[104] Designed to be read by ecclesiastical and civil authorities, members of Opus Dei, cooperators, and others who attend its activities, its name had been chosen many years earlier by the Founder, "to underline the Catholic, universal character, of the pastoral mission of Opus Dei." *Romana* is available in many libraries and by subscription.

Each issue begins with an "Editorial," commenting briefly on some aspect of Christian life from the point of view of the spirit of Opus Dei. The second section, "From the Holy See," reproduces selected documents of the Roman Pontiff and of organizations within the Holy See. It is followed by the section "From the Prelate," which reports on the naming of new members of the prelature's various governing bodies and the creation of new centers, regions, and other similar territorial divisions of Opus Dei. The same section includes some texts of homilies, speeches, and interviews given by the Prelate and reports on his pastoral trips. The next section, "The Founder of Opus Dei," contains information on new editions of the works of the Founder as well as books about him and about Opus Dei. It is followed by a "News" section that offers short articles about events in the life of Opus Dei. The next section, "Some Apostolic Activities Promoted by Members of Opus Dei" reports on apostolic activities of some of the members "in civil society and their professions, in an effort to impregnate temporal realities with a Christian spirit." The penultimate section, "In Peace," consists of brief obituaries of a few members who died recently and a full list of other members who died during the period covered by the issue. Finally, "Studies" generally offers a theological essay on some aspect of the spirit of Opus Dei.

Romana represents a significant step toward greater transparency. It offers a great deal of information about the activities of the Prelate as well as the composition of Opus Dei's governing bodies both in Rome and in the Regions. Since 2019, it has also given an overview of the prelature's economic situation. It does not provide much information about the many educational and social activities promoted by members, but ample information about them can be found on Opus Dei's website as well as on the websites of the individual endeavors.

Notes

1. See chapter 7.

2. Study Report sent to Cardinal Baggio with Álvaro del Portillo's letter of April 23, 1979, reproduced in Amadeo de Fuenmayor, Valentín Gómez-Iglesias, and José Luis Illanes, *El itinerario jurídico del Opus Dei. Historia y defensa de un carisma* (Pamplona: EUNSA, 1990), pp. 601–610. Hereafter cited as Study Report.

3. The Second Vatican Council's discussion of secular institutes, for instance, forms part of its document on the renewal of religious life. See Second Vatican Council, Decree on the Adaptation and Renewal of Religious Life *Pefectae caritatis*, (October 28, 1965), 11. *http://www.vatican.va/archive/hist_councils/ii_vatican_council/documents/vat-ii_decree_19651028_perfectae-caritatis_en.html.*

4. Pius XII, Apostolic Constitution *Provida Mater Ecclesia* (1947), III, 2. *http://www.vatican.va/content/pius-xii/en/apost_constitutions/documents/hf_p-xii_apc_19470202_provida-mater-ecclesia.html*. The commitment to live poverty, chastity, and obedience could also take forms other than that of a vow, for instance a promise.

5. Study Report sent to Cardinal Baggio with Álvaro del Portillo's letter of April 23, 1979, n. 7, reproduced in Fuenmayor, pp. 601–603.

6. Second Vatican Council, Decree on the Ministry and Life of Priests *Presbyterorum Ordinis*, (December 7, 1965), 10, 1. *http://www.vatican.va/archive/hist_councils/ii_vatican_council/documents/vat-ii_decree_19651207_presbyterorum-ordinis_en.html*. Pope John Paul II, Apostolic Constitution *Ut Sit* (November 28, 1982), English version *https://opusdei.org/en-us/article/apostolic-constitution-ut-sit/*.

7. Congregation for Bishops, Declaration *Praelaturae personales* (August 23, 1982), English version: *http://prelaturaspersonales.org/vatican-declaration-on-opus-dei-english/*. Latin text: AAS 75 (1983), pp. 464–468. Letter of Cardinal Baggio to Álvaro del Portillo dated January 17, 1983, communicating the mind of John Paul II on the question of the canonical character of personal prelatures manifested to Baggio in an audience on January 8, 1983. AGP L 1.2, 1418. Quoted in Pedro Rodriguez, *Opus Dei: Estructura y Misión. Su realidad eclesiológica* (Madrid: Ediciones cristiandad, 2011), p. 52.

8. Study Report, pp. 601–604.

9. Study Report, pp. 601–604

10. Medina Bayo, Álvaro del Portillo. Un hombre fiel (Madrid: Rialp, 2013), p. 481.

11. Medina Bayo, p. 481.

12. Quoted in Del Portillo, Letter to Bishop Augustin Mayer, OSB, Secretary of the Congregation for Religious and Secular Institutes, January 11, 1979, reproduced in Fuenmayor, pp. 594–595.

13. Letter of Del Portillo to Pope John Paul II, February 2, 1979, reproduced in Fuenmayor, pp. 595–596.

14. Julián Herranz, *Nei dintorni di Gerico*, p. 298.

15. Study Report.

16. Study Report.

17. Study Report.

18. Study Report, pp. 603–605. On the secular character of Opus Dei, See Congregation for Bishops, Declaration *Praelaturae personales* (August 5, 1982), part 2, published in *L'Osservatore Romano*, November 28, 1983 and in AAS 75 (1983), pp. 464–468, reproduced in Fuenmayor, pp. 618–621.

19. Study Report.

20. Study Report.

21. Letter of Álvaro del Portillo to Cardinal Sebastiano Baggio, June 2, 1979, reproduced in Fuenmayor, p. 610.

22. Letter of Álvaro del Portillo to Cardinal Sebastiano Baggio, June 2, 1979, Study Report, p. 608.

23. Letter of Álvaro del Portillo to St. John Paul II, July 13, 1979. AGP series H.1.

24. Testimony of Bishop Javier Echevarría. AGP APD, T-19544, 488, quoted in Medina Bayo, p. 488.

25. Letter of Álvaro del Portillo to St. John Paul II, July 13, 1979. AGP H.1; Julián Herranz, *Nei dintorni di Gerico,* p. 299.

26. Letter of Álvaro del Portillo to St. John Paul II, July 3, 1979. AGP Sezione giuridica, VIII/15036.

27. Letter of Álvaro del Portillo to St. John Paul II, July 3, 1979.

28. Letter of Álvaro del Portillo to St. John Paul II, July 13, 1979. AGP H.1.

29. Letter of Álvaro del Portillo to St. John Paul II, July 13, 1979.

30. Letter of Álvaro del Portillo to St. John Paul II, July 13, 1979.

31. Testimony of Bishop Javier Echevarría. AGP APD, T-19544, 475-76, quoted in Medina Bayo, p. 486.

32. Testimony of Cardinal Franz Konig. AGP APD, T-15763, 2, quoted in Medina Bayo, p. 487.

33. Letter of Cardinal Sebastiano Baggio to Del Portillo, July 18, 1979, reproduced in Fuenmayor, pp. 612–613.

34. Letter of Cardinal Sebastiano Baggio to Del Portillo, July 18, 1979.

35. Letter of Cardinal Sebastiano Baggio to Del Portillo, July 18, 1979.

36. See Herranz, *Nei dintorni di Gerico*, p. 301.

37. Quoted in Fuenmayor, p. 431, n. 20.

38. Letter of Álvaro del Portillo to St. John Paul II, October 20, 1979. AGP L 1.2, 1403.

39. Letter of Álvaro del Portillo to St. John Paul II, October 20, 1979.

40. Letter of Cardinal Sebastiano Baggio, to Álvaro del Portillo, November 17, 1979. AGP L 1.2, 1403. Quoted in Herranz, *Nei dintorni di Gerico*, p. 302.

41. Letter of Cardinal Sebastiano Baggio, to Álvaro del Portillo, November 17, 1979.

42. Fuenmayor, p. 432.

43. Letter of Del Portillo to Joint Commission, February 6, 1980, reproduced in Fuenmayor, p. 433, n. 24.

44. *"Circa la trasformazione dell'Opus Dei in Prelatura personale. Studio realizzat dalla Commissione paritetica approvata da S.S. Giovanni Paolo III e composta de rappresentanti dell S.C. per i Vescovi e da rappresentanti dell'Opus Dei, Roma, Febbraio 1981,"* n. 20, quoted in Fuenmayor, p. 438.

45. Herranz, *Nei dintorni di Gerico*, pp. 303–306.

46. Summary Report on the Erection of Opus Dei as a Personal Prelature, sent to all the members of the Congregation for Bishops, August 19, 1982. AGP L 1.2, 1414. See also Herranz, *Nei dintorni di Gerico*, pp. 306–310.

47. *"Rapporto urgente e grave sull'Opus Dei. Informe agli emm.mi sign.ri cardinali della Sacra Romana Chiesa, ai Presidenti delle Conferenze Episcopali e ai vescovi residenziali."* AGP L.1.2, 1407.

48. *"Rapporto urgente e grave sull'Opus Dei."*

49. Text of statement attached to note 12225/81. AGP L.1.2, 1407.

50. Summary Report on the Erection of Opus Dei as a Personal Prelature, sent on August 19, 1982 to All the Members of the Congregation for Bishops, August 19, 1982. AGP L.1.2, 1414. Letter from Cardinal Baggio to Álvaro del Portillo, November 9, 1981. AGP L.1.2, 1408.

51. Congregation for Bishops, *"Nota informativa circa l'erezione dell'Opus Dei in Prelatura personale, per opportuna conoscenza dei Vescovi,"* November 14, 1981. AGP L.1.2, 1408. Report entitled *"Vescovi che hanno ricevuto la 'Nota Informativa' della Sacra Congregazione."* AGP L.1.2, 1408.

52. Congregation for Bishops, *"Nota informativa circa l'erezione dell'Opus Dei in Prelatura personale, per opportuna conoscenza dei Vescovi,"* November 14, 1981.

53. Herranz, *Nei dintorni di Gerico*, p. 313.

54. Letter of Gabino Díaz Merchán, President of the Spanish Episcopal Conference, to Cardinal Agostino Casaroli, Vatican Secretary of State, July 2, 1982. AGP L.1.2, 1414.

55. Unsigned report from the nuncio in Spain, Bishop Antonio Innocenti, July 15, 1982, "*Opus Dei e Vescovi in Spagna.*" AGP L.1.2, 1414.

56. Letter of Gabino Díaz Merchán, president of the Spanish Episcopal Conference, summarizing recent events, to Cardinal Agostino Casaroli, Vatican Secretary of State, July 2, 1982. AGP L.1.2, 1414.

57. Innocenti, "*Opus Dei e Vescovi in Spagna.*" See also notes H 1304/82 and H 1309/82. AGP L 1.2, 1414.

58. Innocenti, "*Opus Dei e Vescovi in Spagna.*"

59. Report of Bishop Angel Suquía, quoted in unsigned report dated Rome, August 20, 1982. AGP L 1.2 1414.

60. Unsigned report dated Rome, August 20, 1982. AGP L.1.2, 1414. Congregation for Bishops, Declaration *Praelaturae personales*, August 5, 1982, published in *L'Osservatore Romano*, November 28, 1983 and in AAS 75 (1983), 464 et seq., reproduced in Fuenmayor, pp. 618–621.

61. Letter of Cardinal Baggio to the nuncio in Spain, Bishop Antonio Innocenti, August 11, 1982. AGP L.1.2, 1414.

62. Letter of Cardinal Baggio to Álvaro del Portillo, August 19, 1982. AGP L.1.2, 1414.

63. Report dated June 14, 2005, of Pedro Álvarez de Toledo on a conversation with Bishop Sebastián on April 6, 2005. AGP L.1.2, 1414. In memoirs published in 2016, Bishop Sebastián gave a somewhat different version of the Pope's comments, saying that John Paul II predicted that having a clear legal status would make Opus Dei feel more secure and "they will have better relations with the bishops": Fernando Sebastián, *Memorias con esperanza* (Madrid: Encuentro, 2016), p. 263.

64. Herranz, *Nei dintorni di Gerico*, p. 313.

65. Sebastián, *Memorias*, p. 264.

66. Herranz, *Nei dintorni di Gerico*, p. 317.

67. Letter of Del Portillo to Cardinal Baggio, August 25, 1982. AGP L 1.2, 1414.

68. Letter of Del Portillo to Cardinal Baggio, August 24, 1982. AGP L.1.2, 1414.

69. Congregation for Bishops, Declaration *Praelaturae personales*.

70. Sebastiano Baggio, "*Un bene per tutta la Chiesa,*" *L'Osservatore Romano*, November 28, 1982.

71. Marcello Costalunga, "*L'erezione dell'Opus Dei in Prelatura personale,*" *L'Osservatore Romano*, November 28, 1982.

72. Del Portillo to John Paul II, November 28, 1982. AGP L.1.2, 1415.

73. See, e.g., *Appunto* attached to note from Echevarría to Bishop Eduardo Martínez, Substitute of the Secretariat of State, December 22, 1982. AGP L.1.2, 1415. See also *Appunto* attached to letter from Julián Herranz to Cardinal Baggio, December 23, 1982, and *Appunto* attached to letter of January 4, 1983 from Álvaro del Portillo to Cardinal Baggio. AGP L.1.2, 1418.

74. AGP L.1.2, 1418.

75. Letter from Del Portillo to Baggio, January 4, 1983 (thanking Baggio for the reassurances given to Herranz). AGP L.1.2, 1418.

76. Note prepared by Ernesto Juliá, January 8, 1983, on private audience of Del Portillo with John Paul II on January 7, 1983. AGP L.1.2, 1418.

77. Letter from Baggio to Del Portillo, January 17, 1983. AGP L.1.2, 1418. This letter is reproduced and commented on in José Luis Illanes, "*Lettera del card. Sebastiano Baggio a mons. Álvaro del Portillo del 17 gennaio 1983, sulle prelature personali*," *Studia et Documenta* 5 (2011), pp. 369–380.

78. Especially Gianfranco Ghilanda, SJ, professor of canon law at the Gregorian University.

79. Letter from Álvaro del Portillo to Eduardo Martínez Somalo, Rome, February 15, 1993, quoted in Medina Bayo, p. 503.

80. Del Portillo, Pastoral Letter, November 28, 1982, no. 47. AGP Biblioteca, 17.

81. Del Portillo, Pastoral Letter, November 28, 1982, no. 48.

82. Del Portillo, Pastoral Letter, November 28, 1982, nos. 22–23

83. Del Portillo, Pastoral Letter, November 28, 1982, nos. 22–23.

84. Del Portillo, Pastoral Letter, November 28, 1982, nos. 22–23.

85. Del Portillo, Pastoral Letter, November 28, 1982, no. 18.

86. Medina Bayo, pp. 647–648.

87. Medina Bayo, p. 648.

88. Medina Bayo, p. 648.

89. Medina Bayo, p. 649.

90. Fernando Ocáriz, "*Reflexiones teológicas sobre la ordenación episcopal del Prelado del Opus Dei*," *Palabra* 310 (1991/II), pp. 92–95.

91. As early as 1979 Aymans expressed these views in a lengthy article in the *Frankfurter Allgemeine Zeitung* with the title "*Die ganze Welt als Personaldiözese für das Opus Dei?*" (December 13, 1979).

92. See, e.g., Robert Ombres, OP, "Opus Dei and Personal Prelatures," *The Clergy Review*, LXX (August 1985), pp. 292–295. Fr. Ombres taught canon law at the University of St. Thomas in Rome and theology at Oxford University.

93. Among his articles were "*De differentia Prelaturam personalem inter et Ordinarium militarem seu castrensem*," *Periodica* 76 (1987), pp. 219–251, and "*Natura delle Prelature personali e posizione dei laici*," *Gregorianum*, 69/2 (1988), pp. 299–314.

94. Giancarlo Rocca, SSP, *L' "Opus Dei." Appunti e documenti per una storia* (Rome: Edizioni Paolini, 1985).

95. Giancarlo Zizola, "*L'Opus Dei/ Come e perché difende i suo Segreti. Don Rocca, ti cancellerò*," *Panorama* (February 16, 1986), pp. 66–68.

96. Del Portillo to Cardinal Agotino Casaroli, February 22, 1986. AGP L 1.2, 1420.

97. Del Portillo to Casaroli, February 22, 1986.

98. See Note signed by Ernesto Juliá and dated April 22, 1985, on private audience of del Portillo with John Paul on April 20, 1985. AGP L 1.2 1420.

99. See Note by Ernesto Juliá, April 22, 1985.

100. Report of Julián Herranz, January 6, 1986, "*Explicación y defensa de las Prelaturas personales*," AGP L. 1.2 1420.

101. *http://prelaturaspersonales.org/ordinariatos-militares/preguntas-frecuentes/*.

102. Fuenmayor, *Itinerario*. English version: *The Canonical Path of Opus Dei* (New York: Scepter, 1994).

103. See Fuenmayor, *Itinerario;* Rocca, *L'Opus Dei.*

104. An English version began in 1997. Its title is *Romana: Bulletin of the Prelature of the Holy Cross and Opus Dei*. Back issues in English, Spanish, and Italian can be found at *https://en.romana.org/archive/*.

CHAPTER 8

⌒∽

Growth

Section 1. Numerical Growth

During the two decades that Del Portillo headed Opus Dei, it grew by 140 percent, increasing from 32,800 in 1975 to 78,500 in 1994. During that period, the number of women nearly tripled, growing from 17,200 to 45,900. The men's branch doubled from 15,600 to 32,600. Growth was slower from 1984 to 1994 (16,800) than from 1975 to 1984 (28,900). The slowing of growth was especially sharp in the men's branch, which added 12,400 members during the first decade and 4,600 during the second. The women's branch grew by 16,500 in the first decade and 12,200. By the end of Del Portillo's tenure, the women's branch constituted 58 percent of Opus Dei.*

Large numbers of people continued to join Opus Dei during the later years of Del Portillo's tenure. Many people also left, however, often shortly after asking to be admitted. In Spain, for instance, in the three years 1983–1985, some 3,400 women joined Opus Dei, but 1,700 left, 850 of them in the first eighteen months after asking to be admitted.[1] From a legal point of view, those who left during the first eighteen months or before they reached the age of eighteen never were members of Opus Dei, but in a period of discernment. The central governing organs of Opus Dei responded to this situation by urging the members of the Work to cultivate a deeper interior life of

---

* These statistics are based on the numbers Opus Dei submitted to the Holy See in its Five-Year Reports. AGP, E.4,1. In press releases issued in connection with the Founder's death in the 1975, Opus Dei's offices of information said that 60,000 people belonged to Opus Dei. That number included 28,000 cooperators and people involved in the formation activities organized by the Works of St. Gabriel and St. Raphael and the Priestly Society of the Holy Cross.

prayer and sacrifice, to be more selective about whom they allowed to ask for admission to the Work, and to be more careful in providing formation to the new vocations, but did not go into specifics.[2] These tasks fell primarily to local councils, often made up of young people who had themselves joined Opus Dei only recently.

At least in Spain, the number of numerary vocations among male high school students remained steady. In the 1981–1982 school year, 172 young men studying in schools connected with Opus Dei asked to be admitted to the Work.[3] During the 1991–1992 school year, the number was 174.[4] A growing portion of the high school students who joined Opus Dei came from families already connected with the Work. For example, in Spain in the late 1980s, 80 percent of the young people who joined Opus Dei as numeraries were children of supernumeraries.

The number of vocations of college students, however, fell dramatically during the second half of Del Portillo's tenure. In 1978, a total of 208 Spanish male university students joined the Work as a result of their contact with students of the centers of studies.[5] In the 1991–1992 school year, that number had dropped to twelve.[6] Only thirty-six male college students joined the Work that school year in the seventeen university residences and twenty-two other centers for university students in the Spanish region.

The decline in vocations of college students in Spain was especially significant because the Spanish region made up half of Opus Dei and provided most of the numeraries who started the Work in new regions or went to recently founded regions to expand activities there. In addition, the Spanish region was beginning to need large numbers of new vocations to continue the apostolic activities started by those who retired, died, or were infirm.[7]

Retaining vocations of associates became particularly difficult during Don Álvaro's tenure. Between 1983 and 1985 in Spain, for instance, 385 women asked to be admitted as associates, but 332 women associates left the Work.[8]

Between 1975 and 1992, 873 priests of the presbyterium of Opus Dei were ordained, including 842 numeraries and 31 associates. The number of diocesan priests who belonged to the Priestly Society of the Holy Cross grew by six hundred from some 1200 to some 1800.[9] Beginning in 1983, seminarians who had not yet been ordained could become "candidates" of the Priestly Society and receive formation in the spirit of the Work to prepare them to join the Priestly Society after their ordination as deacons.[10]

Throughout Don Álvaro's tenure, the Central Advisory paid particular attention to the numerary assistants. The number of vocations of numerary assistants in a given country varied, of course, with the overall size of Opus Dei in the country, but also with the degree to which the social and economic structure made domestic work and the hospitality industry attractive options for young women. In Spain, Mexico, and other countries with large poor, rural populations, training which led to professional qualifications for the hospitality industry or for working in homes offered girls a way to acquire an education and escape from rural areas where they had very few opportunities. In these settings, it was easy to find students for boarding schools that offered training in hospitality. The students took classes in general education and home economics while they worked part-time in the Administration of the residence or conference center to which the schools were attached.[11] In the process they became acquainted with Opus Dei and some of them discovered a vocation as a numerary assistant.

In 1978, 355 young women joined Opus Dei as numerary assistants, including 129 in Spain, 78 in Mexico, and 35 in the Philippines. The next largest number was nine in Argentina and Brazil. In France, Holland, Switzerland, and Nigeria only one person joined Opus Dei as a numerary assistant and in a few countries there were no vocations of numerary assistants that year.

A fairly large number of the young women who initially felt attracted to the vocation of a numerary assistant soon changed their minds, often due to opposition from their parents and friends, or because they had not fully understood the degree of sacrifice involved in being a member of Opus Dei. In twelve out of twenty-eight regions for which there are statistics, the number of numerary assistants who left the Work during 1978 exceeded one-third of the number who joined. In Spain the problem was dramatic. During 1978, a total of 129 Spanish young women joined the Work as numerary assistants and 102 left.[12]

In some regions, a cause of concern was the growing need for women numeraries to work as full-time directors (whether in the regional commissions, the delegations, or the local councils), as administrators of centers, or as teachers and school administrators in corporate apostolates and personal works. Although working in these various positions was a good thing, it reduced the number of numeraries exercising their vocation in other professional settings. In some cases, this phenomenon reached dramatic proportions. In the Region of Central America, only 10 percent of the women numeraries worked in professions outside Opus Dei. Central America was closely followed by Peru at 14, Mexico at 17, and Italy at 22. Spain reported 36 percent of women numeraries and 50 percent of male numeraries in outside jobs, but this number included those in both corporate and personal works.[13]

This issue affected only the numeraries, who, of course, represented a small percentage of the members of Opus Dei. The vast majority of supernumeraries worked in the same job or profession they would have if they had not joined Opus Dei. Nonetheless, given the visibility of the numeraries, the high percentage of numeraries working in institutional jobs could easily lead people to form a distorted idea of the nature of the vocation to Opus Dei. The Central Advisory collaborated with the regions to try to correct the situation, but it had no easy solution other than somehow increasing the number of numeraries without proportionately increasing the number needed for the government of the Work, the staffing of the household Administrations, the corporate works, and personal apostolates.

Section 2. New Countries

At Escrivá's death, Opus Dei had centers in thirty-two countries. During the next two decades it added twenty-one additional countries: 1978 Bolivia; 1980 Honduras, Hong Kong, Zaire (Congo), and Ivory Coast; 1981 Trinidad-Tobago; 1982 Singapore; 1984 Sweden;

Workshop in Tajamar School, Madrid, 1963. Situated in what was at the time a shantytown, Tajamar opened up educational opportunities for boys and young men of the area, providing both technical training and traditional high school education. In addition to a day section, it offered night classes to students who worked during the day.

Cooking class in Lakefield Center for Hospitality Training in London, 1968. During the 1960s, Lakefield and similar schools in other countries won governmental recognition for their hotel and tourism training programs.

Class for farmworkers at ERPA (Andes Radio Schools for Workers) in Peru, 1968. ERPA relied heavily on the radio to offer to the impoverished indigenous population of the province of Cañete, Peru classes on agriculture, livestock care and breeding, basic culture, and religion.

Congress members Marisa Vaquero, Carmen Puente, Rita di Pasquale, and Ameila Díaz Guardamino in Rome during Opus Dei's Special General Congress, 1969. The Congress approved requesting the Holy See to transform Opus Dei into a Personal Prelature.

Josemaría Escrivá de Balaguer consecrates the main altar of the Marian shrine of Torreciudad in Spain, 1975. A month before his sudden death, the founder visited the shrine during the final phases of its construction and prayed that it might be a place of encounter with God through the intercession of his Mother.

Catechism class sponsored by Tanglaw University Center in Manila for a group of girls preparing for their First Communion, 1981. From its very beginning, Opus Dei's apostolic activities with young people have included the teaching of the catechism.

Julián Herranz, Javier Echevarría, Alvaro del Portillo, and an unidentified bishop during a 1986 audience with Pope St. John Paul II. The pope had erected Opus Dei as a personal prelature in 1982 and would beatify (1992) and canonize (2002) its founder.

A group of supernumerary members during a course of formation in Alabang Conference Center near Manila, 1990. Super-numerary men and women see their marriage and family life as an integral part of their path to God.

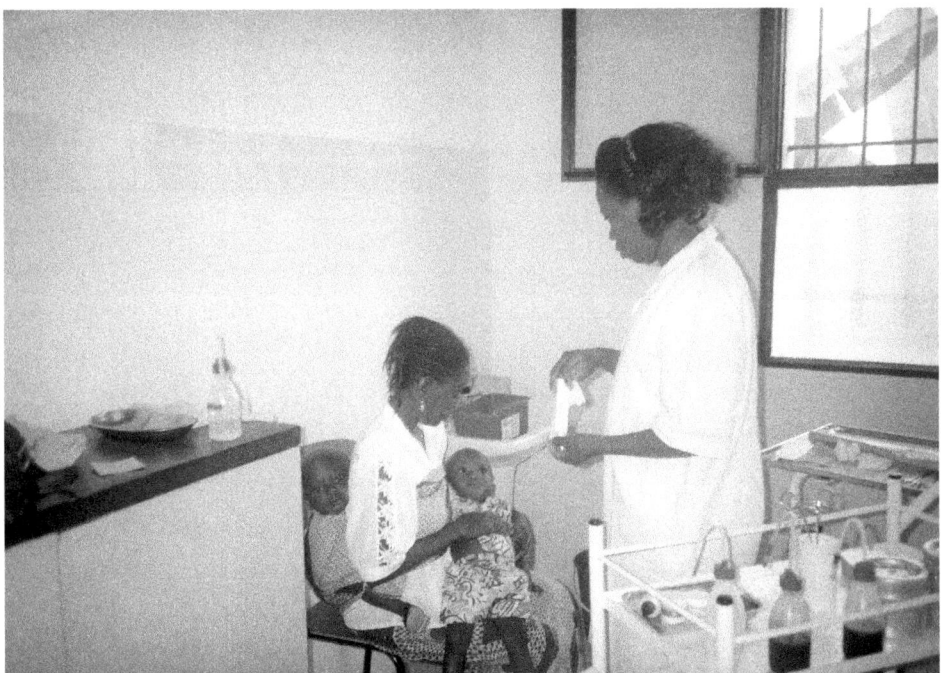

St. Peter's Square during the beatification of Josemaría Escrivá de Balaguer on May 17, 1992.

A pediatric visit in Monkole Hospital in Kinshasa, Democratic Republic of the Congo, 1992. Monkole offers quality care to patients regardless of their ability to pay. Its nursing school prepares professors of nursing who are helping to raise the standard of nursing care in the country.

A conference organized by the Priestly Society of the Holy Cross in the Seminary of Madrid to mark the hundredth anniversary of the birth of St. Josemaría, 2002. The Priestly Society helps diocesan priests seek sanctity through their ministry, offering them spiritual accompaniment and the family spirit of Opus Dei.

A work camp in Maggona, Sri Lanka, 2005. In many countries and together with other people, the faithful of Opus Dei have created associations to promote volunteer activities and to contribute to development in disadvantaged countries and areas.

The church of the parish of St. Josemaría in Mexico City was consecrated in 2009. Its two curved walls suggest the shape of a fish, a symbol of Jesus Christ. The parish sponsors a community center that offers help to vulnerable communities in the area.

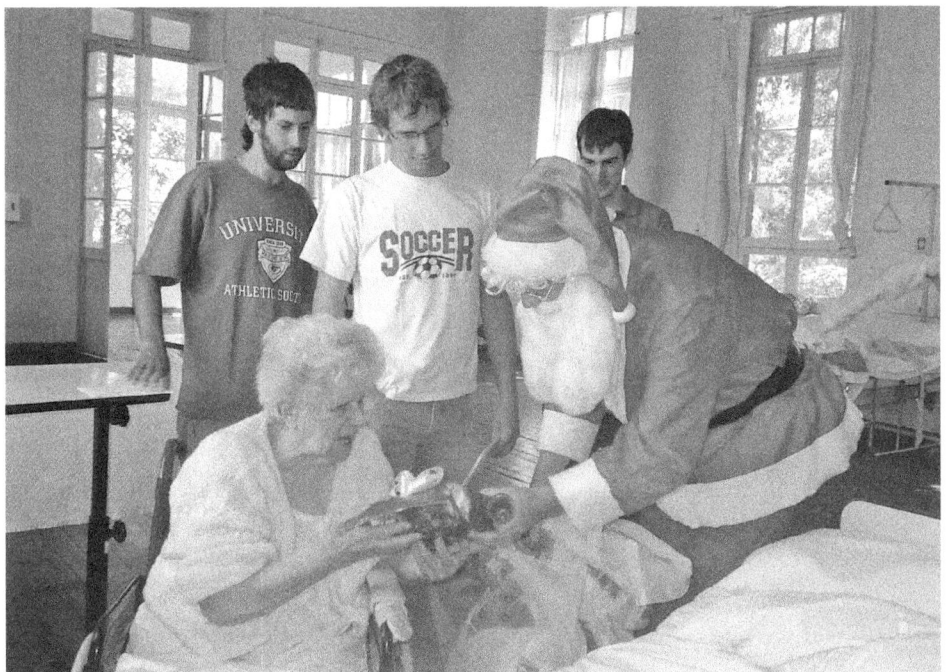

College students distributing Christmas presents in a senior home in Santiago de Chile, 2007. Volunteer activities, including taking care of and accompanying vulnerable persons, help young people develop a social conscience and challenge them to be generous in giving of their time and talents.

The Museum of the University of Navarra in Pamplona, Spain, opened in 2015, was designed by the Pritzker Architecture Prize-winning architect Rafael Moneo. Its collections include works by Picasso, Rothko, Tápies, and Chillida. Through expositions, theater, and a master's in curatorship, it attempts to connect the world of culture with faith.

The Heights School outside of Washington, D.C. is one of three hundred schools promoted by members of Opus Dei around the world. In addition to striving for academic excellence, these schools encourage parents to play an active role in the life of the school and rely on mentoring to help students fully develop their abilities.

1985 Taiwan; 1987 Finland; 1988 Republic of Cameroon, Dominican Republic, and New Zealand; 1989 Macau; 1990 Poland; 1991 Czech Republic; 1992 Hungary and Nicaragua; 1993 Israel and India; and 1994 Lithuania.[14]

Members of Opus Dei throughout the world tried to get to know people from countries where Opus Dei still did not have a corporate presence or was just beginning its activities, with the hope that some of them might have a vocation to Opus Dei and eventually be able to help start or expand the Work in their native countries.[15] Nonetheless, the bulk of the people who started Opus Dei's activities in new countries were foreigners. The Region of Spain continued to provide most of the personnel. In the period from 1977 to 1985, more than three hundred numeraries left Spain for other regions.[16] By the late 1980s, although on a much smaller scale, the Region of the Philippines was becoming an important source of people not only to begin Opus Dei's activities in other Asian countries but also for expansion outside of Asia. In 1987, for instance, the women of Opus Dei in the Philippines were preparing college-age members of the Work to go to Australia, the United States, and Canada, and eleven young Filipino women were scheduled to attend the center of studies in other regions.[17]

The normal pattern was that the first center in a new country was opened by members of the men's branch. Once the men had gotten started in a country and were able to guarantee the availability of Opus Dei priests, the women's branch followed suit. The first center of the men's branch was usually an apartment for five or six people (one or two priests and four or five laymen) and an oratory. Whenever possible, the initial group included at least one native of the country who had joined Opus Dei elsewhere. In the Dominican Republic, for instance, Fernanda Mallorca, a citizen of the country who had joined Opus Dei in Barcelona in 1959, was a member of the group that started Opus Dei's activities in 1989.[18] In any case, an effort was made to avoid having the group composed of people from a single foreign country.

At the beginning, the activities of the first center in a new country were limited to get-togethers (sometimes with a locally famous professor or other speaker), meditations, and days of recollection. As time went by, the people of the Work, together with local people they had met, began to think of a larger project: a conference center for workshops and retreats, a training center for domestic employees, a language academy, or perhaps a school.

The members of the group who were going to start Opus Dei in a country typically spent a few days in Rome with the Prelate and the members of the General Council preparing for their adventure. Del Portillo urged them to cultivate a deep interior life of prayer and penance above all. He gave them a picture or statue of Our Lady for the first center and encouraged them to have recourse to her.[19] Members of the General Council or the Central Advisory gave talks about apostolic activities they might consider undertaking and outlined some of the difficulties they might expect to encounter.

Many of the countries in which Opus Dei began during Del Portillo's tenure presented special challenges. They were culturally very different from the home countries of the members of Opus Dei, and the process of acculturation was daunting. The languages were not only different, but in many cases notoriously difficult. It was often hard to get work visas and to find work.[20] Before 1975, with the exception of Japan, all of Opus Dei's centers were in countries where the Catholic Church had a significant presence. In the two following decades, centers opened in eight countries where Catholics were a tiny minority: Israel, India, Hong Kong, Singapore, Taiwan, Macau, Sweden, and Finland.

Why did Opus Dei choose to open centers in these countries? Israel responded to a longstanding desire for a presence in the Holy Land. As the second largest country in the world, India was simply too important to ignore, even though Catholics were less than 2 percent of the population. Hong Kong, Singapore, Taiwan, and Macau were dynamic countries in Asia where English speakers could get along well initially, although to become part of the society and to make real friends it would be necessary to learn Cantonese or Mandarin. Del Portillo and others at Opus Dei's headquarters in Rome viewed the four countries not only as individually important, but as beachheads in Asia that would eventually facilitate the beginning of Opus Dei's apostolic activities in China.

Starting in 1984, members of the Work from Australia and the Philippines actively investigated the possibility of starting a center of higher education in the city of Zhuhai, a Special Economic Zone located in southern China on the border of Macao in Guangzhou province. Local government officials were favorable to the project and willing to give oral assurances of the religious freedom and autonomy needed to make it feasible. After much back and forth, however, it became clear that they could not provide written guarantees and were quite unlikely to obtain the necessary permissions from Beijing.[21]

Finally, ICU, an Italian not-for-profit organization in which members of Opus Dei were active, managed to interest the Italian government in taking advantage of the goodwill of local Chinese university and government officials to undertake some projects involving maintenance engineering. ICU arranged for experts from Italy and other European countries to work with researchers from the University of Canton. It also established a student residence at the University of Canton, but without a chaplain. When the project was over, the University of Canton took over the residence.

If many of the countries where Opus Dei opened its first center under Del Portillo's leadership presented serious challenges, there were also factors that facilitated the projects. In many cases, people from the country had been in contact with Opus Dei elsewhere. Netherhall House, for instance, an international student residence in England that had opened in 1952, had an extensive list of former residents, particularly from countries of the British Commonwealth.[22] In several countries, some of them helped locate an apartment, settle in, find work, and begin meeting more people.

The factors that triggered the opening of the first center of Opus Dei in a country varied. In some cases, one or more married members of the Work found themselves in a country for professional or other reasons and began to spread Opus Dei's message among their colleagues and friends.[23] In other cases, members of the hierarchy requested Opus Dei's presence in their countries.[24] As previously mentioned, the Nordic countries were an unusual case. In a December 1982 audience, Del Portillo told John Paul II about Opus Dei's first steps on the mainland of Asia and of his desire to reach China. The Pope responded that he was happy to hear this but was more concerned about the Nordic countries. Del Portillo immediately began to focus on them and to ask the members to pray for Opus Dei's future apostolate there, even though Catholics were a small minority and many people were completely irreligious.[25]

Del Portillo could not leave Rome before the promulgation of the bull establishing Opus Dei as a personal prelature. The very day following the promulgation in March 1983, however, he set out on an exploratory trip to Norway, Finland, Sweden, and Denmark.[26] The following year Opus Dei opened its first center in Sweden.[27] In August 1987, Opus Dei opened its first center in Finland, Bulevardi Foorumi Cultural Center, in an apartment in downtown Helsinki. A year later, the women of Opus Dei began activities in Vanha Puisto center. From the beginning they were helped by a number of Lutheran cooperators. The first Finnish man to join Opus Dei, Dr. Seppo Rotinen, had come into contact with Opus Dei in Vienna while studying medicine there. The first woman to join Opus Dei in Finland was Lissy Clement. At the beginning of the twenty-first century both the men and the women of Opus Dei started university residences in Finland. In 2011 Malminharju conference center opened, and in 2016 Oskari Juurikkala was ordained as the first Finnish priest of the Prelature.[28]

Although Opus Dei could not open centers behind the Iron Curtain, some members had traveled occasionally to the Communist countries of Eastern Europe for professional or other reasons. Starting in 1986, European student residences connected to Opus Dei began to organize summer work camps there. After the fall of the Berlin Wall in 1989 and the collapse of the communist regimes in the Soviet Union and its satellites, Opus Dei moved quickly to begin in Poland with the support of Bishop Majdanski of Szczecin, opening centers in Warsaw and Szczecin. The regional commission and the regional advisory of Austria took responsibility for beginning Opus Dei in Czechoslovakia (1991) and Hungary (1992).

In many cases, there was little possibility that the new outposts would become self-sufficient either financially or in terms of personnel for many years. Beginning in those countries represented a long-term commitment to provide financial support and to send people from other countries to help expand Opus Dei's presence and apostolic activities.

Notes

1. AGP Q 1.9, 2-12. Report entitled "*España (Datos al 31-XII-1985).*"

2. See, e.g., Report prepared for the President General by the Central Advisory on apostolate with Numerary Assistants in 1978. AGP R6.1, 1-2. We have not been able to carry out the in-depth analysis of the working papers of the General Council and the Central Advisory which would be required to know what the central directors thought about the effects of the evolution of social, cultural, and religious life on the process of vocational discernment. The 1992 General Congress pointed out that the lack of formation of many young people made it necessary to be more careful in the selection and formation of new vocations (AGP D.1), but did not provide specific analysis or guidance. Ten years later, the 2002 General Congress went into greater depth. See chapter 13, section 2.

3. H 1967/82, and H 179/92. AGP G 3.2.2, 3151 and 3152.

4. H 179/92. AGP G 3.2.2, 3151.

5. Background material for note 2252/89. AGP G 3.2.2, 3151.

6. H 179/92, Attachment. AGP G 3.2.2, 3152.

7. Based on statistics of the women's branch. See background material prepared for briefing of the prelate by vicar of Spain. AGP Q1.9, 11-1.

8. Report entitled "*España, datos al 31-XII 1985.*" AGP Q 1.9, 2-12.

9. AGP I.4, 1350.

10. AGP I 4, 1136, "*Informe de la labor de aspirantes de la sss+.*"

11. Report prepared for the President General by the Central Advisory on apostolate with Numerary Assistants in 1978. AGP R6.1, 2, 1.

12. Ibid.

13. Report prepared for the President General by the Central Advisory entitled "*Trabajo Profesional de las Numerarias.*" AGP R 4.3, 2, 1.

14. *http://opusdei.org/en-us/article/historical-overview*. Last consulted July 16, 2020. See Carlo Pioppi, *"Verso le aree marginali del cattolicesimo contemporaneo. La diffusione internazionale dell'Opus Dei sotto la guida di Álvaro del Portillo (I),"* *Studia et Documenta* (2015), pp. 101–143.

15. Note 253/84. AGP E.1.3 (urging members to get to know people from South Korea, Taiwan, Singapore, Malaysia, Indonesia, and New Zealand).

16. Report entitled *"España (Datos al 31-XII-1985)."* AGP Q 1.9, 2-12.

17. Report of Delegate for the Women's Branch in the Philippines, May 4, 1987. AGP Q 2.2, 1-5.

18. Isabel Pareja Roldán, *"Comienzos en República Dominicana (marzo 1989–1994)."* Memoir dated June, 2016. AGP U2.1, 5-94.

19. Medina Bayo, p. 568.

20. See AGP M.2.1, 38-1-1 (discussion of beginnings in Poland) and AGP M.2.1, 33-3 (discussion of beginnings in Singapore).

21. See large number of documents in AGP M 2.1, 35-1-1.

22. James Pereiro, "Netherhall House, London (1960–1984): The Commonwealth Dimension," *Studia et Documenta* (2011), p. 13. Available at *http://opusdeihistory.org/articles/netherhall-house-london-1960-1984-the-commonwealth-dimension/*. Last consulted April 17, 2018.

23. This was the case, for instance, in Trinidad and Tobago. AGP M. 2.1, 33-2, and in the Dominican Republica. Pareja Roldán, *"Comienzos en República Dominicana."*

24. This was the case in Poland, for example. AGP M. 21, 38-1-1 and 2.

25. Medina Bayo, pp. 556–557

26. Medina Bayo, p. 557

27. *http://opusdei.org/en-us/article/historical-overview*. Last consulted April 16, 2018.

28. Electronic interview of the authors with Raimo Goyarrola, October 6, 2020. Goyarrola, a numerary priest of the Prelature, is the vicar general of the Diocese of Helsinki.

CHAPTER 9

Doctrinal Formation

scrivá often stressed that Opus Dei's principal apostolate consists in transmitting Catholic doctrine to its members and other people.[1] It is impossible to document the most important vehicle of this apostolate, which Escrivá called the apostolate of friendship and confidence: the example of members' lives and their countless personal conversations with colleagues, friends, neighbors, and relatives. In this chapter, we focus on activities designed to transmit doctrine.*

Section 1. Cooperators and Young People

Since Opus Dei began its first corporate activity in the early 1930s, the Work has offered courses, lectures, and talks at student residences, schools, and conference centers, about the Church's teaching on publicly debated areas like bioethics, marriage, and family.[2] Opus Dei's activities in these areas took on a new urgency in response to Pope John Paul II's call for a New Evangelization. The Pope was deeply concerned about the growing secularism in Europe and America and called on the Church to engage the many people in traditionally Christian and Catholic countries who were gradually becoming secularized.[3] At the close of a symposium of the Council of European Episcopal Conferences held in Rome in October 1985, he invited the church to a renewed missionary zeal focused on the growing secularized sector of society.[4] Del Portillo immediately wrote a pastoral letter to the faithful of the Prelature, urging them to collaborate in this task, especially in Europe and

---

* In chapter 16 we attempt to illustrate some aspects of the members' personal apostolate.

North America.[5] He redoubled his own pastoral efforts in this sector, making frequent trips throughout Europe.

In February 1986, Opus Dei held a workshop in Rome for regional directors of the women's branch from Europe, the United States, and Canada, to stimulate the participation of supernumeraries in the New Evangelization. That apostolate would begin with their Christian testimony at work, at home, and in the rest of their life, but it would also include explaining the teaching of the Church in an opportune way and at the right time to colleagues, friends, and relatives. To study how this might be done better, parallel workshops were held in Torreciudad for supernumeraries from English-speaking regions and in Hohewand Conference Center in Austria for German speakers.

As a way of contributing to the New Evangelization, many of the student residences connected with Opus Dei invited Catholic scholars to give lectures on the history of the Church and on the contribution of the Church to the development of European culture. In cities throughout Europe and in the United States and Canada, numerous conferences and lectures explored papal documents like *Reconciliatio et Paenitentia* and *Familiaris Consortio* as well as the instruction of the Congregation for the Doctrine of the Faith on Christian Liberty and Liberation.[6]

In regions where Opus Dei had a large presence, many of the young people who took part in the formational activities of the St. Raphael Work attended schools that were corporate or personal apostolates of Opus Dei or came from families where the husband or wife was a member of the Work.[7] The members of Opus Dei tried to encourage young members and their friends to think about careers in teaching, journalism, publishing, and other areas that lent themselves to communicating a Christian view of human life and society. They also encouraged students to consider thesis topics that were of doctrinal interest. They prepared supernumeraries to teach basic courses and run family clubs.

The circles which members had been giving to young men and women since the beginning of the Work were intended to help the participants develop an interior life of prayer, sacrifice, and sanctification of work, and to carry out an apostolate of friendship and confidence with their peers. They presumed a basic understanding of Catholic doctrine about God, the sacraments, and morality. Beginning in the late 1970s, members of the Work in different parts of the world noticed that many of the people who attended the circles in fact knew almost nothing about their religion. Even in countries with a long Catholic tradition, it was becoming frequent to meet young people and college graduates who did not know the most basic prayers or truths of the faith, or whose conscience was ill-formed regarding even the principles and precepts of the natural law.[8]

To remedy this situation, they began experimenting with courses on the fundamentals of Catholic faith to prepare students for the circles. Building on this experience, the General Counsel put together a detailed syllabus for a course on Christian doctrine aimed primarily at young men and women who were interested in developing an interior life but who lacked the necessary background to benefit from the traditional circles. In 1980, what was called within Opus Dei the "Basic Course" was launched throughout the world.[9] The classes were taught in formats ranging from lectures for large groups to one-on-one personal explanations. In most cases, however, they took the form of informal classes for small groups which met once a week, every other week, or once a month. Usually, things were arranged so that the entire syllabus would be covered in the course of one year, after which the students who were interested could join a circle. In 1982, the General Counsel sent out detailed notes to help members of the Work prepare the classes.[10] Over the following years, the Basic Course became a staple part of Opus Dei's apostolate, especially with young people. For instance, in 1987, some five thousand students and almost two thousand young women working in the hospitality industry or providing domestic services attended Basic Courses organized by members of the Women's branch.[11]

Taking his inspiration from the volumes of meditations prepared by the General Council for use in Opus Dei centers, a priest of Opus Dei, Francisco Fernandez Carvajal, published a seven-volume series between 1986 and 1991 entitled *In Conversation with God*, designed to help people practice mental prayer. The books contain 450 meditations which usually focus on the texts of the Mass for each day. The straightforward style and rich content of the meditations made them popular with Catholics all over the world—from housewives to members of contemplative religious orders. They have been published in nine languages and have sold more than two million copies.[12]

Section 2. Formation of Members of the Work

Under Del Portillo's leadership, Opus Dei continued to focus on making sure that all its members had a firm grasp of the Church's teaching. This would enable them to develop their own interior life based on doctrine rather than exclusively on emotions, carry out a doctrinal apostolate with their colleagues, friends, and relatives, and recognize positions contrary to the Church's teaching when they encountered them in their conversations and reading. One way Opus Dei did this was arranging for all its members to systematically review the Catechism of Pius X with a supplement covering the magisterium of subsequent Popes and of the Second Vatican Council. Part of the Catechism was reviewed each year in the formational courses organized for the members. After its publication in 1992, the *Catechism of the Catholic Church* became the text.[13]

Naturally, doctrinal formation of members was not limited to study of the catechism. The annual workshops for the supernumeraries and associates included classes of philosophy and theology adapted to the educational background of the participants. In regions where the number of members made it feasible, two-year programs of more intensive formation called "Courses of Studies" were arranged for some of the supernumeraries. According to a note sent by the General Council, the first objective of the Courses of Studies was to "give the supernumeraries more solid doctrinal religious formation and a broader and deeper understanding of the spirit of the Work." In addition, the Courses of Studies aimed "to help the participants develop their personal apostolate of friendship and confidence and their spirit of initiative to promote and support apostolic undertakings." The courses were also designed to "give the appropriate preparation to coordinators."[14] To achieve all this, the curriculum included classes of philosophy and theology as well as an in-depth study of the message of Opus Dei.

For numeraries, doctrinal formation included a systematic multi-year study of philosophy and theology. For men, this was structured to meet the requirements for ordination, even though only a small percentage would ever be ordained. Most numeraires received this philosophical and theological training in their own country, but some men went to the Roman College of the Holy Cross and some women to the Roman College of Holy Mary. Virtually all the men who were eventually ordained studied in the Roman College of the Holy Cross.

At the beginning of Del Portillo's tenure, the Roman College of the Holy Cross moved from Villa Tevere, where it had shared space with the General Council for twenty-five years, to a newly constructed campus in the outskirts of Rome called Cavabianca. The new location offered more modern and less crowded residential facilities as well as better classrooms, library, and sports facilities. The move also freed up space in Villa Tevere for the offices of the General Council. Del Portillo followed closely the operations of the Roman College which prepared new groups of priests and directors. Between 1975 and 1994, he called almost eight hundred numeraries to the priesthood. Starting in 1981 smaller numbers of associates were also ordained after having earned an ecclesiastical doctorate.

The Roman College of Holy Mary moved in 1992 from Castelgandolfo to Villa Balestra, located in Rome about half a mile from Villa Tevere. In addition to being larger and more modern than the old one, the new location made it easier for the members of the Central Advisory to visit frequently. It also sharply reduced the commuting time for students who were pursuing advanced degrees in theology at the Pontifical Athenaeum (later University) of the Holy Cross. A few years earlier, in 1989, the International Institute of Educational Sciences had ceased operations because by that time virtually all the women who came to the Roman College of the Holy Cross already had a college degree. This permitted them to focus more intensely on their studies of theology and of the spirit of Opus Dei, preparing them to become directors of Opus Dei and professors in the *Studium Generale* of their region.[15]

In the formation of its members and of the cooperators and other people who attended classes and other means of formation, Opus Dei continued to be concerned about doctrinal confusion in parts of the Church and stressed orthodoxy rather than being up-to-date. In 1978, for instance, the General Council suggested the use of two classic theology textbooks written well before the Second Vatican Council.[16] The Work also discouraged members from reading many contemporary philosophical and theological treatises and articles which it feared defended propositions contrary to the teaching of the Church.*

Opus Dei took seriously *Libertatis nuntius*, the Holy See's 1989 warning against the doctrinal errors contained in the writings of some authors connected with the Theology of Liberation.[17] Del Portillo described the issues raised by Liberation Theology as "something

---

* Among the authors whose works members were required to request permission to read was Joseph Ratzinger. This measure can be traced to the Vatican's reaction to a declaration on the freedom and function of theologians in the Church published in 1969 by 38 theologians, including Ratzinger. When *L'Osservatore Romano* said the declaration was subject to serious reservations, Escrivá decided that as a measure of prudence the members should ask for permission before reading the works of the theologians who signed the declaration. See Nota general 3/69, January 22, 1969. AGP, series E.1.3, 246-1.

Álvaro del Portillo, who was a consultor of the Congregation for the Doctrine of the Faith from 1966 to 1983, felt that it was not yet clear in the 1980s what was valuable and what not in contemporary theology. He, therefore, left these provisions in place for a while both with respect to the *Studia Generale* of the Work and the School of Theology of the University of Navarra. Prolonging the exceptional measures taken by the Founder in the 1960s undoubtedly made it difficult for members of Opus Dei to be in the vanguard in philosophy, theology, and canon law.

An important project during the mid-1970s to mid-1980s was the publication by Magisterio Español of more than sixty books in a collection it called Crítica Filosófica. The books were designed to summarize and evaluate from a Catholic perspective the principal works of modern and contemporary philosophy. The majority of the philosophers and theologians who wrote the studies were members of the Work.

very important which influences the life of society and of people" and urged the regions to carry out a "profound, constant and capillary catechesis" of *Libertatis nuntius,* to combat errors about the nature of redemption and of the Church.[18] He asked that in all the means of formation for members and cooperators of the Work, stress be laid above all on "the primacy of supernatural realities over natural and earthly realities; on the reality of sin and of the Redemption; on the essentially theological nature of Christian life; on the hope for eternal life; on the Christian meaning of suffering; and on the supernatural character of the Church's mission." At the same time, he insisted that Christians must "feel the responsibility of living seriously justice with charity, each one in his place in the world."[19]

As the years went by, Opus Dei's reception of the teaching of John Paul II explaining Catholic doctrine to the contemporary world, the establishment of the Pontifical University of the Holy Cross, and the growing relationship of Opus Dei theologians with other theologians all brought with them increasing reflection on modern authors. A clear sign that the times had changed was the University of Navarra's conferral of an honorary doctorate on Cardinal Ratzinger in 1998.

Part 1. Formation of Numerary Assistants

In many countries during the late 1980s and early '90s, the role of women in society and in the home changed greatly. This change in social structures was one of the factors that led many young women who originally thought they had a vocation as a numerary assistant to change their minds in a few months or years. Clearly a new professional and formative approach to domestic work was needed. Under Del Portillo, the Central Advisory made a major effort to understand in greater depth and explain better the vocation of numerary assistants while improving their formation.

An important part of the formation of numerary assistants took place at the center of studies, a boarding school exclusively for members of the Work. It was usually connected to the Administration of a conference center or a large university residence. The central point of the formation given in the center of studies was the same as that given to any other member of the Work at any stage of their vocation: meeting Christ and developing a profound interior life based on a thorough knowledge of the teaching of the Church and the spirit of Opus Dei. At the same time, they received the technical training necessary to become qualified professionals.

A distinctive feature of the formation of young numerary assistants was coming to understand work in the Administration not just as a job, but as an essential part of the apostolate of Opus Dei—a way of taking care of persons and creating a family atmosphere in the centers where they worked. In the center of studies, they learned to understand that they were not just cooks or cleaners but literally homemakers who put their hearts at the service of others.

Wherever possible, the center of studies tried to obtain recognition of their programs so that the graduates could receive an official certificate or diploma in home or hotel services or catering. This often involved modifying the curriculum to meet official standards as well as lengthy and often tedious negotiations with government or university officials.[20]

During the years of Don Álvaro's tenure, rapid changes in social conditions in many countries required major changes in the curriculum of the center of studies for numerary assistants. As late as the mid-1970s, a significant number of numerary assistants had not finished their primary education when they began at the center of studies. They needed to complete their primary education, something many of them would not have done had they remained in the small villages where their families lived. As the years went by, the general level of education increased in Spain and other countries, and it became unnecessary to offer primary education in the center of studies.[21] In more highly developed countries, the girls who joined Opus Dei as numerary assistants were all at least high school graduates.[22]

Because of the importance of the Administration for the family life of Opus Dei, Escrivá wanted all the numeraries of the women's branch to have some experience working in an Administration. The 1968 plan of studies for numeraries of the women's branch called for them to work part-time in an Administration during the two years of the center of studies and to spend a month and a half working full-time there at the end of the center of studies.[23] In 1989, this was made more flexible.[24] All of the women numeraries were asked to spend "some time" working in the Administration as part of their formation in keeping with the Founder's desires.*

Part 2. Formation of Administrators

Opus Dei needed not only numerary assistants but also women who wanted to direct the work of the Administration as a career while understanding their work as a way of creating a home for the members of both branches of the Work. To carry out their work at a professional level, they needed education in home economics or hotel management not offered in many universities until the mid-to-late 1980s. Therefore, during Del Portillo's tenure, a number of regions began four-year courses for administrators within their *Studium Generale*. This was the case in Argentina (1976), Brazil (1977), Italy (1981), the Philippines (1983), and the United States (1987). The school in Argentina, for example, was called the *Instituto Superior de Administración de Servicios en Hogar e Instituciones*. The professors had earned their doctorates in Mexico, Colombia, and Spain. The four-year course, which included practical sessions, led to a private degree. Each year, five to eight women graduated.

By the late 1980s, it was becoming more common for universities and other institutions to offer degrees in home economics and hotel management. Most of the numeraries of the women's branch, including those who wanted to be Administrators, were university students and could acquire the necessary training at the university. The smaller schools of home economics of the regional *Studium Generale*, therefore, closed in 1989. Some of the more established schools became

---

* In recent years, a growing awareness of the importance for both men and women of a culture of care has led to the numeraries of the men's branch spending more time on housework, taking on some of the tasks previously carried out by the Administration.

part of universities that were corporate works. The *Escuela de Administración de Instituciones* in Mexico City became part of the *Universidad Panamericana*. The *Instituto Femenino de Estudios Superiores* in Guatemala City entered into an agreement with the state-run *Universidad de San Carlos* which enabled it to give officially recognized degrees for thirty years. In 1997 it became affiliated with the newly founded *Universidad del Istmo*. The *Escuela Superior de Administración Montemar* in Lima, Peru, which gave bachelor's degrees, became an *Instituto de Educación Superior* of the University of Piura.

In Spain, the *Centro de Estudios e Investigación de Ciencias Domésticas* (CEICID) moved from Madrid to Pamplona in 1989. The move brought with it a new and much improved approach. Previously, numeraries who wanted to be administrators of Opus Dei centers needed to spend four years in Madrid studying home economics without receiving an officially recognized degree. In Pamplona, they could study for a degree in many different subjects while also taking specialized courses at CEICID on managing and working in the Administration of an Opus Dei center. CEICID itself thus became an institute of studies focused on the professionalization of family life and care for persons.

In other regions, numeraries who wanted to be administrators studied home economics or institutional management in public or private universities. The Work continued to provide the special training needed to be the administrator of a center, such as instruction in how to care for the oratory.[25]

Section 3. Service to the Church

Part 1. Training Priests for the Dioceses

The roots of what is now the Pontifical University of the Holy Cross in Rome can be traced to the ecclesiastical schools of the University of Navarra in Spain. By 1988, the university was offering the full range of ecclesiastical studies required for those preparing for the priesthood.[26] At the express request of Pope John Paul II, Opus Dei created that same year an international seminary, Bidasoa, for seminarians sent by their bishops to study at the University of Navarra.[27]

In 1983 Del Portillo decided that the time had come to lay the first stones of an ecclesiastical university in Rome. Although he knew the project had the full backing of Pope John Paul II, the obstacles were formidable.[28] In addition to finding a building and putting together the faculty, it would be necessary to obtain the formal approval of the Holy See and find students at a time when there were few priestly and religious vocations and when it seemed to many that there was already a surfeit of ecclesiastical universities and schools in Rome.

The problem of a building was solved through an agreement with the Holy See to lease a temporary location. The administrative difficulties were overcome with a transitional formula that treated the nascent institution in Rome as part of the ecclesiastical schools of theology and canon law of the University of Navarra.[29] The Roman Academic Center of the Holy Cross opened for classes in October 1984 with forty students. The Vatican Congregation for Catholic Education approved it as a Pontifical Athenaeum in 1990.[30] That same year it moved to its present site in the fourteenth-century Palazzo dell'Appolinare near Piazza Navona.[31]

Establishing and operating these facilities required large amounts of money, particularly since many of the students came from dioceses in South America, Asia, and Africa that could not afford tuition in Rome. To help meet these needs, in 1989 members and cooperators of Opus Dei founded CARF (*Centro Académico Romano Fundación*).

Opus Dei's contribution to the formation of diocesan priests was not limited to these institutional efforts. At the request of local ordinaries, by1986 some thirty numerary priests of Opus Dei were working as professors and spiritual directors in the seminaries of a number of dioceses.[32]

Part 2. Public Churches

During Don Álvaro's tenure, priests of Opus Dei took responsibility for a number of public churches in different parts of the world. In some ways, the most significant was the parish of *San Eugenio a Valle Giulia* located a little less than one kilometer away from Opus

Dei's Rome headquarters. The church had been completed in 1951 with funds collected from Catholics throughout the world to commemorate the twenty-fifth anniversary of the ordination of Pope Pius XII as a bishop. It was entrusted to the priests of Opus Dei in 1981, and quickly became the preferred location for major liturgical ceremonies connected with Opus Dei such as ordinations and memorial Masses for the Founder. It would be the site for Don Álvaro's funeral in 1994.[33]

On the occasion of Escrivá's beatification, Opus Dei undertook to build a parish in the outskirts of Rome whose patron saint would be the Founder. Construction of the parish of Blessed (later St.) Josemaría Escrivá began in 1994 and was completed in 1996.[34]

The parish of St. Mary of the Angels in Chicago, Illinois, had begun in the early twentieth century as an ethnic Polish parish, but gradually many of the Polish parishioners had moved away and the mammoth church, which seats almost twice as many people as Chicago's Catholic cathedral, had fallen into serious disrepair. In 1988, the Archdiocese of Chicago decided to demolish the church, which had become unsafe. In the face of protests, Cardinal Bernardin asked Opus Dei to take over the parish. Thanks to an energetic fundraising effort, the church was fully restored by 1999. Over the years, Latin American immigrants and young professionals have moved into the neighborhood, and the parish has become a multicultural and multiethnic community with Masses in English, Spanish, and Polish.[35]

Several other churches were entrusted to priests of Opus Dei during Del Portillo's tenure: the parish of St. Pantaleon in Cologne, Germany; the parish of St. Ambrose in Montreal, Canada; the Church of Our Lady of Peace in Guatemala City, Guatemala; and the Church of the Holy Family of Nazareth in Caracas, Venezuela. Each of the churches entrusted to priests of Opus Dei developed its own parochial groups and ministries as well as supporting devotions popular in the area. In addition, they offered days of recollection directed by priests of Opus Dei and became known as places where it was easy to find a confessor.

Notes

1. See, e.g., Josemaría Escrivá, interview in *ABC*, Madrid, March 24, 1971. See also Escrivá, *Christ is Passing By* (New York: Scepter, 2002), n. 149.

2. Note 3713/91. AGP K1, 2454.

3. See Committee on Evangelization and Catechesis of the United States Conference of Catholic Bishops, *Disciples Called to Witness, Part II. Historical Context of the New Evangelization. https://www.usccb.org/beliefs-and-teachings/how-we-teach/new-evangelization/disciples-called-to-witness/disciples-called-to-witness-part-ii*. Last consulted, October 28, 2020.

4. John Paul II, "*Discorso ai Partecipanti al VI Simposio Del Consiglio delle Conferenze Episcopali d'Europa*," October 11, 1985. *https://www.vatican.va/content/john-paul-i/it/speeches/1985/october/documents/hf_jp-ii_spe_19851011_partecipanti-simposio.html*. Last consulted April 23, 2020.

5. Álvaro del Portillo, Pastoral Letter, 25-XII-1985. AGP Library, P.17.

6. Report entitled "*Labor recristianización Europa: informes de las asr y estudio Asesoría Central 1987 (después de cve 1986)*." AGP R1.1.3, 32 2.

7. "*Resumen del acta de la comisión de servicio a España*," 4-II-1989. AGP E.2.1.

8. Note 15/80, n. 3. AGP E. 1.3, 1138.

9. Note 15/80.

10. Regional note 139/82 and background information. AGP E1.31138.

11. AGP R 1.1.3, 2-32.

12. See Francisco Fernández Carvajal, *Hablar con Dios*, 7 vols., 26th ed., (Madrid: Palabra, 2017).

13. General Note 12/92. AGP E1.3, 1146.

14. Note 138/76. AGP E 1.3, 1137.

15. 4817/89. AGP R 42.2, 7-58.

16. Note 118/78. AGP E 1.3, 1137.

17. Congregation for the Doctrine of the Faith, *Libertatis Nuntius, Instruction on Certain Aspects of the "Theology of Liberation."* (1984). *www.vatican.va/./congregations/cfaith/documents/rc_con_cfaith_doc_19840806_theology-liberation_sp.html - 73k- 1984-08-06*. (Last consulted July 17, 2020).

18. Note 160/84. AGP E 1 3,1137.

19. Note 140/84. AGP E 1 3, 1137.

20. See, e.g., the experience of Montemar in Peru. PF 209/79. AGP L. 4.5.

21. HF 86/81. AGP R 6.2.2, 8-01. HF 517/84, R 6.2.2, 4-28.

22. Ample information for the year 1985 in AGP R 4.5, 38-2. See also Euf 196/79. AGP R 6.2.2, 4-28.

23. See AGP series R. 6.2.2, 3-21.

24. *Consulta de la Asesoría Central*, 10-X-1989, in AGP series R. 4.2.4, 2-20.

25. Note 162/89. AGP R. 42.4, 20-2.

26. *http://www.unav.edu/web/facultad-eclesiastica-de-filosofia/origen-desarrollo-y-fines*. Last consulted, July 17, 2020.

27. *http://www.ceibidasoa.org/01/espanol-quien-somos/*. Last visited April 20, 2018.

28. Medina Bayo, pp. 543–544.

29. The Congregation for Catholic Education approved this arrangement with a decree dated January 8, 1985 but effective October 15, 1984. General Note 111/85. AGP E 1.3 1139.

30. General Note 101/90. AGP E 1.33, 1145.

31. Antonio Miralles, "*Il germe di una nuova istituzione universitaria*," in *Pontifica Università della Santa Croce. Dono e Compito: 25 anni di attività* (Milan: Silvana, 2010), pp. 40–47.

32. AGP I.4, 3116.

33. *https://www.parrocchiasanteugenio.it/storia/*. Last consulted August 27, 2020.

34. AGP G1.5, 3237.

35. *https://en.wikipedia.org/wiki/St._Mary_of_the_Angels_(Chicago)*. Last consulted April 20, 2020.

CHAPTER 10

～∽

Apostolic Activities

pus Dei, as we have seen, exists to spread a Christian message. Each member and cooperator of the Work is invited to try to be holy and a witness to Christ in his work and other ordinary occupations. This goal is permanent because evangelization through the example of professional life will always be necessary, although it is as varied as the personal circumstances of each person.

The institutional activities of the Work are concrete ways in which some of its members transmit gospel values and the spirit of Opus Dei. They contribute to continuity in the apostolate across time and make it possible to bring together the efforts of many people. Any given collective activity begins, develops, and terminates to the extent that it contributes to the diffusion of Christian truth and can be sustained economically.*

All the Work's collective undertakings share certain essential characteristics. They have a Christian and apostolic identity which is reflected in their vision and mission. The members who work in them try to incarnate that spirit in their personal lives and spread it. They are "civil and professional, not confessional [in] character."[1] They involve education, social assistance, charity, or health. The not-for-profit entities that own and run them are responsible for their technical legal and economic aspects and name their officers. They "use the goods and resources derived from their activities [for instance,

---

* This chapter describes only a small number of corporate activities, mostly ones that are of special interest because of where they carry out their activities or because of their degree of development. Further information on corporate activities is found in chapters 3 and 15.

from tuition] and other civil resources that they have obtained or can obtain [for instance, from grants and donations]."[2] At the petition of the directors, the Prelature of Opus Dei names the religion professors and the chaplains who provide pastoral assistance to these activities.

After establishing the common characteristics of all institutional activities, the Statutes of the Prelature distinguish between two types of institutional activities: "corporate works," which are also referred to as "works of corporate apostolate," and "personal works."

Corporate works, in the words of the statutes, are "undertakings promoted by Opus Dei as such,"[3] in the sense that the directors of the Work identify a particular social or educational need in the community, encourage some members to create an institution that will help meet that need, and provide spiritual attention to the people involved and to the institution they start. They are "founded and directed by members of the Work together with other people. Opus Dei as such, corporately takes official responsibility for their doctrinal and spiritual orientation."[4] Opus Dei is responsible for animating them with a Christian spirit through suitable doctrinal and spiritual orientation, as well as for appropriate pastoral assistance, with full respect for the legitimate freedom of the consciences of the students, the residents, and all other involved parties."[5]

In some cases, the primary goal of the corporate apostolate is to contribute to the wellbeing of disadvantaged members of the society. Even where this is not the case, the directors of the Work take steps to make sure that every corporate apostolate contributes in a significant way to the "human, cultural, and social advancement"[6] of underprivileged members of the communities in which it operates.

When necessary, the directors of Opus Dei channel the financial contributions of members of the Work to these activities. The people of the Work who are directors or trustees of the corporations that carry out the activities attempt to guarantee continuity in their apostolic goals. When they retire, they try to see to it that they are replaced by another member of Opus Dei or a cooperator.

In the case of schools that are corporate works, Opus Dei creates a center and names a local council made up of at least three numeraries.

This local council takes responsibility for the doctrinal and formational activities of the school. Until 2000, the directors of the Work asked the not-for-profit entities that owned and operated the schools to name the members of the local council to the principal leadership positions of the school. In this way, the members of the local council became responsible for the "overall governance of the corporate work." They played a role in "all the management" of the school and "were responsible to the regional commission or delegation for its management."[7] Although the reason why the directors of the Work were interested in a school was its apostolic and formative activities, this practice made it difficult for them not to intervene in other areas of the school's life, especially if they had an impact on its doctrinal and formational activities. Their authority to name the local council gave them indirect authority to name the school's headmaster and other principal managers and a degree of influence over the life of the institution that exceeded what was foreseen in the Statutes of the Prelature.[*]

Opus Dei refers to the second type of institutional activities as "personal apostolates." According to the statutes, the members of the Work and other people who promote them "ask Opus Dei for spiritual help."[8] Their directors take responsibility for the Christian character of their teaching and ask the local bishop for permission to have an oratory. They sign an agreement with the Prelature's vicars to appoint chaplains and in the case of schools, religion teachers. Opus Dei offers orientation and, pastoral assistance and assures that the chaplains and religion teachers follow Church teaching. It does not, however, "direct or govern these undertakings and does not take responsibility for them," other than for the Christian teaching given by the chaplains and religion teachers.[9]

Opus Dei does not own the corporate or personal apostolates and neither the regional vicar nor his councils play a role in their day-to-day operations.

---

[*] As we will see in chapter 15, this practice changed by 2000. Today those who run corporate activities are not always numeraries, and if they are, they are not necessarily members of the local council that coordinates apostolic activities.

Seen from the outside, say by a couple looking for a school for their son or daughter, the difference between a school that is a corporate work and one that is a personal work normally does not seem very important. Probably most people think of both as institutions that offer high quality education with a Catholic character because they are associated with Opus Dei.

Section 1 Educational Activities

Part 1. Higher Education

At the death of the Founder, there were two universities that were corporate activities of Opus Dei: the University of Navarra in Pamplona, Spain, with satellite campuses in Barcelona and San Sebastian, and the University of Piura in Piura, Peru, some six hundred miles north of Lima.[10] In addition, there was a women's college known as the *Instituto Femenino de Estudios Superiores* in Guatemala. Founded in 1964, it eventually came to offer a bachelor's degree in interior design, a degree in hospitality, and various other certificate and diploma programs. Men were admitted only to its culinary arts program. In 1991 it merged into what would become six years later the *Universidad del Istmo,* with headquarters in Guatemala City.[11]

During Del Portillo's tenure, the University of Navarra grew rapidly. The faculty doubled in size from 700 to almost 1,600. The number of undergraduate students went from 9,000 to 11,500 and the number of graduate students from 1,300 to 2,900. The university hospital more than doubled its number of beds from 225 to 475. The annual number of patient visits in the hospital and the outpatient clinics grew from 40,000 to 89,000.

Under Del Portillo's leadership, Opus Dei started five new universities. In some cases, these instituions began offering courses in a specialized area like business administration and gradually added new areas of instruction until they reached a level at which they could be called a university. In others, they started as universities, albeit small. The path followed varied from place to place and depended on local needs and resources and on the legislative framework in the country.

In 1978, *Universidad Panamericana* was founded in Mexico City, building on the foundation of a business school (IPADE) that had been started in 1967 and an institute of humanities begun in 1968.[12] In Bogotá, Colombia, the nucleus for what would become in 1979 the University of the Sabana was an institute of education which had begun in 1971.[13] By contrast, the University of the Andes, in Santiago, Chile, opened as a university in 1989,[14] as did the Austral University in Buenos Aires, Argentina, which opened its doors in 1991, although the Institute of Higher Business Studies had been offering classes since 1978.[15]

The roots of today's *Università Campus Bio-Medico di Roma* lie in a suggestion Del Portillo made in 1988, that a group of doctors in Rome investigate the possibility of establishing a medical school and university hospital. The project was challenging both because of the human and financial resources needed for a medical school and hospital and because of a virtual state monopoly of higher education in Italy.[16] In 1990, a group of doctors, many of whom were members of Opus Dei, established two not-for-profit entities to support the project, and in 1993 the medical school and the school of nursing opened their doors. A year later, a nascent university hospital began admitting patients.[17]

In the Philippines, two young economists who had recently earned PhDs at Harvard started a think tank for applied research in economics and statistics in 1967. At first, the Center for Research and Communication (CRC) largely did research for Philippine businesses, but it soon began to offer graduate level classes in economics and a master's degree in industrial economics. In 1989 it added a college of arts and sciences and in 1993 a school of economics.[18]

Part 2. Primary and Secondary Education

During the two decades in which Del Portillo headed Opus Dei, members continued to work with other interested parents to found and expand grade schools and high schools. The General Council summarized the goals of these schools as "giving the students an integral education with a Christian inspiration, and a solid doctrinal and spiritual formation, as well as trying to see to it that as many parents, professors, and students as possible come to know the basic spirit of the Work."[19] In many cases, they began small, offering only one or two primary grades, and added a new grade each year until they finally had a full high school.

Some drew their students primarily from working-class families. The *Ciudad de los Niños* in Monterrery, Mexico, switched in 1986 from being an orphanage to being an educational center. It eventually developed four schools, a center for family formation, and a clinic. Some 1,200 working-class students are enrolled in its grade school, high school, and technical school.[20]

Other schools catered to the upper middle class and upper class. Some of them had a day section for students from comparatively well-to-do families and an evening section for students who had to work during the day.[21]

The financial arrangements of the schools varied greatly from country to country and even within a specific country. Some received significant governmental aid both for construction and operation. The generous support the Spanish government provided to groups interested in establishing and running private schools made possible the rapid growth of a network of schools started by parents connected with Opus Dei and their friends. In other countries like the United States, by contrast, private schools received virtually no government assistance.

A common arrangement was to establish a corporation or limited partnership whose owners were some of the parents of students currently enrolled in the school. In schools that adopted this system, parents purchased shares when they enrolled their children and were able to sell the shares back to the entity or to new parents when their children left the school. In addition, they paid tuition which was often capped when they had three or more children in the school.[22]

Most schools related to Opus Dei are personal works; a few are corporate apostolates of Opus Dei. For corporate works, in addition to naming a chaplain, the regional commission, as we have seen, also names a local council made up of numerary members. They are responsible for the doctrinal and apostolic aspects of the schools. The principal or headmaster and other key administrators who are in charge of all aspects of the life of the school are appointed not by the regional commission or advisory, but by the corporation which runs the school. It was understood for many years, however, that they would be chosen from among the numeraries selected by the regional commission or advisory to serve on the local council. The local council reports to the regional commission on the apostolic and formational aspects of the school, but its individual members in their capacities as the principal administrators of the school are responsible for all facets of its life.[23]

Schools which are corporate works often have nearby or attached to them a center of Opus Dei which serves as a residence for some of the members of the Work who teach there. In both corporate and personal work schools, an effort is made to have a significant number of members of Opus Dei among the teachers. In Spain in 1978, for instance, members of the Work averaged around 45 percent of the faculty in corporate works and around 35 percent in personal works.[24]

All the schools to which Opus Dei provided chaplains, whether corporate works or personal works, shared three characteristics. They were single sex; they strove to have a high degree of parent involvement; and they used personal mentoring as a way of helping the students to develop in all aspects of their lives.

The schools explain their choice of a single-sex education in terms of the developmental differences of boys and girls and their different needs.[25] The choice may also have something to do with the separation between the two sections of Opus Dei, which would be impossible to maintain among the members of a close-knit school faculty.

The Catholic Church has long taught that "parents have the first responsibility for the education of their children"[26] Consequently, St. Josemaría stressed that parents were the most important components in the life of a school. In a study carried out for the European Parents' Association, a Scottish professor of education examined the role of parents in fourteen personal work schools in Italy. He found that each of the schools was created in response to local parent demand and through parent action. The schools all placed "parents at the center of a practical scheme of parent-teacher cooperation."[27] He found an "interweaving of active family participation in education with school-based education," and "a capacity to achieve a high degree of professional autonomy for teachers in their presentation of formal classwork, despite emphasis on parental contributions to education in a broader sense and parental influence on school management."[28] The schools offered "educational training for parents (and for teachers)."[29]

In Spain and Italy, professional educators who belonged to Opus Dei formed not-for-profit corporations that offered advice and guidance to groups of parents interested in starting schools. In some cases, these corporations directly ran the schools, hiring principals and teachers, choosing textbooks, and designing curriculum. Even in these cases, however, parents played a large role in the life of the school and were central to its operations.[30]

A final feature of the schools connected to Opus Dei is their emphasis on one-on-one mentoring as a way of helping the students not only learn academic subjects but also develop their character. The Heights School, outside Washington, DC, for instance, relies on mentors to bring together all the different aspects of the school's programs—academic, athletic, spiritual—into one single conversation. Mentoring is intended to help each student reach his or her full potential both in academic endeavors and in personal growth as a human being. Mentoring is intended to complement the training the students receive from their parents.[31]

In many cases, the mentors are teachers who have the students in class. They try to get to know the students well and become genuine friends with them. In addition to mentoring, the school chaplains offer personal spiritual guidance to students who want it.

Both corporate and personal works are urged to organize courses, talks, and conferences for teachers. Faculty members are are urged to reach out to their colleagues in other schools, and some schools offer seminars and other training courses for teachers.[32]

In many cases, Opus Dei also has a St. Raphael center near the school. These centers have an oratory and a study room that help to create an environment of serious study. They provide high school students supplementary educational and recreational activities, usually including sports. They offer the traditional means of Opus Dei's St. Raphael Work with young people: formational classes in interior life called circles, guided meditations led by the chaplain, days of recollection and retreats, and personal spiritual guidance with a priest of Opus Dei.

These centers are often organized as a club which charges members modest dues. They usually have a division for younger students who come to the club for recreational and formative activities and to study a few times a week. The older students are encouraged to come frequently after class to study and participate in activities. Like the schools connected with Opus Dei, the clubs have mentors whose responsibilities are very similar to those at the schools. The directors of the Work stress the fact that in the clubs the mentors need to deal with the students one-on-one and really get to know them personally. Many centers also offer formative activities for the parents of the students.[33]

Helping parents to found and run schools involved a significant commitment of personnel. In Spain in the late 1970s, approximately four hundred members of Opus Dei taught in schools for boys that were either corporate apostolates of Opus Dei or personal works founded and directed by members.[34] It seems safe to assume that a similar number of members taught in schools for girls connected to Opus Dei. In Mexico in the mid-1980s, 18 percent of the numeraries and 25 percent of the associates worked in corporate apostolates or personal works which were primarily schools of various types.[35]

Some supernumerary members and cooperators sent their children to corporate or personal work schools, but many others sent them to public schools or to private schools unrelated to Opus Dei. The Work urged them to play an active role in the lives of those schools, participating in parent-teacher organizations and other similar groups. It suggested that by working with other parents they might be able to influence the selection of textbooks and teachers, especially for religion in schools where religion was taught. Opus Dei also urged parents to be attentive to subjects like history, literature, and social studies, which could be as important as religion in shaping the students' outlook on life.[36]

Some supernumeraries and cooperators whose children were in schools where religion was not taught at all or taught inadequately tried to play an active role in the school's parent-teacher associations to influence the teaching of religion. Some of them also organized catechism classes at home for their own children and their friends. In Spain in 1981, members of the women's branch had organized many such catechism classes with a total of almost eight thousand students.[37] In New York City, a supernumerary began the Narnia Clubs (now known as Adeo Clubs), a home-based program of religious instruction for Catholic students attending non-Catholic schools.[38]

During the 1930s and, 40s, Opus Dei's apostolic activities focused largely on college students. In the 1950s, it expanded both to married people and to high school students. During the 1960s and, 70s, apostolic activities with high school students grew to the point that it became necessary for the directors to stress the importance of apostolate with college students.[39]

Section 2. Social Works

Del Portillo frequently pointed out that social problems were questions of justice, not only of charity. He stressed that a materialistic and hedonistic vision of life which lacked sympathy for the poor often exacerbated social differences. In 1990, he reminded the members of the Work that "being sensitive to social problems is an integral part of our spirit." Everyone shares in the responsibility of building up the social order and is called to play an active role. "No one can be indifferent in the face of the material and human needs of their neighbor, the situations of misery, ignorance and suffering which are often the product of injustices." "We must all do what we can to remedy these evils."[40]

In the formation of its members and of cooperators and other people who attended its activities, Opus Dei stresses the social doctrine of the Church. A note sent from the General Council to all the regional commissions in 1985, for instance, underlined the need to "spread and teach the social doctrine of the Church."[41] It urged the members to insist on the "serious obligation which all Christians have not only to live justice and charity faithfully in our personal activities and relations with others, but also to try to make political, social, economic and professional structures just and in conformity with the dignity of each human person."[42] In a 1990 Pastoral Letter, Del Portillo urged the members to do everything they could

> to make the principles of Catholic Social Doctrine known and practiced. We must respect everyone's opinion in matters that are open to debate but also do what we can to avoid freedom's being used as a pretext for avoiding doing what they can to contribute to the solution of many unjust situations.[43]

The most important result of these efforts may well be the greater social consciousness of people working in businesses throughout the world, but it is impossible to measure or even document the ways in which this contributes to a more just society. During Del Portillo's tenure as the head of Opus Dei, many members of the Work started or expanded a variety of institutions to help people in need, the majority of which continue today. Most are schools of various sorts designed to prepare young people from impoverished backgrounds to find jobs and earn a good living. Even in countries where it was difficult to obtain government approval of private schools, almost all of them eventually obtained government recognition of the diplomas and certificates they give their students.

Kinal began in 1961 in a small, rented house in an extremely poor area on the outskirts of Guatemala City. By 1994 it was providing high school education combined with technical training in fields like graphic arts, welding, and bricklaying to almost eight hundred students. In addition, it was providing technical training courses to close to 1,500 adults. It also had developed a consulting service for small businesses, and a clinic which offered medical and dental care.[44]

The Dualtech Training Center in Manila, established in 1982, introduced to the Philippines the Dual Training System, a German model of technical education in which students alternate between theoretical classes and practice at companies which partner with the school. By 1993 it had more than three hundred students, almost all from poor families. Its graduates find employment as shop floor leaders, often at the companies where they had done their practical training.[45]

In the impoverished area around the town of Jonacatepec in the state of Morelos south of Mexico City, members of Opus Dei worked with local leaders and other people to begin courses on agricultural and livestock techniques in the 1960s. In 1973, working with a government agency, they added a televised secondary school. Building on these foundations, they opened El Peñón Agricultural and Livestock High School for boys and Colegio Montefalco for girls in 1984. The schools offered a high school education to the sons and daughters of the farmers in the area. Despite the poverty-stricken background of the students, in recent national exams El Peñón had the best results in mathematics of any school in its state. Only 6 percent of students in Mexico scored excellent in mathematics, but 44 percent of the young women from Colegio Montefalco did so. Ninety-five percent of the young women who graduated from Colegio Montefalco in a recent year went on to university: 33 percent in biological and health sciences and 21 percent in physical sciences, engineering, and math.[46]

In Chile, Las Garzas offers a free technical high school education which prepares the students to work as agricultural technicians. In 1980, the school had more than one hundred fifty applicants for forty places. More than 80 percent of the students already had a job when they graduated. In an outreach program, the physical education teacher at the school began offering sports training to students from the public primary schools in the area.[47]

Members of Opus Dei tried to help indigenous Peruvian subsistence farmers who lived in the territory of the Prelature of Yauyos improve their lives. Valle Grande, a corporate apostolic activity of Opus Dei, worked primarily with adults, many of whom cultivated small plots of land on steep hillsides located high up in the Andes. It offered instruction in simple, practical agricultural techniques that gave immediate visible results. In 1977, its various programs for adults reached some 2,500 people. In addition, it sponsored a youth club for boys between ten and fifteen years of age with training in sports, sports theory, and sports medicine. Condoray, a women's center for professional and technical training, offered a wide range of classes for peasants, employees, and students in higher education.[48]

Building on the experience with family agricultural schools in Spain, members of Opus Dei in Argentina established a number of *Centros de Formación Rural*. By 1987, there were three schools for boys and one for girls with a total of some 225 students and 25 teachers. The Argentine government recognized their courses as equivalent to the first three years of high school and consequently began to provide financial assistance. In addition, members of the Work established a school that offered the last two years of high school to graduates of the lower-level schools. For ongoing education of adults, they formed twelve *Centros de Estudios Técnicos Agrícolas*, groups of eight to ten graduates of the schools who met with an agricultural engineer to explore topics of immediate interest using the case method. The nonprofit organized to run the schools, the Pedro Antonio Marzano Foundation, organized monthly pedagogical meetings in Buenos Aires and annual two-week courses on educational methods for faculty members. It participated actively in the *Association Internationale de Maisons Familiales Rurales*.[49]

In many parts of the world, women members of Opus Dei ran schools of hospitality, catering, and home economics. Their activities varied according to the social conditions of the countries in which they were located. Kibondeni School of Management in Nairobi, Kenya, offered a program of hospitality and catering to girls from poor families who would not otherwise have been able to finish high school. The school aimed "primarily at improving the standards of living of young women from low-income families equipping them with the knowledge, skills, and attitudes to enable them to secure employment to meet their needs and those of their families and make them self-reliant."[50] Demand was so high in the mid-1980s that Kibondeni received six hundred applications for twenty places.

Although schools of various sorts for economically disadvantaged groups were the most common social activities sponsored by members of Opus Dei, there were many others. Responding to Don Álvaro's urging to reach out more decisively to the poor and the marginalized, members of the Work in Spain set up several foundations to sponsor a wide variety of social undertakings.[51] *Cooperación Social* began tutoring and mentoring for students with academic difficulties. Gradually it expanded into supporting development projects in underdeveloped countries, humanitarian aid in the case of natural disasters, as well as the promotion of volunteer activities and training of volunteers.[52] *Cooperación Internacional* focused its attention on college students, offering them training in social services and opportunities to volunteer both in Spain and in other countries.[53] The *Fundación Promoción Social de la Cultura* began in 1987 and has grown considerably. Today, it sponsors programs in the Middle East focusing on the role and status of women, the availability of clean water, and social development. It partners with local groups in Africa, South America, and India and currently receives financial assistance from a wide range of groups including the European Commission, Google, and many financial institutions.[54]

By 1991, Opus Dei had been carrying on apostolic activities in Zaire (later renamed Democratic Republic of the Congo) for a decade. The country under the rule of Mobutu was suffering a prolonged economic crisis and ranked close to the bottom of the United Nations Human Development Index. In Kinshasa, the largest city in the country, unemployment reached 80 percent and poverty was rampant. Pillaging by soldiers who had not been paid was common. The people who lived in the Mont-Ngafula neighborhood, one of the poorest in Kishasa, desperately needed medical care.

The situation might have seemed literally hopeless, but a handful of physicians and other medical personnel associated with Opus Dei decided to do what they could. They started an outpatient clinic they called Monkole, with a facility for outpatient surgery and three observation beds. Realizing that malnutrition lay at the root of many maladies, they began asking every patient when he or she had last eaten and provided food. Although the beginnings were modest, its founders were determined to do something much bigger and to provide high quality health care to their patients regardless of their economic situation. After Del Portillo's death, Monkole grew into an important hospital center.[55]

Toshi, located about 120 miles from Mexico City, opened its doors in 1959 when doctors and nurses from the capital began to offer their services to the impoverished indigenous population on Sundays. Like the staff of Monkole, they soon realized that many of the medical problems they were seeing were caused by malnutrition, so they began distributing food. Toshi has not experienced the dramatic growth of Monkole, but more than fifty years later its services have expanded to include dentistry, pediatrics, endocrinology, ophthalmology, dermatology, gynecology, optometry, and family medicine. Several nursing students from the Pan-American University fulfill their social service requirement each year by participating in Toshi's health care programs and by giving health education classes in the local schools. Additionally, a new medical unit is now under construction, where medical graduates will be able to carry out residency programs. Volunteers also offer classes to help local residents develop job skills that will make it possible for them to obtain better-paying jobs.[56]

Junkabal is located on the edge of a huge municipal dump in Guatemala, and many of the families it serves scratch out a living combing through the trash for items they can use or sell. Junkabal offers training in dressmaking and other trades for adult women as well as primary and secondary education for girls. In addition, Junkabal has a medical dispensary that offers basic medical services and medication and distributes milk to needy families. In the mid-1980s, some two thousand people benefited from its programs.[57]

Notes

1. *Codex iuris particularis Operis Dei*, 1982, n. 121, § 1.

2. *Codex iuris particularis Operis Dei*, n. 122.

3. *Codex iuris particularis Operis Dei*, n. 121, § 2. Ordinarily, the regional vicar informs the local bishop before making the appointments.

4. General Note 100/80. AGP E.1.3.

5. *Codex iuris particularis*, n. 123.

6. Josemaría Escrivá de Balaguer, *Conversations with Monsignor Escrivá de Balaguer* (New York: Scepter, 2002), n. 119.

7. General Note 5/86. AGP G4.4.2, 2612.

8. *Codex iuris particularis*, n. 121, § 2.

9. H 544/76. AGP K. 1, 614.

10. *http://udep.edu.pe/conocedlaudep/*. Las consulted July 19, 2020.

11. *https//unis.edu.gt/en/identidad*. Last consulted July 29, 2020.

12. *http://www.up.edu.mx/en/about*. Last consulted August 21, 2020.

13. *https://www.unisabana.edu.co/nosotros/nosotros/historia/*. Last consulted August 21, 2020.

14. *https://www.uandes.cl/la-uandes/historia/*. Last consulted October 15, 2020.

15. *http://www.austral.edu.ar/la-universidad/historia/*. Last consulted August 21, 2020.

16. Henry Hansmann, *The State and the Market in Higher Education*, law.yale.edu/system/files/documents/pdf/Faculty/Hansmann_The_State_and_the_Market_in_Higher_Education.pdf. Last consulted July 7, 2018.

17. *https://www.unicampus.it/ateneo/mission-e-storia*. Last consulted August 21, 2020.

18. *https://en.wikipedia.org/wiki/University_of_Asia_and_the_Pacific#History*. Last consulted August 21, 2020.

19. Note 156/85. AGP E 1.3, 1139.

20. *https://ciudaddelosninos.edu.mx/quienes-somos/*. Last consulted August 12, 2020.

21. This was the case, for instance, in Gaztalueta, the first school started by members of Opus Dei in Spain. *https://www.gaztelueta.com/es/nosotros*. Last consulted August 21, 2020.

22. Report entitled "*Algunas experiencias de colegios en Chile.*" AGP G 4.4.2, 2612.

23. General Note 5/86. AGP G 4.4.2, 2612.

24. General Note 156/85, Appendix. AGP G 3.2.3, 3152. H 2002/78 Table II. AGP G 3.2.3, 3152.

25. See, e.g., Victor García Hoz, *"El debate sobre la coeducación,"* Aceprensa, November 8, 1995. *https://www.aceprensa.com/educacion/el-debate-sobre-la-coeducaci-n/.* The author was a well-known professor of education and one of the founders of *Fomento de centros de enseñanza.* Last consulted April 19, 2022.

26. *Catechism of the Catholic Church,* n. 2223.

27. Alastair Macbeth, *FAES: A Parent-Teacher Educational Structure* (Brussels: European Parents' Association, 1991), p. 4. A copy in AGP G 4.4.3, 1547 (FAES was the not-for-profit corporation that oversaw personal work schools in Italy.)

28. Macbeth, pp. 4–5.

29. Macbeth, p. 6.

30. The entity in Spain was called *Fomento de centros de enseñanza.* The Italian entity was called FAES.

31. *https://heights.edu/mentoring/.* Last consulted April 15, 2020.

32. General Note 134/80. AGP E 1.3 1138.

33. General Note 77/77, Attachment. AGP E 1.3, 11137.

34. H 2002/78, Table I. AGP G3.2.3, 3152. This number does not include priests of Opus Dei who served as chaplains nor other members who were administrators.

35. Report from members of a Service Commission to the Region of Mexico, November 1985, Appendix XXI. AGP G 4.4.3, 1977.

36. General Note 134/80. AGP E 1.3, 1138.

37. HF 2092/81. AGP R 2.4.2, 1-1.

38. *www.adeoclubs.org.* Last consulted October 28, 2020.

39. See, e.g., Notes 109/78 and 154/79. AGP E 1.3, 1137.

40. General Note 119/90. AGP E 1.3, 1145.

41. General Note 120/85. AGP E 1.3, 1137.

42. General Note 120/85. AGP E 1.3, 1137.

43. Álvaro del Portillo, Pastoral Letter, August 1, 1990. AGP Biblioteca, P. 17.

44. *http://opusdei.org/es-gt/article/kinal-un-centro-educativo-tecnico-y-laboral-en-guatemala/.* Last consulted July 20, 2020.

45. *http://www.dualtech.org.ph/*. Last consulted April 19, 2022.

46. *http://www.colegiomontefalco.edu.mx*. Last consulted August 22, 2020. *https://colegiomontefalco.edu.mx/wp-content/uploads/2019/12/Informe-Anual-Montefalco-2016-web.pdf*. Last consulted August 22, 2020.

47. Ch 73/80. AGP G 4.4.3 1547.

48. Material in AGP G 4.4.3, 2674 and R 4.5, 2-38.

49. Arg 210/87 and Note 7298/87. AGP G 4.4.3, 2674.

50. *http://kibondeni.ac.ke/*. Last consulted July 9, 2018.

51. *https://ciong.org*. Last consulted March 17, 2020.

52. *https://www.cooperacionsocial.org*. Lasted consulted March 17, 2020.

53. *https://ciong.org*. Last consulted March 17, 2020.

54. *https://promocionsocial.org*. Last consulted March 18, 2020.

55. *http://monkole.cd/*. Last consulted March18, 2020.

56. *https://opusdei.org/en-us/article/a-medical-clinic-in-mexico/*. Last consulted July 9, 2018.

57. *http://junkabal.edu.gt/*. Last consulted April 20, 2020. Amcf 65/85 appendix. AGP R 4.5, 28, 02.

CHAPTER 11

~

Public Opinion

As a follow-up to the 1984 General Congress, the General Council urged the regions to pay particular attention to the apostolate of public opinion, including encouraging the faithful of the Prelature to consider working professionally in the media and taking special care of the formation of media professionals to make their work more apostolically effective. The General Council also suggested that members and cooperators who were not media professionals could consider writing letters to the editor and articles about topics connected with their professions. They could also get to know journalists, publishers, bookstore owners, and other media professionals and carry out with them an apostolate based on authentic friendship.

The information offices of Opus Dei in the various regions gradually acquired more experience and professionalism. In some regions, the regional advisory developed a separate office of communications staffed by women. The offices worked to spread the teachings of the Pope and make the Founder and his writings and teachings known. They provided information to the central office of the apostolate of public opinion in Rome to be used in writing *SIDEC*, a bulletin with articles about topics of general interest that had some doctrinal relevance. In 1987, the central office began sending to the regions a bulletin entitled *Documentación,* made up of clippings from the international press about the Church, the Pope, and the Work and its apostolic activities, especially its efforts to contribute to social development.[1]

During the two decades that Del Portillo directed Opus Dei, many new people came to know about it through their participation in activities organized by its centers and by personal contact with members who were their friends, neighbors, relatives, or colleagues. Many others learned about it through newspaper and magazine articles and radio and television programs about the Founder and his beatification, about Opus Dei's becoming a personal prelature, or about local apostolic activities. Some people became aware of Opus Dei because the director of the Vatican Press Office from 1984 to 2006, Joaquín Navarro-Vals, was a member.

The global Catholic television and radio network EWTN frequently broadcast information about Opus Dei. The state-owned Italian television network showed programs produced by Alberto Michellini, a well-known Italian documentary maker, in primetime slots. Information about activities in the area of social promotion carried out by centers of Opus Dei began to appear more frequently in the media. During the period 1984–2006, Joaquín Navarro-Valls was quoted frequently by the media in his capacity as director of the Holy See's press office. From time to time the fact that he was a numerary member of the Work was discussed.

In quite a few countries, including those like Mexico and the Philippines where Opus Dei had a significant presence, this type of information was dominant and created a positive overall image of Opus Dei among those who knew something about it. Even in those countries, however, many people knew little or nothing about the Work. In countries where Opus Dei's presence was still small, the media largely ignored it. This was true especially in countries like the United States and Canada, where local general circulation newspapers were not interested in publishing articles about the Founder or the activities of Opus Dei's centers.

In some European countries, the media was highly polarized and some socialist, communist, or sensationalist organs of public opinion were openly hostile toward the Catholic Church and the Pope. Not surprisingly, these publications criticized Opus Dei, especially in the final years leading up to Opus Dei's transformation into a personal prelature and in the months preceding the Founder's beatification. The criticism related to the transformation into a personal prelature are discussed in chapter seven, section one, parts two and three, and those related to Escrivá's beatification in chapter twelve, section two.

Here we will discuss negative press coverage of Opus Dei related to events in Spain, Great Britain, Germany, and Italy.

Section 1. Spain: The Rumasa Affair

In the early 1980s, the giant holding company Rumasa accounted for 2 percent of Spain's gross national product. It had more than sixty thousand employees and controlled some four hundred companies including twenty banks, industrial and service companies, and shell companies used to channel bank loans to other members of the group. Its founder and principal owner, José María Ruiz-Mateos, was a supernumerary member of Opus Dei. He was known for his generous contributions to charitable, religious, and social organizations, including educational and social centers founded and directed by members of Opus Dei. One of the Rumasa companies gave a long-term, no-interest loan of 1.5 billion pesetas ($10–$15 million) to the *Instituto de Educación e Investigación, S.A*, created in 1981 by Gregorio López Bravo to provide scholarships to needy students who wanted to study at the University of Navarra.[2]

In February 1983, the Socialist government of Spain headed by Felipe González announced that Rumasa owed 200 million euros in taxes and was on the verge of collapse. It was later revealed that the banks that formed part of the group had engaged in unusually risky activities on a large scale. The group had accumulated losses of some 350,000 euros and had enormous debts. Citing the damage its failure would do to the Spanish economy, the government expropriated Rumasa with an executive order (*decreto ley*). The government paid nothing to the owners, who vigorously contested the claim that Rumasa was on the verge of collapse or was worthless as well as the legality of the executive order. Ruiz-Mateos was charged with numerous financial crimes.[3]

The decision to expropriate Rumasa was based on technical reports, but it was one of the most politically significant early actions of the Socialist government formed after the 1982 elections. It attracted great attention in the Spanish press not only because of its economic importance, but also because it signaled the attitude of the newly formed Socialist government toward the banks, the Church, and especially Opus Dei, which had just become a personal prelature. The press also debated vigorously the constitutionality of the use of an executive order to expropriate a private business. An evenly divided Constitutional Court eventually upheld it thanks to the tie-breaking vote of its president.[4]

Large parts of the media claimed that the directors of Opus Dei were involved in Ruiz-Mateos's decisions both before and after the expropriation and that Rumasa companies had made generous contributions to the Prelature. This incited suspicion in Spanish public opinion that Opus Dei was involved in large-scale dubious or illegal schemes that benefited it directly or indirectly.

The information office of Opus Dei in Spain issued formal statements denying that the directors of the Work had been involved in Ruiz-Mateos' decisions. It stressed that he, like all members of the Prelature, enjoyed complete freedom in his business decisions and was solely responsible for them. It also denied that Rumasa had made large contributions to the Prelature. These statements had little effect, in part because they rested on distinctions most people did not make between Rumasa and Ruiz Mateos and between financing Opus Dei itself and the University of Navarra and other schools and social centers connected with Opus Dei.[5]

The Rumasa financial scandal occupied the Spanish press for years, both because of its sheer scale and because of attention-grabbing incidents like Ruiz-Mateos' flight to London, his escape from a Spanish court disguised by a wig and raincoat, and his coming to blows with the Minister of the Economy, whom he considered responsible for the expropriation.

Ruiz-Mateos launched numerous verbal attacks on people whom he considered responsible for his plight or who he thought should have stepped up to defend him or help him financially. Among the targets of his attacks were several regional directors of the Prelature. He also excoriated several prominent members including the bankers Luis Valls-Taberner, president of Banco Popular, and Rafael Termes, president of the Spanish Association of Bankers. He accused them of failing to provide him the loans he needed with the excuse of protecting the banks they led.[6]

As the tension he suffered mounted over the years, Ruiz-Mateos' press attacks on those he felt had wronged him or failed to come to his assistance became more virulent and increasingly incompatible with his spiritual obligations as a member of the Work. He bitterly and publicly criticized the directors of Opus Dei in Spain and stopped receiving spiritual assistance from the Work. He threatened to create a scandal if Opus Dei and its members continued to withhold the support he felt they owed him. Eventually this behavior became so incompatible with his obligations as a member of the Work that in 1986 he was expelled from Opus Dei following the procedures laid down in its statutes.[7] Ruiz Mateos then filed suit against two regional directors of Opus Dei in Spain. In 1989, the judge dismissed the case on grounds that there was no evidence of improper behavior on the part of Opus Dei's directors.

After many years of litigation and some time in jail, in 1999 the Spanish Supreme Court found Ruiz-Mateos not guilty of the criminal charges brought against him. By that time, he had established a new business he also named Rumasa. Eventually, he apologized for some of his accusations against Opus Dei.

Twenty-five years after the scandal first arose, most people had forgotten its details. But despite Opus Dei's attempts to disassociate itself from the controversy, the Rumasa Affair left a lingering suspicion in the minds of many of involvement in doubtful if not illegal financial deals on a large scale.[8] Opus Dei might have been more successful in its efforts had it relied less on fine points like the distinction between donations from Rumasa and from Ruiz Mateos and donations to Opus Dei and to the University of Navarra or other corporate activities.

Section 2. Great Britain: Cardinal Hume Speaks

In January 1981, *The Times* published a lengthy article which criticized Opus Dei as secretive and authoritarian.[9] The article was based on material provided by an Irish former member, John Roche, who may have hoped to prevent the Holy See from making Opus Dei a personal prelature.[10] Opus Dei responded with a generic statement which proclaimed its love of freedom, its rejection of secrecy, and its full obedience to the hierarchy, but which did not enter into detail.

In addition to providing material to *The Times*, Roche also urged the archbishop of Westminster, Cardinal Hume, to investigate Opus Dei.[11] Hume may also have been upset by accusations made by the mother of a woman that Opus Dei was separating her from her family. In December 1981, he issued a memorandum on the pastoral practices of Opus Dei in his diocese, which he released to the press.[12] It included a recommendation that no one under eighteen should be allowed to make a long-term commitment to Opus Dei, and that young people who wished to join Opus Dei should first discuss the matter with their parents. In addition, the cardinal recommended respecting the freedom of people who wished to leave Opus Dei and clearly identifying all activities connected in some way with Opus Dei.

The publication of the guidelines was taken as criticism of Opus Dei,[13] although Cardinal Hume, who must have been aware of John Paul II's strong support of Opus Dei, took pains to say that his recommendations "must not be seen as criticism of the integrity of the members of Opus Dei."[14] Opus Dei, for its part, published a statement in which it "welcome[ed] this memorandum and the recommendations made by the Cardinal, which," it said, "are in line with what members of Opus Dei have always sought to do in Britain and worldwide."[15] Eventually Hume seems to have changed his mind about Opus Dei. In 1998 he was the principal celebrant at a public Mass of thanksgiving for its seventieth Anniversary,[16] but this, unlike his earlier memorandum, received almost no attention in the press.

Section 3. Germany: Opus Dei Defends Itself in the Courts

In the first fifty years of its existence, Opus Dei had never sued an author or a media outlet for libel, but attacks in the German press and television in 1984 led it to change that policy. Matters began in 1983, when Klaus Steigleder, a former member of Opus Dei, published a book entitled *Das Opus Dei: Eine Innenansicht* (*Opus Dei: An Inside View*). The book used statements from former members to produce a picture of Opus Dei as a dangerous cult.[17] Had things stopped there, it probably would have been a tempest in a teapot, but the influential left-wing news magazine *Der Spiegel* published lengthy excerpts from the book in three consecutive issues, starting with its September 5, 1983, publication.[18] Between September 1983 and November 1984, the local German public radio and television station Westdeutscher Rundfunk (WDR) aired twenty-five radio and television programs which characterized Opus Dei as a secretive sect, with declarations of former members, lurid critiques of corporal mortification, and statements by parents who were unhappy about their children's decision to join Opus Dei. One program accused Opus Dei of a whole range of misconduct, even including arms trafficking.[19] These critiques were picked up by some progressive publications and some politicians called for an investigation of Opus Dei as a cult.

The majority of the programs and of the articles were highly polemical and made no effort to present a balanced view. As the media and culture critic for the *Frankfurter Allgemeine Zeitung*, Germany's second-most-widely-read newspaper, pointed out, they interviewed no happy members of Opus Dei nor any parents who approved of their children's decision to join. One program which purported to be about Opus Dei's formational activities gave, he pointed out, "virtually no information" about its subject. Rather it criticized "the fundamental convictions which undergird a Christian way of life."[20]

The information office of Opus Dei attempted unsuccessfully to enter into a dialogue with the producers of the programs. It sent information about Opus Dei's activities to some forty thousand people and institutions including all German parishes, religion teachers, newspapers, magazines, radio stations, and press agencies. Several bishops, including the president of the Bishops Conference, Cardinal Höffner, made public statements in support of Opus Dei, and some of these statements were reported in the Catholic press.[21] Numerous people who were personally familiar with Opus Dei's activities registered protests with the TV station.[22]

Various bishops, including Höffner, urged Opus Dei to take legal action, since the accusations that Opus Dei was involved in clandestine commercial and political activities including arms dealing were manifestly false. The directors of Opus Dei in Germany decided that the time had come for it to have recourse to the courts. They filed seven suits: three against publishing houses, three against WDR, and one against an individual. The courts held for Opus Dei in six of the seven suits. For example, in the case of a numerary who was criticized, the judge held that WDR violated the right of personal integrity by entering the sphere of personal intimacy. In August 1988, a German court issued an unprecedented decision which required WDR to publicly retract its false assertions that Opus Dei was involved in arms trafficking. [23]

Although Opus Dei prevailed in the courts, its public image and its activities were seriously damaged in Germany, Austria, and Switzerland. Several priests of Opus Dei were forced out of positions in which they had been teaching religion and giving spiritual guidance to high school students. Attendance at activities in Opus Dei's youth clubs dropped sharply because parents were frightened off. Ernst Burkhart, who was the chaplain of a high school in Vienna, says "practically all the students who had been coming for spiritual direction fled. What had been closeness and enthusiasm became rejection and contempt."[24] A few parents, moved by what they perceived as exaggerated criticism, looked into Opus Dei and testified in the media about their positive experiences,[25] but overall German public opinion was left with a negative image of Opus Dei.

Section 4. Italy: A Parliamentary Inquiry

In Italy, what began as a lengthy article published in an academic journal read primarily by a handful of specialists in canon law ended up triggering a parliamentary inquiry.[26] The author, Giancarlo Rocca, a priest of the Society of St. Paul, criticized Opus Dei for having secret statutes. The influential Italian magazine *L'Espresso* picked up Rocca's accusation of secrecy in an article which claimed to be based on what it described as the "secret code [which] rules the life of Opus Dei." This "top secret code bound in red" and revealed according to the *L'Espresso* article for the first time by Rocca, was in fact a copy of the 1950 Constitutions of Opus Dei, which had been superseded three years earlier by the 1982 Statutes. Opus Dei, the articles claimed, "governed . . . the professional careers of its members" and urged them to seek "public offices," which it interpreted to mean positions in the government or the bureaucracy.[27]

The Opus Dei Secretariat responded by denying the existence of secret codes and pointing out that the statutes approved three years earlier by the Holy See specifically established that members should not hide their membership. It also clarified that when the 1950 Statutes talked about a "*munus publicum*" [a public position], they meant any profession or job which would define the members' place in the world, not necessarily a position in the government or the bureaucracy.[28]

The article in *L'Espresso* triggered formal parliamentary calls (*interpellanza*) from Socialist and Communist members of the Italian Chamber of Deputies for an investigation of Opus Dei. Specifically, they focused on its alleged secret character, which they said violated the constitutional prohibition of secret societies.[29] They also expressed their concern that Opus Dei was a Catholic power that infiltrated society to dominate it. Several Independent Socialist deputies went further to suggest that Opus Dei ought to be declared illegal, and that as a precautionary matter, members who occupied governmental or bureaucratic positions should be immediately suspended. Over the next few months there were further calls for investigations as well as calls from other deputies for respect of the Church and of religious freedom.[30]

In response to the Italian government's request for information, the Holy See—which was deeply involved in the matter since it had approved Opus Dei—gave assurances that Opus Dei was not a secret organization and that it was governed only by its publicly available statutes, not by any hidden code.[31] On November 24, 1986, Oscar Luigi Scalfaro, the Minister of the Interior, gave a lengthy response to the questions put to the government. He concluded: "Opus Dei is not secret as a matter of fact or as a matter of law. Obedience in Opus Dei covers only spiritual matters. There are no rights or duties other than those laid out in the *Codex Iuris Particularis*, all of which are also spiritual in nature."[32] This formal reply from the government put an end to the investigation and the whole matter gradually died out.

Notes

1. General Note 106/87. AGP E 1.3, 1145.

2. See "*El ministerio fiscal acusará a Ruiz-Mateos de irregularidades penales*," *El País*, April 13,1983.

3. See "*El Gobierno expropia los bancos y todas las empresas del Grupo Rumasa*," *El País*, February 24, 1983.

4. See "*García-Pelayo afirma que hay sentencia definitiva sobre Rumasa*," *El País*, October 6, 1984.

5. Interview with Antonio Hernández Deus, Madrid, November 4, 2019, and electronic communications of the authors with him in October 2020.

6. See "*Ruiz-Mateos declara que no piensa rectificar lo que dijo sobre algunos miembros del Opus Dei*," *El País*, May 29, 1986.

7. See "*El Opus Dei pide a Ruiz-Mateos que rectifique sus declaraciones*," *ABC*, May 29, 1986.

8. For example, in 1988, approximately 25 percent of all critical references to Opus Dei in the Spanish press referred to in the text it is Rumasa. *Comisión de servicio in España*, January 4, 1989. AGP E.2.1.

9. Clifford Longley and Dan van Vat, "A Profile of Opus Dei," *The Times*, January 12, 1981.

10. John Roche, "The Inner World of Opus Dei," *https://odan.org/tw_inner_world_of_opus_dei*.

11. Roche, "The Inner World of Opus Dei."

12. "Guidelines for Opus Dei in Westminster Diocese: Statement by Cardinal Basil Hume," December 2, 1981, *Cultic Studies Journal*, 1985, 2, 2, pp. 284–285. *https://www.icsahome.com/articles/statmnt-by-cardinl-hume-guidelines-for-opus-dei-csj-2-2*.

13. See, e.g., "Cardinal Lays Down Ground Rules for Opus Dei," *Catholic Pictorial*, December 13,1981.

14. "Guidelines for Opus Dei," 2.

15. Statement of the Secretariat of Opus Dei in Britain, quoted in "Cardinal Lays Down Ground Rules."

16. "Cardinal Hume Celebrates Mass for 70th Anniversary of Opus Dei," *https://www.youtube.com/watch?v=41cJBWOUiVw*.

17. Klaus Steigleder, *Das Opus Dei: Eine Innenansicht* (Zürich: Benziger, 1983).

18. Klaus Steigleder, "*Jeden Tag eine Abtötung: Opus Dei—die heimliche Elite der Katholischen Kirche?*" *Der Spiegel* 36 (5-IX-1983), 37 (12-IX-1983), 38 (19-IX-1983). See also "*Opus Dei—Stoßtrupp ottes oder Heilige Mafia?*" *Der Spiegel* 37 (12-IX-1983).

19. WDR's first program was broadcast on September 10, 1983, with the title "*Mit heiliger Unverschämtheit.*" Opus Dei first began to consider legal remedies after the broadcast of a program entitled "*Gott und die Welt: Opus Dei—Irrenhaus Gottes?*" on May 4 1984. Electronic inverview of the authors with Han Thomas on August 4, 2020. Thomas worked during the 1980s in Opus Dei's information office in Germany.

20. Eberhard Straub, "*Opus Dei—Irrenhaus Gottes,*" *Frankfurter Allgemeine Zeitung*, May 7, 1984.

21. See, e.g., *Katholische Nachricten Agentur*, August 25, 1984, and August 30, 1984.

22. AGP M 24, 3274.

23. See G 251/85, 2-X-1985, en AGP M.24, 3274.

24. Quoted in Medina Bayo, p. 576.

25. Electronic interview with Hans Thomas on August 4, 2020.

26. Giancarlo Rocca, "*L'Opus Dei: Appunti e documenti per una storia*" *Claretianum* 25 (1985), pp. 5–227. Giancarlo Rocca, *L'Opus Dei: Appunti e documenti per una storia* (Roma: Edizioni paoline, 1985).

27. Sandro Magister, "*Santa Facciatosta,*" *L'Epresso*, March 2, 1986, 22 et seq. Since March 1983, three years before the publication of the article, Opus Dei had had a new set of statutes, those of the personal prelature. The 1950 Constitutions had not been published because shortly after their approval Escrivá became convinced that they did not adequately defend the secular spirit of Opus Dei, and he did not want to give publicity to legislation that did not reflect the true character of the Work.

28. AGP E 44, 1401, Statement of Secretariat of Opus Dei, February 24, 1986.

29. Italian Constitution, Article 18. *https://www.constituteproject.org/constitution/ Italy_2012.pdf?lang=en*. Last consulted April 28, 2020.

30. See Marco Tosatti, "*Opus Dei troppo segreta. Richiesta una indagine*," *La Stampa*, 2-III-1986. The parliamentary questions can be found in *Atti Parlamentri, Camera dei Deputati, IX Legislatura*, November 24, 1986, pp. 4–8. See also Tosatti, *"Opus Dei troppo segreta"*

31. *Atti Parlamentari, Camera dei Deputati*, IX Legislatura, November 24, 1986, p. 49,461.

32. *Atti Parlamentari, Camera dei Deputati*, IX Legislatura, November 24, 1986.

CHAPTER 12

⟜⟝⟞

The Beatification of the Founder

scrivá's legacy is found less in his writings than in the lives of the members of Opus Dei and in the record of his behavior and spoken comments. He passed on the spirit of Opus Dei primarily through his example, his informal conversations with individuals and small groups of people, and his preaching. This is not to say that his publications, were unimportant in the life of Opus Dei. *The Way* was many people's first introduction to Opus Dei's spirit, and although short, the book was a significant source of material for personal mental prayer, preaching, and preparing talks and classes about seeking sanctity and carrying on an active apostolate in ordinary life. By Escrivá's death in 1975, he had published three other books which reflected aspects of the spirit of Opus Dei: *Holy Rosary, Conversations with Msgr. Escrivá de Balaguer*, and *Christ is Passing By*. All of them had been translated into most major European languages.*

Between 1977 and 1987, five posthumous works appeared in Spanish and were promptly translated into other languages: *Friends of God* (a book similar to *Christ is Passing By*, with eighteen homilies given between 1941 and 1968), *Furrow* (a book similar to *The Way*, with one thousand points for meditation), *The Forge* (another book similar to *The Way*, with 1055 points for meditation, many of them taken from the *Apuntes íntimos* the Founder had written in the 1930s), *The Way of the Cross* (considerations on each of the stations supplemented with additional points for meditation), and *In Love with the Church* (three homilies on the Church and the priesthood). These posthumous publications, which were finalized under Del Portillo's direction, more than doubled the amount of readily

---

* See volume 1, chapter 9, section 1.

available material which members of the Work and others interested in its spirit could use.

Many of the get-togethers Escrivá had during his catechetical trips to Spain and Portugal in 1972 and to Latin America in 1974–1975 were captured on film. In total, there are nearly one hundred hours of raw film. Originally Escrivá consented to the filming on the condition that the material would be kept in the archives and used only after his death. But by 1973, Del Portillo had convinced him to allow them to be shown in centers of the Work. The first releases were full-length versions in the original Spanish. Soon, however, subtitled versions appeared. Gradually, abbreviated versions as well as documentaries that focused on specific topics were prepared. During the 1980s it became quite common to organize showings in the centers and corporate activities of Opus Dei.

In the films one can easily appreciate Escrivá's ability not only to communicate the spirit of Opus Dei but also to establish a personal contact with people, even when large crowds are present. Many who haved watched the films have found them helpful in establishing a more personal and direct contact with him.[1]

Section 1. Escrivá's Process of Beatification

Part 1. What is Beatification?

In the words of St. John Paul II, the Church "proposes to the faithful for their imitation, veneration and invocation, men and women who are outstanding in the splendor of charity and other evangelical virtues."[2] In the act of canonization, the Church enrolls them in the canon, its official list of saints who are in heaven with God, and authorizes their public remembrance at liturgies throughout the whole Church. Canonization is preceded by beatification, in which the Pope allows the candidate for sainthood to be venerated publicly as Blessed in places closely associated with their life and ministry.[3]

Reform of the process of canonization to make it shorter and less cumbersome was already underway when John Paul II became Pope in 1978.[4] In January 1983, he issued a set of guidelines for causes of beatification and canonization designed to produce "a simpler process while maintaining the soundness of the investigation."[5] These changes were implemented in greater detail the following month by the Congregation for the Causes of Saints. The goal was to make it possible to propose models of sanctity who are close in time and to whom contemporary people can relate.[6]

The new procedures gave a greatly expanded role in the process of beatification to the local bishop, normally in the diocese where the candidate died.[7] The new guidelines for both the diocesan and the Roman phase of the process of beatification were designed "to conduct the inquiry [into the sanctity of the candidate] in the light of dogmatic, spiritual, and pastoral theology and on the basis of well-founded historical methods,"[8] giving less emphasis to legal models of procedure. The move away from a courtroom model brought with it the elimination of the official popularly known as the "devil's advocate," who had been charged with arguing against the candidate no matter what he personally thought about the merits of the case. As one author has said, the model changed from a trial with a prosecutor and a defense attorney to something more like the preparation of a doctoral thesis in history.[9] In terms of speeding up the process, the most significant single change was eliminating the requirement that at least fifty years pass between the candidate's death and the issuance of the decree on heroic virtue.[10]

Under the new procedures, a crucial first step is naming a postulator who is charged with moving the cause forward. Unlike the other officials, the postulator is normally someone who has a vested interest in the cause—although the postulator should be even more deeply committed to the truth than to the success of the cause. With the help of the postulator, the diocese gathers as much information as possible about the candidate by collecting documents and by having a tribunal take the testimony of people who knew the candidate, including those who oppose the beatification. The members of the tribunal are diocesan officials with no vested interest in the cause. Once the information is amassed, the bishop asks a group of theologians, again unconnected with the cause, to determine whether, in light of all the evidence, the candidate lived the Christian virtues in a heroic manner. If their answer is positive, it is up to the bishop to decide whether to forward the cause to the Congregation for the Causes of Saints for further consideration.[11]

In Rome, the Congregation for the Causes of Saints appoints a relator from among its pool of specialists to oversee the rest of the process. Under his direction, an official report, entitled the *Positio*, is prepared and transmitted to a theological commission composed of nine theologians chosen by the congregation. Each theologian votes affirmatively or negatively on the cause. The recommendation of the theologians is then passed on to the members of the congregation (a group comprised of cardinals, archbishops, and bishops). They decide whether to recommend that the Holy Father issue a Decree of Heroic Virtues, a document which describes the life of the candidate and issues a judgment that he or she lived Christian virtues in a heroic degree.

In addition to this historical-theological inquiry into the life of the candidate, the Church looks for a miracle attributable to the candidate's intercession. Alleged miracles are examined first by scientific and theological commissions at the diocesan level. If the scientific commission determines that there is no natural explanation for the alleged miracle, the theological commission rules on whether the phenomenon can by its nature be attributed only to God and whether it resulted through the intercession of the candidate alone. If all of these processes lead to a conclusion that a miracle has occurred through the intercession of the candidate for canonization, the material about the purported miracle is forwarded to the Congregation for the Causes of Saints, which carries out a similar process.[12] If the congregation's conclusion is positive and the Pope approves, a Decree of a Miracle is issued and, the candidate can be beatified in a public ceremony of beatification.[13]

Perhaps surprisingly, the process of canonizing someone who has already been beatified (declared Blessed), is much shorter and simpler. No new investigation into the life of the person is carried out. The only essential requirements are a second miracle which took place after beatification, evidence that the person is widely known among the faithful for holiness, and a decision of the Holy Father to go ahead.

Part 2. First Steps Toward Escrivá's Beatification

Opus Dei had many reasons for wanting to see its founder beatified and canonized. Members viewed him with the affection of sons and daughters and naturally wanted to see his merits and accomplishments recognized. They were convinced that God had called him to heaven and wanted to have that conviction corroborated by the Church. In addition, his beatification and canonization would make many more people aware of his message. Finally, since Escrivá had lived the spirit of Opus Dei, his beatification and canonization would confirm that the spirit of Opus Dei is a path to sanctity in the world.

During the five years after Escrivá's death, Opus Dei collected and catalogued his writings as well as notes taken on his preaching and other comments. The Work received numerous testimonies about incidents of the Founder's life from members and many other people who had known him over the years. More than six thousand people from more than one hundred countries wrote to the Holy See requesting the opening of his cause for canonization. Among them were 69 cardinals, 241 archbishops, and 987 bishops—more than one-third of all the bishops in the world. In addition, forty-one letters asking for his cause to be opened were received from superiors of religious orders and congregations.[14] Pope Paul VI himself told Del Portillo in 1976 that he considered the Founder "one of the men in the history of the Church who had received the most charisms and had corresponded with the greatest generosity to God's gifts."[15] Thousands of reports of favors received through Escrivá's intercession by people from all backgrounds testified to how many people all over the world had taken him as an intercessor for their needs both great and small.

Starting almost immediately after Escrivá's death, Opus Dei established offices in Rome and in the countries where it had a significant presence to disseminate information about Escrivá and to collect data about favors people attributed to his intercession. These offices prepared and distributed cards in many languages with a picture of Escrivá, a brief prayer asking for favors through his intercession, and a very short biography. Similarly, bulletins with information about his life and about favors received through his intercession were published. By 1984, twenty-three million prayer cards had been printed in thirty-six languages; and nineteen million bulletins had been printed in seven languages. Some three million people had subscribed to the bulletin.[16] The prayer cards and bulletins helped make people around the world more aware of Josemaría Escrivá as a model of Christian life and as an intercessor.

The historical office in Madrid collected and organized large amounts of material about the life of the Founder, including recollections written down after his death by people who knew him and documents from civil and ecclesiastical archives. It provided information to a number of people who wanted to write Escrivá's biography. The first appeared in Spanish in 1976.[17] Between 1982 and 1992, five others were published: one in French,[18] one in German,[19] one in Portuguese,[20] and two in Spanish.[21] Most of these books were eventually translated into the major European languages.

Escrivá's own works, his biographies, and the prayer cards and bulletins contributed to his reputation for sanctity—an essential prerequisite for opening a cause for canonization. In support of the official request for the opening of the cause, the postulator presented two volumes of testimonies that demonstrated Escrivá's reputation for sanctity both during his lifetime and after his death. In a second book, he presented 1500 accounts of favors attributed to the Founder's intercession. A third six-hundred-page volume reproduced some of the articles published in the international press about Escrivá during the first four years after his death, including nine written by cardinals.[22]

Part 3. Diocesan Phase of Escrivá's Cause

Because Escrivá had died in Rome, Church law assigned his cause to the Archdiocese of Rome. The Pope's Vicar for Rome, Cardinal Poletti, officially decreed the introduction of the cause in February

1981. Testimony in Rome was taken by a tribunal charged with hearing many different cases. Over the next five years, that tribunal would hear twenty-six witnesses in Escrivá's case; among them three cardinals, two archbishops, one bishop, eleven priests, and nine laypersons, including two former members of Opus Dei.[23] Among the witnesses heard in Rome were Álvaro Del Portillo and Javier Echevarría. Because of their close association with Escrivá over many years, their testimony was very lengthy.[24]

The Rome tribunal received seventeen letters from persons opposed to the beatification. Some were from parents who were unhappy that their children had joined Opus Dei. The Roman tribunal, made up entirely of specialists unconnected with Opus Dei, responded that the circumstances under which young people had joined Opus Dei were not sufficiently related to Escrivá personally to be of interest in a cause for beatification. Other writers sent texts of Escrivá's homilies which they had interpreted as critical of the Pope and the Church. The tribunal responded that the homilies had already been included in the documentation presented by the postulator and showed that Escrivá was a man of faith and interior life. One person showed up unannounced at a meeting of the tribunal wishing to testify against the cause, but the tribunal decided that what he wished to contribute was irrelevant.[25]

Because many of the potential witnesses lived in Spain and others were Spanish-speaking, a second tribunal was created to gather testimony in the Archdiocese of Madrid. Its members were named by Cardinal Tarancón of Madrid, who was not known to be particularly sympathetic to Opus Dei. Unlike the Rome tribunal, which had to hear witnesses in many different causes, the Madrid tribunal was charged only with taking testimony in Escrivá's case, and so was able to proceed much more quickly. To preside over its proceedings, Cardinal Tarancón chose Fr. Rafael Pérez, an Augustinian friar who had previously worked in the Congregation for the Causes of Saints. This tribunal examined sixty witnesses, among them two archbishops, six bishops, seventeen priests, five religious, and thirty lay men and women, including eight former members of Opus Dei.[26] Less than half the witnesses heard by the two tribunals were members of Opus Dei.[27] Naturally, no members of Opus Dei were members of either tribunal.

The witnesses called by the two tribunals had known Escrivá at different times that covered virtually the entire arc of his life. Some testified at great length, others much more briefly, but among them they presented a complete picture of the Founder's life and his virtues. Most of them stressed his message about the call to holiness in ordinary life. Many talked about how his charity manifested itself in genuine affection for them. Married people related how he had helped them to see their married life as a path to sanctity. Several members of religious orders testified about how he helped them in their vocations. One of the bishops explained in some detail how Escrivá had helped him focus on his priestly vocation rather than on the academic career he had been planning. Among those who testified favorably about Escrivá's virtues were several former members of Opus Dei who had known Escrivá personally.[28]

Among the documents presented to the Holy See were publications critical of Escrivá written by two authors who had known him personally, Alberto Moncada and María Angustias Moreno.[29] The postulator proposed both as witnesses. Moncada testified in November 1982. In a letter to the Congregation for the Causes of Saints, the judges who heard his testimony concluded that it was unreliable and should not be considered because it was moved by vehement hatred for Escrivá.[30]

Moreno's publications were included in the record. Her writings and appearances on television suggested that her testimony would not be reliable, and she failed to answer the tribunal's invitation to testify.[31] For these reasons, the tribunal told the congregation that her oral declaration was not needed. The congregation concurred. Considerably later, after the tribunal had concluded its investigations, Moreno asked to testify, but the tribunal decided not to reopen its proceedings. According to the *Newweek* journalist Kenneth Woodward, the postulator, a priest of Opus Dei, proposed nine other critical witnesses whom the tribunal chose not to hear.[32]

While the Madrid tribunal was still hearing witnesses, Cardinal Taráncon commented to Fr. Pérez that several persons had told him they wanted to testify. Fr. Pérez asked him to provide a list of names and information about any documentation they had presented, but the cardinal still had not done so when he resigned. Sometime later, after the official closing of the Madrid phase of the process, some of the people involved approached the new archbishop of Madrid, Angel Suquía, who informed the tribunal. Among those who had told Cardinal Tarancón that they wished to testify were María del Carmen Tapia and Miguel Fisac, both prominent former members of Opus Dei and highly critical of Escrivá.

After considering the information they provided and their public declarations, the tribunal decided that none of the people who had approached Cardinal Tarancón would be reliable witnesses and recommended to the congregation that nothing further be done about their request. Once again, the congregation concurred. Fr. Pérez explained the decision on grounds that it would be a waste of time to hear those whose aversion to the candidate was so strong that it would vitiate their testimony.[33]

The two tribunals collected a total of almost eleven thousand pages of transcribed oral testimony. They received from the postulator thirteen thousand pages of Escrivá's writings and eleven volumes of documents collected from 390 public and private archives. They entrusted the study of Escrivá's writings to theologians, who gave positive assessments.[34] One of them wrote: "The proofs in this case are so rich that one could not desire more."[35]

In 1982, Cardinal Tarancón had established another tribunal to study the sudden cure attributed to Escrivá's intercession of a Carmelite nun suffering terminal cancer. That tribunal finished its investigations in April 1982, concluding that the cure had no natural explanation and should be attributed to Escrivá's intercession.[36]

Cardinal Suquía decided that the information collected about Escrivá's life and about the purported miracle was sufficiently clear to justify forwarding the materials collected to Rome for further study by the Congregation for the Causes of Saints.

Part 4. The Vatican Phase of the Cause

For Escrivá's case, the congregation chose from its pool of seven rela-tors Fr. Ambrogio Eszer, OP, a veteran of the congregation, who has been described as "deadly earnest about the importance of making new saints."[37] The postulator put together a group of Opus Dei mem-bers who were specialists in theology, Church history, and canon law, as well as a number of computer experts. This team, working under Eszer's general direction, prepared the official report to the congrega-tion, technically known as the *Positio super Vita et Virtutibus* or more briefly the *Positio.* The six-thousand-page study was completed in June 1988. The relator concluded that it was complete and that fur-ther investigations would not significantly enrich the picture it drew of Escrivá's life.[38]

The *Positio* was delivered to a group of nine theological consul-tants, drawn from the pool of consultants regularly engaged by the congregation. Seven of the nine consultants voted in favor of moving forward, in some cases with great enthusiasm. One described Escrivá as "a finished and attractive model of the sanctity that the contempo-rary world most needs." Another called him "the Master of the spiri-tuality for our time . . . the man sent by God to renew and revivify the Christian spirit in an indifferent world distant from God."[39]

One of the consultants, however, voted against going forward, and another voted to delay. Without revealing the author's name, an Italian journal published a leaked copy of the opinion that suggested delaying. The consultant summarized his objections by saying that it would be prudent to let more time pass to allow for further investi-gation into three questions: tensions between Escrivá and the Jesu-its; what he perceived as Escrivá's apparent lack of humility; and the abundance of asserted mystical phenomenon in Escrivá's life.[40]

Despite the reservations of the two consultants, the relator, Fr. Eszer, concluded that no further studies or testimony were needed because "the procedural processes, the collection and analysis of the documents and the subsequent studies of the documents are mod-els of scrupulous exactitude, with a solid critical apparatus and a wise and careful in-depth study."[41] Eszer determined that the cause was ripe for consideration by the cardinals and bishops who were members of the Congregation for the Causes of Saints. In March 1990, they recommended that the Holy Father issue the Decree of Heroic Virtues. On April 9, 1990, the Pope promulgated the decree. After a lengthy summary of Escrivá's life at the head of Opus Dei, the decree found "his most characteristic features not only in his extraordinary gifts as a man of action, but also in his life of prayer and in the assiduous unitive experience that made him an itinerant contemplative."[42]

In June 1990, the medical consultants of the congregation concluded unanimously that the instantaneous cure of a Spanish Carmelite suffering from terminal cancer could not be explained through natural causes. The congregation's theological consultants concluded unanimously that the cure was miraculous and attributable to Escrivá's intercession. In July 1991, the Holy Father promulgated a decree about the miraculous cure and decided to proceed to Escrivá's beatification. The date of the ceremony was set for May 17, 1992.

Part 5. Beatification Ceremony

Seventeen years after Escrivá's death and eleven years after the opening of the cause, some 200,000 to 300,000 people filled St. Peter's Square and spilled over into Via della Conciliazione for the beatification. Thirty-five cardinals and some three hundred bishops participated in the Mass of Beatification celebrated by Pope John Paul II for Josephine Bakhita and Josemaría Escrivá.[43] In his homily at the Mass, John Paul II stressed Escrivá's message:

> With supernatural intuition, Blessed Josemaría untiringly preached the universal call to holiness and the apostolate. Christ calls everyone to become holy in the realities of everyday life. Hence, work too is a means of personal holiness and apostolate when it is lived in union with Jesus Christ, for the Son of God, in the incarnation, has united himself in a certain way with the whole reality of man

and with the whole of creation (see *Dominum et vivificantem*, n. 50). In a society in which an unbridled craving for material things turns them into idols and a cause of separation from God, the new Blessed reminds us that these same realities, creatures of God and of human industry, if used correctly for the glory of the Creator and the service of one's brothers and sisters, can be a way for men and women to meet Christ. "All things of the earth," he taught, "including the earthly and temporal activity of men, must be directed to God" (Letter, 19 March 1954).[44]

Section 2. Controversy over the Beatification

Escrivá's beatification was received joyfully not only by the immense crowd in St. Peter's Square but by members, cooperators, and friends of Opus Dei throughout the world, as well as by many people who had no direct contact with Opus Dei but had become familiar with Escrivá and his message through his writings and articles about him in the press. Both before and after the ceremony, many articles appeared in newspapers and magazines throughout the world celebrating his life and his holiness.

The beatification, however, also gave rise to negative comments in the press. Some had little to do with Escrivá as a person and seemed motivated primarily by opposition to Opus Dei based on the fact that twenty years earlier a number of its members had served in Franco's cabinet,[45] or on its purported conservative influence in the life of the Church.[46] Other articles reflected the negative experiences of some former members of Opus Dei, which may have been the result of the mistaken actions of other members but which usually did not involve Escrivá personally.

Criticism aimed directly at Escrivá and his suitability for canonization can be summarized under four headings, although any summary will necessarily leave out some things and miss some nuances: 1) that he had a bad temper which he sometimes lost; 2) that he supported Franco; 3) that he was sympathetic to Hitler and the Nazis; and 4) that he lacked humility.

The major critic of Escrivá's temper was María del Carmen Tapia, who published shortly before his beatification an exposé which depicted him as a vain tyrant who dealt with her unjustly and in grossly insulting terms.[47] Her criticisms were picked up by the US weekly magazine *Newsweek*[48] and by other international publications. Some of the details of her account seem highly questionable. *Newsweek*, for instance, highlighted her charge that Escrivá threatened that if she ever spoke ill of Opus Dei "I, Josemaría Escrivá de Balaguer, who have the world press in my hands . . . will publicly dishonor you." At the time this incident purportedly took place, Opus Dei was meeting with very little success in its efforts to clarify that its members who belonged to the Franco government were acting with personal freedom and initiative. Escrivá would have had to have been delusional to believe that he had "the world press in his hand," and even his most severe critics do not depict him as delusional.

Whatever the reliability of the details of Tapia's stories, it is clear that Escrivá did have what Spaniards describe as a "strong temperament" and what English-speakers would call a "temper." He freely admitted that he lost his temper. He said it happened sometimes because it, was called for, and sometimes "because I am a poor man." If, however, one struggles to control his temper, sometimes losing it is not incompatible with the love of God which is the essence of sanctity. Tapia herself, despite the negative picture she painted in her pre-beatification book, issued a declaration shortly before Escrivá's canonization saying she had "never considered his strong character an obstacle to his sanctity and consequent canonization." It would be, she continued, "a grave error to make use of the information contained in my book to put in doubt the sanctity of the Founder of Opus Dei."[49]

The charge of being pro-Franco is not based on statements Escrivá made or things he did, but on the fact that a number of Opus Dei members served in Franco's cabinet and in other important positions in his government and that Escrivá did not prohibit them from doing so. Respect for the political freedom of its members is a central tenet of Opus Dei. The most careful student of the question, the Vaticanist John Allen, writes:

> A charge [against Escrivá] of being "pro-Franco" cannot be sustained, except in the generic sense that most Spanish Catholics were initially supportive of Franco. For one thing . . . there was widespread participation by Opus Dei members in anti-Franco activity. The most one can say is that Escrivá was not "anti-Franco" either. His main concern seems to be the stability of Spanish society in order to hold radical movements at bay that might renew the horrors of the Civil War. Escrivá did not attempt to dictate particular political solutions, either to his members or to the Spanish authorities.[50]

The charge of being sympathetic to the Nazis,[51] and the related charge of anti-Semitism, are based exclusively on the allegations of one former member, Fr. Vladimir Feltzmann. He reports that Escrivá told him that Hitler had been unjustly accused of killing six million Jews when in fact he had killed only four million.[52] No other source has been offered for this allegation, which seems implausible on its surface. A Nazi sympathizer might say Hitler had good reason for killing the Jews, or deny that he did kill Jews, but it is hard to believe he would consider it a defense to say that Hitler did not kill six million Jews but "only" four million.

The accusation that Escrivá was anti-Semitic is also derived exclusively from Feltzmann's statement. Feltzmann does not point to any specific anti-Semitic comment or act on Escrivá's part. In fact, Escrivá's frequent public manifestations of affection for the Jewish people and for individual Jews are well documented.[53] Rabbi Leon Klenicki, director of interfaith affairs at the Anti-Defamation League, who had ongoing contact with Opus Dei for more than a decade, said he has "never discovered any anti-Semitic reference in any of Opus Dei's writings here in the US or abroad."[54] Rabbi Angel Kreiman, international vice president of the World Council of Synagogues and a cooperator of Opus Dei, testified that "Opus Dei members helped me, right from the beginning of my seminary studies, to persevere with my vocation, and I have also seen them do it with other rabbis, for which

I am deeply grateful."[55] In a later statement, Feltzmann said he did not mean to suggest that Escrivá was anti-Semitic but rather that because of his anti-Communism, he was pro-Hitler and pro-Germany.[56]

The charge that Escrivá lacked Christian humility turns in large part on whether or not one accepts Escrivá's claim that the foundation of Opus Dei was a charismatic event in which he received an illumination from God. His insistence that he and he alone could determine what constitutes the genuine spirit of Opus Dei and on his unique role in guiding the institution will appear as a lack of humility to anyone who does not accept that claim. In beatifying Escrivá, the Church accepted the claim and therefore was untroubled by statements and attitudes which would certainly indicate a lack of humility if Opus Dei were merely Escrivá's invention.[57]

Some critics focused not on whether Escrivá was a genuinely holy person, but on the process of his beatification. They objected to: 1) the small number of critical witnesses heard and the refusal to hear some critical witnesses who presented themselves; 2) the absence of a "devil's advocate"; 3) Opus Dei's influence on the process; and 4) the speed of the process. We will address them here in turn.

Although the postulator, who was a member of Opus Dei, proposed eleven critical witnesses, the members of the Madrid tribunal, none of whom belonged to Opus Dei, chose to hear only a few of them because they considered that the others had such strong aversion to Escrivá that their testimony could not be trusted. No detailed evidence is available about how or why the tribunal made this decision. Looking back at some of the media treatment of the process, it seems that it would have been desirable to hear additional contrary witnesses. But at the time, the responsible officials did not see things that way. The Dominican priest who was in charge of the cause during the Vatican phase carried out by the Congregation for the Causes of Saints concluded: "This *Positio* is complete. Possible further supplementary studies would not significantly enrich it."[58] It is possible that the members of the tribunal did not think about the importance of hearing a larger number of contrary witnesses to protect the process from criticism, even if their testimony ultimately added little of value.

Or perhaps they did consider it but were deterred by the rule that "all witnesses . . . must be trustworthy" and their own conviction that the potential negative witnesses were not.[59]

The absence of a "devil's advocate" was still a novelty at the time of Escrivá's beatification but is an integral part of the new procedures established by the Vatican for all causes of beatification. The devil's advocate played a role similar to that of the prosecuting attorney in a criminal trial but has no place in the new procedures which are based on the methods employed in historical research rather than on those used in courtroom settings. Under the new legislation, the relator is charged with making sure that the postulator adequately address the weak points of the candidate. The promoter of justice is responsible for ascertaining that all legal procedures are properly followed. Whether or not the new procedures are better than the old ones,[60] the procedures used in Escrivá's case were the ones required by the new law for all causes for canonization at the time. According to the relator, Fr. Eszer, "the investigations [during the diocesan phase of the cause] were carried out with the most rigorous respect for the legal requirements and the scientific methodology required by Church . . ."[61]

Critics made numerous accusations of undue influence by Opus Dei on the cause. Most were generic: Opus Dei "bought" the beatification; Opus Dei "pressured" Church officials; and so forth. As the Vaticanist John Allen wrote, the success of the cause has a far simpler and less sinister explanation. Pope John Paul II's well-known support of Opus Dei and devotion to Escrivá is, Allen wrote, "probably the single most telling argument against the hypothesis that Opus Dei 'bought' or 'manipulated' the beatification and canonization. There was no reason why they had to. John Paul was positively inclined and was just waiting for the paperwork to reach his desk."[62]

Escrivá's beatification twelve years after the opening of the cause was the quickest modern beatification on record at the time, thanks in large part to the new rules instituted by John Paul II. Recently those rules have made other causes even faster: Mother Teresa, four years; Ceferino Giménez Malla, "El Pelé," a Spanish Romani, four years; Chiara Badano, a young lay member of the Focolare movement, eleven years; Pope John Paul II, six years. Escrivá's case did move quickly, but that is hardly surprising. The reformed procedures applied to his case were designed to be speedy. John Allen, in an article on the beatification of Pope John Paul II, listed five factors in addition to a reputation for personal holiness and miracle reports that make for a "fast track" saint.[63] Four of the five seem to have been present in Escrivá's case.

First, "an organization behind them, fully committed to the cause, with both the resources and the political savvy to move the ball."[64] Opus Dei was certainly fully committed to the cause. It was able to find among its members a skilled postulator, the Italian priest Flavio Capucci, and put together a team of people with the requisite knowledge of theology, canon law, history, archival science, and computers. Second, "a 'first,' usually to recognize a specific geographical area or unrepresented constituency." This factor was not present in Escrivá's case since there is no lack of Spanish priests among the saints. Third, "a political or cultural issue symbolized by the candidate . . . that lends a perceived sense of urgency." Escrivá's message and the Church's desire to encourage the laity and diocesan priests to seek sanctity rather than being content with mediocrity helps explain the Church's diligence in moving forward quickly the man whom John Paul II would describe as "the Saint of the ordinary." Similarly, Escrivá's well-known loyalty to the bishops, the Pope, and the Magisterium of the Church was a welcome message. Fourth, "causes sometimes make the fast track because the sitting pope feels a personal involvement." Pope Paul VI had known Escrivá personally since the 1940s and had affection for him. During Del Portillo's audience with him in June 1978, the Pope told him that he planned to ask the Congregation for the Saints to act quickly in Escrivá's case because he was "extraordinary."[65] Pope John Paul II knew and admired Escrivá's writing and the organization he had created and had personal devotion to him. A striking sign of his interest in the cause was his decision to make St. Peter's Square and the papal altar available for the Mass of Thanksgiving celebrated by Del Portillo the day after the canonization. Fifth, "fast-track cases generally enjoy overwhelming hierarchical support." One-third of all the bishops in the world took the trouble to write to the

Holy See requesting that Escrivá's cause be opened. More than forty cardinals and three hundred bishops took part in the beatification. A final factor, not mentioned by Allen, was the postulator's ability to identify and document early on potential miraculous cures attributable to Escrivá's intercession. Even before the tribunal finished hearing witnesses, the postulator had identified two, and by the end of the diocesan phase even more.[66] Given all these factors, it is not surprising that Escrivá's cause moved quickly.

After the beatification, devotion to Escrivá continued to grow. Increasing numbers of books by and about him were sold, and it became easier to find statues of him in churches and his name on streets and squares throughout the world.

Notes

1. See Juan José García-Noblejas, "*Grabaciones audiovisuales*," in *Diccionario de San Josemaría Escrivá de Balaguer*.

2. John Paul II, Apostolic Constitution *Divinus perfectionis Magister http://w2.vatican.va/content/john-paul-ii/en/apost_constitutions/documents/hf_jp-ii_apc_25011983_divinus-perfectionis-magister.html*. Last visited June 27, 2018.

3. See C. Beccari, "Beatification and Canonization," in *The Catholic Encyclopedia* (New York: Robert Appleton Company, 1907). Retrieved June 28, 2018 from New Advent: *http://www.newadvent.org/cathen/02364b.htm*.

4. See Paul VI, *Motu Propio Sanctitas Clarior* (1969), *http://w2.vatican.va/content/paul-vi/la/motu_proprio/documents/hf_p-vi_motu-proprio_19690319_sanctitas-clarior.htm*. Last visited June 27, 2018.

5. John Paul II, *Divinus perfectionis*.

6. Sacred Congregation for the Causes of Saints, "Norms to be Observed in Inquires made by Bishops in the Causes of the Saints," n. 17, AAS 75 (1983), pp. 396–403.

7. *New Law for the Causes of the Saints*, 5 a.

8. Paolo Molinari, SJ, and Peter Gumpel, SJ, "*L'istituto della beatificazione. A proposito d'uno studio recente*," *Gregorianum* 69, 1 (1988), pp. 133–138, at 133.

9. Kenneth L. Woodward, *Making Saints* (New York: Simon and Schuster, 1990), p. 91.

10. See *Code of Canon Law* of 1917, Canon 2101.

11. *http://www.vatican.va/roman_curia/congregations/csaints/documents/rc_con_csaints_doc_07021983_norme_en.htm*, 6–31.

12. Congregation for the Causes of the Saints, "New Law for the Causes of the Saints," *http://www.vatican.va/roman_curia/congregations/csaints/documents/rc_con_csaints_doc_07021983_norme_en.html*, 33–34. Last visited June 15, 2022.

13. John Paul II, *Divinus perfectionis*, 13–15.

14. Flavio Capucci, *Josemaría Escrivá, santo. El itinerario de la causa de canonización* (Madrid: Rialp, 2009), p.18. Fr. Capucci was the postulator of Escrivá's cause.

15. Quoted in Álvaro del Portillo, *Entrevista sobre el fundador del Opus Dei* (Madrid: Rialp, 2014), p. 213.

16. General Congress of Men's Branch, 1984, Outline used by Del Portillo in addressing the Congress. AGP D.2, 6940f, 8.

17. Salvador Bernal, *Mons. Josemaría Escrivá de Balaguer. Apuntes sobre la vida del Fundador del Opus Dei* (Madrid: Rialp, 1976).

18. François Gondrand, *Au pas de Dieu. Josemaría Escrivá de Balaguer, fondateur de l'Opus Dei* (Paris: France-Empire, 1982).

19. Peter Berglar, *Opus Dei. Leben und Werk des Gründers Josemaría Escrivá* (Salzburg: Otto Muller, 1983).

20. Hugo de Azevedo, *Uma luz no mundo: vida do Servo de Deus Monsenhor Josemaría Escrivá de Balaguer* (Lisbon: Prumo—Rei dos livros, 1988).

21. Andrés Vázquez de Prada, *El fundador del Opus Dei: Mons. Josemaría Escrivá de Balaguer (1902–1975)* (Madrid: Rialp, 1983); Ana Sastre, *Tiempo de caminar* (Madrid: Rialp, 1989).

22. Capucci, *Josemaría Escrivá, santo*, p. 19.

23. Capucci, *Josemaría Escrivá, santo*, p. 44.

24. Some sense of the content of Del Portillo's testimony can be derived from his book-length interview about Escrivá. Álvaro del Portillo and Cesare Cavalleri, *Intervista sul fondatore del Opus Dei* (Milan: Ares 1992). English edition: *Forty Years with a Saint* (New York: Scepter Publishers, 1996). Similarly, Javier Echevarría, *Memoria del beato Josemaría Escrivá* (Madrid: Rialp, 2000).

25. Electronic mail with Constantino Ánchel, January 23, 2019. Ánchel worked in the historical office of the Spanish regional commission and as a procedural expert. In 1987 he was part of the team that prepared the *Positio* under the direction of the relator and the postulator.

26. Capucci, *Josemaría Escrivá, santo*, p. 43.

27. Capucci, *Josemaría Escrivá, santo*, p. 20.

28. For a general overview, see Capucci, *Josemaría Escrivá, santo*.

29. Alberto Moncada, *Opus Dei: una interpretación* (Madrid: Índice, 1974); and *Los hijos del Padre* (Barcelona: Argos Vergara, 1977). María Angustias Moreno, *El Opus Dei. Anexo a una Historia* (Barcelona: Planeta, 1976); and *La otra cara del Opus Dei* (Barcelona: Planeta, 1978). Moreno had also published several articles in the magazine *Interviú* that were included in the documentation.

30. Electronic mail with Constantino Ánchel, January 23, 2019.

31. Electronic mail with Constantino Ánchel, January 23, 2019.

32. Woodward, *Making Saints*, p. 10.

33. Electronic mail with Constantino Ánchel, January 23, 2019.

34. See Capucci, *Josemaría Escrivá, santo*, pp. 21–23.

35. *Relatio et vota Congressus peculiaris super virtutibus, die 19 septembris 1989*, Roma 1989, 19, quoted in Capucci, *Josemaría Escrivá, santo*.

36. Capucci, *Josemaría Escrivá, santo*, pp. 30–31.

37. Woodward, *Making Saints*, p. 104.

38. Capucci, *Josemaría Escrivá, santo*, p. 75.

39. Brief excerpts without the names of the authors, including the two quoted here, can be found in Capucci, *Josemaría Escrivá, santo*, pp. 26–28.

40. "Voto I," *Il Regno*, May 1, 1992, pp. 301–304.

41. Ambrogio Eszer, OP, "Actualidad eclesial del mensaje de Josemaría Escrivá," *El Norte de Castilla*, Valladolid, January 9, 1992, reproduced in *https://opusdei.org/es-es/article/actualidad-eclesial-del-mensaje-de-josemaria-Escriva/*. Last consulted June 29, 2018.

42. *Decree on Heroic Virtues*, April 9, 1990, reproduced in Capucci, *Josemaría Escrivá, santo*, pp. 80–84. Quoted material at 83.

43. *https://opusdei.org/en-us/article/the-process-of-canonization-for-josemaria-escriva./*

44. John Paul II, Homily at the Mass for the Beatification of Josephine Bakhita and Josemaría Escrivá, May 17, 1992. *http://w2.vatican.va/content/john-paul-ii/it/homilies/1992/documents/hf_jp-ii_hom_19920517_beatifications.html.* (Italian). English versión *https://opusdei.org/en-us/article/homily-of-john-paul-ii-at-the-beatification-of-josemaria-Escrivá/*. Last consulted July 3, 2018.

45. See chapter 5.

46. See section 1 of volume 2, chapter 9.

47. María del Carmen Tapia, *Tras el umbral. Una vida en el Opus Dei* (Barcelona: Ediciones B, 1992). English version: *Beyond the Threshold: A Life in Opus Dei* (New York: Continuum, 1997). A second English edition was published in 2006 with the title *Inside Opus Dei: A True, Unfinished Story* (New York: Continuum 2006).

48. Kenneth L. Woodward, "A Coming-Out Party in Rome," *Newsweek*, May 18, 1992, p. 62.

49. "Maria del Carmen Tapia, "Non ho mai considerato il suo carattere forte un ostacolo alla sua santità e conseguente canonizzatine," *ANSA*, 24 December, 2001.

50. John L. Allen, Jr., *Opus Dei* (New York: Image, 2007), p. 61.

51. Kenneth L. Woodward, "A Questionable Saint," *Newsweek*, January 12, 1992.

52. Woodward, "A Questionable Saint."

53. See generally Allen, *Opus* Dei, pp. 66–69.

54. Quoted in "Conservative Catholic Group Denies Candidate for Sainthood Hated Jews," Jewish Telegraphic Agency, January13, 1992, *https://www.jta.org/1992/01/13/archive/conservative-catholic-group-denies-candidate-for-sainthood-hated-jews*. Last consulted November 12, 2018.

55. "How Does a Rabbi Gauge the Ideas of Opus Dei Founder Josemaría Escrivá de Balaguer?," Zenit, January 13, 2002. *https://zenit.org/articles/how-a-rabbi-views-blessed-escriva*. Last consulted, November 12, 2018. Further information on Escrivá's attitude toward the Jews can be found at *https://www.temesdavui.org/node/6985?lang=es&*.

56. Allen, *Opus Dei*, p. 67.

57. Cardinal Angelo Felici, *Decree on Heroic Virtues*, April 9, 1990, in Capucci, *Josemaría Escrivá, santo*, p. 80.

58. Eszer, "Actualidad ecclesial."

59. Sacred Congregation for the Causes of Saints, "Norms to be Observed in Inquires made by Bishops in the Causes of the Saints," n. 17, AAS 75 (1983), pp. 396–403.

60. Gray, for instance, while recognizing many merits of the new procedures, feels that something was lost in eliminating some of the trial type procedures.

Jason A. Gray, *The Evolution of the Promoter of the Faith in Causes of Beatification and Canonization: A Study of the Law of 1917 and 1983*. Doctoral Thesis, Pontifical Lateran University, 2015. *www.gray.org/docs/promoterfaith.html*.

61. Eszer, "Actualidad eclesial."

62. Allen, *Opus Dei*, 265.

63. John L. Allen, Jr. "With Beatification of John Paul II, What Makes a 'Fast Track' Saint?," *National Catholic Reporter*, February 1, 2011, *https://www.ncronline.org/news/vatican/beatification-john-paul-ii-what-makes-fast-track-saint*. Last visited July 5, 2018.

64. This and all the quoted material in this paragraph are taken from Allen, "With Beatification of John Paul II."

65. Account of Audience on June 19, 1978. AGP E.4.1, 227-4-6.

66. See Flavio Capucci, *Cures: Through the Intercession of Saint Josemaría Escrivá* (New York: Scepter, 2002).

PART III

The Third Generation
(1994–2016)

Toward the end of the twentieth century, just over six billion human beings inhabited the planet. By 2011, the number exceeded seven billion. The two largest countries, China and India, each accounted for some 1.4 billion people.

The era of electronic communication, which began at the end of the last century with laptops and Internet access, allowed new forms of contact. The technological infrastructure has made mobile devices and social networks available to the masses. Large parts of the world's population have continuous access to data hosted in the cloud. The processing and sending of information, ideas, and images in real time and at low cost has changed the social and cultural paradigms of an increasingly global world. The big American and Chinese electronics and computer companies—Amazon, Apple, Google, Microsoft, Alibaba, and Huawei—dominate the technology market.

There have also been remarkable advances in medicine and engineering. Scientists have determined the sequence that makes up DNA and have identified and mapped all the genes. Since 2000, there has been a permanent human presence on the International Space Station, and there are already plans for a permanent base on the moon and another on Mars.

China has progressively challenged the United States as the world's leading economic power. In 2008, a global financial crisis broke out that has not yet been fully resolved. Governments organized financial bailouts to save large companies, but this greatly increased public debt—especially in the Eurozone countries. Economic austerity programs brought with them severe cuts to social spending.

The Earth suffered major natural disasters, such as the earthquakes in Kashmir (2005) and Haiti (2010), Cyclone Nargis (2008), the tsunami in Japan (2011), the epidemics of dengue fever (several years) and Ebola (2014), and the Covid-19 pandemic which by the end of 2021 had killed more than 5 million people and inflicted enormous damage on the world economy. Other calamities have been man-made, in particular, wars and terrorism in West and Central Asia and in North and Central Africa. Fundamentalist Islamist terrorist groups such as al-Qaeda perpetrated serious attacks in the United States (2001) and other Western countries, followed by wars in Afghanistan and Iraq. The new century was also marked by tensions between Russia and the United States, which showed that political peace had not been achieved after the Cold War. Instability in the Arab world led to demonstrations such as the Arab Spring (2011), with major with major protests and insurrections in favor of democracy and social rights in North Africa and the Middle East.

In many countries, there was increasing stress on the values of transparency, sensitivity to ecology, the importance of the emotional dimension of human life, the recognition of other ways of thinking, and social awareness in the face of racial, gender, or social inequalities, particularly for migrants and refugees. Many sought actively to give meaning to human existence and to share values that orient and ennoble life.

At the same time, culture suffered from the crisis of postmodernity, characterized by the loss of the concept of identity, the radicalization of individualism, the supremacy of exteriority and material comfort over spiritual cultivation, confidence in scientific progress and capitalism, and the hope that the welfare state would solve all social problems. The "I" increasingly dictated people's desires and ways of life. Many came to reject the normative criteria offered by the Church and other institutions, and ultimately, rejected God as absolute. This found expression in the Italian philosopher Gianni Vattimo's *pensiero debole* [weak thought] which is based on a practical agnosticism and on the impossibility of reaching universal and absolute certainties. Because of what it defined as tolerance and diversity, this school of thought accused those who defended any form of absolute, objective, or universal truths of being dogmatic. What we should do, it contended, is conform to the rules dictated by the majority at any given moment. But, contrary to their own principles, these forms of liberalism and subjectivism made relative values a universal criterion and stifled the freedom of thought of those who did not accept them. They justified appealing to emotions without regard to facts, thereby making it easier for individuals to be indifferent to those who do not interact with them directly and allowing markets to transform people's claim to be different into an object of consumption.

The Catholic Church suffered greatly from the clergy sexual abuse scandal, which contributed to a steep decline of church attendance among young Catholics. John Paul II rallied Christians at the turn of the millennium and asked each member of the Church to bring faith and fraternal charity to society as the fruit of openness and a vital relationship with the transcendent. The baptized, he stressed, were called to a new evangelization that would humanize a vulnerable world.

Benedict XVI (2005–2013) spoke of a crisis of truth, goodness, and beauty. He went so far as to refer to the "dictatorship of relativism," which stigmatizes those who accept and spread absolute truths. For the Pope, this was a failure of reason, which has given up on discovering the truth about the nature of reality and the morality of human acts. To get out of the crisis, he called for uniting faith and reason more deeply and more explicitly.

Pope Francis has taken up these proposals pastorally with original formulas that are the fruit of his intellectual and life experience. Since his election, he has invited every Christian to transmit Jesus Christ—the essence of the gospel—and to alleviate the physical and interior suffering of others, especially that of migrants and those discarded by the welfare society. Francis proposes a Church that "goes out" to the peripheries and becomes a "field hospital" for a broken world.

This part of our monograph summarizes the development of Opus Dei over the last twenty-five years. Some questions are dealt with in a very general way, both because of a lack of historical perspective and because few sources are available. For the same reasons, we sketch out the facts with little effort to evaluate them. In chapter fifteen, we use some data from after 2016 to complete what is essentially a snapshot of some formative and apostolic activities.

$$\sim\!\!\mathcal{D}$$

Central and Regional Government

A fter the death of Del Portillo, the procedures for the election of a new prelate laid out in the Statutes of the Prelature of Opus Dei were applied for the first time. The process has three phases: a plenary meeting of the Central Advisory council, in which each participant proposes the name or names of those priests considered most suitable for the office of prelate; a general elective congress, in which the congress members, taking into account the proposals of the plenary meeting of the Central Advisory, vote for the prelate; and appointment of the new prelate by the Holy Father.[1] On April 19, 1994, the plenary session of the Central Advisory, made up of thirty-two women numeraries from regions all over the world, met. Each member proposed one or more candidates whom she considered appropriate. These proposals were then passed on to the elective General Congress, composed of 138 men, both priests and laymen. They elected Javier Echevarría Rodríguez as the new Prelate on the first ballot. After Echevarría accepted election, the secretary of the congress informed Pope John Paul II, who confirmed Echevarría's election and named him Prelate of Opus Dei.

Section 1. A Prelate Prepared by the Founder

Both the older electors, some of whom had been appointed in the 1950s, and the newer ones chose the person who had been formed by St. Josemaría and whom Del Portillo had continued to form with the obvious hope that he would succeed him. The fact that Echevarría had been so close to the Founder made him an authorized interpreter of Escrivá's thought and a guarantee that the Work would maintain the spirit of its beginnings. Moreover, the electors were confident that he would follow Del Portillo's example as "the Father" for the members of the Work.

Echevarría was born in Madrid on June 14, 1932, the youngest of eight children. He joined Opus Dei in September 1948 and moved to Rome to study two years later. He obtained a doctorate in canon law at the Pontifical Athenaeum Angelicum and in civil law at the Lateran University. He was ordained to the priesthood in August 1955. From September 1956 on, Echevarría served as the Founder's *custos* for material matters. He became a member of the General Council of Opus Dei as vice-secretary of St. Raphael in May 1966. He held these positions until Escrivá's death. In September 1975, the General Congress appointed him Secretary General of the Work and Del Portillo chose him as the Father's *custos* for spiritual matters. When the Work became a prelature in 1982, his title changed to Vicar General. He held these positions until Del Portillo's death.

The twenty-five years Echeverria spent with the Founder, both at Villa Tevere and in his travels through Europe and America, shaped his mind and his actions. First as his personal secretary, and then as a member of the central government, Echevarría learned from Escrivá how to pray, work, direct the Work, and relate to others with the ultimate goal of personal sanctity and spreading the call to Christian perfection in ordinary life. During Del Portillo's tenure as head of the Work, all important matters of Opus Dei's government passed through Echeverria's hands before they were dealt with by the Prelate. Del Portillo frequently ratified the decisions he proposed.

According to his successor, Fernando Ocáriz, Echevarría prayed a great deal: "Although nothing about his behavior was unusual or strange, it was perfectly obvious that his piety was continuous."[2] The people who lived and worked with him learned from his example to base their lives and their way of seeing things on faith, and he often encouraged them to have confidence in prayer. He frequently reminded them that the Church, and Opus Dei as a part of the

Church, would reach people through each one's personal dedication to God, generously fulfilling the tasks entrusted to him.

Becoming the Father of Opus Dei was obviously a turning point in his life. His paternal concern for the members mellowed his character.[3] He said that he loved his spiritual children with human and supernatural affection and that he felt that affection was reciprocated. He accompanied with his prayers the sick, the unemployed, and those who suffered in other ways. He tried to give primacy to individual people over projects and responded personally whenever someone asked him for prayer or advice. He read a great number of the letters sent to him by his spiritual children from all over the world and answered many of them. As the years went by, Echevarría became increasingly insistent on encouraging the members of the Work to care for one another and to live a Christian fraternity full of kindness.[4] "Love one another" was a frequent refrain on his lips.*

In his role as head of the Work, Echevarría demonstrated his capacity for leadership and hard work. He maintained cohesion and stability in Opus Dei, while at the same time proposing new challenges with a vision of the future. He liked to follow the progress of projects and to analyze in detail those submitted to him for review. He had an excellent memory that permitted him to remember many people and events. He relied on the collegiality of the central governing bodies and, when he did not see clear solutions, he expressed his doubts. After weighing the facts and circumstances, he moved forward with faith, audacity, and a desire to help.

---

* One of the most painful moments of Echevarría's life was September 13, 2016. Nine numerary assistants and two numeraries died and four others were seriously injured in a traffic accident in Guadalajara, Mexico. As soon as he received the news, Echevarría sent a letter to the regional vicar in which he said: "When I read the names, and right now, my eyes filled with tears. It is not sentimentality, but the reality that we are a splendid family which is very united, and for that reason this situation is always very difficult." He asked the vicar to "reassure those who have survived. Help them not be overwhelmed by what has happened, and to offer their efforts to return to normal life" (Letter of Javier Echevarría to Francisco Ugarte, Rome, September 14, 2016. AGP, series B.2.3).

From the first moment, Echevarría felt the responsibility of being the successor of two men of holiness of life and remarkable vision. His chief point of reference was the Founder. He prayed to him insistently, studied his writings, thought about how he would have solved the problems he faced, and recalled in public and private conversations anecdotes illustrating Escrivá's relationship with God and affection for others.

Being faithful to the original substance of the Work while adapting the nonessential elements to the changing times and finding new possibilities in the patrimony received were to be a continuous challenge in his life as Prelate. In addition to the changes occurring in civil society and the Church, Opus Dei itself was undergoing its first generational change. Although many of the older directors had experienced part of the foundational period, most younger ones had joined the Work after the Founder's death, and the youngest after Del Portillo's. Echevarría considered himself a member of the "third generation," made up of those "who received the Work already outlined, as a precious legacy from our Father through the first generations of his children. The Work, now, is in our hands."[5]

As soon as he was elected, he called a press conference where he stressed, as he did in his first pastoral letter, that "the time has come to delve more deeply into the message we have received, to live it with loyalty, to transmit it with integrity, and to spread it everywhere." He signaled three areas of special interest, in accord with the priorities of Pope John Paul II: 1) the family, so that "it may walk along the paths that the Creator has marked out for it;" 2) the apostolate with youth, "in accord with the charism proper to Opus Dei [helping them to feel] the need to draw close to Christ, to know him and love him and to meet him as they prepare themselves to work well and be responsible citizens;" and 3) the evangelization of culture through apostolate with men and women who "are the moderators of civil society, those who are in a position to profoundly influence the ways of thinking and living of future generations."[6]

Following Del Portillo's practice, he decided to write a monthly pastoral letter to the members and cooperators of the Work. Beginning in 2006, this letter was published on Opus Dei's institutional website. Echevarría also wrote long letters for special events, such as the preparation for the Jubilee of the year 2000, the centenary of the birth of Escrivá (2002), the ordinary General Congresses (2002 and 2010), the Year of the Eucharist (2004), the Year of Faith (2012), and the Year of Mercy (2015). Each letter revolved around a spiritual theme. They generally contained doctrinal elements, requests for prayers for particular intentions, and proposals for how readers might improve in their Christian life.

Echevarría undertook numerous pastoral trips to meet with the members of the Work, cooperators, and others connected with the Work's activities. He called for Marian years of thanksgiving in the Work to celebrate the Founder's canonization (2002), the twenty-fifth anniversary of the erection of Opus Dei as a personal prelature (2007), and the eightieth anniversary of the presence of women in the Work (2010). He proclaimed a final Marian year in 2015 to pray for the Synod of Bishops about the family

He published five books: *Memoria del Beato Josemaría* (2000), a personal recollection of the Founder which groups the ideas and phrases he heard from him thematically; *Itinerarios de Vida Cristiana* (2001), which expounds the principal truths of the faith; *Getsemaní* (2005), on the prayer of Jesus in the Garden of Gethsemane; *Por Cristo, con El, y en El* (2007), a collection of essays on St. Josemaría; and *Vivir la Santa Misa* (2010), which follows the rites of the Mass and offers ideas for its preparation. He also published articles, made statements, and gave interviews to the press, radio, and television.

As the Prelate of Opus Dei, Echevarría met regularly with the Pope and other Vatican authorities, participated by pontifical designation in various synods of bishops, and was a consultor, and later a member, of the Congregation for the Causes of Saints, a consultor to the Congregation for the Clergy, and a member of the Supreme Tribunal of the Apostolic Signatura.

Echevarría encouraged the faithful of the Work to be united in mind and heart to the Pope. He had regular meetings with the three popes who led the Church during his years as head of Opus Dei. He was grateful to John Paul II for his solicitude for the Work, which manifested itself, among other things, in the establishment of Opus Dei as a personal prelature, the beatification and canonization of the Founder, and the establishment of the Pontifical University of the Holy Cross. He tried to follow the teaching of Benedict XVI in religious and cultural matters, promoting studies on the natural law and the relationship between faith and reason, and he seconded Pope Francis' solicitude for the marginalized and his preaching on mercy.

The Prelate joined the popes on some apostolic journeys and World Youth Days: Kazakhstan (2001), Cologne (2005), Sydney (2008), Madrid (2011), Rio de Janeiro (2013) and Krakow (2016). He also traveled to participate in special celebrations at the request of local bishops. For example, he concelebrated with Cardinal James Hickey of the Archdiocese of Washington, DC, in 2000. A year later, Juan José Omella, bishop of Barbastro-Monzón in Spain, invited him to the inauguration of a church dedicated to St. Josemaría. When the Founder was canonized, Bishop Echevarría participated at meetings in Seville and Logroño, Spain, which were organized by the local ordinaries. In 2005, he traveled to Helsinki with Bishop Józef Wróbel for the commemoration of the arrival of the Church in Finland; and in 2009 and 2010 he participated in the dedication of churches in honor of St. Josemaría in Mexico City and Toruń (Poland).

A few weeks after a trip to Finland and Estonia at the end of October 2016, Bishop Echevarria was diagnosed with a lung infection associated with the pulmonary fibrosis he had been suffering from for years. On 12 December, he died in the hospital of the Università Campus Bio-Medico in Rome at eighty-four. His last words were a plea to God for the fidelity of the people of the Work to their Christian vocation.

Section 2. Governing the Work

After Pope John Paul II appointed Echevarría Prelate of Opus Dei on April 20, 1994, the General Congress continued. The congress members studied the situation of the Work, established the main lines of expansion of the message and activities for the next eight years, and appointed the members of the central governments.

The members of the General Council were: Fernando Ocáriz, vicar general; Francisco Vives, vicar central secretary; Pedro Pérez Botella, vice-secretary of St. Michael; Roberto Dotta, vice-secretary of St. Gabriel; Antoine León, vice-secretary of St. Raphael; Carlos María González, prefect of studies; and Federico Riera-Marsá, general administrator.

The directors of the Central Advisory were: Marlies Kücking, central secretary; María Teresa Iglesias, secretary of the advisory; María Dolores Alonso, vice-secretary of San Miguel; Concepción Ramos, vice-secretary of San Gabriel; María Pía Chirinos, vice-secretary of San Rafael; Monique David, prefect of studies; Sylvia Bacharach, prefect of numerary assistants; and Mercedes Gascó, central procurator.

Echevarría asked Fernando Ocáriz to be his most direct collaborator as vicar general of the whole Prelature and his personal confessor.* The central vicar secretary, Francisco Vives, helped him in the formation and apostolic activities of women members. At the regional level, the vicars collaborated with the Prelate in the territories entrusted to them.

During the years in which Echevarría was the head of Opus Dei, two ordinary General Congresses were held in Rome. The first, from October 11–22, 2002, was marked by the joy of the recent canonization of the Founder. One hundred forty men and 107 women participated. They reviewed the Work's apostolic activities since the previous

---

* Born in Paris on October 27, 1944, Ocáriz studied physics at the University of Barcelona. Afterward, he studied theology at the Pontifical Lateran University (1969) and received his doctorate at the University of Navarra (1971). He was ordained a priest in 1971. For more than twenty years he worked in the department of spiritual direction at the central headquarters of Opus Dei, where he focused on bibliographical orientation and the preparation of doctrinal texts. He was a professor of fundamental and dogmatic theology in the Work's Roman Colleges of the Holy Cross and of Holy Mary and in the Roman Athenaeum of the Holy Cross. He joined the General Council of Opus Dei in 1992 as prefect of studies. He is a consultor to the Congregation for the Doctrine of the Faith and to the Pontifical Council for the Promotion of the New Evangelization. He has published dozens of books and articles related to fundamental theology and Christology.

General Congress and made plans for the next eight years. Echevarría thanked God for John Paul II's trust and affection for Opus Dei and stressed the idea of continuity in the spirit received from the Founder. At the end of the congress, he wrote a pastoral letter to all the members transmitting its conclusions: to grow in personal virtue and in culture; to make Christ more visible through the revitalization of the family and social customs and through a sober life; to rediscover work as an area of personal sanctification and Christian witness; and to deepen one's own knowledge and ability to explain Christian teaching in relation to critical topics such as marriage and the family, education, bioethics, and ecology. At the same time, Echevarría proposed

> interdisciplinary studies on how to promote a mobilization of many people and institutions throughout the world, to promote, following the example of the first Christians, a new culture, a new legislation, a new fashion, consistent with the dignity of the human person and his or her destiny to the glory of the children of God in Jesus Christ.[7]

The Eighth Ordinary General Congress of Opus Dei took place in April 2010. Two hundred fifty-five congress participants took part, with one phase for men and another for women. At the end of the congress, Echevarría presented the conclusions reached by the congress in a pastoral letter. These stressed individual formation and the study of the sacred sciences; sobriety and detachment from material goods to facilitate the contemplative life; showing the beauty and importance of the virtue of chastity and Christian celibacy; cultivation of friendship; increasing the involvement of parents in the schools and youth associations that receive pastoral assistance from Opus Dei; and "the participation of well-formed Catholics in public life so that, according to their free personal preferences and convictions, they may contribute to the influence of the Christian spirit in the making of laws and in the government of peoples.[8]

The statutes provided for the possibility of an "auxiliary vicar" who could exercise the authority of the Prelate in matters reserved to him, but until 2014 there had never been one.[9] In June 2014,

Echevarría had turned eighty-two years old. Both his age and the growth of the Work were making it difficult for him to meet all the demands made on him. In December 2014, he named Fernando Ocáriz auxiliary vicar of the Prelature and appointed as vicar general Mariano Fazio who had been the regional vicar of Argentina since 2010.[*]

Echevarría was pleased with the state of Opus Dei's management structures when he took over as Prelate. Over the years, he worked at the progressive renewal of the government teams in the Work, incorporating more young men and women. He also encouraged the exchange of opinions among the central, regional, and local levels.

As Prelate, Echevarría met regularly with the General Council and the Central Advisory to study and resolve major issues. He also met, although less frequently, with the regional vicars and the regional secretaries, as well as with other members of the regional governments. Most of these meetings were held in Rome, but some were held in Argentina, Brazil, Spain, Mexico, and Portugal. Every eight years, the Prelate received a report about each of the regions from a small group, called a service commission, which traveled to the region, studied the situation on the ground and reported back to Rome. Every ten years, each region held a regional assembly. A recurring topic in many of these meetings was the importance of the local councils, which are responsible for the direction and organization of the centers of the Prelature. The regional directors often stressed the importance of not changing the members of the local councils too often and of trying to see to it that they had enough time to dedicate to their tasks.

---

[*] Born in Buenos Aires in 1960, Fazio graduated in history and received a doctorate in philosophy. He was ordained to the priesthood in 1991. He served as rector (2002–2008) of the Pontifical University of the Holy Cross and president of the conference of rectors of Roman pontifical universities. He was pontifical expert at the general conference of the Latin American and Caribbean Episcopate held in Aparecida (Brazil, 2007) and synod father by pontifical appointment at the synod of bishops for youth and vocational discernment (2018). From 2010 to 2014, he served as regional vicar of Opus Dei in Argentina. He has published numerous works on the history of thought, the Church, Latin America, and on literary classics.

Echevarría worked to increase the role of women in the government and activities of the Work. His goal was to achieve full equality between men and women within the constraints inherent in the hierarchical structure of the Prelature, which required that certain positions be held by priests. From the beginning of the Work, the Founder had wanted women to carry out the full range of apostolic activities conducted by men and to govern themselves and their activities autonomously. As a result of historical and organizational factors, however, this had not yet been achieved. Echevarría encouraged women members to aspire to a leading role in all fields of human life and asked that the central and regional government teams of women, as well as those of men, work collegially to study and resolve issues that arose. He also encouraged greater participation of women in the faculty and academic administration of the colleges and universities connected with Opus Dei.[10]

These developments within Opus Dei accelerated at the beginning of the new millennium in response, in part, to growing social awareness of women's dignity, rights and legitimate demands, such as work-life balance, the wage gap, legal parity, and social opportunities. In order to foster a public awareness of the dignity of women and their role in society on an equal footing with men, Echevarría thought it was necessary to start with the family itself and build from there.[11] He encouraged "mature women, courageous women, [to] set the tone in all areas of society."[12]

Regarding the liturgy, Echevarría decreed with the approval of the Holy See that in Masses celebrated in centers of the Work, the prelate would be mentioned in the Eucharistic prayer after the Pope and the bishop. Again with the approval of the Holy See, he decided to celebrate the Chrism Mass in Holy Week with the clergy of the Prelature and to establish a liturgical calendar proper to the Prelature, similar to that of the dioceses. In 2002, the Prelate sent to the Work's centers a booklet entitled *Experience with Liturgical Ceremonies* that gave guidance on the celebration of the Mass and other acts of worship in light of the new edition of the Roman Missal. The goal was to deepen the Eucharistic piety of those in attendance. Echevarría reminded the priests of the Prelature that, within the options approved by the Church, they should try to celebrate the Mass and fulfill the liturgical norms on worship in a way that fosters contact with God. They should avoid both complete uniformity that would amount to a kind of distinctive Opus Dei liturgy, an idea rejected by the Founder, and arbitrary spontaneity.

At the General Congresses of 2002 and 2010, the directors asked the members of Opus Dei to consider possible responses to the central themes of social life that the popes had been stressing: the value and dignity of human life, marriage, the family, education, social customs, communications, and politics. The Congresses reminded members that the Christian vivification of the world in the face of secularization depended, in large part, on the action of Christians in their work, and in their family and social relationships. The spirit of the Work invited the individual members to participate from their own place in society in the vanguard of the solutions proposed to improve society.

Echevarría concentrated on promoting the spread of the spirit of Opus Dei because he understood that in this way he was making an effective contribution to evangelization. The three popes with whom he met during his term of office, John Paul II, Benedict XVI, and Francis, all encouraged him in this regard.

In May 2016, Echeverría called together in Rome a small group of faithful of the Prelature from around the world to reflect on how the faith could be transmitted more effectively and to more people, particularly in non-Christian or secularized societies. He asked them to take into account the contemporary environment and the accumulated experience of the Work in various parts of the world as they thought about attractive ways of presenting traditional Christian principles. He hoped this would make it possible for the Work to respond more effectively to Pope Francis' challenge to the Church to reach the existential peripheries, including those who were far from God and from religious practice.

Following that meeting, the central governing bodies of the Work called for a "new evangelizing effort, which requires a major development of the apostolate to facilitate many more people coming to know Christ."[13] In particular, they urged the members to reach out to family members and friends with little or no faith or religious practice or who found themselves in irregular situations within the Church. They suggested that, along with the witness of personal life, the centers of the Work could schedule more formation courses based on what it means to be fully human, as a preamble to a proclamation of the Christian faith. Other possibilities they suggested for bringing the Christian message to new people were catechesis, formation of couples for married life, providing legal advice, and parish volunteer undertakings.[14]

They stressed that the means of formation should emphasize contemplation and then ascetical struggle. Primacy should be given to Eucharistic adoration and meditation on the gospel, without neglecting spiritual combat. A positive and witnessing style of faith, far removed from voluntarist formulas and defensive attitudes, would facilitate the interior freedom of each person to reflect and adopt in conscience his or her own resolutions.

Section 3. Day-to-Day Developments

In addition to stressing the broad themes we have just examined, Opus Dei sought new ways of spreading its message on a day-to-day basis. In the words of Monica Herrero, director of the office of the apostolate of public opinion of the Central Advisory:

> Evolution is something inherent in any institution, and even more so for an entity whose message is the sanctification of daily realities, which are always changeable. Throughout these years, some changes in Opus Dei have arisen spontaneously from the base, for example, increased stress on the care and attention of the elderly as the population has aged. Others have been the result of the directors' study and reflection. Some have been fully implemented and some have not yet been fully incorporated. Sometimes these positive institutional changes have been slower than social trends or legislative developments, partly because the solutions are complex. We also listen to and deal with the comments and criticisms of former members. In

this sense, Opus Dei is a young, learning institution. And we learn as much from what goes well as from what goes wrong.[15]

Doctrinal assistance to the members of the Work and cooperators was carried out primarily by the central and regional offices of spiritual direction. The publication of studies on philosophy and theology was encouraged, and brief overviews of doctrinal topics, lists with bibliographical guidance, and doctrinal ratings of books were drawn up. As the founder of Opus Dei had established, a bibliographical guide was sent periodically to the centers with evaluations of books on philosophy, theology, spirituality, thought, and literature, according to their adherence to the Christian message and the magisterium of the Church. In 2008, this list was transferred to the Internet so that people outside the Prelature could also benefit from the information it contained in deciding in conscience what they should read. This information was hosted for a time on the website almudi.org, run by some priests of Opus Dei in Valencia. Since 2014, it has been accessible on delibris.org, open to anyone who wishes to collaborate. In addition to the evaluation of publications, the guide offers reviews and bibliographical lists of literature, thought and spirituality.

The central office of spiritual direction also oversees the website collationes.org, which provides resources for priests on Christian faith and life and the art of spiritual accompaniment. It includes seven annual *collationes*, or ongoing formation conferences, for priests of the Prelature on a variety of topics in systematic theology, biblical theology, canon law, liturgy, Church history, and moral cases. Professors from universities and pastoral formation centers, especially from the Pontifical University of the Holy Cross, contribute to this page.

During the last decade, the directors of Opus Dei have reflected on how the Work as an institution and its members can deal more constructively with former members. In 2009, they created two working groups, one at the central headquarters and the other in Spain, to study how to improve the care given to former members who want to maintain some contact with the Work or with some of its members. According to Carlos Cavazzoli, the General Council's vice-secretary for St. Gabriel,

We are moving in three directions. First, we try to adopt a spirit of listening and respect for the life journey of each person, avoiding passing judgment on intentions while trying to contribute in a positive way to the individual's decision making. Secondly, we want to learn from past mistakes and rectify them when necessary: for example, by asking forgiveness if we realize that there was haste in planning someone's vocational process or carelessness in spiritual accompaniment. At the same time, we strive to facilitate the process of leaving the Work, appreciating the suffering of both the persons concerned and those who know them. And, thirdly, we leave the door open to continuing friendship and collaboration, offering spiritual direction, Christian formation, personal meetings, etc. In fact, there are many cases of men and women who had been numeraries or associates but who sometime after leaving the Work rejoin as supernumeraries.[16]

Misunderstandings and complaints to the Holy See from a few former members and some people who had never been part of the Work presented Echevarría with a particularly delicate challenge regarding spiritual guidance. The priests and other faithful of Opus Dei who spiritually accompanied another person naturally treated what they were told as confidential and subject to silence of office, much as lawyers protect the confidential information shared with them by clients. At the same time, it was understood by both parties that the person providing spiritual guidance might, when appropriate, consult someone else, just as a lawyer might consult another lawyer, who would in turn treat the information as confidential. Usually, the person consulted was the the director of the center and other members of the local council or perhaps a regional director who could help resolve a difficulty. This practice, which came from the tradition of the Church, was lived in accordance with the family spirit of the Work.[17]

Over time, however, a greater sensitivity had developed in society and in the Church to privacy and the distinction between the realm of individual conscience and the governance of the Church and its institutions. To avoid any impression of intrusion into the conscience of individuals, and after studying these issues with the Holy

See, Echevarría addressd these questions in a 2011 pastoral letter. In response to the concern about privacy, he established that priests and others providing spiritual guidance should not normally discuss with anyone else what they had been told. If, in some exceptional case, they felt in conscience that the person speaking with them needed guidance they could not give, they should urge that person to seek it directly. Alternatively, they could offer to seek advice on their behalf, but only with their explicit permission.[18]

In response to the concern about possible confusion between spiritual guidance and the governance of the Work, he stressed that the local directors and the priests who impart spiritual direction have no power of governance over the people they guide. Their role in the governance of the Work extends only to apostolic activities and the organization of the center.[19]

At the beginning of the twenty-first century, the Holy See became aware of the dimensions of the tragedy of clerical abuse of minors. Popes John Paul II, Benedict XVI, and Francis adopted measures to protect and support the victims, to prevent future abuse, to cooperate with civil authorities, to speed up the judicial process, and to ensure transparency in the follow-up of the cases. Opus Dei had traditionally established strict norms of prudence in dealings between priests and women and between adults and minors. In response to the new situation, it further strengthened its measures for the protection of minors and other potentially vulnerable persons. For example, Echevarría established that in all schools and youth entities there should be a confessional with a grille for hearing confessions, with separate spaces for the priest and the penitent; that conversations between an adult and a minor should take place in the open air or in rooms with transparent glass in the door; and that in overnight activities, such as camps, adults should not sleep in the same room or tent as minors. As of March 2021, four cases of abuse of minors involving priests incardinated in the Prelature had been processed with the Apostolic See, according to law.[20]

From the beginning, the Work has formed its individual members to practice the virtues of poverty and temperance in the world, living a life that is sober and in keeping with each person's social position. Some manifestations of this spirit, like the concern to earn enough to support oneself, one's family, and the apostolates, are permanent and stable across time. As economic and social circumstances change, however, new challenges appeared. For example, widespread Internet access and its increasing importance in professional life and personal relationships led the directors of the Work to stress the importance not only of technical measures such as filters to avoid offensive content but also "the formation of responsibility and temperance" to guarantee that the Internet serves the development of each person.[21]

In the early twenty-first century, Opus Dei continued to be financed through the contributions of the faithful of the Prelature, cooperators, and other benefactors. With these resources it covered the operating expenses of the prelatic curia and of the regional governing bodies, the support of its priests, the causes of canonization of the Work's faithful, and, in case of need, the support of the parents of the numeraries and associates. The operating expense of the central headquarters in Rome, where 150 people live, currently run approximately 1.7 million euros a year.[22]

Members of the Work also help support its apostolic activities such as conference centers, schools, and social centers through contributions for capital and operating expenses.[23] Schools and colleges and universities connected with the Work try to establish endowments.

Approximately 10 percent of the donations made to support the Work in each region are put at the disposition of the Prelate for apostolic projects in poorer countries. The funds are usually loaned at low or no interest and with favorable repayment schedules. Only rarely are outright grants made.

As we have seen, the Founder established that the Prelature does not normally own the buildings and facilities that house its centers or corporate apostolic activities. Currently, even Villa Tevere, the site of the prelatic curia, belongs to a company that allows the Prelature to use it. It is encumbered by a prohibition on sale, so that in the event of a transfer, the property would revert to the donors.

An especially important corporate activity undertaken during Echevarría's tenure was the construction of a retreat house in the Holy Land. Although Escrivá was never able to make a pilgrimage to the Holy Land, he wanted many Christians to deepen their faith by meditating on the gospel in the places where the events took place. During Del Portillo's pilgrimage there in March 1994, he talked about the Founder's desire to build a retreat house in the Holy Land. A few weeks later, the General Congress of the Work, which met for the election of Del Portillo's successor, approved the project.

After a decade of bureaucratic red tape and looking for a suitable site, land was purchased in Abu Gosh, some ten miles (eighteen kilometers) northwest of Jerusalem. Christians, Jews, and Muslims worked on the design and construction of the project, which began in 2007. Some of the Work's faithful organized a campaign to finance the construction and raise a thirty million dollar endowment fund to ensure stability of the center and help people of limited means who wished to make a pilgrimage to the Holy Land.

From the beginning, the undertaking was called *Saxum* (Latin for "rock"), a nickname given to Álvaro Del Portillo by the Founder during the Spanish Civil War. The purchase of the land and the construction cost $56 million, a sum contributed by more than one hundred thousand people all over the world. The project was inaugurated in 2017. It has a visitors' center, a retreat house, and a services center. The visitors' center offers a virtual tour of the Holy Land to orient and enrich the spiritual experience of pilgrims who are not otherwise connected to Saxum and whose tour guides may not always be able to explain adequately the Christian significance of the places they visit. The visitors' center also provides professional training to tour guides as part of the training offered by the Israeli government. The retreat house offers retreats and workshops on an ongoing basis to members of the Work, cooperators, and other people from all over the world. The activities are conducted in many languages. The annual weeklong Holy Land Dialogues combine elements of a pilgrimage with an educational program designed to promote interreligious dialogue and contribute to the participants' knowledge of the culture and spirituality of the Holy Land.

The sanctuary of Torreciudad in Spain, is now half a century old. It focuses on devotion to the Eucharist and to the Blessed Virgin and on the sacrament of penance. Among the events that attract large numbers of pilgrims are Marian days for families and pilgrimages along the Marian route, which includes the sanctuaries of Lourdes, El Pilar, Torreciudad, Montserrat, and Meritxell. In a country where many Catholics have special devotion to a particular image of the Blessed Virgin located in or near their hometown, visits of some of those images to the sanctuary of Torreciudad draw many families from the particular image's hometown.

In recent years, between two and three hundred thousand people have visited Torreciudad every year. In 2018 a strategic plan was launched to adapt the sanctuary to the needs of twenty-first century pilgrims. Thanks to generous contributions from many people, Torreciudad has established a thirty-million-euro fund to cover the costs of maintenance and visitor services and to guarantee the sustainability of future projects.

Section 4. Numerical Growth and New Countries

When Echevarría was elected prelate in 1994, 78,500 people belonged to Opus Dei: 45,900 women (58.5% of the total) and 32,600 men (41.5%). There were 1,500 priests incardinated in the Prelature. In addition, another 1,800 diocesan priests were members of the Priestly Society of the Holy Cross. Geographically, 46,500 faithful of the Work resided in Europe (59%), 27,000 in North, Central, and South America (35%), 4,000 in Asia and Oceania (5%), and 1,000 in Africa (the remaining 1%).

Over the next twenty-two years, the net growth of the Prelature (incorporations minus deaths and departures) was 14,400 persons, reaching 92,900 faithful in 2016. The average annual increase was 650 persons. The number of associates and supernumeraries of the Priestly Society remained constant at about 1,800 members.

During Echevarría's tenure, the Work began to have many elderly and sick members and had to find ways of caring for them. Deaths increased sharply from 48 faithful of the Prelature and 34 members of the Priestly Society in 1997 to 919 and 41 in 2016.[24]

Compared to previous periods, new members declined not only as a percentage of the total but in absolute numbers. Although Opus Dei continued to grow every year under Echeverría's leadership, the pace was much slower than during the 1980s when it occasionally reached three thousand new members a year. Especially since 2000, in many cases there has been a decline in vocations to celibacy.

The shrinking of the base of the demographic pyramid of Opus Dei reflects the demographic changes in the population of many countries as well as the increase of secularization. Vocations to the Work, as well as to other Church institutions, have been impacted by cultural changes in people's understanding of family and marriage and an increasing reluctance to make personal commitments.

Opus Dei came to recognize that it needed to update its formative activities and to correct mistakes made in the past. A 1997 service commission in Madrid reported, for instance, that increasing secularization and loss of the vigor of faith among Catholic families and communities were reflected in a lack of interest in spiritual values, sentimentalism, an individualism that makes true friendship difficult, a loss of intimacy and modesty, a decrease in religious practice, and difficulty in discerning a call to follow Christ. As a solution, they suggested trying to develop new ways of promoting Christian virtues among families and young people, giving priority to qualitative growth over quantitative growth, striving to go deeper in the Christian formation of each person, giving precedence to individual action without taking refuge in collective achievements, and fostering true friendship that respects the time that each person needs to understand and accept a Christian approach to life.[25]

During the years of Bishop Echevarría's tenure, the Prelature added fifteen regional circumscriptions to those the Work already had, bringing the total to forty-nine. This gave Opus Dei an official presence in seventy-one countries and more than three hundred fifty dioceses. In eight regions where the Work was more developed, it had delegations to facilitate activities. In 2016 there were ten delegations in Spain, four in Mexico, four in Argentina, three in the United States, two in Brazil, two in Italy, and one in Northern Central America.[26]

At Echevarría's death, the Work had sixty-six full-fledged retreat houses with an ordinary Administration in addition to about a hundred somewhat less-developed conference centers and some thirty still smaller ones in all parts of the world—including in countries with small Christian minorities. The centers of studies for numeraries and courses of studies for associates were in some cases consolidated because of fewer vocations. This was especially marked in Spain, where the centers of studies for male numeraries, female numeraries, and auxiliary numeraries went from eight, eight, and five to four, five, and three respectively.

The passage of time has also necessitated the renovation of retreat houses, residences, and centers. In addition, in several countries the Work built new facilities for formation and government. These included the headquarters of the regional commissions and advisories in the United States (New York, 2001), Italy (Milan, 2005), and Mexico (Mexico City, 2010). As families moved from the historic center of many cities to the suburbs leaving the city centers heavily commercial, Opus Dei centers also relocated to the suburbs. In Madrid, for example, several centers moved from the downtown districts to the expanding areas of the metropolis to better serve the activities of the Works of St. Raphael and St. Gabriel.

The parishes and other churches entrusted by diocesan bishops to Opus Dei priests in large cities around the world numbered more than fifty at the end of Echevarría's mandate.* The Onze Lieve Vrouw

---

* In Echevarría's first years, four churches were added: the parish of Blessed Josemaría (Rome, 1996), the parish of San Ildefonso (Granada, Spain, 1999), the church of Tres Cruces (Montevideo, 2001), and the parish of St. Mary Star of the Sea (Melbourne, 2001). Years later, others followed, such as the parishes of St. Thomas More (Archdiocese of Westminster, London, 2005), Our Lady Queen of Peace (Dublin, 2008), Saint-Wandrille de Le Pecq (Versailles, 2010), San Gioachimo (Milan, 2013), St. Agnes (New York, 2016), and the church of the Holy Cross (Vilnius, 2016). Some were left after a while, such as the church of Santa Veracruz (Santiago de Chile, 1998-2018) or Santa Rosalia (Palermo, 1998–2004).

church, in Amsterdam, stands out because it is owned by the Syrian Orthodox Church and accommodates Orthodox worship as well as Catholic worship entrusted to priests of Opus Dei. The two communities use the church at different times and collaborate in the upkeep of the building.

The Holy See and local bishops sometimes asked Opus Dei for priestly and professional help. Echevarría accepted the requests whenever he could, even though doing so reduced the availability of priests for the ordinary pastoral needs of the Work. Specifically, thirty priests of the Prelature work in the Roman Curia and some two hundred (ten percent of the clergy of the Prelature) have assignments in parishes, tribunals, educational centers, diocesan seminaries, and communities of religious women. In addition, during this period nineteen numerary priests were ordained diocesan bishops.* The Pope created two cardinals who came from the clergy of the Prelature: Juan Luis Cipriani (2001), Archbishop of Lima; and Julian Herranz (2003), President of the Pontifical Council for Legislative Texts.

The Prelate entrusts to his vicars and the personnel of the central and regional governing bodies institutional relations with the Vatican, dioceses, religious orders, movements, and ecclesial communities. Since the earliest days, the Work has maintained a particularly close relationship with communities of consecrated religious, especially contemplatives. Almost six hundred religious communities in thirty countries are cooperators of Opus Dei.

The 1994 General Congress proposed opening a center in eleven countries where the Work still had none and in a significant number of new cities in countries where the Work was already established

---

* For example, José Gómez, auxiliary bishop of Denver (2001) and since 2011 archbishop of Los Angeles; Anthony Muheria, bishop of Embu, Kenya (2003); Jaume Pujol, archbishop of Tarragona (2004); Philippe Jourdan, apostolic administrator of Estonia (2005); Jaime Fuentes, bishop of Minas, Uruguay (2010); Stephen Lee Bun Sang, auxiliary bishop of Hong Kong (2014); Levi Bonatto, auxiliary bishop of Goiânia, Brazil (2014) and Richard James Umbers, auxiliary bishop of Sydney (2016). The Prelature of Opus Dei continues to care for them spiritually after their episcopal ordination, although they cease to be incardinated in the Prelature.

in at least one city. In the late twentieth century, Opus Dei opened its first center in eight countries: Lithuania (1994), Estonia, Slovakia, Panama, Lebanon, and Uganda (1996), Kazakhstan (1997), and South Africa (1998). In the new millennium, eight more countries were added: Slovenia and Croatia (2003), Latvia (2004), Russia (2007), Indonesia (2008), Korea and Romania (2009), and Sri Lanka (2011). Although the General Congress also called for beginning in Angola, Vietnam, and Cuba, political conditions in those countries have made that impossible thus far. Faithful of Opus Dei, nevertheless, reside for professional or family reasons in a number of countries where the Work does not have a center, including Saudi Arabia, Bulgaria, Denmark, Dubai, Greece, Madagascar, Malta, Thailand, and Tanzania. They try to travel periodically to places where they can receive formation from the Work, as well as maintaining contact through digital media.

Beginning in Russia and in former communist satellites put Opus Dei in contact with large numbers of Orthodox Christians and with many Byzantine-Rite Catholics. In Lebanon, it reached out to Maronites who who make up the majority of the country's Catholics, as well as to the smaller number of members of other Eastern Catholic churches. In many other places, Orthodox Christians and Muslims, well as nonbelievers, come into contact with the Catholic faith through members of the Work and its centers.

Echevarría implemented the project of establishing the Work in Kazakhstan with the opening of two centers, one for men and another for women, in Almaty, the largest and most cosmopolitan city of the republic. Baybulak, a retreat house, is located in the outskirts of the city. Since 2011, Joseph Louis Mumbiela, a member of the Priestly Society of the Holy Cross, has been bishop of Almaty. In addition, two priests of the Priestly Society, with the permission of their respective bishops, have moved to Shymkent, the third-largest city in the country, to minister to the Catholic community.

Although Catholics represent only 10 percent of the population of Korea, a significant number of adults are baptized each year in the country. In August 2009, faithful of Opus Dei settled in the city of Daejeon, whose bishop, Nazarius Heung-sik Yoo, had previously been in contact with Opus Dei. After two years, they opened men's and women's centers in Seoul. Given the notorious difficulty of the Korean language, it took special effort and perseverance to learn as well as to become familiar with Korean customs. The women's center, Saint Hill, is a small residence near Sookmyung Women's University, while the men are currently building their first student residence. One of the first Koreans to join Opus Dei was Professor Kim June-Hong, a cardiologist from Busan, in the southern part of the country. The first woman, Ellie Kim, joined in 2015.

Section 5. Consolidation of the Personal Prelature

When Echevarría became its Prelate in 1994, Opus Dei had been a personal prelature for twelve years. During his tenure, Echevarría worked to establish the legal category of personal prelatures more firmly in canonical doctrine and to consolidate the position of the Opus Dei Prelature in civil and ecclesiastical law.[27]

He often invited bishops and nuncios from all over the world to visit Opus Dei's headquarters when they were in Rome. When the Prelate traveled to other countries, he made a point of visiting local bishops. His vicars also maintained regular contact with bishops and other Church authorities as well as with the leaders of religious communities and other Catholic institutions in their countries. Over time, a number of the bishops who had once feared that the personal prelature would distance their faithful from diocesan life came to be convinced that those fears were unfounded.[28]

In November 1994, the Vatican announced that John Paul II had called the Work's Prelate to the episcopate. On January 6, 1995, the Pope ordained him bishop in St. Peter's Basilica. Echevarría's episcopal ordination helped establish the Prelature of Opus Dei in the pastoral ministry of the universal Church and of the particular churches in which it was active. It also strengthened the Prelate's communion with the other bishops.

Over the years, the Work was recognized as a legal corporation by the governments of almost all the countries where it carried out pastoral activities on a stable basis. In many cases, the Holy See requested legal recognition of the Prelature, certifying that it had canonical legal status in the Catholic Church.[29] In addition, many of the recent concordats signed by the Holy See explicitly include personal prelatures among the ecclesiastical circumscriptions that the Church can erect, thereby facilitating Opus Dei's civil recognition.[30] Among the first nations to grant Opus Dei legal recognition were Italy (1990), France (1996), and Spain (1996). The form this recognition takes varies from country to country. In the United States, for instance, Opus Dei is a religious corporation organized under the laws of the State of New York.

Many legal scholars who have written about personal prelatures see them as fitting naturally into the broad category of ecclesiastical circumscriptions which form part of the jurisdictional and hierarchical structure of the Church. The Vatican curia has recognized the jurisdictional character of personal prelatures in the *Annuario pontificio*, where the Prelature of Opus Dei appears within the hierarchical structure of the Church.[31] Some canonists, mostly associated with the Pontifical Gregorian University, have, however, understood personal prelatures as merely administrative entities of an associative character that incardinate clerics and, consequently, deny that they are part of the ordinary structure of the Church, or that the laity belong to them fully.[32]

Some authors have suggested that personal prelatures be erected to care for migrants whose pastoral needs are not easily met by the normal diocesan structures which presuppose some degree of geographic stability. Similar suggestions have been made regarding the pastoral care of other social minorities. John Paul II referred to possible personal prelatures for these pastoral needs in the post-synodal apostolic exhortations *Ecclesia in America* and *Ecclesia in Europa*,[33] but nothing came of these suggestions.

John Paul II clarified the legal nature of the Prelature of Opus Dei in a March 2001 address to a congress organized by the Work to study possible social and apostolic applications of the apostolic letter *Novo*

Millennio Ineunte. The Pope explained the theological and canonical foundation of the hierarchical nature of Opus Dei and of its mission in the Church. He pointed out that the Prelature was organically structured of priests and laity, headed by its prelate, and stressed that

> the fact that the lay faithful belong both to their particular Church and to the Prelature, to which they are incorporated, means that the special mission of the Prelature converges with the evangelizing commitment of every particular Church, as the Second Vatican Council foresaw when it established the figure of personal prelatures.[34]

During the early years of the twenty-first century, the Vatican created some ecclesiastical circumscriptions based on personal criteria. It made use of legal categories similar to personal prelatures, but did not erect any more personal prelatures. The most significant case involved the 2009 creation of *personal ordinariates* for Anglican communities seeking full communion with the Catholic Church that wished to maintain some of their specific characteristics and patrimony. Subsequently, the Holy See erected three personal ordinariates: Our Lady of Walsingham, for the territory of the Bishops' Conference of England and Wales (2011); St. Peter's Chair, for the territory of the Bishops' Conferences of the United States and Canada (2012); and Our Lady of the Southern Cross, for the territory of the Bishops' Conference of Australia (2012).[35]

In 2011, the Holy See announced that it was considering readmitting the followers of Archbishop Lefèbvre, who belonged to the Priestly Fraternity of St. Pius X, into the Catholic Church. It said that the channel for canonical recognition could be a personal prelature. The process was derailed, however, by doctrinal issues. A few years earlier, in 2002, Pope John Paul II admitted into full ecclesial communion, under the figure of a *personal apostolic administration*, a group of faithful from the diocese of Campos (Brazil) coming from the Fraternity of St. John Mary Vianney (equivalent to the European Priestly Fraternity of St. Pius X). The decision to use the category of personal apostolic administration is probably due to the exceptional nature of the case and to the fact that the jurisdiction of the personal apostolic administrator is limited to the territory of Campos.

The internal consolidation of the Opus Dei Prelature was reflected in Echevarría's establishment of the Prelature's trail court, a necessary element in ecclesiastical structures to resolve legal conflicts and the channel for the exercise of the judicial power that pertains to the prelate. The Prelature's court of appeals is the appeals court of the Diocesan Vicariate of Rome.[36] In practice, even after the establishment of the court, the Prelate has resolved almost all questions through administrative rather than judicial channels.

At the procedural level, Echevarría's most important activities involved the ongoing causes for canonization of Álvaro del Portillo and Dora del Hoyo, and the requests received from diocesan tribunals for the instruction of the causes for canonization of Antonio Zweifel, José María Hernández Garnica, and José Luis Múzquiz. At the legislative level, Echevarría promulgated various laws or general decrees which form part of the Prelature's particular legal norms.

Experience suggested that the glosses and *vademecums* drawn up at the end of the 1980s might in some cases lead to a certain rigidity and voluntarist attitudes, in part because they were overly detailed. In addition, the procedures they called for gradually became outdated because of social and technological change. For these reasons, in the 2000s, the central governing bodies of the Work revised and condensed them into a relatively small number of documents called *Experiencias* [Experiences] to guide regional and local governing bodies about ways of living the Christian virtues in accordance with the spirit of the Work and organizing corporate activities and life in the centers of the Work. These texts incorporate points drawn from the Work's permanent normative documents, including its Statutes, and other points that refer to living its spirit in current circumstances and are therefore subject to change over time. Several points of the Catechism of the Work were also updated.[37]

Under Echevarría, the official bulletin of the Prelature of Opus Dei, *Romana*, continued to publish two issues each year in Italian, Spanish, and English. It prints about two thousand copies of each issue.

Section 6. Causes of Canonization and Studies on Opus Dei

More than twenty thousand members of the Work have died since its foundation. Many have given a witness of Christian coherence throughout their lives, right up to their final moments. At times, people from Opus Dei, from other ecclesial institutions, and even non-Catholics have asked the Church to recognize their sanctity. The Work has prepared causes for the beatification and canonization of various members to reflect the broad spectrum of people who seek to identify themselves with Christ by living the Work's spirit: women and men, priests and laity, single and married,

For the Founder to be canonized, a miracle that occurred after his 1992 beatification was needed. In November of that year, a medically inexplicable healing took place when a Spanish physician was cured of a chronic skin cancer he had contracted in the course of his work. Once the medical evidence was examined, the Holy See certified the miracle in September 2001.

On October 6, 2002, John Paul II canonized Josemaría Escrivá in St. Peter's Square. Numerous civil and ecclesiastical authorities and, according to media reports, more than 250,000 people, were present. Twenty-nine television networks transmitted the ceremony to all five continents. Escrivá's canonization implied the Holy See's judgment that the spirit of Opus Dei, which he had lived and proclaimed, was a path to holiness in daily activities. The Pope summed up in the Founder's own words his advice on how to put in practice his ideal of "raising the world to God and transforming it from within: 'First prayer, then atonement; in the third place, very much in the third place, action' (*The Way* 82)." "It is not a paradox," John Paul II continued, "but a perennial truth: the fruitfulness of the apostolate resides, first of all, in prayer and in an intense and constant sacramental life. This is, in the end, the secret of holiness and of the true success of the saints."[38]

The following day, Echevarría celebrated a Mass of thanksgiving in St. Peter's Square. At its conclusion, John Paul II received the pilgrims in audience. He defined Escrivá as the "saint of the ordinary," a priest who "was convinced that, for those who live in a perspective of faith, everything offers an opportunity for an encounter with God, everything becomes a stimulus for prayer. Daily life, seen in this way, reveals an unsuspected greatness."[39] The Pope concluded the audience with a reception for the Patriarch of the Romanian Orthodox Church, Teoctist I, and with a prayer for the full unity of Christians.

Devotion to St. Josemaría and knowledge of his life and message have grown rapidly. His published works have sold more than nine million copies, including five million copies of *The Way*. The website escrivaobras.org allows his writings to be consulted in various languages and searched electronically. At the beginning of this century, more than two million prayer cards were being published annually to help people pray to God through his intercession, and a total of a million copies of information bulletins about his life were published in various languages each year. Today the bulletins have been largely displaced by information on the Internet and social networks. The Office for the Causes of Saints receives some two thousand reports of favors attributed to St. Josemaría every year. The Beta Films Foundation (Madrid) has a large archive of meetings with Escrivá on film.

The Vatican approved texts in twenty-seven languages for the Mass of St. Josemaría. Some dioceses and episcopal conferences have included his feast day, which is celebrated on June 26, in their liturgical calendars. More than forty churches have been named for him and there are thousands of statues, plaques, and pictures of him in churches and chapels throughout the world. In September 2005, Pope Benedict blessed a larger-than-life-sized statue of St. Josemaría in a niche on one of the outside walls of St. Peter's Basilica. Dozens of streets, squares, public gardens, schools, hospitals, and libraries bear his name.[40] In some places, members of the Work have created societies that recall events of his life, such as the Associació d'Amics del Camí de Pallerols de Rialb a Andorra (2002), which recalls his crossing of the Pyrenees at the end of 1937.

The organizing committee for the canonization promoted a fundraiser among the participants at the ceremony to support the Harambee Project 2002, which promoted solidarity undertakings in sub-Saharan African countries. Over time, the project has expanded into the current Harambee Africa International Foundation which provides support to local groups that run social programs for the promotion of women, strengthening of family agricultural schools, social integration of youth, construction of primary schools, training for sustainable agriculture, and the fight against mother-to-child transmission of AIDS. Harambee has also helped give visibility to other social undertakings of African Catholics. Commenting on the first ten years of Harambee's activities, Echevarría reminded its supporters that social charity "constitutes a substantial part of the mission of the Church" and is manifested in a preferential way in the care of the poor, "promoting forms of cooperation for development that overcome religious, racial, ideological and territorial divisions."[41]

At the request of bishops, priests, religious, and laypeople from all over the world, Echevarría prepared the necessary documentation to initiate the cause of canonization of Álvaro del Portillo. He also asked that holy cards and information bulletins be prepared to facilitate private devotion to Escrivá's first successor. By 2010, ten million prayer cards and four million information bulletins had been distributed in many languages. From very early on, reports of favors attributed to his intercession were received.

Del Portillo's cause of canonization began in 2004. In 2010 the Congregation for the Causes of Saints was given the *Positio*, which includes a documented biography. Two years later, with the approval of Pope Benedict XVI, the congregation declared that Del Portillo had lived the Christian virtues to a heroic degree. Later, it certified a miracle attributed to his intercession, the healing of a Chilean infant. A few days after being born with a serious clinical condition, the baby suffered a cardiac arrest. His mother prayed to Álvaro del Portillo and, after forty-five minutes, the little boy's heart began to beat again, and in the following days he recovered from the hemorrhage he had suffered. Although he has experienced some aftereffects, the child grew up normally.

Del Portillo was beatified on September 27, 2014, in Madrid. Cardinal Angelo Amato, prefect of the Congregation for the Causes of Saints, presided at the Mass; seventeen cardinals and one hundred fifty bishops concelebrated. During the ceremony, a letter from

Pope Francis was read. The Pope repeated a phrase Del Portillo often addressed to God: "Thank you. Pardon me. Help me more." In those words, the Pope added,

> the new Blessed tells us to trust in the Lord, that he is our brother, our friend who never lets us down and who is always at our side. He encourages us not to be afraid to go against the current and to suffer in order to proclaim the Gospel. He also teaches us that in the simplicity and everydayness of our lives we can find a sure path to holiness.[42]

Another process that advanced rapidly was the cause for the canonization of Guadalupe Ortiz de Landázuri, who held a doctorate in chemistry. She was one of Opus Dei's first women and had started the activities of the women's branch in Mexico. The cause was opened in the Archdiocese of Madrid in 2001; the *Positio* was delivered in 2009, and the Decree of Heroic Virtues was promulgated in 2017. A year later, the Holy See approved a miracle attributed to Guadalupe's intercession, the instantaneous cure of a malignant skin tumor. On May 18, 2019, she was beatified in Madrid.

Causes for the canonization of fifteen other faithful of the Work have been officially opened, and several other possible causes are being studied. They reflect the variety of the Work's faithful and include married and single men and women, priests, and laity. The causes of Isidoro Zorzano and Montserrat Grases had been begun by the Founder, but they moved slowly in the Congregation for the Causes of Saints and suffered a serious setback in the 1980s when changes in the legislation governing the causes of the saints required reworking the documents that had been submitted. The new documentation was finally submitted for Montserrat in 1999 and for Isidoro in 2006. In 2016 the Holy See approved separate Decrees of Heroic Virtues for both of them. The next step in their beatification would be the certification of a miracle attributed to their intercession.

At the time of this writing, the Prelature has also presented to the Congregation for the Causes of Saints the *Positio* of Eduardo Ortiz de Landázuri (a supernumerary doctor from Spain 2007), José María

Hernández Garnica (a numerary priest, 2017) and Ernesto Cofiño (a supernumerary doctor from Guatemala, 2021).

The other causes of members of the Work promoted by the Prelature itself are: Antonio Zweifel, a numerary Swiss engineer; the married couple Tomás Alvira, a supernumerary Spanish professor of education, and his wife Francisca, a supernumerary Spanish housewife; José Luis Múzquiz, a Spanish numerary priest who helped begin Opus Dei in the United States; Dora del Hoyo, a Spanish numerary assistant who work in the Administration of a number of centers; and Laura Busca, a Spanish supernumerary housewife who was the wife of the previously mentioned Eduardo Ortiz de Landázuri. In addition, the causes for canonization of several members of the Work have been sponsored by other entities: Bishop Juan Ignacio Larrea of Guayaquil, Ecuador, and Bishop Adolfo Rodríguez Vidal of Santa María de los Ángeles, Chile, are being promoted by their respective dioceses. The Diocese of Abancay (Peru) is looking into opening the cause of its bishop, Enrique Pèlac, a Spanish associate of the Priestly Society of the Holy Cross. The cause of a Brazilian supernumerary, Marcelo Henrique Câmara, a lawyer and state prosecutor who died at the age of twenty-eight, was begun in 2018 by the Marcelo Henrique Câmara Association formed by his friends.

The mortal remains of three Servants of God have been transferred to churches for the private devotion of the faithful: Zorzano to the parish of San Alberto Magno in Madrid, Grases to the oratory of Santa María de Bonaigua in Barcelona; and Hernández Garnica to the church of Santa María de Montalegre, also in Barcelona. Cofiño rests next to his wife in the church of Nuestra Señora de la Paz (Guatemala City).

Numerous studies on the life and teaching of Escrivá have been published. Of particular note are the three-volume biography of the Founder, *El Fundador del Opus Dei* [English translation, *The Founder of Opus Dei*], written by Andrés Vázquez de Prada based on the *Positio*; the account of Escrivá's Roman years, written by Pilar Urbano under the title *El Hombre de Villa Tevere* [English transaltion, *The Man of Villa Tevere*]; and the *Diccionario de San Josemaría Escrivá de*

Balaguer, with 288 entries, some of a theological-spiritual nature and others historical-biographical. Also of special interest are the three volumes of *Vida Cotidiana y Santidad en la Enseñanza de San Jose-maría* [English translation, *Ordinary Life and Holiness in the Teaching of St. Josemaría*], the first systematic explanation of the message of Opus Dei from the perspective of spiritual theology.[43] In addition, there are more than a hundred books of testimonies and recollections of faithful of Opus Dei.

In January 2002, when the canonization of Josemaría Escrivá had already been announced, the Pontifical University of the Holy Cross held an international congress in Rome to commemorate the centennial of his birth and to study how his teachings could be applied in everyday life. People from different countries, cultures, and religions took part. The presentations and debates explored the potential of Escrivá's message and teachings from many angles, including theology, history, art, family, youth, and education.[44] The meeting received some attention in the media because of the speakers and the topics explored.

Eight years later, Echevarría acknowledged that although Escrivá's teaching constituted a "catechesis on holiness in ordinary life," the professors of theology and other ecclesiastical subjects who belonged to the Work had made little progress in making it known to their colleagues and appreciated by them. "Among the authors who study his doctrine from a theological perspective," he confessed, "almost all are faithful of the Work, although there are notable exceptions, such as Cornelio Fabro, Leo Scheffczyk, and a few others."[45] He urged the professional theologians who belonged to Opus Dei to work harder at helping their colleagues appreciate the richness of Escrivá's life and writings.

The Pontifical University of the Holy Cross created the Chair of St. Josemaría Escrivá, which has offered courses on spiritual theology in light of Escrivá's teaching, and has awarded a number of doctoral degrees. In November 2013, the university hosted an international congress on St. Josemaría and his theological thought, with the participation of renowned theologians who are not members of the

Work, such as François-Marie Léthel and Robert Wielockx.[46] Other congresses have analyzed the contribution of Escrivá's charism to theology, some from an academic perspective and others from a more popular point of view.

Journalists who do not belong to the Work have published valuable articles and books about its spirit and activities, including *Opus Dei: Un'indagine* (1994) by Vittorio Messori; *Escrivá, Fondatore dell'Opus Dei* (2002) by Andrea Tornielli; and *L'Opus Dei: Enquête sur le « Monstre »* (2006) by Patrice de Plunkett. Perhaps the most important was *Opus Dei: An Objective Look Behind the Myths and Reality of the Most Controversial Force in the Catholic Church* (2005), by the well-known America journalist John Allen, a specialist in Vatican affairs.

In 2001, Echevarría established the St. Josemaría Escrivá Historical Institute (ISJE) with the goal of promoting the publication of historical and academic studies on the Founder and Opus Dei. The ISJE has its headquarters at the Pontifical University of the Holy Cross in Rome. It also has a section at the University of Navarra called the Josemaría Escrivá Documentation and Study Center.

One of the first tasks undertaken by the ISJE was beginning the publication of Escrivá's complete works.* After the books that had been published during his lifetime (*Camino, Santo Rosario, Conversaciones con Mons. Escrivá de Balaguer, Es Cristo que Pasa, Amigos de Dios, La Abadesa de las Huelgas,* and *Escritos Varios*), the ISJE has

---

* The editors have chosen to call them "critical" editions. For ancient texts where different manuscripts offer different versions, sometimes diverging in important ways, editors prepare critical editions which report the variations and attempt to reconstruct the original text, giving reasons for preferring one reading to another. For Escrivá's works, there are few questions about the correct text. The editions prepared by the ISJE offer extensive introductions and explanatory footnotes, and a critical apparatus which clarifies the few minor variants in the text. For *Camino*, the editor traces the growth and evolution of the text from its first brief version under the title *Consideraciones Espirituales* to its final form. Even this, however, is not a "critical" edition in the usual English sense of the term because there is no need for a critical edition when the author himself gave final form to the text and there is no doubt about what he intended. In English they might better be called "authoritative editions."

begun to release the previously unpublished works. The first two volumes contained a collection of meditations, *In Dialogue with the Lord*, and four pastoral letters.

Since 2007, the ISJE has published a journal entitled *Studia et Documenta*, which brings together academic articles on the Founder, members of the Work, and the history of the institution; a documentary section that publishes texts from the General Archives of the Prelature of Opus Dei; a news section with short articles on recent cultural and social activities related to the Work; a bibliographical section; and a theological essay on some aspect of the spirit of Opus Dei. The ISJE maintains a library that collects historical monographs and other printed resources about Opus Dei. It has also created an online library of works on St. Josemaría.[47]

The main documentary basis for research about Opus Dei is the General Archives of the Prelature of Opus Dei (AGP), established by the Prelate in December 2017. It holds the documentation of Escrivá de Balaguer, his successors, and the organizations of the Prelature, with government documents, letters, diaries, and photographs.

Notes

1. See *Codex iuris particularis Operis Dei*, 1982, n. 130.

2. Recollections of Fernando Ocáriz, in Álvaro Sánchez León, *En la tierra como en el cielo. Historias con alma, corazón y vida de Javier Echevarría*, 3rd ed., (Madrid: Rialp, 2018), p. 187.

3. See Ernesto Juliá, *Instantáneas de un cambio. Javier Echevarría, Prelado del Opus Dei* (Madrid: Palabra, 2018).

4. See Recollections of Isabel Sánchez, in Sánchez León, *En la tierra*, p. 239.

5. Javier Echevarría, Pastoral Letter, November 28, 1995, n. 12. AGP Biblioteca, P17.

6. Javier Echevarría, Pastoral letter, May 1, 1994, nn. 4 and 5. AGP Biblioteca, P17 and "Declarations of the New Prelate of Opus Dei" (undated). AGP D.1.

7. Javier Echevarría, Pastoral Letter, November 28, 2002, n. 11. AGP Biblioteca, P17.

8. Javier Echevarría, Pastoral Letter, May 17, 2010, n. 23. AGP Biblioteca, P17.

9. See *Codex iuris particularis Operis Dei*, 1982, nn. 134–135.

10. According to Isabel Sánchez Serrano, central secretary of Opus Dei, Javier Echevarría encouraged women to occupy "the most important positions in the world, working there to create home-like environments and humanizing the world. But he also wanted women at the center of the home, performing there the most important task in society: caring for persons" (quoted in Sánchez León, *En la tierra como en el cielo*, p. 317). Sánchez Serrano has been the central secretary of the Central Advisory since 2010.

11. Because of its great social influence, members of Opus Dei gave special importance to fashion, which permits men and women to reveal who they really are through what they wear. Echevarría recalled that Christians are invited to ensure that a pleasant and elegant exterior reflects their inner attunement with God and responds to the truth about man, created in the image of God, who is absolute beauty. He encouraged fashion professionals to try to be present in the places where new trends are born and spread. Members, cooperators, and friends responded, trying in various ways to spread styles of clothing that dignified the person, to contribute to decorum in shows and advertisements, and to present in an attractive way the sense of modesty. Concrete undertakings include anthropology seminars, congresses and publications, fashion shows, and courses in aesthetics. See lecture of Javier Echevarría at a meeting on fashion and Christian apostolate, Rome, February 17, 1996. AGP R.2.4.2, 4-245. Some specific undertakings related to fashioned are described in chapter 16.

12. Javier Echevarría, Pastoral Letter, November 28, 2002, n. 11. AGP Biblioteca, P17. For example, 150 Opus Dei members and cooperators, both men and women, participated in the International Conference on Women in Beijing (1995) as members of their country's official delegations or representing associations and NGOs. They were moved by a desire to promote equality between men and women and mutual interpersonal solidarity (see AGP R4.1, 1-263).

13. General Note 102/16 (September 21, 2016), n. 1.

14. See General Note 103/16 (September 21, 2016). These ideas go back to the foundation and the earliest period of the Work's history. In 1980, the General Council reminded all the members that "we cannot limit our apostolate to those who already have a good Christian foundation: we must reach every corner and spread the living Christian doctrine of Jesus Christ among people of the most diverse backgrounds" (General Note 15/80, n. 5. AGP E.1.3, 1138.).

15. Author's interview with Monica Herrero, Rome, April 6, 2011. Herrero has been director of the Opus Dei information office since 2018.

16. Authors' interview with Carlos Cavazzoli, Rome, January 20, 2021.

17. See for example, General Note 7/89, n. 4. AGP Q.1.3, 9-59; Javier Echevarría, Pastoral Letter, October 2, 2011, n. 18 . AGP Biblioteca, P17.

18. Echevarría, Pastoral Letter, October 2, 2011, n. 18 . Two years earlier, indications along these lines had already been given. See General Notes 103/09 (March 13, 2009) and 104/09 (November 5, 2009). AGP E.1.3.

19. Echevarría, Pastoral Letter, October 2, 2011, n. 15.

20. In 2013, Bishop Echevarría published guidelines for the management of possible cases of abuse. Msgr. Ocáriz revised them in 2020 to bring them into line with the new regulations and recommendations of the Holy See. In every region there is an advisory committee and a coordinator for the protection of minors. Their mission is to receive and study accusations and carry out investigations of possible cases: *https://opusdei.org/es-es/article/proteccion-de-menores*. Last consulted, November 10, 2021.

21. H 417/99 (16-III-1999). AGP G3.2.4, 3153.

22. See *https://romana.org/68/notizie/alcune-informazioni-economiche-del-2018/*.

23. The members often do so by contributing to foundations and other not-for-profit entities that support the social and cultural centers. Some of these foundations are relatively large and support a wide range of activities. An example is the *Fundación Casatejada*. *www. https://www.fundacioncasatejada.com*. Last consulted, November 10, 2021. Others are small and may concentrate on just one or two projects.

24. See *Romana* 24 (1997), p. 154; *Romana* 25 (1997), p. 350; *Romana* 42 (2006), p. 136; *Romana* 43 (2006), p. 250; *Romana* 62 (2016), p. 172; *Romana* 63 (2016), p. 376.

25. This summary was prepared by the authors drawing on the ideas in the report of the Service Commission to the Madrid East Delegation, February 22, 1997. AGP Q.2.1, 81-307.

26. During this period, six countries became full-fledged regions: Brazil, Chile, Colombia, the United States, Portugal, and Venezuela. Two preexisting units, technically classified not as regions but as delegations dependent on the General Council or quasi-regions were divided, creating a total of five units: the East Asia delegation covering Hong Kong, Macao, Canton, Taiwan, and Korea; the Southwestern Asia delegation, covering Singapore, Malaysia, Thailand,

and Vietnam; the North Central America delegation, covering Guatemala and Honduras; the South Central America delegation covering Costa Rica, Nicaragua, and Panama; and finally the delegation of El Salvador.

27. See Javier Echevarría, "L'esercizio della potestà di governo nelle prelature personali," *Folia Canonica* 8 (2005), pp. 237–251.

28. See Fernando Sebastián, *Memorias con* esperanza (Madrid: Encuentro, 2016), pp. 261–266.

29. See José María Vázquez García-Peñuela (ed.), *El Opus Dei ante el Derecho estatal. Materiales para un estudio de Derecho comparado* (Granada: Comares, 2007), p. 154. The book explains the process by which the recognition of the civil personhood of the Prelature was acquired in different countries.

30. This is the case, for example, of art. 6 §1 of the concordat between the Holy See and the Republic of Poland, July 28, 1993; art. 5 of the agreement on juridical matters between the Holy See and the Republic of Croatia, December 19, 1996; additional protocol to the agreement between the Holy See and the Republic of Gabon on principles and juridical provisions concerning their relations and collaboration, December 12, 1997; and of art. 5 of the Agreement between the Holy See and the Republic of Lithuania concerning juridical aspects of the relations between the Catholic Church and the State, 12 May 12, 2000.

31. It appears in a similar way in ecclesiastical yearbooks and practical documents such as the one used to prepare the quinquennial reports of *ad limina* visits (see Congregation for Bishops, *Formulario per la relazione quinquennale*, Libreria Editrice Vaticana, 1997).

32. Among the important studies in this doctrinal debate are: Eduardo Baura, "Le attuali riflessioni della canonistica sulle Prelature personali," in Sandro Gherro, ed., *Le Prelature personali nella normativa e nella vita della Chiesa* (Padova: CEDA, 2002), pp. 15–53; Gaetano Lo Castro, "Le Prelature personali nell'esperienza giuridica e nel dibattito dottrinale dell'ultimo decennio," in *Studi in onore di P. Bellini*, vol. 1, (Soverria Mannelli: Rubbetino, 1999), pp. 423–456; Julián Herranz Casado, "La razón pastoral de las prelaturas personales: consideraciones a los 50 años del Concilio Vaticano II," *Ius communionis* 3/2 (2015), pp. 245–260; Antonio Viana, "El contexto doctrinal sobre las prelaturas personales. (Con ocasión de unas recientes páginas de Gaetano Lo Castro)," *Ius Canonicum* 40 (2000), pp. 289–306; Antonio Viana, *Introducción al estudio de las Prelaturas* (Pamplona: EUNSA, 2006). A relatively exhaustive bibliography with links to many articles on personal prelatures, ordinariates and other personal circumscriptions can be found at *https://prelaturaepersonales.org*.

33. See John Paul II, Post-Synodal Apostolic Exhortation *Ecclesia in America*, (January 22, 1999), AAS 91 (1999), pp. 717–815, n. 65, n. 237; John Paul II, Post-Synodal Apostolic Exhortation *Ecclesia in Europa* (June 28, 2003), AAS 95 (2003), pp. 649–719, n. 103, n. 166. This suggestion was echoed in the Instruction *Erga Migrantes* (May 3, 2004), n. 24, of the Pontifical Council for the Pastoral Care of Migrants and Itinerant People.

34. *http://www.vatican.va/content/john-paul-ii/es/speeches/2001/march/documents/ hf_jp-ii_spe_20010317_opus-dei.html*. Last consulted, May 25, 2020. See Jorge Miras, "Notas sobre la naturaleza de las prelaturas pesonales. A propósito de un discurso de Juan Pablo II," *Ius canonicum* 42 (2002), pp. 363–388.

35. On the relationship of this new legal category with personal prelatures, see Antonio Viana, "Ordinariatos y prelaturas personales. Aspectos de un diálogo doctrinal," *Ius canonicum* 53 (2012), pp. 481–520.

36. See *Romana* 22 (1996), pp. 26–28; John Paul II, Apostolic Constitution *Ecclesia in Urbe* (January 1, 1998), AAS 90 (1998), pp. 177–193, art. 40.

37. See AGP E.1.9 and AGP Q.1.7. The latest edition of the Catechism of the Prelature of the Holy Cross and Opus Dei (the 8th edition) is from 2010.

38. *http://www.vatican.va/content/john-paul-ii/es/homilies/2002/documents/ hf_jp-ii_hom_20021006_escriva.html*. Last consulted October 8, 2020.

39. *http://www.vatican.va/content/john-paul-ii/es/speeches/2002/october/documents/ hf_jp-ii_spe_20021007_opus-dei.html*. (last accessed on October 8, 2020).

40. See Aldo Capucci, "La memoria di san Josemaría Escrivá nello spazio urbano in Italia," *Studia et Documenta* 4 (2010), pp. 439–451.

41. Javier Echevarría, "Speech at the 10th Anniversary of Harambee, Pontifical University of the Holy Cross, Rome (October 5, 2012)," *Romana* 55 (July–December 2012), pp. 316 and 318.

42. *http://www.vatican.va/content/francesco/es/letters/2014/documents/papa-francesco_20140927_lettera-beatificazione-Álvaro-del-portillo.html*.

43. Ernst Burkhardt and Javier López, *Vida cotidiana y santidad en la enseñaza de San Josemaría*, 3 volumes (Madrid: Rialp, 2010–2013). English version of volumes 1 and 2: *Ordinary Life and Holiness in the Teaching of St. Josemaría* (New York: Scepter, 2017 and 2018).

44. *La grandezza della vita quotidiana*, 13 vols. (Rome: Edizioni Università della Santa Croce, 2002–2003).

45. Javier Echevarría, Pastoral Letter, April 23, 2010, n. 395. AGP Biblioteca, P17.

46. See Javier López Díaz (ed.), *San Josemaría e il pensiero teologico*, 2 vols. (Rome: EDUSC 2014–2015).

47. See María Eugenia Ossandón, "*Instituto Histórico San Josemaría Escrivá de Balaguer*," in Illanes (ed), *Diccionario de San Josemaría Escrivá de Balaguer*, pp. 644–645. Virtual Library: *https://www.unav.edu/web/centro-de-estudios-jose-maria-escriva/biblioteca-virtual/index.vm*. Last consulted November 10, 2020.

CHAPTER 14

Formational Activity

As we have seen, from the beginning the spirit of the Work has been transmitted in an institutional way through the formative activities that constitute the Works of St. Raphael, St. Gabriel, and St. Michael and through the activities of the Priestly Society of the Holy Cross. In each case, the means employed, both individual and collective, are based on foundational ideas such as the sense of divine filiation, knowledge of and devotion to Jesus Christ, and the sanctification of work as a means of holiness and Christian witness.

The formation Opus Dei offers seeks to prepare people to face perennial human questions in a fully Christian way. It attempts to present the truth about God and humankind in ways that can be understood by men and women who live in a constantly changing cultural and social environment. For this reason, formation plans in Opus Dei have been frequently updated to help the member transmit Christian principles and outlooks to individuals in ways that help them to internalize them and spread them in a personal way in their own environment.

Section 1. Formation of Youth

Opus Dei directors have always encouraged all members of the Work to take care of the Work of St. Raphael, which seeks to bring the message of holiness in the midst of the world to young people through personal friendship. They have reminded members that the Founder used to talk about it as "the apple of his eye."

The centers of the Work which carry out St. Raphael activities are often linked to an educational entity for youth. These educational undertakings, promoted by faithful of the Prelature in collaboration with other people, are of a professional and civil nature, and rely on the Prelature for their Catholic orientation. They can take various forms, depending on their purpose, the age of the young people to whom they are directed, and other factors. These forms include a youth association that offers activities for young people in their free time; a residence for college students; a center for the academic and character education of adolescents; and a cultural center for university students. They are designed to meet specific needs of the society where they are located, and their activities are meant to provide a useful service in a Christian spirit, facilitate personal apostolate with many people, and foster the growth of apostolic work with young people.

There are some eight hundred youth organizations and associations connected with Opus Dei around the world, from the Liepkiemis and Vilnelės cultural centers in Vilnius (Lithuania), to Huayna and Hontanar in La Paz (Bolivia) and Hodari and Faida in Nairobi (Kenya). A majority are intended for boys or girls in middle school, high school, or college, but a good number serve young people in manual trades. Among the most frequently offered activities are leadership courses, language classes, opportunities for social volunteering, cooking classes, sports, and excursions. They normally have a board of directors, which includes some parents of the young people who are involved in their activities, and a management council which runs their programs.[1]

The directors of the Work urge all these centers and associations to develop their own educational projects in ways that help families create Christian homes and which complement the instruction participants receive at school. The centers' staff encourages parents to play important roles in the tutorials and other activities, since they are primarily responsible for the formation of their children. Active participation in the centers' activities also provides parents an opportunity to grow closer to their children in an environment other than the home. Both in their programs and through tutoring, these organizations focus on helping students develop good study and reading habits. To facilitate this, they usually have a dedicated study room.[*]

From the beginning of Opus Dei, residences for college students have figured large in its apostolic activities. As we have seen, during the 1930s and 1940s, its apostolate concentrated mainly on university students. Starting in the 1950s, the Work expanded among married people and high school students. During the 1960s and 1970s, apostolic undertakings with high school students grew to such an extent that the directors of the Work felt compelled to stress the importance of not neglecting the apostolate with university students.[2] Today there are about two hundred student residences, some for men and others for women. For example, in Italy the Fondazione RUI runs thirteen university residences in six cities. In addition to residences, there are some nine hundred other university centers of various kinds that offer programs of cultural enrichment, opportunities for participating in social outreach activities, and Christian formation.

Some of the young people who attend the activities of the various centers also take part in the formational activities, which constitute what Opus Dei refers to as the Work of St. Raphael. At their core are always what Opus Dei calls "traditional" St. Raphael activities: a preparatory course or circle, teaching catechism to young children, visits to "the poor of Our Lady," meeting Christ in personal prayer, retreats, and spiritual accompaniment. These are carried on in an environment which encourages study and enthusiasm for the participant's future career or profession as a path to holiness and a service to society. They foster a desire to bear witness to the faith among the student's friends, even among those who do not lead a Christian life.

At the heart of these traditional St. Raphael activities are the practical classes in Christian life Opus Dei calls "circles." The most

---

[*] In addition to these corporate activities, many individuals connected to the Work have felt inspired to run informal clubs for their own children and their friends starting at a young age. They gather on a regular basis in the family's home for a brief catechism class, a few minutes of prayer, and other educational and recreational activities.

important part of the circle is an examination of conscience made up of twelve questions composed by St. Josemaría. They focus on the participants' personal relationship with God, their study, and their relationship with others. For example: "Do I often realize that I am in the presence of God?" "Have I devoted the necessary hours to study, knowing that studying is a serious obligation for me?"" Have I neglected, through selfishness, apathy, or carelessness, my fraternal duties?"[3] The questions are read aloud, pausing briefly between each question to allow each person to reflect silently on his or her own life.

In addition to the traditional means of formation, each center organizes a variety of "auxiliary activities," which vary over time in response to local needs and preferences, and which often include professional seminars, retreats, individual tutoring, sports, and camps. Since John Paul II started the World Youth Days in 1986, many Opus Dei centers have formed groups to attend them. It is also very common for centers to organize volunteer work during the academic year as well as domestic or international work camps during vacations, sometimes in places that have suffered natural catastrophes such as Hurricane Mitch, which hit Honduras (1998), the earthquakes in El Salvador (2001), and the floods in the province of Santa Fe, Argentina (2003).

During Holy Week, many regions organize formative meetings for secondary school students. The largest of them, the International Fatima-Ourém Meeting, is attended every year by more than a thousand young people from various European countries. In addition to celebrating Holy Week in Fatima, the students enjoy sports and cultural activities.

The annual international UNIV meeting brings together in Rome about two thousand university students, both men and women, during Holy Week. Conferences and round tables explore possible solutions to the challenges posed by contemporary culture. Since most of the participants are young people involved in the Work of St. Raphael, UNIV offers the participants an opportunity to attend the Solemn Easter Vigil celebrated in St. Peter's Basilica by the Holy Father and the rest of the Holy Week liturgy. There are formative meetings and cultural tours of the Eternal City as well as an audience with the Pope and a meeting with the Prelate of Opus Dei.

From 1991 to 2019, a simultaneous second meeting was organized in Rome by the Associazione Centro ELIS under the title *Incontro Romano* to promote study and research in the field of hospitality, home management, and other professions dedicated to the service of the person in public and private spaces. It was attended annually by about four hundred students and people working in the sector. It now forms part of the UNIV meeting.

Other themes especially stressed in Opus Dei's activities among adolescents during Echeverría's tenure were character formation, affectivity and the integration of the emotions, and good use of free time. Youth entities have convened talks and seminars on true love, purity of heart, Christian chastity, and the value of waiting until marriage to become sexually active. Another important focus has been on the use of the Internet, social networks, and multimedia resources.

St. Raphael centers have recruited well-known academics and leaders in the professions to participate in conferences on the humanities and seminars on current cultural themes including the dignity of the person and bioethics, science and faith, artistic creation and religion, ethics and economics, and finance and social responsibility.

The atmosphere of Opus Dei centers and the formation they received there has helped many young people to discover the Christian meaning of their lives. Some of them received God's calling to celibacy as numeraries or associates of Opus Dei, in the priesthood or in consecrated life. Others have come to appreciate the Christian vocational sense of marriage, some of them as supernumerary members of the Work. To encourage prayer and the desire for more people to follow Jesus Christ with the gift of celibacy in Opus Dei, for years Echevarría asked the members of the Work to pray that there would be five hundred vocations in their region.[4]

Echeverria reminded all the members of the Work that the Prelature's Statutes provide that a minor cannot be a member of the Prelature or legally bound to the Work.[5] To make even a commitment for a period one year, and thereby be admitted as a member (referred to as "making the oblation"), a person must be at least eighteen years of age. To make a lifetime commitment (referred to as "making the fidelity"), a person must be at least twenty-three years old.

This means that young people between fourteen and sixteen-and-a-half who think they have a vocation to the Work can only become "candidates" for admission (*aspirantes*). They are able to begin receiving appropriate formation immediately,* but may request admission only when they reach sixteen-and-a-half years of age. Neither becoming a candidate nor requesting admission has any legal effect. Neither makes a person a member. Only by making the oblation (at age eighteen or older) does anyone become a member. Despite the lack of legal significance of becoming a candidate and requesting admission, Echevarría established that to do either, a minor needs the parents' permission. This, he said, "besides being a measure of prudence, will help confirm the selection and maturity of these young men and women."[6]

During Echevarría's tenure, half of the new numerary members and one-third of the new associates had been candidates for admission for some period of time between age fourteen and age sixteen-and-a-half. Some people who embraced celibacy in the Work when they were young, however, later realized that celibacy was not their vocation and asked to be admitted as supernumeraries.

Section 2. Primary and Secondary Education

In 1994, there were just over two hundred schools connected with the Work. By 2016, there were three hundred, with 150,000 students. One hundred twenty are located in Spain. Eighty percent are personal works and the rest are corporate works. At present, in the countries where Opus Dei has been established for decades, the effort is concentrated on consolidating and improving the schools that already exist rather than on starting new ones. The Work focuses on

---

* The significance of being sixteen-and-a-half is that the Statutes provide that the soonest the oblation can be made is a year and a half after requesting admission to the Work. Working back from the requirement of being at least eighteen to make the oblation, one reaches sixteen-and-a-half as the youngest age for requesting admission.

providing advice to the schools on catechetical and religious texts, programs of education in affectivity and temperance, the use of digital media and social solidarity, and the sense of responsibility.

The Work has urged all schools connected with it to offer large numbers of generous scholarships to ensure that they are open to families who cannot afford the full tuition. A number of schools have gone well beyond this in their social commitment. For example, in Santiago de Chile, the Nocedal Foundation (1996) has established four schools in very poor neighborhoods. Two are technical schools that teach electronics, telecommunications, nursing care, and administration. In San Salvador, the secondary school Citalá (2011) offers full scholarships to all its students who come exclusively from poor neighborhoods.

Maintaining and developing the Christian identity of these schools and their commitment to character and religious formation has required an ongoing effort on the part of the Work. The schools were born thanks to the commitment of parents who were enthusiastic about the values-based, personalized education they would offer and felt personally responsible for their success. Once they were established and had won a reputation, they began to have a growing number of students whose parents did not closely follow their children's education and were content to leave matters in the hands of competent teachers. Other parents took an interest in their own children's education but showed little interest in the overall progress of the school. Faced with this reality, the directors of the Work have encouraged the staff of the schools to try to engage the parents actively and to renew the enthusiasm and entrepreneurial spirit of the beginnings through interviews, family counseling, and active parents' associations.

From the beginning, the schools connected with the Work have tried to tailor education to the needs of individual students. They were convinced that the differences in the pace of development between boys and girls and their way of learning and of processing emotions and motivations in childhood and adolescence meant that this would be easier in single-sex schools. They are not alone in this belief. Although coeducation is now the norm in most countries, significant numbers of experts in many English-speaking countries argue in favor of single-sex schools. In the United States many highly respected private schools are single-sex and in the last decade there has been a small but significant movement toward single-sex public schools. Currently, there are several hundred single-sex public schools in the US.

In other parts of the world, single-sex schools have been severely criticized. Their opponents claim that they are associated with conservative ideologies, resistance to the advancement of gender equality, and outdated pedagogical methods. The critics ignore considerable evidence that many single-sex schools have evolved with society, enjoy academic prestige, are in demand by families, obtain excellent results, and excel in terms of the indices and parameters by which equality objectives are usually measured.

Despite social, political, and economic pressure to move to coeducation, the boards of directors and management of virtually all the schools associated with Opus Dei have decided, in agreement with the authorities of the Work, to continue single-sex education. In support of their decision, they point to the academic results obtained, the satisfaction of the families of the students, and the quality of the formation of the students.* In pedagogical journals, in public debates, and in general circulation publications, the backers of these schools have explained that they encourage the active participation of men and women on equal terms in all areas of society, and that they are

---

* A few personal work schools have moved to coeducation, generally because of financial difficulties caused by a shrinking pool of school-age children. In those cases, the directors of the Work have stoped classifying them as personal works, even though the schools maintain their Christian identity and people of Opus Dei continue to work there and have a personal relationship with the authorities of the Prelature in the area. When possible, priests of the Prelature or of the Priestly Society of the Holy Cross continue to provide spiritual care for teachers, employees, and students. This is the case, for example, of Institució Igualada (Barcelona), which merged its boys' school and girls' school. The nursery, primary, and middle school students have classes together. The high school is housed in a single building with several common spaces, but boys and girls are taught separately.

far removed from earlier approaches that taught different subjects to boys and girls to prepare them for different roles in society.

In Spain, the government has made several efforts to cut off funding to single-sex schools, but its efforts have been rejected by the courts. In 2018, the Constitutional Court ruled that single-sex education is "a pedagogical option voluntarily adopted by the schools and freely chosen by the parents." It cannot, the court said, "be conceptualized as discriminatory," and therefore single-sex schools must be able to "access the system of public funding on equal terms with the rest of the educational centers."[7]

Historically, significant government subsidies have made it possible for private schools in Spain, including those associated with Opus Dei, to keep their tuition low enough that low-income families have been able enroll their children. In 2020, the Parliament passed an education law cutting back on aid to private schools generally and prohibiting aid to single-sex private schools. The government of Madrid decided to continue providing subsidies at more or less their existing level. It remains to be seen how this will play out in Spain and what effect it will have on the schools associated with the Work.

Section 3. The Development of the Work of St. Gabriel

Supernumeraries and cooperators are engaged in all kinds of professions and trades throughout the world. Through their work and family and social relationships, they individually help give a Christian orientation to social, economic, cultural, and political institutions and help their colleagues and acquaintances to discover their own human and supernatural vocations. Echevarría frequently reminded the supernumerary members that they had the same call to holiness and to spreading the message of the Work as the rest of the faithful of Opus Dei, since there is no such thing as a "second-class" vocation. Dedication to God places each person on the front line of the spiritual struggle for Christian perfection, whatever his or her personal circumstances.

The doctrinal, religious, and apostolic formation given in the Work of St. Gabriel has naturally evolved over time to adapt to changing social circumstances. The directors have increasingly encouraged parents to play active roles in the lives of the schools their children attend and to develop programs and activities outside of school that foster their children's growth, including youth groups and meetings with other families. Groups of supernumeraries have taken a larger role in running the St. Raphael centers' activities for young people and their parents. Bishop Echevarría encouraged them to join "with other fathers and mothers of families to help their children learn to use their free time well, and to provide opportunities for recreation and amusement and suitable places for their daughters and sons to mature humanly and spiritually."[8]

Monthly days of recollection, retreats, workshops, circles, spiritual direction, and classes of Christian doctrine have increasingly focused on themes related to holiness in the family, stressing both the underlying theory and practical ways to foster the education of children and unity between spouses. Some of these formative activities are given at the centers of the Work, others in parishes and in the houses of supernumeraries. The St. Gabriel centers also began to offer more events for people in the final years of their studies and the early phases of their careers who are not yet married.

Supernumeraries regularly attend Mass in their parishes and have their children baptized and confirmed there. Many play an active role in the life of the parish, teaching catechism to children or giving RCIA classes, taking part in in marriage preparation courses, accompanying the sick, participating in parish Caritas or St. Vincent de Paul Societies, as well as in diocesan synods.

Many, though not all, supernumeraries receive two years of especially intense formation in "courses of formation." There are currently about 120 of these courses spread around the world. Participants take classes in philosophy and theology, the teachings of the Church, the spirit and apostolates of Opus Dei, and practical aspects of Christian life—especially family, marital morality, the education of children, social justice, and the meaning of suffering. A special effort is made to enroll young supernumeraries to equip them to meet the challenge of seeking sanctity in marriage and family life and carrying out a vibrant apostolate with other young families.

An ongoing effort in the St. Gabriel Work has been creating closer connections among the supernumeraries, especially those who belong to the same group. The directors regularly remind the members of local councils, group leaders, and coordinators to make sure they give each person the help they need. Some supernumeraries with the necessary aptitude and time are asked to help care for other supernumeraries, especially those who might otherwise be isolated by illness or old age. A few supernumeraries are entrusted with the spiritual accompaniment of other members as group leaders or coordinators.*

Another focus in the formation given in the St. Gabriel work is the apostolic mission of the lay faithful. Being an apostle who is aware of having received a mission from God gives meaning to one's personal vocation to Opus Dei. The current 65,000 supernumeraries and the more than 170,000 cooperators are invited to discover Christ's call to be a leaven in society through a joyful and sober life that sometimes goes against the dominant way of thinking. They are frequently reminded that God wants them to speak about him to family members, colleagues, relatives, and friends in a personal manner that goes well beyond inviting them to participate in religious or social activities.

Section 4. Numeraries, Numerary Assistants, and Associates

Part 1. Numeraries

The numerary members have college or graduate degrees or on their way to earning them, have embraced celibacy, generally live in centers of the Work, and are ready to dedicate all or a large part of their efforts to carrying out internal tasks in the Work. All of this puts them in a position to strengthen the family bonds of the Work, to give formation to other members, and to fill management positions in corporate

---

* On the group leaders and coordinators see chapter 13, section 4.

activities and in the government of Opus Dei. Some take on these tasks as their full-time job. Others work at an outside job but spend much of their free time on these tasks, sometimes working part-time at their jobs to have more time available. To do all of this effectively, they need training in philosophy and theology at least equivalent to that required of priests.

In 1989, with the approval of the Congregation for Catholic Education, Del Portillo promulgated a *Ratio Institutionis Sacerdotalis* which specifies the content of the ongoing formation for the clergy of the Prelature and for numeraries and associates who are candidates for Holy Orders. Attached to this document was an *Ordinatio Studiorum* which focused on the academic content of the formation given to members. In accordance with canonical legislation, new editions of this *Ratio* were promulgated in 1996 and 2007. In addition, Del Portillo promulgated a *Ratio Institutionis* for the Prelature of Opus Dei that established the plan for the doctrinal, spiritual, and apostolic formation of all its faithful. This was revised years later by Bishop Echevarría.

The interregional centers for men annually welcomed more than one hundred students who studied for a bachelor's, master's, and eventually a doctoral degree in theology, philosophy, canon law, or some other branch of the sacred sciences. Almost all of them studied at the Pontifical University of the Holy Cross or at the University of Navarra. While carrying on their studies, numeraries of the men's branch resided in Rome at Cavabianca or in Pamplona at Aralar. Associates lived at the Iturgoyen residence in Pamplona. These interregional centers are the Prelature's international seminaries and offered their residents in-depth formation in the spirit of the Work. When they finished their studies, some returned to their regions or moved to other regions as directors of regional governments or local councils and as professors of the *Studium Generale*. Others, who had expressed their willingness to be ordained, were called to the priesthood. During Echevarría's tenure more than six hundred members became priests of the Prelature. In a normal year, some twenty to thirty numeraries and two or three associates were ordained. From 1995 until his death, Echevarría personally ordained the priests and deacons of the Prelature.

More than a thousand numerary women have studied at the Roman College of Holy Mary, an interregional center for women. Since 1992, it has been located in Villa Balestra, in the Pinciano district of Rome. Some eighty students take undergraduate courses in philosophy, theology, canon law, and communications in addition to receiving specific training in the spirit and activity of Opus Dei. In 2005, the University of the Holy Cross entered an agreement with the Roman College of Holy Mary for its faculty to teach classes there. Since 2015, classes and seminars have been held at a nearby location, Rocca Romana, which has classrooms and a specialized library.

Only a small number of numerary members go to one of the interregional centers of studies. The vast majority attend one of the eighty regional centers of studies for numeraries or one of the twenty regional centers of studies for numerary assistants. Currently many of the young people who attend the centers of studies come from schools that are in some way linked to Opus Dei, from St. Raphael centers, or from families related to the Work of St. Gabriel. They are encouraged to cultivate relationships and friendships with their university and professional colleagues who have had no previous contact with Opus Dei, and to organize activities in the centers and residences to get to know more people

Each year, some young numeraries go, with their parents' permission, to study in colleges and universities in countries where the Work is taking its first steps. Their youth makes it easier for them to learn the language, to assimilate culturally, and to find their way in the academic and professional environment of the place. When their parents grow older and need help, it is not uncommon for them to return to their native country to take care of them.

Part 2. Numerary Assistants

Finding the best approach to the formation of women who plan to work in the Administration, whether as numerary assistants or as administrators, has proven especially complex. It has required an effort to understand more deeply the role of the Administration in changing social environments marked by the full incorporation of women into public life in the vastly different cultures of different countries and even different social groups in a single country, All of this has required the women who work in Administrations to develop above all a clearer understanding of their work as centered on the care of persons. At the same time, they need a professional approach and the extensive theoretical and practical knowledge needed to embrace flexibly cutting-edge methods in ways that reflect ecological responsibility and sustainability. Through the professional competence they place at the service of each person, the women who work in the Administration aspire to become a focus of light for society on the way of being and creating family.[9]

Since the mid-1990s, in developed countries, the majority of numerary assistants have come from cities and have university or other higher education. In other places, such as Central America, Kenya, or the Philippines, a significant number of numerary assistants still come from rural backgrounds and have less education when they join the Work. No matter what their background, the formation offered the numerary assistants strives to help them see their work as a worthwhile person-centered profession which contributes decisively to making Opus Dei a family and is in no way reducible to providing the services which might be done by a housekeeping company. The numerary assistants' approach to their work also helps the men and women who live in the Work's centers understand that they are cared for not only with professional competence but also with real affection.

These developments have naturally been reflected in the syllabus that outlines not only the organizational and technical components of the training of numerary assistants, but more importantly the vision of spiritual, human, and family life that inspires their work. The current syllabus stesses self-confidence and on developing competences in communication, teamwork, innovation, and proactivity.[10]

In 2006, the *Centro de Estudios e Investigación de Ciencias Domésticas* (CEICID) [Center for Studies and Research in Domestic Sciences] of the University of Navarra began to offer a special vocational training program for the numerary assistant who held or were study-ing for a college degree. The program took its current shape in 2010 as a three-year *Programa de Desarrollo en Administración de Servicios* (PDA) [Service Management Development Program], a dual training program offering classes and on-the-job training as well as online sup-port and mentoring of students by professors who work with them in the Administrations.[11]

As we have seen, in Mexico future administrators can take a degree in administration and hospitality at the School of Adminis-tration of Institutions at the Universidad Panamericana; the same is true in Colombia for those who study administration and ser-vice at the Universidad de La Sabana. In several countries, train-ing sessions and refresher courses led by experienced professionals are organized in both large and small Administrations. Even in places where there are few members of the Prelature, as in Almaty (Kazakh-stan), courses of specialization in hotel and catering services have been offered.

In the past, in many countries it was common for housekeepers, maids, and other domestic workers not to have the same access as other workers to public or private insurance, retirement plans, and even medical coverage. Some women working in the Administra-tion of Opus Dei centers at times found themselves in this situation, although Opus Dei took on the obligation of supporting the numer-aries and numerary assistants in illness and old age. In recent decades, the directors of Opus Dei have established that the authorities of the foundations and other entities that run the centers must make certain that all the people who work in the Administration have appropriate health coverage whether under public or private plans.[12]

Women related to Opus Dei have contributed to research and educational theory in the caring professions in the hotel, home, and healthcare sectors. The Home Renaissance Foundation, for example, a British-based think tank founded in 2006, promotes new under-standing of the professional dimensions of housework and the task of creating welcoming homes that contribute to the humanization of society. It conducts interdisciplinary academic research and organizes international conferences related to domestic work and family care. It also fosters dialogue with public authorities about ways "to promote education and communication strategies that raise awareness that family tasks are a matter of shared responsibility."[13]

Part 3. Associates

Associates are men and women with a commitment to celibacy who carry out all kinds of work from scientific research to banking, from operating a lathe to being a clerk in a store. In the more developed countries, the majority have college degrees. A few work in corporate apostolates, but the majority work for companies that have no connection with Opus Dei. They bring to the places where they live and work the message of holiness in everyday life.

The associates receive ongoing formation in the same ways as other members do, through circles, day of recollection, retreats, workshops, classes, and personal spiritual direction. In the seven regions where there are courses of studies for associates, they receive a more intense formation in the spirit of Opus Dei for two years. At the end of this stage, it is common for those who have the time available to oversee the formation of groups of supernumeraries and to participate in the spiritual accompaniment of other associates as well as of supernumeraries and cooperators. Some also play an active role in corporate or personal apostolic activities.[14]

Each associate decides where and how he wants to live. When they are students or starting their careers, many live with their parents. After that, most of them have their own homes or apartments. Some, however, prefer to have a room in a residence for professional people with shared areas and services. Others choose to have an individual apartment in a building where a few other associates also live and which offers some common spaces. Finally, some groups of three or four associates live together in an apartment or house. Whatever the specific arrangements, the directors of the Work try to make sure that they are suitable to the character, age, and needs of each associate.[15]

Section 5. The Secular Clergy

Today the Priestly Society of the Holy Cross has almost 4,000 members: 2,000 numeraries and 80 associates ordained for the Opus Dei Prelature, and 1,300 associates and 600 supernumeraries who belong to a large number of dioceses spread throughout the world. This section focuses on the activities of the Priestly Society with the diocesan clergy.

Since the 1980s, many vocations to the Priestly Society have come from the large group of young men who, before entering the seminary, received formation in schools and centers related to Opus Dei and were attracted to its spirituality. Many of them join the Priestly Society shortly after being ordained deacons. In addition, many priests who have studied in the ecclesiastical schools of the University of Navarra and the Pontifical University of the Holy Cross join the the Priestly Society or become cooperators.

There are a little more than two hundred centers of the Priestly Society. They offer circles, spiritual accompaniment, monthly days of recollection, and retreats for diocesan clergy as well as classes and seminars on theology and canon law. Most have a physical and digital library with books and periodicals on spiritual and priestly themes. From time to time, they invite the local bishop and other ecclesiastical personalities to give a lecture or to attend a gathering.

The centers vary greatly in size and in the number and type of activities they organize. In Prague, about ten priests meet regularly at the Terasa Center. The meetings foster priestly fraternity and help overcome possible temptations to discouragement in the face of pastoral difficulties in a highly secularized society. For over ten years the Strėvadvaris Conference Center in Lithuania has offered monthly days of recollection for priests. In Barcelona, the Centre Sacerdotal Rosselló organizes the annual *Jornades de Qüestions Pastorals de Castelldaura*. Similar seminars take place at Thornycroft Hall Conference Center in Manchester, UK. In Mexico, the Priestly Society organizes an International Course of Theological Updating. Each year, Dworek (Poland) offers a weeklong seminar for seminarians on a topic of special interest. The Midwest Theological Forum (Chicago) organizes, with the advice of a committee of American bishops, a program called the Rome Experience, which brings together seminarians from different American diocese for a week in Rome. In addition to benefiting from advanced classes on select topics in theology, the participants develop a more universal vision of the Church.

The formation seminarians and priests receive from the Priestly Society helps them meet contemporary challenges by developing a personal prayer life, fostering a desire for holiness, and growing in the virtues of fortitude, mastery of feelings, empathy, and the ability to forgive. In addition, priests benefit from the Christian family atmosphere characteristic of Opus Dei and found in the centers of the Priestly Society. Lunches and dinners, get-togethers, and other informal gatherings facilitate the cultivation of priestly friendship and fraternity.[16] The founder of the Work always saw the dioceses as the principal beneficiaries of the apostolate of the Priestly Society of the Holy Cross. The spiritual improvement of priests has repercussions for the faithful to whom they render their pastoral service and, consequently, on the evangelization of the citizenry.

Just as the personal apostolate of individual members of Opus Dei is the most important part of its apostolate, the same is true of the Priestly Society. Each member tries to reflect in his own life the universal call to holiness and spread it among his priest friends. He also disseminates it among the parishoners and other people entrusted to his care through homilies, spiritual accompaniment, catechesis, and meetings. The priests of the Priestly Society are encouraged to take special interest in promoting vocations to the diocesan seminary. They also collaborate with the Works of St. Raphael and St. Gabriel, especially in larger cities, where they assist many families spiritually. The great majority dedicate themselves exclusively to the pastoral tasks entrusted to them by their respective bishops. The few who exercise part of their pastoral ministry in corporate apostolates of Opus Dei do so only with the explicit permission of their bishop.

Naturally the day-to-day activities of most diocesan members of the Priestly Society are very similar to those of other priests in their diocese. Some, however, find themselves in unusual circumstances which call for unusual activities. For example, the pastor of the parish of St. John the Baptist in Pushkin, Russia, south of St. Petersburg, had to wage a campaign to recover the use of the parish church which had been confiscated by the Communist government. Not content with success in this, he enlisted the help of other people to purchase a house in the nearby town of Kolpino, where he started a new parish.

Notes

1. Since 1990 numerary auxiliaries have run St. Raphael centers and taken a more active role in the St. Gabriel apostolate with married women. See AGP R6.2.2, 4-28.

2. See, for example, General Notes 109/78 and 154/79. AGP E.1.3, 1137.

3. Outline for St. Raphael circles. AGP A.3, 186-1-17.

4. Echevarría was inspired by some words spoken by the Founder on January 1, 1951. At a time of great expansion of Opus Dei throughout the world, Escrivá asked for "five hundred new student vocations." Quoted in *Crónica*, January, 1977, p. 49. AGP Biblioteca, P01.

5. See *Codex iuris particularis Operis Dei*, 1982, nos. 17 and 20, §1.

6. General Note 100/08 (December 16, 2008). AGP E.1.3 and Q.1.3. This indication represented a change. In the mid-1980s, a note from the General Council said: "It should be explained to the youngest that their vocation is no secret. For example, it would *never* make sense to tell them not to talk about it with their parents. However, when it is considered opportune, they should be advised not to be too hasty and to be prudent" General Note 121/84 April 27, 1984. AGP Q.1.3, pp. 13–85.

7. *http://hj.tribunalconstitucional.es/es-ES/Resolucion/Show/25628*. Last consulted July 12, 2020.

8. Javier Echevarría, Pastoral Letter, November 28, 2002, n. 12. AGP Biblioteca, P17.

9. "If your families, your friends and acquaintances see that you are cheerful, helpful, and always happy, they will end up wondering about the cause of this joy and will feel moved to follow your example, taking care of their own homes or the homes in which they work." Javier Echevarría, Pastoral Letter, October 23, 2005. AGP Biblioteca, P17.

10. See General Note 106/09, May 17, 2009. AGP E.1.3 and Q.1.3. Authors' interview with Isabel García-Jalón, Pamplona, Janury 30, 2019.

11. Authors' interview with Isabel García-Jalón, Pamplona, January 30, 2019. Since 2006 CEICID has published a series of books entitled *Trasfondos*, comprising anthropological, aesthetic, and moral studies on the underpinnings of the care of persons, the family, and the home: see *https://ceicid.es/categoria-producto/publicaciones/trasfondos/*. Last consulted, March 5, 2021.

12. Decree of Javier Echevarría approving the seventh edition of the "Internal Regulations for the Administration," September 15, 2014. AGP Q.1.7. See General Note 157/94, June 23, 1994. AGP E.1.3, 1146.

13. https://homerenaissancefoundation.org/about/. Last consulted July 22, 2020. There are numerous scholarly and popular publications in various languages. See, for example, *Mujer y hogar. Manual de administración familiar* (Mexico City: Edac-Trillas, 1996); Claire Mazoyer, Béatrice Carrot, *Je suis débordé(e) à la maison!* (Paris: Carnets De L'info, 2008); Elisa Tumbiolo, *Casalinga in carriera* (Milan: Ares, 2008); Mariángeles Nogueras, *Mi familia. Mi mejor empresa* (Madrid: *Ediciones Internacionales Universitarias* (EIUNSA), 2009).

14. See H 1112/95. AGP G3.2.4, 3153.

15. See Hf 320/02. AGP R1.4.

16. Authors' interview with Rev. José Ramón Vindel, November 3, 2020. Vindel is director of a center of the Priestly Society of the Holy Cross in Madrid.

CHAPTER 15

Collective Apostolic Activities

We have seen that one way Opus Dei carries out its mission is to give pastoral attention to certain collective educational and social undertakings of its members which it classifies as corporate apostolic works or personal apostolates.* Under Echevarría's leadership, the nature and mechanisms of the relationship between the Prelature and these undertakings were clarified. More of an effort was also made not to allow enthusiasm to lead to starting apostolic projects without adequate personnel or finances.

In any corporate or personal apostolic activity, three entities and groups of people are involved. Before turning to specific corporate and personal apostolic activities, we will briefly outline the current status of the three groups. For the sake of clarity and ease of understanding, we will focus on schools, but the same principles apply, with appropriate modifications, to other types of activities (social centers, student residences, conference centers, clinics). Even in the case of schools, what we outline is a general approach that varies from case to case. The day-to-day relationship between Opus Dei and a particular school is more collegial and nuanced than the outline that follows might suggest.

At the first level, a foundation or other not-for-profit entity organized under local law owns and operates the school. Its board is responsible for the school's strategic orientation as an educational

---

* See the introduction to chapter 10 ("Apostolic Activities"), where the similarities and differences between corporate works and personal works are described. All the undertakings mentioned in this chapter have web pages explaining their relationship with Opus Dei.

institution, its apostolic mission, and its financial viability, while leaving day-to-day operations in the hands of the school's management team. These boards seek to ensure that the new generations who become involved in the not-for-profit entity as well as the management of the school preserve their purpose and character as well as the goals the school was founded to achieve, while adapting to changing social and economic circumstances.

The board of the nonprofit entity that owns and operates the school usually signs an agreement with the authorities of Opus Dei specifying how Opus Dei will support the school from a spiritual and apostolic point of view and how relations between them will be managed. This normally involves providing a chaplain and religion teachers. The agreement typically calls for regular discussions of the apostolic aspects of the school between the directors of Opus Dei and the school's managers. The board usually agrees to seek the opinion of Opus Dei's directors about the suitability from an apostolic point of view of candidates for the most important managerial positions including the headmaster and assistant headmaster, although the ownership/management entity has the last say in these matters and makes the actual appointments.

A second level is made up of the management of each school: a headmaster, principal, or president and his or her staff. They run the school on a day-to-day basis and are answerable for their professional decisions about curriculum, staffing, admissions, and so forth. to the entity that hired them. They consult the authorities of Opus Dei about issues like religious instruction, character formation, and overall Christian environment including a culture of understanding and forgiveness, as well as collegiality in decision-making. On occasion they may also consult them about other questions like the fairness of salaries and grants.

The third level comprises the regional vicar of Opus Dei and his councils. To contribute to the Christian identity of the corporate work or personal apostolate, they meet regularly with the members of the board, the headmaster and other managers, and the chaplains and teachers of religion whom they have appointed. In these meetings, they approve the subjects and programs related to Christian teachings.*

Under Echevarría's leadership an effort was made to ensure that the people at all three levels act with initiative and take full responsibility for their areas without offloading decisions onto others or interfering in their sphere. For example, the requirement that had been established by the central government of Opus Dei that the headmaster and other top managers of the school be chosen from among the members of the local council appointed by the regional government, which had not always been applied, was dropped. This helped ensure that the attention of the Work's governing bodies focuses on the apostolic aspects of each school and reduced the number of occasions on which the Work's directors inadvertently intervened in other areas.

The collective apostolic activities of Opus Dei have evolved over time to reflect larger social changes in the roles of women. In the past, it was common for men to play leading roles in the governing bodies of private girls' schools, whether connected with Opus Dei or not. Today, schools for girls connected with Opus Dei are managed and directed by women and their boards are made up largely of women. In universities and other centers which serve both men and women, a serious effort has been made to promote equality and co-responsibility of men and women in governing bodies and management positions, as well as in the faculty and nonteaching staff. Much has been accomplished, although much remains to be done. At the most important corporate work, the University of Navarra, for instance, 38 percent of the faculty, and 42 percent of the doctors in the university clinic are women. In 2021 for the first time, a woman became the university's president.

---

* In both corporate works and personal works, if the Catholic identity or apostolic purpose disappears or if the institution does not follow the guidelines that the Prelature considers necessary to fulfill its mission, according to the established agreement, the authorities of the Work can suspend the agreement.

Section 1. Higher Education*

At Del Portillo's death in 1994, seven universities were corporate works of Opus Dei: Universidad de Navarra (established as a university in Pamplona in 1960), Universidad de Piura (Piura, Peru, 1969), Universidad Panamericana (Mexico City, 1978), Universidad de La Sabana (Bogotá, 1979), Universidad de los Andes (Santiago de Chile, 1989), Universidad Austral (Buenos Aires, 1991), and Università Campus Bio-Medico (Rome, 1993).

Under Echeverría's leadership, eight additional corporate work universities were established: University of Asia and the Pacific (Manila, 1995), Universidad del Istmo (Guatemala City, 1997), Universidad de Montevideo (Montevideo, 1997), Pontifical University of the Holy Cross (Rome, 1998), Universidad Monteávila (Caracas, 1998), Pan-African University (Lagos, 2002, renamed Pan-Atlantic University in 2013), Universidad de los Hemisferios (Quito, 2004), and Strathmore University (Nairobi, 2008). Some of them had begun earlier as specialized centers of research and teaching but had developed sufficiently after 1994 to become universities. In addition to these corporate works, members of the Work established the Universitat Internacional de Catalunya (Barcelona, 1997) and the Universidad Villanueva (Madrid, 2020), which are classified within Opus Dei as personal apostolates.

The nonprofit entities that own and operate each of the universities, together with their academic authorities, have established agreements with the Prelature of Opus Dei, which supports their Christian character and apostolic orientation.

All these universities strive to achieve academic and professional excellence, rooted in Christian teachings and the social doctrine of the Church. They encourage their faculty and students to conduct research in areas of special social impact including bioethics, the family, human life, communication, the formation of youth, and the causes and remedies of poverty. All have established scholarship

---

* For information on primary and secondary schools, see chapter 14, section 2.

systems for students from low-income families and volunteer programs. From a governance and economic point of view, each university is autonomous.

To reinforce the Christian identity of these apostolic undertakings, Opus Dei's central governing bodies organized meetings in 2003
and 2004 with directors of universities, clinics, and business schools.
They studied the Christian impact they could have on society, on the
teaching and nonteaching staff, on students, and on patients.

The University of Navarra is the best-known corporate work of
Opus Dei. It has achieved national and international recognition in a
number of areas. Its business school, for instance, has been ranked by
the *Financial Times* (London) as best-in-the world in executive education every year since 2015. It has fifteen schools spread over four campuses (Pamplona, San Sebastian, Madrid and Barcelona), six research
centers, and more than twelve thousand students. Its alumni number
almost 130,000. It offers thirty-eight undergraduate majors, fourteen
double degrees, thirteen bilingual courses, forty-two master's degrees,
and twenty doctoral and specialization programs. It publishes twenty
journals and holds more than one million volumes in its main library.[1]

Over time the university has striven to find new ways of expressing its Christian identity and transmitting Christian values. It offers
theology classes for university students and has a Core Curriculum
Institute, an Institute for the Family, and a Research Group on Science, Reason, and Faith. Several humanities professors have made
significant contributions to their fields. Among the best known, is
the proposal for methodological renewal of philosophy of Professor
Leonardo Polo.

The university hospital, Clínica Universidad de Navarra, has
more than two thousand employees. It serves one hundred thousand
patients annually and has received numerous awards for the quality
of its medical care and for its patient services. The Applied Medical
Research Center brings together two hundred researchers who study
degenerative, oncological, and cardiovascular diseases. The School
of Engineering works with the medical school in offering a degree
in bioengineering. Of special interest to many developing countries

is the work of the Institute of Tropical Medicine, which draws on the resources of the schools of medicine, pharmacy, nursing, and sciences as well as of the university hospital and the Applied Medical Research Center. It collaborates with researchers and health centers in Peru, Argentina, Costa Rica, Mali, Nigeria, Mozambique, Mongolia, Congo, France, Portugal, Switzerland, and Tanzania.

The university's Tantaka program strives to promote an ethos of volunteering and to make available to civil and religious nonprofit social service groups the skills and efforts of volunteers from the university community. During the 2019–2020 academic year, some 1,500 volunteers worked with 160 groups and associations in 181 projects, caring for people with disabilities, carrying out programs accompanying the sick and the elderly, and participating in international cooperation programs.

In recent years, the university has stressed multidisciplinary work in both the humanities and the social sciences. The Research Group on the Golden Age fosters research and publications in this period of Spanish culture. The Institute of Culture and Society strives to bring to bear on pressing contemporary social challenges the varied expertise of some one hundred specialists in the humanities and social sciences.

The collections of the Museum of the University of Navarra have been built around two important legacies: the works of important twentieth-century artists including Picasso, Rothko, Tàpies, and Chillida, donated by Josefa Huarte, and the photographs of José Ortiz-Echagüe, perhaps the most important twentieth-century Spanish photographer. Through its permanent collection, exhibitions, performing arts performances, film screenings, and classes in curatorial studies, the museum attempts to establish a dialogue between culture and Christian faith. The university also has a Science Museum, focused on the protection and care of the environment, and on recognizing and promoting the contributions of women in science.

The Pontifical Athenaeum of the Holy Cross became a pontifical university in July 1998. By 2016, about 1,200 priests, seminarians, and laypeople studied each year in its four schools: theology (with departments of dogmatic, moral, spiritual, and biblical theology, liturgy, and Church history), canon law, philosophy, and institutional social communications. In addition, three hundred more studied catechetics, pedagogy, and didactics of religion in the Higher Institute of Religious Sciences. Because of the large number of priests and seminarians, 79 percent of the students are men. A good part of the laity are members of Opus Dei.[2]

Navarra and Santa Cruz are supported by tuition and fees, endowment income, and donations for operations and earmarked projects. Almost 70 percent of the income of the University of Navarra comes from fees charged patients by the university clinic and tution. By contrast, 80 percent of the funding of the Pontifical University of the Holy Cross comes from contributions from private entities and student fees. In 2018, the CARF foundation raised five million euros in donations and indirect aid for the ecclesiastical schools of the University of Navarra and for the Pontifical University of the Holy Cross. More than half went to student scholarships and another two million were used for structural and teaching expenses.[3]

Between them, the two universities have more than eight hundred theology and two hundred canon law students. Over the years, some 2,300 students have been ordained priests and one hundred, from thirty-one different countries, have been ordained bishops.

To contribute to the ascetical and spiritual formation of the seminarians and diocesan clergy who attend these universities, Opus Dei runs three institutions in Rome and two in Pamplona. In Rome, the International Ecclesiastical College *Sedes Sapientiae* (1991) educates almost a hundred seminarians; and the priestly residences Tiberino (2004) and Altomonte (2012) houses a total of almost a hundred priests and deacons. At the University of Navarra, the Colegio Mayor Echalar serves fifty priests, and the Colegio Eclesiástico Internacional Bidasoa houses one hundred diocesan seminarians studying in the ecclesiastical schools.[4]

A large proportion of the universities connected with the Work are located in Latin America. The Universidad Panamericana has more than twelve thousand students at campuses in Mexico City,

Guadalajara, and Aguascalientes; the Universidad de La Sabana in Bogotá, Colombia, has eleven thousand students. The Universidad de Piura in Peru has seven thousand students at campuses in Piura and Lima. The Universidad de los Andes (Santiago de Chile) has some eleven thousand students. The Universidad Austral, with campuses in Buenos Aires and Rosario, Argentina, also has a total of about eleven thousand students with a high percentage of nondegree students in its prestigious business school.

L'Università Campus Biomedico is a corporate work in Rome with about 1,500 students. Despite being classified as a university, thus far it has concentrated on medicine, the health sciences, and bio-medical engineering. It was the first Italian school to offer nursing at a university level.

In Africa, Strathmore College became a university in 2002. It now has five thousand students and schools of law, business, mathematics, business technology, information technology, tourism and hospital-ity, humanities, and social sciences. In Lagos, Nigeria, the Lagos Busi-ness School and several other schools merged into the Pan-Atlantic University in 2002. It offers degrees in communications, business, and science and technology. It has some 1,100 degree candidates and more than 3,500 students enrolled in nondegree programs. In the Philippines, the University of Asia and the Pacific has seven schools and some 6,500 students.

Two universities founded by members and cooperators of Opus Dei with their colleagues sought the spiritual assistance of the Prelature, but are classified as personal apostolates, not corporate works. The Universitat Internacional de Catlyunya in Barcelona, Spain, has twelve schools plus an Institute of Bioethics, an Institute of Higher Studies of the Family, and a University Dental Clinic. The Universidad Villanueva (Madrid) was begun on a very modest scale by Francisco Ansón and Juan Gutiérrez Palacio as an academy that prepared for university entrance exams and offered tutoring to students. In 1990, Centro Universitario Villanueva was attached to the Complutense University of Madrid; in 2020, it was approved as a university.

The universities connected with the Work tend to focus on fields that offer especially clear opportunities to spread a Christian view of life in society. Almost all have a school of communications or at least an institute of media studies and advertising. Ten have business schools that stress the principles of Catholic social doctrine and business ethics.[5] The most prestigious is the Instituto de Estudios Superiores de la Empresa (IESE) of the University of Navarra, with nineteen hundred students and campuses in Barcelona, Madrid, Munich, New York, and São Paulo.[6] Two prepare students to work in the fashion industry. In 2001, the journalist Covadonga O'Shea started a specialized business school, the *Instituto Superior de Empresa y Moda* (ISEM Fashion Business School). In 2012, it became part of the University of Navarra. It currently offers an executive master's degree in fashion business management. Villanueva University offers a diploma in fashion communication and management to students pursuing an undergraduate degree in some other field.

The Universidad de Navarra, Universidad de La Sabana, and Universitat Internacional de Catalunya have family science institutes that do research on family values and offer courses and programs on subjects like work-family integration and the equality of men and women.

Five universities have a university hospital: Clínica Universidad de Navarra (with hospitals in Pamplona and Madrid), Policlinico Universitario Campus Bio-Medico (Rome), Clínica Universidad de La Sabana (Bogotá, Colombia); Hospital Universitario Austral (Buenos Aires, Argentina); and Clínica Universidad de los Andes (Santiago de Chile).

In addition to medical schools and university hospitals, members of Opus Dei have started numerous other undertakings in the field of healthcare. The Laguna Hospital-Care Center was founded in Madrid to commemorate the hundredth anniversary of the birth of the Founder of Opus Dei. It provides specialized care for the elderly including palliative care, treatment of neurodegenerative diseases, ortho-geriatrics, long-term nursing care, family respite care and day-care centers. In Santiago de Chile, the *Policlínico El Salto* began as a volunteer activity in an impoverished area of the city. It has expanded to offer medical, dental, mental health, and alcohol rehabilitation services to underserved populations in the area. In Paris, the *École du Service à la Personne* (2014) offers a baccalaureate in care for children, the elderly, and persons with disabilities, whether in their homes or in institutional settings.[7]

The Monkole Medical Centre (Kinshasa, Democratic Republic of the Congo, 1989) now has a hospital with one hundred fifty beds, eight operating rooms, and three outpatient clinics in the slums of Kinshasa. It was the first hospital in the country to provide its patients meals, bed linens, and assistance in personal hygiene and has become a benchmark for other Congolese hospitals. It currently provides high-level treatment to more than twenty thousand patients a year. Thanks to aid from a number of international foundations, it is able to give the same medical care to people of all social levels, adjusting its charges to each family's abilitiy to pay. Monkole's reputation for quality care leads some upper- and upper-middle-class families, both local and foreign, to go there for treatment instead of traveling to European hospitals as they used to do. Since 1997, it has had a Higher Institute of Nursing Sciences with a hundred students, almost all of them with scholarships. In cooperation with the Canadian NGO Lincco, this school offers a master's degree to future nursing professors, an important service to society in a country where many people still do not have access to modern medicine.[8]

At Del Portillo's suggestion, in 1993, faithful of Opus Dei started the Niger Foundation Hospital in Enugu, Nigeria, to help meet the basic health needs of the city. In the Ivory Coast, in 2004, some members of the Work and cooperators started the *Centre Médico-Social Walé*, a primary care establishment located in Yamoussoukro. It offers general medicine, pediatrics, gynecology, and care for chronic illnesses such as diabetes and AIDS. A similar center operates in Toumbokro, near the Ivorian capital.

Polis—The Jerusalem Institute of Languages and Humanities—is an independent university-level institute dedicated to the teaching of humanities and ancient and Semitic languages. It began its activity in

Jerusalem in 2011. It offers courses in five ancient languages (Latin, Classical Greek, Syriac, Biblical Hebrew, and Coptic), a master's degree in ancient philology and another in Near Eastern languages, and classes in spoken Arabic, Modern Standard Arabic, and Modern Hebrew. Polis applies the complete immersion method of instruction, even in ancient languages. A student of Syriac, for instance, receives instruction, speaks, writes, and reads in Syriac.[9] In addition to Jerusalem, the institute teaches courses at Christendom College (Virginia, USA) and at the Pontifical University of the Holy Cross (Rome). Every two years it organizes an international congress for humanists.*

Section 2. Vocational and Technical Centers

Members of the Work run more than a hundred vocational training centers all over the world. Some have been in existence for decades, such as the Kinal and Junkabal in Guatemala City. The same is true of the Centro ELIS vocational school in Rome, which offers courses in mechanics, industrial electronics, marketing, computer science, and technical design. It also has a division that offers higher level courses in material handling, telecommunications, multimedia technology, office management, and land use planning. The *Istituto Alberghiero Enogastronomico Safi ELIS*, which forms part of the larger ELIS operation, is a professional institute for the hotel and catering industry that offers a five-year secondary education with alternating periods of classroom instruction and work in hotels and restaurants in Rome.[10]

In Brazil, a number of schools and centers offer education to impoverished students. AFESU provides free education and professional training to socially vulnerable women. It has three divisions located in a poor area on the outskirts of São Paulo. Morro Velho

---

* The first venture of members of Opus Dei in the field of language teaching, Seido Language Institute (Ashiya, Japan), found after five decades that the market for its services had dried up due to social changes and improvements in language instruction in Japanese schools and colleges. In 2013 the foundation that sponsored Seido decided to close the language institute and focus its efforts on the student residence it managed and on other educational, cultural, and spiritual activities.

(1963) trains young women to enter the labor market and offers classes for young mothers. Casa do Moinho (1998) has two technical courses for young people between seventeen and twenty-three years of age, one in hotel management and the other in cooking. It also offers tutoring and mentoring to help girls stay in school and finish their education. Veleiros (2001) provides professional training to nurses and family assistants as well as a range of general educational activities for girls.[11] Pedreira educational and welfare center provides more than four hundred boys from an impoverished neighborhood of Sao Paulo with vocational training in electricity, electronics, and computers.[12] The Instituto Profesional Madero (Buenos Aires) stresses character development and interpersonal relations while providing technical training in fields like telecommunications and automation to young people who have only completed primary education. It works with industry leaders like Toyota, Siemens, and Mercedes Benz to guarantee that its graduates will have the skills demanded by today's market as well as the educational base needed to adapt to future conditions.

Xabec, begun in 2006, is a vocational training center in Orriols, the neighborhood with the largest foreign population in Valencia (Spain). Its sponsor, the Eifor Foundation, aims to provide the education and training that young people, unemployed persons, immigrants, and others at risk of social exclusion need to enter the labor market. In addition to providing training classes for unemployed individuals in a wide variety of fields like heating and air-conditioning, solar energy, telecommunications, and warehousing, Xabec collaborates with local companies to provide training that will permit their employees to advance professionally.

There are many more technical schools on five continents. Dual-tech Training Center in the Philippines (with branches in Manila and Canlubag) offers course in electromechanical technology combining classroom learning and internships with companies. Its graduates often become shop-floor leaders in the companies where they did their internships. The Institute for Industrial Technology in Legos, Nigeria, located in a poor neighborhood of the capital, has nine hundred students most of whom specialize in electromechanics. Eastlands College of Technology began its activities in 1993 with the help of the Austrian NGO ICEP. It is located in one of poorest and most densely populated areas of Nairobi, Kenya. It began life as the Informal Sector Business Institute (ISBI). Its aim was to train micro entrepreneurs in basic business skills and to offer classes in Information and Communications Technology (ICT) to local young people. Over the years, over five thousand young people took ICT courses and more than five hundred entrepreneurs participated in capacity building activities to improve their earning potential. When it added to its activities technical training for industrial workers, ISBI adopted its current name. In addition to continuing its original activities, Eastland now offers courses in automotive technology, electrical technology, and mechanical maintenance technology, as well as short courses and refresher courses in a wide variety of areas. They are a powerful tool for escaping poverty as an unskilled worker and developing a career in a technical field.[13]

In addition to technical training schools like the ones we have just mentioned, members of the Work and cooperators with their colleagues and friends have started a variety of other undertakings to help poor and marginalized people improve their situation. Parts of the Casavalle neighbourhood of Montevideo (Uruguay) are slums made up of shacks without sewers or running water, known for crime and drug trafficking. Several decades ago, some residents got in touch with Glenda Vilela, a numerary member of Opus Dei who worked in a government office dealing with housing problems. She began organizing volunteer activities in the neighborhood with the help of college students who lived in a residence connected to the Work. This led in 1992 to the construction of the *Centro de Apoyo al Desarrollo Integral* (CADI) [Center for the Support of Integral Devlopment]. CADI's mission is "promoting women by contributing to their human, cultural, professional and social development from infancy to old age." It has a kindergarten, a health clinic, a social and legal assistance clinic, workshops for mothers, and professional training courses for adolescents. In 2015, Los Rosales school was started in the CADI building to offer girls from the neighborhood a quality bilingual grade school and high school education, including cutting-edge math instruction using the Singapore method. The school describes its goal as "making it possible for women from the area to develop their potential, educate themselves, and construct their life project."

In the same Casavalle neighborhood, two members of the Work, Pablo Bartol and Santiago Altieri, started in 1998 an after-school center for boys called Los Pinos. The project was made possible by a Jewish businessman who donated the land, and the German government which provided construction funding. Los Pinos offered programs to supplement the often-limited instruction provided by local schools as well as mentoring to help students tempted to drop out of school. Gradually it added an array of job training courses and beginning in 2016, a technical school with courses in cooling systems, industrial maintenance, and telecommunications.[14]

The Siramá Foundation (El Salvador) organizes workshops in cooking, sewing, and cosmetology for single mothers, the unemployed, and retired women. Eight out of ten graduates set up small businesses.[15] Las Gravileas training center for artisans, located in Santa Catarina Bobadilla, a village in Antigua Guatemala, began its activities in 1997. It offers two- and three-year courses in professional cooking, upholstering, floral design and event planning, and fashion and dressmaking. It also has three- to ten-month courses in jewelry making, calligraphy, and basketmaking. Most of its four hundred students are Kaqchikel-speaking indigenous women.

Iniciatives de Solidaritat i Promoció tries to help immigrants and unemployed people in the Raval neighborhood (Barcelona) though two centers: Braval, for men, and Terral, for women. Each center has about 150 volunteers who offer school support, attention to families, and assistance in entering the world of work.[16]

Many centers scattered around the world offer remedial education through after-school programs in underprivileged neighborhoods. Among them are Baytree Centre in London; Midtown Center and Metro Achievement Center in Chicago; and Crotona Center and Rosedale Center in the Bronx, New York. Their academic, human, spiritual, and athletic mentoring programs aim to help students from impoverished areas overcome their environmental disadvantages.

Under Echeverría's leadership, the women's branch continued to offer a wide variety of training in the fields of catering, hotel services, home economics, and personal care of individuals, especially those with special needs. By the end of the 1980s, the focus of these programs had shifted away from training offered by residences for domestic workers to vocational schools and programs offered by universities and other centers of higher education. Increasingly, the students were young women who were interested in studying in a college or other postsecondary institution. Some of them hoped to pursue careers in the hotel and catering industry (including the Administrations of Opus Dei Centers), while others wanted to acquire housekeeping skills which they would then apply in their own homes.

The study and work centers (CET) begun during the 1988–1989 academic year aim at the second group. They offer young women who are studying in a university or other professional school an opportunity to earn money to help finance their studies while learning professional-level cooking and housekeeping skills by working part-time in the Administration of a large Opus Dei center, usually a student residence or conference center. These centers include La Chacra (Buenos Aires), La Loma, Fontana and Navacerrada (Madrid), and Yarraton (Sydney). Typically, these centers also offer other extracurricular educational, cultural, and sports programs.

Schools and centers of higher education in the field of hospitality, home economics, and catering strive to meet the changing needs of future professionals in these areas. Kenvale College (Sydney) has been closely associated with the tourism and hospitality industry since its inception, offering courses in event management, hospitality, and commercial cooking.[17] Punlaan Vocational School (Manila) also specializes in the hospitality and tourism sector and offers students training in hotel and food service. The Institute of Management and Services (Byblos, Lebanon) aims to expand job opportunities for women from rural villages. It offers development, awareness, and training programs for the creation and management of micro and small businesses with a focus on tourism services. The students of Kimlea School (Kenya) come mainly from rural families who scratch out a living in tea and coffee harvesting. It began in 1989 with classes in literacy, sewing, and agriculture but now focuses on a two-year course in hospitality studies which offers the students a way out of rural poverty.[18]

Some schools and training centers which originally offered almost exclusively home economics and related subjects have greatly increased the scope of their offerings. An outstanding example is Ribamar, a secondary school and vocational training center in Seville, Spain. It now prepares students to work as pharmacy and drugstore technicians, nursing assistants, dietitians, managers of tourist accommodations, oral and dental hygienists, specialists in child education, and caregivers for dependent persons.

Some freestanding technical schools begun by members of the Work have become part of corporate universities, such as the Strathmore School of Tourism and Hospitality at Strathmore University (Kenya) and the School of Service Business Administration at the Universidad de los Andes (Santiago de Chile). The Universidad de La Sabana (Colombia) and the Università Campus Bio-Medico (Italy) developed diploma programs in various areas of human services on their own.

The programs we have been describing frequently seek recognition of their programs and diplomas from the government or from independent accrediting bodies including the National Vocational Qualification. This can be especially important to young people from impoverished backgrounds in poor countries. For example, in the Ivory Coast, where only half the population completes primary school and where illiteracy among girls is especially high, the National Vocational Qualification in catering offered by Yarani Professional Training School virtually guarantees the graduates a well-paying job. Ninety percent of them find employment immediately in hotels and embassies, and many of the rest start their own small businesses.

In rural areas, seventy schools that are personal works offer vocational training and contribute to the economic and social development of rural families. They are located in Latin America, the Philippines, Spain, and Portugal. The largest number are in Peru, where the Pro Rural organization comprises forty rural schools. In Machetá (Colombia), the Guatanfur family agricultural school offers a technical baccalaureate to five hundred young people. The *Instituto Superior de Ciencias Sociales y Económico-Familiares* (ICSEF, located in Fusagasugá, Colombia) has been training women since 1969.[19] It offers degrees in commercial cooking and hotel management and administration. The Marzano Foundation in Argentina has eleven rural training centers, which provide secondary education to more than six hundred students.[20] The twenty-nine Family Farm Schools in Spain have more than four thousand students. They offer high school diplomas as well as government-recognized vocational training in administrative management, intensive farming, gardening, ecology, and foreign trade.[21]

Section 3. Apostolate Involving Public Opinion

Escrivá repeatedly asked all the members of the Work to "always proclaim, day and night, deeds and doctrines of mercy and truth."[22] He urged every member of Opus Dei and indeed all Christians to make Jesus Christ known and to bring the gospel to their professional work, whatever that might be. He also invited them to contribute to shaping public opinion through the media. Of course, only a relatively small number would do so as media professionals or as experts in various areas. The majority could, however, express their opinion in the media in the many ways open to nonspecialists, including writing a letter to the editor or calling in to a radio talk show.

In the last two decades, Opus Dei's institutional efforts in the area of communications have focused on spreading the Christian message of the Church and the Pope; on explaining the spirit, history, and life of the Work and its members; and on making known the Founder's life and writings.

Escrivá's beatification brought the Work to the attention of people all over the world, in many cases for the first time. Photographs of an enormous crowd gathered in St. Peter's Square for the ceremony marked a certain paradigm shift in the focus of public opinion with regard to Opus Dei. Prior to the beatification, there had been, as we have seen, a certain amount of criticism of John Paul II's decision to beatify the Founder. Once the beatification took place, the Church and the Christian faithful welcomed the new Blessed without much further controversy. Subsequently, the tone of information about events like the death of Del Portillo, the election of Echevarría (1994), the congress commemorating the centenary of the birth of the Founder, and his subsequent canonization (2002) demonstrated that there had been a substantial improvement in the worldwide public understanding of the ecclesial phenomenon of Opus Dei.[23]

In subsequent years, the Prelature's institutional communications team worked to gain a reputation for being a reliable source of information that could be counted on to provide clear, straightforward answers to questions from the media. It took the initiative in confronting persistent stereotypes and tried to address head-on misunderstandings about what it meant to be a personal prelature, the life of the numeraries, the work of the Administration in the centers, the meaning of corporal mortification for a Christian, the supposed elitism and wealth of the Work's faithful, and its alleged connection with political conservatism. Greater transparency and a less self-referential attitude in the Work's official communications reduced the level of controversy and made it easier for it to be recognized as a reality in the Church as a whole, although much still remains to be done.[24]

Under Echevarría's leadership, Opus Dei began to dedicate more resources to institutional communications. In 1992, it had communications offices in six countries: Spain (Madrid and Barcelona), Italy, Portugal, Germany, the United States, and Mexico. Ten years later, almost every large or medium-sized region had at least one person working professionally in the communications office; in the larger regions a number of men and women of the Prelature were involved.

In 1999 the Work opened an international press office in Rome. Today, that office regularly provides information to the five hundred journalists accredited to the Holy See. In addition to furnishing information about Opus Dei, it has helped inform the media on events affecting the entire Church, including the Jubilee of the Year 2000, the death of John Paul II and the election of his two successors, the beatification of Archbishop Oscar Romero, and the dignity of the priesthood and lay celibacy. It has also provided professional advice on communications to Catholic educational and social institutions that have seen their ability to carry out their mission compromised by legal or social pressure to act in ways opposed to human dignity. Every two years, the School of Institutional Church Communication at the Pontifical University of the Holy Cross organizes a professional seminar on institutional Church communication, a global forum for Church spokespersons.

The central offices of Opus Dei periodically organize international seminars with directors of the schools of communications of universities inspired by the message of St. Josemaría, focusing on how to provide the best professional training and to help students see their future work in communications as a way to spread Christ's message. Meetings have also been held with communication directors of large universities, colleges, hospitals, and business schools to reflect on the Christian roots of these centers.[25]

Technological change has, of course, affected Opus Dei's internal communications. It continues to print two magazines intended to inform members about the activities of the Father and the apostolates of members in different parts of the world: *Crónica* for the men's branch and *Noticias* for the women's branch. In December 2018, however, it stopped publishing two other magazines (*Obras* and *Iniciativas*) intended to inform not only members but also cooperators and friends about the spirit of the Work and its apostolic undertakings. By then, the kind of information those publications had provided was available to a much broader public "on the Opus Dei website (www.opusdei.org). For the same reason, *Documentation* ceased publication in 2004. It had provided centers of the Work with reprints of selected articles about the Church and Opus Dei as well as an occasional original article about welfare activities and educational undertakings for the disadvantaged carried out throughout the world by faithful and cooperators of Opus Dei.

The institutional website *opusdei.org* was launched in 1996 in French, German, Italian, Spanish, and English. By 2021, there were website administrators in seventy-three countries who update the local content of the site in thirty-three languages. On the occasion of Bishop Echevarría's death and the election of his successor in 2017, the website had for the first time more than one million unique monthly visitors. In April 2020 it had more than 1.5 million. Currently, ten million unique visitors per year visit the site.

At first, *opusdei.org* was a static page very much focused on the Work and its activities. It explained what Opus Dei was and offered some press clippings and a contact email address. Little by little, the site became more dynamic and shifted focus from institutional aspects of Opus Dei to the boader Christian message. For example, in 2006 it published "54 Questions about Jesus Christ," answered by theologians from the University of Navarra. Since then, these pages have been consulted or downloaded eight million times. A section entitled "Summaries of Christian Faith" offers, as its name implies, a series of articles on the teaching of the Church which reflects the initial theological training offered to all new members of the Work.

A major focus of the website is now Christ's call, echoed so forcefully by Pope Francis, to reach out to the poor and the disadvantaged. The section "Just Start: Ways of Helping Others" comprises eleven videos prepared during the Year of Mercy (2015). They show specific ways in which one hundred people from twelve countries exercise mercy, ranging from learning to forgive, to visiting those in prison, to providing work. The video *The Creativity of Charity* offers brief interviews with people who collaborate in collective and personal social undertakings that alleviate the suffering of those around them. The videos focus on single individuals who have found in the spirit of Opus Dei a way to respond to God in daily life.

The website also brings together material on the lives of members of Opus Dei who have been beatified or canonized (Escrivá, Del Portillo, and Ortiz de Landázuri) and others whose causes for canonization are under way.

Today *opusdei.org* is a portal with online and audiovisual resources on the Christian life, a medium that massively disseminates content on spirituality, a contemporary way to fulfill the Founder's desire to "wrap the world in printed paper."[26] It has become the easiest way to get to know the Work and to find out about its formative activities. It provides Opus Dei a way to present its message without passing through the filter of third parties, a voice of its own, a direct connection with many members of the public. All of this helps reduce the feeling of a lack of information about the Work which people sometimes had, in part because Opus Dei made few corporate statements and gave priority to individual members' transmission of its message through their professional work, family, and social life.

Since 2005, the advent of Web 2.0 has made it possible to increase interaction with users, thanks to digital platforms such as Facebook, Twitter, Instagram, YouTube, and Flickr. These channels allow members to show some facets of the spirit of Opus Dei using their own digital languages: images, audio, videos, and animations. They allow people who follow members on these various platforms to ask questions, express their approval, and spread what they find interesting.

Information on Opus Dei began appearing on YouTube in 2005. A Facebook channel was opened in 2009 in Spanish, with other languages following. The first Opus Dei Twitter channel (@opusdei_es) also dates to 2009. Instagram, which caters primarily to younger users, has offered information on Opus Dei since 2011. Since 2014, audio recordings of the Founder's homilies, messages from the Prelate, commentaries on the gospel, and meditations by priests of the Work have been accessible on Sound Cloud. High-resolution photographs can be found on Flickr.[27]

Naturally the web has also given voice to critics of Opus Dei. Perhaps the two most significant critical websites are *odan.org* in the United States and *opuslibros.org* in Spain. They gather testimonies about negative experiences with Opus Dei and criticize what they consider the distance between the ideal and the real life of the organization, which they describe as rigid, characterized by lack of respect for individual conscience, pervasive inequality between men and women, and an outdated practice of corporal mortification.

Mónica Herrero, the director of the central office of the Apostolate of Public Opinion of the Women's Branch sums up Opus Dei's reaction to this criticism:

> Although some critics have recourse to personal attacks which are sometimes unjust, they do reveal the point of view of people who feel they have been injured. This has led Opus Dei to critical self-analysis, creating a better understanding of what caused these wounds, contributing in some cases to calm dialogue with the individuals, and helping us to explain better some aspects of the Work which previously we may have thought did not need much explanation. . . . As a result of criticism and of some negative experiences, we have tried to improve in various ways. For example, in the personal formation given in the Work, we have made more of an effort to avoid fostering voluntarism or a misunderstood spirit of sacrifice. In the life of the centers, we have taken more into account the needs of older people.[28]

During Echevarría's years as the head of Opus Dei, a significant number of films and novels made reference to Opus Dei, some quite inaccurately. The 2003 publication of Dan Brown's *The Da Vinci Code* sparked an unprecedented amount of media interest in Opus Dei. The novel presents the Work as a religious sect that helps the Church cover up the secret of an alleged marriage between Jesus Christ and Mary Magdalene and their two children. The book sold more than eighty million copies in forty-four languages. Three years later, a film adaptation was made, starring Tom Hanks. With a $120 million budget, the film grossed more than $750 million.

During the run-up to the premiere of the film in May 2006, Opus Dei experienced more attention in world public opinion than at any other time in its history. The Prelature's information office in the United States adopted as its motto the saying "Make lemonade out of lemons." Resisting the temptation to react defensively to patently false and offensive statements, it adopted a serene tone with touches of humor. The novel features an albino assassin named Silas. Opus Dei introduced to the media the only American member named Silas, a mild-mannered stockbroker originally from Nigeria. All over the country it made numerous members available for interviews and it allowed one of the major national TV networks, ABC, to broadcast live from the Work's national headquarters in Manhattan. By the time the film debuted, over one hundred members had appeared on talk shows and interviews, some with very large audiences. Opus Dei's communications office asked the production company, Sony Pictures, as a "gesture of respect for the figure of Jesus Christ, the history of the Church, and the religious beliefs of viewers," to present at the beginning of the film a statement to the effect that it was fiction.[29] Sony refused.

As soon as the film was released, the media turned to other topics and the controversy ended. The novel and the film unfortunately left many readers and viewers with a false idea about Jesus Christ and the true nature of Opus Dei, but they did serve to encourage many members and cooperators, especially in English-speaking countries, to bear witness to Christ and to try to convey an accurate picture of Opus Dei at least to their colleagues and acquantances.

A 2008 Spanish film, *Camino*, narrates the life of Alexia González-Barros, the daughter of two members of Opus Dei, who died of cancer at age fourteen and currently has a cause for canonization underway. The film, which met with critical acclaim although modest box-office success, portrays Alexia's family as peculiar people who dress, behave, and above all pray in ridiculous ways. It even depicts them, and the doctors and nurses of the Clinic of the University of Navarra Hospital where Alexia died, applauding at the moment of her death. The family asked the film's director, Javier Fesser, not to identify Alexia by name and to cut the scene which falsely portrays them as applauding her death, but he refused.

There Be Dragons (2011) is a feature film written and directed by Roland Joffé, director of *The Mission*. It features Charlie Cox, Wes Bentley, Olga Kurylenko, Derek Jacobi, and Geraldine Chaplin. Set during the Spanish Civil War, this historical drama is about friendship and forgiveness. Escrivá helps a fictional character find peace with himself and with God. The film was released in theaters in thirty countries and on several television stations around the world. Some critics and viewers praised the quality and values of the film, although a complex script made it hard for many people to follow. In the year of its release, the film grossed $4.5 million at the box office. Later, the Colombian distribution company Tayrona, in agreement with Joffé and the producers, made a simplified version that was released in some countries under the title *Secretos de Pasión* (*Secrets of Passion*).

Notes

1. *https://issuu.com/universidaddenavarra/docs/un_memoria_curso_2018_19_web*. All websites cited in this and the following chapter have been consulted as of January 2021.

2. *http://www.universityholycross.org/santa_croce_101*.

3. *https://carfundacion.org/indicadores-cifras/*.

4. *https://carfundacion.org/indicadores-cifras/*. The definitive headquarters in Bidasoa was financed by a Basque businessman, not connected with Opus Dei, who was interested in the formation of the clergy.

5. *Instituto de Estudios Superiores de la Empresa* (IESE) (Universidad de Navarra), *Instituto Panamericano de Alta Dirección de Empresas* (Universidad Panamericana), *Instituto de Altos Estudios Empresariales* (Universidad Austral), *Instituto de Alta Dirección de Empresas* (Universidad de La Sabana), Lagos Business School (Pan-Atlantic University), *Escuela de Alta Dirección* (Universidad de Piura), *Instituto de Desarrollo Empresarial* (Universidad de los Hemisferios), *Instituto de Estudios Empresariales* (Universidad de Montevideo), UNIS Business School (Universidad del Istmo), and *Estudios Superiores de Empresa* (Universidad de los Andes). To these schools are added the *Associação de Estudos Superiores de Empresa* (Porto and Lisbon) and the CEU Law School (São Paulo).

6. IESE is widely considered one of the best business schools in the world. In 2021, its MBA program was ranked best in the world by *The Economist* and among the top five MBA programs in the world by the *Financial Times*. Its executive education programs have been ranked by the *Financial Times* best in the world every year since 2015.

7. *https://policlinicoelsalto.cl/*; *https://www.esp-paris.fr/*.

8. *http://monkole.cd/*.

9. Authors' interview with Christophe Rico, June 14, 2020. See *https://www. polisjerusalem.org/*.

10. *http://safi.elis.org/home/*.

11. *https://www.afesu.org.br/*.

12. *https://ceappedreira.org.br/*.

13. *https://cite.edu.ph/*; *https://www.iit.edu.ng/*.

14. Authors' interview with Santiago Altieri, November 22, 2020.

15. *https://www.american-initiatives.org/sirama*.

16. *https://www.braval.org/es*.

17. *https://kenvale.edu.au/*.

18. Also noteworthy are the Pinhais vocational education center (Curitiba, Brazil), *https://ospinhais.org.br/*; the Surí training center (San José, Costa Rica), which offers secondary education and a wide range of courses to women with limited financial resources, *https://proyectosuri.org/*; the Cefim technical institute (La Paz, Bolivia), which offers a higher technical degree in gastronomic services administration, *https://sites.google.com/a/instituto-cefim.com/test-cefim/*; the Sorawell vocational training center (Yaoundé, Cameroon), *https://www. sorawell.com/*, specializing in hotel management and catering; the Altaviana vocational training center (Valencia, Spain), *https://www.altaviana.com/*; and the Zunil technical baccalaureate school in hotel and catering (Guatemala City) *http://escuelazunil.blogspot.com/*.

19. *http://www.icsef.edu.co/*.

20. *http://www.fundacionmarzano.org.ar/*.

21. *https://unefa.org/*.

22. Letter 12, n.74. AGP A.3, 92-5-1.

23. See Juan Manuel Mora, "Eco de la canonización en la opinión pública internacional," *Anuario de Historia de la Iglesia*, 11/1 (2003), pp. 609–628.

24. See Gianni Riotta, "L'arma della trasparenza. L'Opus Dei batte il Codice da Vinci," *Il Corriere della Sera*, May 20, 2006.

25. See Dirección de Publicaciones de la Universidad de la Sabana (eds.), *Comunicación e identidad cristiana en la universidad del siglo XXI—Actas de Redecom II* (Pamplona, April 24–25, 2015) (Bogotá: Publicaciones Universidad de La Sabana, 2015).

26. Words of Josemaría Escrivá, 1958, quoted in AGP K.1, 184-4.

27. Authors' interview with Juan Narbona, Rome, June 29, 2020. Narbona has been webmaster of opusdei.org since 2006.

28. Authors' interview with Mónica Herrero, April 6, 2021.

29. Communiqué from the Information Office of Opus Dei in Japan, April 6, 2006, in Juan Manuel Mora, *La Iglesia, el Opus Dei y El Código Da Vinci. Un caso de comunicación global* (Pamplona: EUNSA, 2009), p. 137.

CHAPTER 16

"A Sea without Shores": Individual Action in Society

ike everybody else, the members of Opus Dei have jobs, families, and social ties. They lead normal lives, wherever they may find themselves. But they also realize that they are called to something that transcends all these things. They offer their activities to God and use them to spread the gospel. They try to live out their Catholic faith in their public and private lives and to spread their ideas and way of life, opening out like a fan. In some ways, the history of Opus Dei is the history of each of the members' individual lives. This chapter, therefore, takes a look at the lives and activities of a number of members of the Work and cooperators. The picture we present is necessarily fragmentary and incomplete. To describe the full range of activities of Opus Dei's faithful, we would need as many biographies as there are people in Opus Dei, but here we can offer only a small number.*

Opus Dei is like an iceberg; people usually see only the tip—some institutional or corporate aspect of the Work, or a renowned member's public actions. They do not perceive the base, the immense majority of its faithful who lead normal and ordinary lives. This

---

* From the methodological point of view, this study is complex because of the variety of people involved, their social situations, and the varied development of each person's spiritual life. For example, it is difficult to quantify the evangelizing impact of a government employee, a cab driver, or a mother who works, raises her children, and talks about God to her friends. Moreover, it would not make sense to lump an employee, cab driver, and housewife who belong to Opus Dei into a single category, because we would lose sight of who they are and what they do. Each one has his or her own personality, lifestyle, and way of thinking, but all are leaven of Christian life brought into the "dough" of their social worlds.

sometimes causes people to make the mistake of interpreting the decisions and actions of a well-known member as if they were attributable to Opus Dei as a whole.

In this chapter, we will focus on two sets of people. First, a number of everyday men and women who, for the most part, will never make the headlines. They are family members, colleagues, and neighbors who lead ordinary lives and carry out the evangelizing mission of the Church in a way that is "capillary" and unnoticed. We interviewed about fifty faithful and cooperators of Opus Dei from Congo, Ivory Coast, Spain, France, Hong Kong, Italy, Nigeria, and the United Kingdom. We asked them how they came to the Work and how they pass on Christian values in their workplaces and in their network of friends.[*]

Then we will relate the professional experiences of a few men and women connected with the Work who work in fields that in some way have a special impact. We decided to organize the stories that make up this second part into four groups involving 1) family, 2) culture and communications, 3)education, and 4) volunteering and development. We will offer a few examples from each of these areas, without trying to make an exhaustive list.

When we asked them if they would be willing to appear in a book on the history of Opus Dei, some of the people we approached hesitated or even asked not to be mentioned. They said that their work and private lives were not corporately linked to Opus Dei, and that they brought the gospel to society in their own way. They stressed that Opus Dei as an institution was not present in their professional activities. We replied that the purpose of this chapter was precisely to offer examples of people who have made the message of the Work their own and freely manifest it. After this explanation almost all of them agreed to share their personal stories.

What does the Prelature offer the people whose stories we tell here? It strengthens their identity, we may say, helping them to

---

[*] The interviews were held in 2020. As they are oral testimonies, we will not give references in the footnotes. We also consulted the brochure *Cooperators of Opus Dei*, prepared by the central offices of the Work in 2012.

become more truly themselves in their own eyes, before others, and before God. And it reminds them of the mission entrusted to them: to identify with Christ and bring him to all social circles, to promote the values of the gospel in their professional work, in public discourse, and in all spheres of their lives.[1] If, in order to promote "a new culture, a new legislation, and a new fashion,"[2] the Work institutionally promotes a few activities (as we saw in the last chapter), it encourages the majority of its members to think and act in society as *individuals*, in a manner consistent with their Christian values.*

Section 1. Individuals in Society

The lives of most members of Opus Dei are as ordinary as those of their fellow citizens. They have a normal job and there they seek to develop professionally. They know that God has called them as Christians to seek him in the varied circumstances of life, which they understand as a great apostolic opportunity.

They describe their initial encounter with the spirit of the Work as a discovery that brought new light to their way of contemplating the world around them. Although their social or professional circumstances remained the same, their relationship with God began to change. They noticed a difference in their prayer life and

---

* There are a few intermediate cases in which the authorities of Opus Dei have encouraged the members to consider getting involved in certain areas, but once the projects begin, the directors of the Work let each one follow its own path and take responsibility for its activities, creating its own style and facing the natural problems of development and succession. For example, after the General Congresses of Opus Dei in 2002 and 2010, the directors encouraged a few experts—thinkers, university leaders, communicators, and businessmen—to initiate interdisciplinary think tanks to create, share, and analyze ideas and their cultural, social, and public opinion impact within a Christian framework. In particular, they stressed the need to transmit values through literature, the media, video games, and social networks. A few international, professionally competent, economically and legally autonomous undertakings emerged, such as the Institute for Media and Entertainment (New York), the Social Trends Institute (Barcelona-New York), Intermedia Social Innovation (Rome), Rome Reports (Rome) and the Thomas More Institute (London).

way of seeing things. Their relationships with others and their daily occupations—beginning with their professional work—were transformed.

Jean-Luc Navarro is a retired radiology nurse. He is married with six children and lives in Paris. For him, praying is the first step in the Christian's apostolic mission. From there he moves on to taking care of everyone he encounters, especially when he volunteers to help the sick.

> My way of approaching the person who is suffering is to get down physically on my knees in front of them. There are patients who arrive very tired, in wheelchairs. I approach them and ask if they can lift their feet. Then, I kneel down in front of them, to remove the plates that support their feet in the wheelchair. Next, I help them put their foot on the floor and tell them that I am going to help them get up. Since people are not used to so much care, they look at me. From the first moment we meet, we are friends. They look at me with affection, and I look at them with affection. We quickly understand each other. And when one of them comes back for another radiology session, because he is hospitalized, he asks me: "Why are you so good to me?" I tell him that it is because he is a person who suffers, that it is something that comes from my heart, and that my faith also leads me to serve him. Faith helps you a lot. After a while the friendship reaches the point where I can say, "Well, you could also pray a little bit." And they answer: "I don't know how to pray." And I explain to them that to pray is to talk to Jesus, to someone who loves you very much.

Gavin Dixon is an Irish auto mechanic. He remembers:

> I received Baptism and Confirmation when I was young but had no deep understanding of the faith. A friend invited me to attend the monthly recollections and, little by little, I discovered the reasons behind the faith. I work in a garage where I paint many vehicles that have been repaired after an accident. In every assignment, I pray to God for some particular intention. I often work on parts of the car

that are not seen but, as I offer my work as a prayer, I pay great attention to detail even in those areas. Learning how to apply the Catholic faith in a practical way and teaching others is something I find really attractive, and it helps me deepen my relationship with Jesus Christ.

Mirian Solís, head of the Department of Obstetrics at the National University of San Marcos' medical school in Lima, Peru says:

> When I got to know the Work, I loved the cordial and cheerful atmosphere I found. The people who welcomed me treated me as if they had known me all my life; I felt at ease. I began to go [to a center] on Saturdays. I attended doctrine classes and then circles. I participated in visits to the sick and elderly, I received confirmation. . . . One day on a retreat, while reading a homily by St. Josemaría on the Christian vocation, I felt nervous because at that moment God made me see that he was calling me to take him everywhere, to place him at the summit of all activities. This stuck in my mind and heart. I decided to ask for admission [as an associate] because I found what I was looking for: God in my life in the middle of the world.

Edwige Topé, is married with five children. She works at a school in Abidjan (Ivory Coast) and is preparing a doctoral thesis on international trade. She says that when she first came in contact with the Work, "I felt like I was part of a family, since the people at the center that I went to asked me to help out in a way that showed they trusted me a lot. In addition, I noticed that they listened to me, encouraged me, and moved me to outdo myself." She explains that God comes first in her life. "In the way I bring up my children and in the formation I offer to parents, I stress the need to avoid traps, to seek what's fair and, above all, to love the person. For me, the Gospel message 'You received without pay, give without pay' has had great resonance."

Alphonsine Nlandu, was born in Kinshasa, Congo. She is a teacher in a hospitality school. She accepted God's call to Opus Dei as a numerary assistant because she was struck by "the joy of the people I lived with at Kibali School" and "the attention given to everyone, to their personal things, their worries, to each one as she is. This way of treating us was not faked."

Fr. Stephen Langridge, a parish priest and until recently vocations director in the Archdiocese of Southwark in England, perceived the same family atmosphere. He recalls his initial contact with priests of the Work:

> I found the formation I received from Opus Dei stood out for two reasons. First of all, there was a human warmth which I was not necessarily experiencing elsewhere. Secondly, whatever the difficulties at the seminary, it kept me focused on Christ. I think it is sometimes difficult to grasp the idea that a group exists for no other reason than the sanctification of its members.

Mariano Sánchez is a retired master industrial electronics technician. He started work at age seventeen installing radio transmitters throughout Madrid. Later, he did technical service work for Canon, Inc. He relates what happened when he met some associate members of Opus Dei: "What attracted me most was that they were people with great enthusiasm for life . . . and who also prayed, something I didn't do." Something similar happened to Aitor Jusdado, thirty years old. He studied industrial engineering and now teleworks in the after-sales service of Renault in Madrid.

> When I began to attend the formational activities in the Work's center for university students, I immediately realized that I had found something made real in people of flesh and blood, a path where the Christian faith becomes consistent with one's life. After a while, the people in the center encouraged me to consider in prayer whether God was calling me to Opus Dei. I did so and eventually joined the Work because I saw that God had led me that way.

Michel Hingase, from Congo, was moved by visiting Loango, a cultural center of the Work: "From my first moments in Loango I knew that these were good people, and that I would like to be like them." By the time he graduated from the university he was an associate member of Opus Dei. Then he spent eighteen months in Senegal to study for a master's degree. In Dakar, he recalls, "I met a group of people who had taken part in the Work's formation programs in different countries and who had decided to promote devotion to St. Josemaría. Shortly afterwards, we started circles with Senegalese professionals and courses in Christian doctrine with Ivorian students living in Dakar." When he returned to Congo, Hingase was hired by Coca-Cola and oversaw the introduction of the brand into his home country. After a few years, Monkole Hospital hired him as director of general services, a post that involves maintenance and security.

Theo Grilli of Foggia, Italy, has worked as a barber since he was sixteen. In the past he has worked as a stylist at companies specializing in hair cosmetic products, but now, at sixty-two years of age, he and his wife are co-owners of a beauty salon. When he first heard that he could sanctify his ordinary work, it changed his way of looking at his profession.

> I am enthused by the idea of imitating Jesus working in Joseph's workshop before the three years of his public life. Jesus had a normal life, and he did things well. I think that he worked well, with dedication, that he took care of his relationships with his clients and colleagues, that he was friendly, attentive to other people, affectionate, humble, understanding, and cheerful. This is the best way of showing the Christian message of Opus Dei.

Pablo Sánchez Jiménez, is married with four children and works at Santander Bank in Madrid in the payments department. He says,

> I have a normal life. Maybe that's why I'm enthusiastic about the possibility of becoming holy in ordinary life, at work, talking with colleagues by the coffee machine, waiting to pick up my children from school. . . . In those moments, listening, taking an interest in the problems of others, and talking about my own are opportunities to be close to God.

Wai-ping Chan (Macau) is an orthodontist and the mother of five children. She opened a dental clinic with her husband in 2013. She says,

> At first, I focused on giving my patients the best care I could. After a year, I realized that every patient was very different, just like my children. I had to learn how to deal with people's problems by

respecting them, patiently listening to their discomfort, under-standing and showing sympathy to them. At the same time, I real-ized I neeed to continue to improve my technical skills. I sanctify my work when I strive to be the best orthodontist I can be.

Sonia Ramoneda, is married and has two children. She explains her trajectory:

Since I was little, I wanted to dance. My parents wanted me to fol-low a more conventional career, but I managed to win them over. I got a degree in dramatic arts at a specialized school. I was now able to be a dancer, a dance teacher, and an actress. And, at the age of twenty-three, my professional adventure began. I opened the Sonia Ramoneda Dance Studio in San Cugat del Vallés (Spain).

Until the outbreak of the coranvirus, I had around 130 young people every year whom I taught to dance and to be respectful with others in the way they relate to each other, move on stage, and dress. In addition to being a dance teacher, many girls see me as an older sister. They often tell me about their problems. I remember one who started cutting herself because she was being bullied. In the musical we do every year, I gave her the lead role because she needed to feel appreciated. And when she saw that the other danc-ers relied on her, she stopped harming herself.

Now, because of the coronavirus health crisis, I have been forced to close the dance studio. But, as soon as this situation passes, I will reopen it because I am passionate about education.

Nkem Emezie-Ejinima works in corporate communications for an oil and gas company based in Lagos, Nigeria. She is married and has four children. She says that when she is with her colleagues, she tries to

truly represent what it is to be a Christian, showing integrity in all that I do, striving to be cheerful, respecting the dignity of all who work in the organization, and showing gratitude at all times. These little gestures and even sacrifices at work help me forge friendships with colleagues, and through these friendships I am able to help them in various ways, from personal favors such as finding a study group or tutoring for their kids, to advice on work and professional matters. The motto for me at work is always *service*: giving of my time, talent, and, where needed, treasure to the positive growth of others.

Józef Morawski has lived all his life in Poland. His job as a shoe-maker is inseparable from his physical limitations:

> I came across Opus Dei thanks to my daughter Agnieszka. She told me that I could bring God into my shoe repairs and that helped me do my job better. Because of my illness I had to reduce my professional commitment. (Three days a week, I have to go to the hospital for dialysis, while waiting to receive a kidney transplant.) Above all, I cooperate by offering the difficulties of the illness and the dialysis sessions, and the Rosaries I pray while taking the long walks the doctors have prescribed.

Sunshine Plata in an artist who lives in the Philippines and uses coffee as her medium. She says:

> Through the formation I received, I learned to love my profession as a painter, because a job well done gives glory to God, and helps you to practice virtue. For example, I learned to speak with the Lord when I'm alone, working on a painting, and perhaps having difficulty concentrating. When I'm struggling with something, I think of someone, perhaps the future owner of the painting, and I offer each stroke of the brush. That way I can ensure that all my painting is done with love and prayers.

The writer José Luis Olaizola is the father of nine children. He has published numerous books in different genres, with more than two million copies sold. In 1983 he won the Planeta Prize in Spain for the book *La Guerra del General Escobar*. He is the founder of the NGO Somos Uno, which has helped more than two thousand Thai girls attend school and avoid falling into child prostitution networks. He explained:

> I can say, succinctly, that God is not absent from the story in any of my eighty-five books, be they novels, essays, or children's books. I don't consider myself a Catholic author in the style of Graham

Greene, but I do consider myself a Catholic who writes, and it is logical that people notice that.

María Gudín is a neurologist and also a writer. In 2006, she published her first novel, *La Reina sin Nombre*, set in the sixth century in Visigoth Spain. She chooses to write because,

> by profession, I am in contact with people who tell me about lives that are more complex and exciting than a thousand novels. The suffering that so many people bring to me must have an outlet in stories. I write as a necessity, as a therapy, as a project, and an attempt at something that does not exist and never will.

Lucía Rodríguez was born in Zamora (Spain). She teaches Latin and Greek. She worked in several high schools before she arrived at the one in Móstoles (Madrid), where she is now. When we asked her how she transmits the Christian message in her work, she answered:

> It's not about setting out to *do* something. I think it is rather what we try to be and live. Maybe you should ask the people around me what they see in me. I try to work the best I can, and when I mess up, I try to fix everything as quickly as possible without getting angry. I try to make friends with people, do favors and help them in any way I can. . . . Most of my work involves students. I help them to be better people, and to solve their problems. I try to bring them closer to the Lord.

Juan José Nieto has also dedicated a good part of his life to public education. Born into a family of limited means—his father was a truck driver and his mother an illiterate housewife—he has always lived in the working-class Vallecas neighborhood of Madrid. For eleven years, he was the principal of a high school and, for another four years, director general of education for the Community of Madrid. He organized the association *Mejora Tu Escuela Pública* [Improve Your Public School]. He comments:

> We have created a personal tutoring network. When I talk to the kids, one by one, I am concerned with improving them as people

in virtues such as honesty and teamwork. I also nurture friendships with my fellow teachers. I send them birthday greetings. I take an interest when people are ill. I go to their loved ones' funerals. They all know that I pray for them. Sometimes someone who claims to be an agnostic says to me: "Pray for me. They hear you more in heaven."

For Peter Green, from the UK, life is a conversion story. He was a hippie in his youth, eventually became an electrician, and is now retired. He has nine children. As a boy, his only experiences with religion were family baptisms, weddings, and funerals. Then he married a Catholic, and the way that a local priest lived his faith attracted him. He later got in touch with Grandpont House at Oxford. "The truth is the guys I saw at Grandpont were always cheerful and positive even when things were difficult. Their attitude to life—doing things well and turning all things into prayer—impressed me a lot." So began a long journey that led him to become Catholic, a cooperator, and later a supernumerary. For the past nine years he has been giving a study circle in Kent. He often reminds people that it was "living your faith in the home, workplace, or any environment" that initially attracted him.

Gustavo Entrala, a numerary member of the Work, is a communications strategist. A specialist in the culture of innovation, he has advised companies such as L'Oréal Group, Diageo, Janssen Laboratories, and Red Bull on their digital services. He has also served as a consultant for the Government of Spain and the NGO Doctors Without Borders. He was CEO and executive director of the advertising agency 101 for fifteen years. "With the idea of helping the Church be more attractive in communicating the truth,"[3] he worked on the Twitter account @Pontifex, which Benedict XVI used to post his first tweet in 2012. He collaborates in the Spanish program *A Vivir que Son Dos Días* (Cadena SER) on weekends.

Habib Moussa is a computer scientist of Lebanese origin who now lives in Spain. He is a Shiite Muslim and a cooperator of Opus Dei. He recalls the day a friend gave him *The Way* as a gift:

> Reading it made me want to contribute to the Work. I really liked the idea that I too could help others. I lend a hand in various activities at

Nerpio Club in Albacete. I think this has helped me to get to know the Catholic Church better. I appreciate the Church a lot. My life has been enriched and my being a Muslim hasn't been an obstacle. Among many things, what has struck me above all is forgiveness in action, something which is far from easy and which I want to learn to live better.

In Galway, Ireland, Nora Heneghan (1910–1994) had the heart of a wife, mother, and friend. She had ten children, fifty-two grand-children, and nineteen great-grandchildren. She knew countless people in her hometown. She came close to Opus Dei through her children, two of whom belong to the Prelature. Nora devoted herself to the care of her family and, in a particular way, to her ailing husband in his final years. Nora passed away while caring for her husband.[4]

Section 2. In Particular Fields

Part 1. Education

Members of the Work teach at public and private schools of all sorts, from universities to nursery schools. Some of them have started educational institutions that are inspired by the spirit of the Work but have no legal or institutional relationship with the Prelature of Opus Dei. We discuss a few of them here.

The International University of La Rioja (UNIR) is a private university based in Logroño (Spain). It was founded in 2009 with the idea of giving access to education to people who cannot attend traditional universities that require students to be physically present. José María Vázquez García-Peñuela has been its rector from the outset. He is a law professor who spent two decades working in public universities before arriving at UNIR. According to Vázquez,

> UNIR's teaching model is based on streamed and recorded classes, enriched study material, and continuous support for students through personal tutorials. We currently offer twenty-five bach-elor's and eighty master's degrees. All our activity has a Christian humanist orientation. With thirty-five thousand students, of which 45 percent live in Latin America, UNIR is the biggest private

Spanish university. A typical student might be a woman in her early thirties, with a dependent child, who is studying for a bachelor's or master's degree in education.[5]

Alfonso Aguiló, an engineer, is a specialist in the management of educational centers. In 2002, he was director of Colegio Tajamar and, a few years later, he was elected president of the Madrid chapter of the Spanish Confederation of Educational Centers. At that time a number of municipalities in the outskirts of Madrid were growing rapidly and needed schools to accommodate the growing population. Aguiló found that very few of the new schools reflected Christian values, even though many parents were looking for such schools. When he discussed this situation with the regional directors of Opus Dei, they told him that they could not support more schools that were apostolic undertakings of the Work, since the existing ones in Madrid consumed considerable amounts of energy.

Aguiló, with some other people, decided to form a foundation to create and support educational centers characterized by a Christian identity, academic excellence, personalized attention to students, and economic sustainability. Its first project was Alborada School (Alcalá de Henares, near Madrid), which opened its doors in 2009 with 350 students, despite a media campaign against it. Other similar schools in various parts of the Community of Madrid joined the group, which gave rise to the Arenales Red Educativa group. Most of these schools are coeducational and are subsidized by the autonomous Community of Madrid.[6]

By 2015, the declining birth rate in Spain had sharply reduced the demand for new schools, but another opportunity arose. Several religious congregations wanted to maintain the identity and mission of their schools but were having difficulties due to lack of personnel and resources. At that time, Aguiló explains,

> Arenales invited them to join the group. The management agreement each one signed with Arenales respected the school's unique identity but was designed to ensure each one's economic sustainability without subsidies from other schools. This required developing the administrators' and parents' sense of responsibility and forming

roots at the local level, as well as collaborating with other schools in the network to reduce expenses and develop better practices. The idea was that different ecclesial realities would collaborate in this way in the new evangelization promoted by the recent popes."[7]

Today, Arenales has more than ten thousand students in twenty-five schools. Most of them are in Spain, but there are others in Munich (Germany), Porto (Portugal), Riga (Latvia), Luanda (Angola), Sofia (Bulgaria), and San Francisco and Miami (USA).

In Poland, a group of parents, some of whom belonged to Opus Dei, founded the Sternik association to promote schools. It eventually established five schools, two in Warsaw and one each in Poznań, Szczecin, and Krakow. Those schools are all classified as personal works. Starting in 2010, groups of parents scattered all around Poland established fifteen other associations to establish schools inspired by by the Sternick model, although in some cases none of the people involved belonged to Opus Dei. Thus far they have started some thirty schools. They have no formal or legal relationship with Opus Dei or with Sternick or its schools. However, according to Dobrochna Lama, who held various management positions in the Sternik association from 2004 to 2018,

> They are united by the same pedagogical foundation, rooted in Christian anthropology: work well done, respect for personal freedom, confidence in the improvement of each person, optimism in the face of difficulties, and openness to innovations. They also take care of the ongoing formation of teachers and administrators and seek a greater involvement of parents in the education of their children.

They are located in Gdansk, Wrocław, Bielsko-Biała, Wadowice, Łódź, Białystok, Olsztyn, and Katowice. Some of them have asked Opus Dei to provide a chaplain.

In London, parents connected to Opus Dei started two co-ed elementary schools, one of which eventually closed, and two secondary schools, one for boys and one for girls. Other educational centers inspired by the Work's message include Stella International School

(Vienna, Austria), the Ružičnjak and Lotrščak schools, and a kindergarten in Zagreb (Croatia), the Parentes and Navisen schools in Prague (Czech Republic), and a kindergarten in Bratislava (Slovakia).

Members of the Work have given life to language schools, such as the Jingdou Language Center in Macau, which has been offering English classes since 1992. The Irtysh Cultural Center, founded in Almaty (Kazakhstan) in 1999, contributes to the opening up and development of the country, offering courses in English, Spanish, and, on a more occasional basis, Italian and Turkish.[8]

Part 2. Volunteering and Social Development

Social programs for the disadvantaged are a traditional way of radiating the gospel. In the earliest days of Opus Dei, the young Fr. Escrivá took college studens with him to visit the sick in the hospitals of Madrid while taking his first steps to found the Work. Together with other people, faithful of the Prelature have set up more than a hundred foundations and nongovernmental organizations (NGOs) that provide assistance to vulnerable social sectors. Some are professional activities; others rely primarily or entirely on volunteers. Some receive state aid, but others are supported exclusively by private funding. Some have become well-known and even serve as models for other institutions, while others are small and go unnoticed. Most arose from the individual initiative of the people who started them, but a few have been encouraged by the directors of the Work.[9] All of them emphasize that they have a Christian origin and an evangelizing mission, which is manifested in companionship and warmth (in addition to material assistance) offered to the needy, the sick, and the marginalized. They are not connected with the Prelature of Opus Dei on the institutional, legal, or economic level.[10]

The *Istituto per la Cooperazione Universitaria* (1966), based in Rome, has completed more than four hundred development projects around the world.[11] In Colombia, the Beatriz Londoño de Arango Foundation has undertaken social integration projects in Medellín since 1982—housing construction in shantytowns, a training center for manual arts, a center providing training to tour guides, and after-school programs for children.[12]

On a trip to Mexico and Guatemala in the early 1980s, images of huge shantytowns were stamped in the Prelate's memory. During a subsequent visit to Spain, Del Portillo encouraged the directors of the Work to consider promoting social works to help the very poor. After a life dedicated to teaching and politics, the former Minister of Development Planning, Laureano López Rodó, made the project his own and shared it with businessmen and professors who were his friends. Together they created the Codespa Foundation (1985), which currently supports seventy projects in various countries. It focuses on four areas: creation of economic infrastructure in remote rural areas, training and integration into the labor market of disadvantaged populations, strengthening of social entrepreneurship to facilitate the transition from subsistence agriculture to a market economy, and microfinancing for development. In addition, along with other foundations and companies, Codespa has set up the Business Observatory for Inclusive Growth, which promotes good business practices. A few of Codespa's projects, such as the Dualtech Training Center (Manila, Philippines), are run by members of Opus Dei, but most are not.[13]

The late 1980s and the 1990s witnessed a flowering of nonprofits and other NGOs dedicated to development and social action in many parts of the world. Increasing numbers of people, especially students, became more aware of how vulnerable the most impoverished members of society were and were moved to try to help them. In this context, a growing number of members of the Work promoted humanitarian and assistance activities.

In 1986, in Madrid, Manuel García Bernal, José Miguel Cejas, and David Palacios started *Solidaridad Universitaria Internacional*, a nonprofit association which, in a short time, brought together several dozen volunteers. The organization existed for seven years. The voluneers dedicated a few hours a week to the social integration of marginalized young people in shantytowns and slum areas. According to García Bernal, many young people tuned in. It was a demanding activity because we went to very poor neighborhoods. We organized school support programs so that the children would go back to school and want to study. We sponsored language and writing classes, catechesis, and sports. We helped the children's parents, many of whom were illegal immigrants, to regularize their legal situation.[14]

Jumana Trad Yunés directs the foundation *Promoción Social de la Cultura* (1987), a Madrid-based NGO which runs development and education projects in the Middle East, Latin America, Africa, and Asia. It also offers humanitarian aid in disaster areas and promotes volunteering. The This institution receives financial support from a wide range of institutions, including the European Commission and Google.[15]

Following the call of John Paul II in his encyclical *Sollicitudo rei socialis*, which encouraged people of good will to become involved in professional and charitable undertakings to combat poverty, Xavier Boutin founded the *Institut Européen de Coopération et de Développement* (IECD) in Strasbourg in 1988. It supports small businesses and technical schools to facilitate the professional integration of unemployed young people in sixteen countries in Africa, the Middle East, and Southeast Asia. For example, it has set up an extensive network of family farming schools in Ivory Coast and Cameroon, several hotel schools in Nigeria, Lebanon, Thailand, and Kenya, and an educational program for middle and high school students from poor rural areas in Madagascar.[16]

The *Organización Navarra para Ayuda entre los Pueblos* (ONAY) was created in Pamplona in 1992 by professors and students from the University of Navarra eager to help build solidarity with marginalized groups and cooperate in promoting their development. Today, ONAY coordinates a dozen international health and educational aid programs. Its main social project is Monkole Hospital in Kinshasa (Congo).[17]

The NGO *Cooperación Internacional* began in Madrid in 1993 to promote social awareness and volunteer work among young people. According to its general director, Rafael Herraiz,

the association works in four main areas: helping schools and universities to foster in their students a mentality of service to others;

training young people to prepare them to engage in social projects; developing cooperative partnerships in various countries; and carrying out volunteer projects such as care for homeless people, housing rehabilitation, and education for children from socially excluded neighborhoods."[18]

Cooperación Internacional brings together more than five thousand student volunteers. Some of its partners are individuals while others are legal entities, such as several youth associations promoted by members of the Work.

In 1995, the economist Daniel Turiel professionalized the existing Belgian NGO ACTEC. It has completed two hundred development projects and invested some one hundred million dollars in projects which have benefited more than two hundred thousand people in Guatemala, El Salvador, Colombia, Ecuador, Haiti, Congo, Kenya, Nigeria, Burundi, Cameroon, and Lebanon. ACTEC's programs support professional training of vulnerable populations so that they can lead change in their communities. Its most important projects involve management training, microcredit, and mentoring of microenterprise creators.

In 2010, Turiel founded a novel business program in the field of developmental cooperation: the microMBA. Based on the virtues of excellence, professionalism, and a spirit of service, this program transforms microentrepreneurs into leaders with an impact on personal and business development: accelerated sales and profit growth, investment capacity, and the creation of decent jobs. Currently, 1,200 entrepreneurs are following this program in Colombia, Guatemala, and El Salvador, and expansion in Africa is already planned.[19]

Desarrollo y Asistencia is an NGO that began in 1995; it was renamed *Nadiesolo Voluntariado* in 2020. Its general director, Isabel Antúnez, explains that

this charitable foundation develops programs to accompany people who suffer from loneliness: sick people in hospitals, elderly people living at home or in retirement homes, people with intellectual disabilities, homeless people who also suffer from loss of the sense of self-worth or have fallen into addictions, and children at risk of exclusion due to failure in school."[20]

Nadiesolo has 2,200 volunteers who assist more than 70,000 people in various cities in Spain.

In 1993, Abel Albino started the NGO CONIN in Mendoza (Argentina) to combat child malnutrition. His method trains mothers to acquire good habits of health, hygiene, nutrition, and psycho-affective and motor stimulation of the child. CONIN currently runs more than one hundred centers in eighteen provinces in Argentina. They have helped some seventeen thousand youngsters. There are also CONIN centers in Paraguay, Peru, and Gambia.[21]

Several retired businessmen and military personnel started a food bank in Madrid in 1994. Thanks to their organizational skills, it quickly grew and was replicated in other cities. Eventually, a Spanish federation of food banks was formed, with branches in each of Spain's fifty provinces. This charitable organization collects surplus food and, with the help of other organizations, distributes it to thousands of people in need.[22]

Tecpán is a municipality located in the Guatemalan highlands. In 1995, the *Fundación para el Desarrollo Integral* established three training centers there to provide training and support to the indigenous population. They offer agricultural education and microcredit programs for small producers in the area; prevention and health services, with community pharmacies selling medicines at low cost; and programs to help women improve their living conditions and participate actively in the development of their community.[23]

In Bolivia, the contrast between rural and urban areas is stark. In 1999, Sergio Elío Marcilla and a number of his friends created the *Asociación Civil para el Desarrollo Ayni*. It provides basic services to thirty highly vulnerable rural areas, such as access to clean drinking water, construction of sewage systems and latrines, and the installation of irrigation systems. In all projects, it asks the local people to contribute labor so that they become the key players in their own development. The group works to improve local organizational capacities so that the people do not have to depend continually on external aid. It especially tries to empower women to occupy decision-making positions in their communities.[24]

In 1999, an Argentine mechanical engineer, Facundo Garayoa, created the FonBec Foundation to provide scholarships to students to prevent them from dropping out of school. Garayoa looks for sponsors to give scholarships to students who are outstanding in their effort and commitment to their studies but are socioeconomically vulnerable. More than one hundred companies and three hundred volunteers make it possible for FonBec to help 1,600 Argentinean and Bolivian students.[25]

González Catán is a city on the outskirts of Buenos Aires contaminated by the garbage that has been dumped there for decades. In 2007, a few members of Opus Dei started Sendas, a center for primary health care, preventive and family medicine, and the promotion of sound nutrition. Activities include first aid courses for children and young people, training for adults, clothing markets, and health care. One volunteer, Isabel Rosón, a doctor specializing in nutrition, explains that she goes to Sendas "because it is a way of doing something to remedy so much misery in our country. As Mother Teresa said, 'You have to give until it hurts.' Going to González Catán 'hurts.'"[26]

Heidi Burkhart spent twenty-six years directing the NGO Hilfswerk International, one of Austria's leading cooperative organizations for development. It promotes health care projects, vocational training, and agricultural programs in more than twenty countries. It also assists children and families left destitute by natural disasters or armed conflicts.

More than 350 volunteers have worked with the NGO Help (Aachen, 1998), visiting orphanages, nursing homes, and foster children. Members of Opus Dei and their friends also promoted AMAL (2015) in Vienna, Austria. The group welcomes immigrants from the Middle East and helps them integrate into Austrian society.[27]

Parishes served by priests from the Priestly Society of the Holy Cross carry out many social aid activities. For example, José Manuel Horcajo, a priest of the Archdiocese of Madrid and pastor of San Ramón Nonato in the Vallecas neighborhood, launched the *Obra*

Social Familiar Álvaro del Portillo which mobilizes two hundred volunteers from the parish. As Horcajo explains, the organization has

> more than forty projects that cover the basic needs of the most vulnerable in the neighborhood, among others a 'family dining room' which serves two hundred fifty hot meals a day, a school for parents, fifteen professional courses, a charitable clothing store, a food pantry that serves two hundred needy families, and a program of visits to elderly people living alone. In addition, it takes in about twenty beggars and fifteen homeless families and provides daycare for children while their mothers are at work.[28]

Part 3. Family, Life, and Bioethics

Like many other individuals, some members of Opus Dei have dedicated themselves professionally or as volunteers to associations and forums dedicated to caring for and strengthening the family, teaching the value and meaning of virginity and celibacy, and promoting human love and the dignity of sexuality and marriage with its features of indissolubility and openness to life.

As we have seen, Family Orientation, which began in the late 1960s, expanded considerably in Europe and the Americas during the following decades.* At the end of the nineties, it developed a more professional structure and began to offer several courses to help parents with children of different ages from infants to adolescents. Later, courses on marital love, courtship, and being a grandparent were also added. It grouped all these activities under the heading "family enrichment." It reorganized as the International Federation for Family Development (IFFD), an independent nondenominational NGO composed of several associations.

In 2004, IFFD held an international congress in New York. Two years later, IFFD appointed the lawyer Javier Antonio Vidal-Quadras as its secretary general. The period of the pioneers came to an end, and another era began, characterized by sustainable expansion made

---

* See chapter 2, section 4.

possible by the development of Family Enrichment's legal structure and economic organization. With these measures, IFFD acquired institutional prestige. Today, organizations from seventy countries are associated with the federation.

To develop themselves personally and as families, parents use a case-study method to discuss the upbringing of their children and their relationship with their spouse. Given its origin—in which several members of Opus Dei participated—and because its vision of the family has its roots in Christian anthropology, many supernumeraries and cooperators have participated in these activities. In addition to strengthening their own family, they help other married couples improve as parents and spouses.[29] Despite the Christian vision that inspires it, IFFD stresses its independent nondenominational character. It does not, therefore, sign agreements with religious institutions.

At the end of the 1980s, the engineer Fernando Corominas rethought his professional life and began to study effective ways families can help their children develop from earliest childhood on. Soon afterward, he created the book series *Hacer Familia*, which now includes more than a hundred books, some of which have been translated into several languages. These books focus on the virtues of family life, the development of children at various ages, and practical solutions to problems parents may encounter. He also started a magazine called *Hacer Familia*.[30] In 1991, he and Alfonso Aguiló started the *Instituto Europeo de Estudios de la Educación*, a nonprofit organization that has extended its family education courses to many countries. The institute prepares teams of family counselors, who, in turn, form teams in schools, parishes, and parent groups.[31]

Identitas, an organization created by Juan José Javaloyes, offers an intensive course in family education, a basic course in personalized education, and a training plan for the harmonious development of personal identity, designed both for educators and parents. It has spread widely in Spain and Latin America.[32]

In 1997, Antonio Affinita and his wife Maria Munizzi (Rome) were expecting twins. At the time, they recall, "we were concerned about the lack of protection that the media offered to minors. The media showed explicit violence, sex, abuse, and discrimination. We had the idea of giving parents a public voice."[33] That's what led to the Italian Parents Movement (*Movimento Italiano Genitori*, or *Moige* for short), a nonprofit, independent, and non-confessional organization.

Moige began by campaigning against the violent and vulgar television programs that could desensitize children and minors. The organization reached agreements with various media outlets and then expanded its range of action by promoting undertakings against drugs, alcohol, bullying, pedophilia, and violent video games. *Moige* currently has a network of eighty thousand parents and operates in thirty-five Italian cities. It is associated with various international federations that work for the protection of minors. One way members raise public awareness is by promoting positive content, Every year, they offer the *Moige* Awards to TV shows, advertising, and YouTube channels that offer high-quality programming that is also family-friendly.[34]

Members of Opus Dei and cooperators are involved in numerous undertakings that defend life, on both a professional and a volunteer basis. Their goal is to promote the dignity of human life from conception to natural death. In the United States, for example, EMC Frontline offers assistance to mothers who are considering the possibility of abortion. Thanks to their help, more than forty-three thousand women have chosen life and given birth. The Guatemalan civil association *Familia Importa*, directed by Pablo Ortiz, proposes positive strategies for promoting life and the family. In Kibera, Kenya, Domtila Ayot runs the St. Martin's Crisis Pregnancy and Prolife Education Centre. A Bolivian doctor who belongs to Opus Dei works in the *Centro de Ayuda para la Mujer*. Every year he helps five hundred women who find themselves facing an unexpected pregnancy. Most of them choose not to abort.

In the mid-1980s, after abortion was decriminalized in Spain, the attorney Benigno Blanco started the *Asociación de Defensa de la Vida*. Years later, he was appointed legal advisor to the *Federación Española de Asociaciones Provida* and later became president of the *Federación Española de Familias Numerosas*. After eight years in politics, Blanco went on to lead the *Foro de la Familia*, a civil and nondenominational platform that brings together the biggest profamily organizations in Spain. In 2005, while the campaign to legalize homosexual marriage was underway in Spain, the *Foro de Familia* called for a demonstration in Madrid. The march brought together one million people under a slogan which translates to, "The family does matter, because of the right to a mother and a father." The organization presented 1.5 million signatures to the Congress of Deputies in favor of their position. Although the petition was ultimately rejected, *Foro's* efforts made the arguments in favor of the family present in the public debate.

In 2007, Blanco created the Mothers' Network (*RedMadre*), a solidarity group that "advises and supports women so that they can overcome conflicts that arise during an unplanned pregnancy or one that brings with it the risk of social exclusion."[35] Every year, it helps ten thousand women carry their pregnancies to term. The foundation has also promoted local popular undertakings, proposing laws in the regional legislatures of Spain that would offer assistance to those expecting a child. In this way, RedMadre gives women a leading role during pregnancy.

Members and cooperators are also active in bioethics. The Bioethics Study Group organized conferences for physicians and specialists in Dublin for a number of years. A family doctor who belongs to Opus Dei is a member of the board of directors for the Scottish Council on Human Bioethics. As part of her work, she promotes cooperation among various prolife organizations.[36]

The *Instituto de Bioética y Ciencias de la Salud* in Zaragoza (Spain) specializes in end-of-life care. A biochemistry professor who belongs to the Work represented the Spanish government on the UNESCO bioethics committee. She later became president of the *Asociación Española de Bioética y Ética Médica*. A Brazilian doctor from Opus Dei represented her country's bishops' conference at debates in the Brazilian legislature when issues related to bioethics and the right to life of the unborn were discussed.[37]

Etienne Montero established the *Institut Européen de Bioéthique*, based in Brussels. Swiss members of the Work created the *Schweizerische Gesellschaft für Biomedizinische Ethik*. In Spain, the *Asociación Nacional para la Defensa del Derecho a la Objeción de Conciencia del*

Personal Biosanitario advocates in favor of the right to conscientious objection on the part of health care personnel.[38]

In Colombia, educator María Luisa Estrada and her husband Juan Francisco Vélez, an engineer, founded *Protege tu Corazón* in 1993. The organization describes itself as "a leading institution in Latin America in programs related to character and sexuality." It has established programs in more than eight hundred denominational and nondenominational educational institutions in fourteen countries. Members "present the content of Christian philosophical anthropology so that parents and children may understand themselves as persons, discover that love is what gives meaning to sexuality, and manage to integrate this into their personality."[39] Similar associations include *Formando Corazones*, a comprehensive training course in affectivity and sexuality in Chihuahua (Mexico), and the *Programa de Educación en Valores, Afectividad y Sexualidad*, founded by the physician Verónica Valenzuela, which has trained more than two thousand teachers from a hundred Chilean educational establishments.[40]

Part 4. Culture, Art, and Communications

Many institutions in cutting-edge fields have been created or run by members or cooperators of Opus Dei in response to St. Josemaría's insistence that lay Catholics should take responsibility for helping build a world that promotes human dignity. This section will introduce some of the men and women involved in these types of projects. None of the projects we will discusss has any formal link with Opus Dei.

Luis Tellez spent much of his early professional years managing NGOs in the United States. In 2003, he founded the Witherspoon Institute in Princeton, New Jersey. The institute offers both academic and popular courses and has publications on various social topics and on the fundamental pillars of society. It is based at Princeton University and offers programs at other American universities.[41]

Carlos Caballé is the president of the Social Trends Institute, a research center based in New York and Barcelona. Focusing on culture, government, and civil society, it provides institutional and financial support to specialists studying social trends and their effects on different communities. In addition to sponsoring publications, the institute organizes symposia and awards scholarships to students researching sociological topics.[42]

In 2002, the historian Andrew Hegarty and several colleagues created the St. Thomas More Institute in London. It organizes conferences about politics and current thought.[43] A similar institution in Cologne, Germany, the *Lindenthal Institut*, promotes interdisciplinary research in philosophy, ethics, work, culture, and the family.[44]

Salvador Bernal and Ignacio Aréchaga created the *Aceprensa* feature article agency in Madrid in 1970. The agency's articles examine the major issues of the day with academic rigor, a journalistic style, and extensive investigation of sources. Individuals, media outlets, and educational centers subscribe to the weekly bulletin. According to Bernal, *Aceprensa's* services aim to provide "reliable points of reference on facts and trends in culture, education, society, and religion, aimed at people without much time: journalists, teachers, family counselors, priests, directors of cultural and educational institutions."[45] In Australia and New Zealand, Michael Cook and Carolyn Moynihan run MercatorNet (founded in 2005), a website that reflects on ethical and anthropological issues relating to culture, family, sexuality, law, and religion.

Firstlife is a German online magazine with articles by young people, which analyzes issues related to human dignity and solidarity. Its target audience is people between fifteen and thirty years of age who are, interested in a proactive approach to social problems.[46]

In the world of fashion and beauty, St. Josemaría's message has inspired stylists, designers, fashion show organizers, beauty shop owners, and others who work in fashion and design to try to develop attractive modern styles that are consistent with the dignity of women as persons and as Christians. Lula Kiah, for instance, founded Style Innovators, "a training and innovation company for image consultants. It has produced programs on fashion for five years on Univision network and, currently, on Telemundo."[47] Elisa Álvarez Espejo is the editor of the fashion, beauty, and lifestyle sections of *Telva* magazine. Paloma Díaz Soloaga is a professor of fashion at the Complutense University of Madrid, honorary director of a diploma program in fashion at Villanueva University, and the author of several books on fashion brand management.[48]

Josefina Figueras has organized fashion congresses for boutique owners and workshops on fashion aimed at broader audiences. Together with a colleague, she started *Asmoda,* a monthly online magazine focused on fashion and culture, the first of its kind in Spain.[49]

Fashion Awareness Direct (FAD) is a London-based group run by María Álvarez. For twenty years its programs have helped creative young people pursue a career in fashion. Working with several fashion companies, FAD has forged a diverse community, with projects that explore British-African heritage and the nexus between education and the design industry.[50]

Enrique Concha heads EC&Co, an international interior design firm based in Santiago, Chile. He explains that he likes "to approach each project as a blank sheet of paper and to have the team use their twenty-five years of experience to obtain a creative, unique result within a reasonable budget." Asked about his call to Opus Dei, he replies: "There are two possibilities regarding this vocation in the middle of the world: either it's madness or it's true. I deeply believe, in the years that I have been here, that it is true. And, in that truth, I am immensely happy."[51]

Javier Muñoz founded Jana Productions in 2000. He has written and directed several musicals, such as *Antígona Tiene un Plan* (recipient of two national Max Awards for the Performing Arts) and *Blancanieves Boulevard*, named best Spanish musical in 2010. Muñoz wants "to make a better world through art."[52] José Gabriel López Antuñano is a professor of drama and directed the Superior School of Dramatic Arts of Castilla y León. He is currently adapting dramatic texts for staging and coordinating a master's program in theater studies.[53] The playwright Pierre Ruthes created in Curitiba (Brazil) an educational show about emotional life. It was staged in several public schools in the State of Paraná.

Talleres de Arte Granda, with its headquarters near Madrid, focuses primarily on sacred art. Sixty artisans and artists produce altarpieces, liturgical furniture, chalices, and other sacred metalwork. The company also provides restoration services. Its associated artisan workshop, Los Rosales, specializes in producing vestments and other embroidery. *Granda* has a large clientele in Europe, the United States, and Latin America. Since 2011, the Sacred Art School of Florence, run by some faithful of the Work along with others, has trained sculptors and painters interested in creating sacred art. The liturgical workshop *Guaicamacuto* in Venezuela and the workshop *Decorações e Artesanato Litúrgico*, started by Maria Laura Faria dos Santos Correia in Brazil, make and restore vestments, chalices, and other liturgical objects.

Fernando Rayón is a journalist with a long professional career. For the last twelve years, he has directed *Ars Magazine*, a prestigious art and collectors' magazine. Its contributors are academics and doctoral students from all over the world. Rayón says, "The art world is exciting. We try to make a high-quality magazine. I believe that doing things well is the best way to transmit the values of the gospel. Undoubtedly, the part of my work I'm most grateful for is the relationships and friendships with the artists. They are people of great human quality."[54]

In the audiovisual world, Ettore Bernabei (1921–2016) was general director of the RAI (*Radiotelevisione Italiana*) between 1961 and 1974. After turning seventy, he started Lux Vide, an audiovisual production company that has released media in a wide range of genres, from comedy to historical drama, including adaptations of the Bible and great literary works. The company's mission is to provide intelligent entertainment in accord with Christian anthropology. The production company is now under the direction of Ettore's son, Luca Bernabei. Another member of the Work, Armando Fumagalli, is a professor at the Catholic University of Milan. To train screenwriters and producers for film and television, Fumagalli launched a master's degree that has formed a large number of Italian and foreign professionals. He is also a consultant for Lux Vide and other audiovisual companies.[55]

Roberto Girault (Mexico) is a director, screenwriter, and producer of films such as *El Estudiante*, *Ilusiones S.A.*, and *Onyx: Kings of the Grail*. He states:

> I try to produce works that reflect gospel values. Thanks to the chisel strokes that life has given me and that I have received in Opus

Dei, I have understood that work is a means and not an end. This is very difficult to understand in my profession, where artists live for and by their work. I am thankful that my wife and children limit my time and help me to organize and prioritize. The most concrete way in which work becomes a means is when I try to see people behind every script, every film, every set or computer screen, and when I really seek to help others, to live the works of mercy in my work. When I was filming *El Estudiante* I came up with an aspiration that was: "My God, may I make something that brings glory to You and that people will like . . ." I think it has come true.[56]

Alberto Fijo studied law and directed several educational centers. When he was forty years old, as he declares,

I reoriented myself professionally. I had always had a passion for cinema, and I started working as a critic in several publications and as a professor of audiovisual narrative and film history at two universities. I wrote a dissertation on the film *The Tree of Life* and was able to talk with Terrence Malick [its director], something very unusual.

Fijo has published some twenty books on contemporary cinema, coordinating the work of a hundred specialists. In 1998, together with journalist Juan Pedro Delgado, he founded *FilaSiete*, a magazine that reviews films, series, and audiovisual culture. In *FilaSiete*, adds Fijo,

I have tried to encourage a healthy critical spirit in the editorial staff and in our readers. I try to be substantive, to contextualize, to listen and not make myself indispensable. I believe we work with rigor, kindness, and a positive sense. I would say that people clearly perceive that we work within a Christian anthropology.[57]

In 2006, the group Estrenos 21 (Madrid) created *Decine21*, a website that specializes in cinematography. José María Aresté is its director and oversees its daily reviews of films, series, premieres, and current events of the industry. *Decine21* has reviews of more than forty-two thousand films and other items. The website encourages viewers to think critically about their audiovisual entertainment and guides them in their choice of movies. Since 2014, it has held the annual Educacine Festival for students in secondary school. The festival shows feature films accompanied by moderated discussions. The goal is to awaken interest in film as something more than entertainment.[58]

On the occasion of Mother Teresa's beatification, Alfonso Nieto and Yago de la Cierva, professors of the Pontifical University of the Holy Cross (Rome), set up *Rome Reports*, a news agency that focuses on the life of the Church, especially the Pope and the Holy See. It provides brief daily TV reports in Spanish and English to more than forty television stations worldwide. It also produces documentaries and other longer pieces.[59] Juan Martín Ezratty, the promoter and director of *Digito Identida* (Buenos Aires), produces audiovisual reports and interviews. Andrés Garrigó (Madrid) of Goya Productions produces, among other things, documentaries and movies related to the history and doctrine of the Church.[60]

InterMedia Social Innovation, based in Rome and Buenos Aires, is an international study group which designs, manages, and evaluates research projects and programs in areas related to child and youth development. To bridge the space between culture and public policy, InterMedia works with several governments and universities to produce practical studies on character and affectivity formation of young people. It organizes international congresses. A spin-off of InterMedia, Interaxion Group provides an educational platform for training parents and educators on the use of information and communication technologies among adolescents. It produces publications and online courses and offers tutorials.[61]

Scott Hahn, a theologian and Protestant convert to Catholicism, is a professor at Franciscan University of Steubenville (Ohio). Author of numerous books, his best-known works are *A Father Who Keeps His Promises* and *Rome Sweet Home*. Through his expertise in Sacred Scripture and the St. Paul Center for Biblical Theology, he has helped thousands of Christians renew their faith.

Fr. Francis J. Hoffman, a priest of the Prelature, directs Relevant Radio, a Catholic radio station with a network of 168 affiliates throughout the United States. Relevant Radio covers spiritual topics such as prayer, but also offers content geared at bringing one's faith to daily life.[62] Another priest of the Prelature, Fr. James Socías, created the Midwest Theological Forum (Chicago) to publish catechetical and spiritual books. Its Didache Series, a collection of textbooks on Sacred Scripture, dogmatic and moral theology, the sacraments, and the history of the Church, have been widely distributed in high schools and parishes, especially to prepare young people for their First Communion and Confirmation.

Catholic Voices was born on the occasion of Pope Benedict XVI's visit to England in 2010. The group's organizers are Jack Valero, director of Opus Dei's UK information office, and Austen Ivereigh, a journalist who had been deputy editor of the *Tablet* and a spokesman for the Archbishop of Westminster. Catholic Voices prepares laypeople and priests to participate, in a positive way, in media discussions on controversial issues related to the Church and the Pope. The project has been established in more than twenty countries and has brought together Catholics from numerous dioceses and ecclesial entities.[63]

Notes

1. For example, in the monthly intention for July 1994, Msgr. Echevarría asked that "we know how to pray and act with generosity, initiative, and fortitude to defend the family and share with those around us (and in public opinion, according to each person's possibilities) the truth about human love, the indissolubility of marriage, respect for human life from conception, and the joy of receiving children as a gift and as a proof of God's trust." (Monthly Intention, Rome, July 1, 1994. AGP E.1.3, 1146).

2. Javier Echevarría, Letter from the Prelate, November 28, 2002, n. 11. AGP Biblioteca, P17.

3. Interview with Gustavo Entrala, March 9, 2020.

4. See *Romana* 10, no. 19 (July/December 1994), p. 368.

5. Interview with José María Vázquez García-Peñuela, June 28, 2020.

6. *https://arenalesrededucativa.es/*.

7. Interview with Alfonso Aguiló, June 21, 2020.

8. Interview with Trinidad Terriza, June 22, 2020. *https://irtysh-center.kz/.*

9. In a 2002 letter, Echevarría points out that, in more developed nations, "apart from the fact that there will always be groups of destitute people, the care of immigrants—our brothers and sisters—who leave their own countries in search of work and better living conditions is particularly important. In the same way, in less developed countries we need to work with many other people, both Catholic and non-Catholic, to develop urgently needed facilities including schools, dispensaries and health care centers, as well centers for agricultural and industrial development, etc." (Javier Echevarría, Pastoral Letter, November 11, 2002, n. 15. AGP Biblioteca, P17).

10. In this section we offer only a few examples. We thank the directors of the various organizations and foundations for allowing us to interview them.

11. *http://www.icu.it/it/.*

12. *https://www.fundacionbeatrizlondono.org/.*

13. Interview with José Ignacio González-Aller, general director of Codespa, November 20, 2020. *https://www.codespa.org/conocenos/historia/.*

14. Interview with Manuel García Bernal, Madrid, November 5, 2019.

15. *https://promocionsocial.org/.*

16. *https://www.iecd.org/.*

17. *https://onay.org/.*

18. Interview with Rafael Herraiz, November 11, 2020 (*https://ciong.org/*).

19. Interview with Daniel Turiel, November 27, 2020 (*https://actec-ong.org/*; *www.micrombaproject.com*).

20. Interview with Isabel Antúnez Cid, November 11, 2020 (*http://desarrol loyasistencia.org/*).

21. *https://www.conin.org.ar/.* A similar undertaking, ReachOut!, was started in the mid-1990s, by members of the Work and cooperators in Manchester, London, and Glasgow. They created a network of tutors to help school-age children living in underserved urban areas. *https://www.facebook.com/ ReachOut-Manchester-106508942742186/.*

22. *https://www.fesbal.org.es/.*

23. *http://www.fudigt.org/.* Similarly, since the mid-1990s, the *Dispensario del Bajo* health-care center has been serving the population living in flood-prone areas along the Paraguay River in Bañado Sur (Paraguay). It offers free outpatient services, a kindergarten, and a school cafeteria. It has signed an agreement with the School of Medicine of the Catholic University of Asunción, which

provides health-care personnel. The Laguna Grande school support center in Asunción offers help to primary and secondary school children and supports parents raising their children (*http://lagunagrande.org.py/*).

24. *https://ayni.org.bo/*.

25. *http://www.fonbec.org.ar/*. Also, in Buenos Aires we find *Impulso Social* and *Universitarios para el Desarrollo* (2002), two NGOs that carry out programs such as service trips to needy communities, educational support, visits to the sick in hospitals and "volunteers for a day" who might spend a day doing repairs in a school in a socially excluded area (*http://universitarios.org.ar/*; *http://impulsosocial.org.ar/*).

26. *https://opusdei.org/es-ar/article/ir-a-gonzalez-catan-duele/*. In Chile, a group of entrepreneurs created the Casa Básica foundation, which helps the most vulnerable families by providing basic foodstuffs and winter clothes (*https://casabasica.cl/*). In the same country, the Banigualdad Foundation (2006) provides microcredits and training to low-income people as a method of promoting social mobility; today, it has more than fifty thousand beneficiaries (*https://www.banigualdad.cl/*).

27. *http://www.hwa-tn.org/*; *https://www.amal-integration.or.at/*.

28. Interview with José Manuel Horcajo, January 25, 2021, *http://www.parroquiasanramonmadrid.com/*.

29. Interview with Javier Vidal-Quadras Trías de Bes, July 14, 2020 (*http://iffd.org/*).

30. *https://www.palabra.es/coleccion/hacer-familia-0005.html*; *https://www.hacerfamilia.com/*.

31. *http://ieee.com.es/*.

32. *https://educarpersonas.com/*.

33. Interview with Maria Munizzi and Antonio Affinita, Rome, July 15, 2020.

34. *https://www.moige.it/*. There are similar associations in other countries, such as iCmedia in Spain (*https://www.icmedianet.org/es/inicio/*). Among other undertakings for the family promoted by faithful of the Work and acquaintances, we might mention *Acción Familiar* (*https://accionfamiliar.org/*), a Spanish civil association that offers training courses, guidance, and legal support to families and care for minors, the elderly, and immigrants, as well as publishing interdisciplinary research; the association *Atout Famille* (*http://atout-famille.over-blog.com/*) in France and the Fase Foundation (*https://www.fasefundacion.org/*, *https://homemanagement. es/*) in Spain offer home management seminars on co-responsibility, the integration of work and family, and the role of young

people. The NGO Institute for Work and Family Integration in Nigeria promotes solutions that make family life and professional activities compatible. (*http://www.iwfionline.org/*). The Polish undertaking *Mama i Tata* advocates for the family in the public debate. The Alliance for the Family Foundation supports the Episcopal Conference of the Philippines (*http://alfi.org.ph/*).

35. Interview with Benigno Blanco Rodríguez, July 8, 2020. *https://www.red madre.es/*.

36. *https://emcfrontline.org/*; *https://afiguatemala.com/*; *https://www.facebook.com/StMartinsCrisisPregnancyProlifeEducationCentre/*; *https://www.schb.org.uk/*. Other undertakings include ISFEM, a Chilean organization that promotes prolife activities and teen pregnancy prevention programs (*https://isfem.cl/*). A similar network is the civil association VIFAC, which has twenty family homes and eighteen support centers in Mexico and Brownsville, Texas, and has helped more than fifty thousand women with financial difficulties in carrying a pregnancy to term. It was founded by Marilú Mariscal de Vilchis, a member of Opus Dei (*https://www.vifac.org/es*). In Germany, 1000plus provides psychological and material assistance to pregnant women with difficult pregnancies (*https://www.1000plus.net/*). In Córdoba (Argentina), the NGO *Portal de Belén* aims to promote life from conception (*https://www.facebook.com/portaldebelenonline/*). The *Universidad Libre Internacional de las Américas* was begun in 1993 in San José (Costa Rica) by several health-care professionals, some of them faithful of Opus Dei. It organizes master's and online courses on social development and the dignity of human life (*https://ulia.org/*). The *Instituto Valenciano de Fertilidad, Sexualidad y Relaciones Familiares* (IVAF), located in Valencia, Spain, sponsors research, training, and clinical assistance (*http://ivaf.org/*). In Chile, the *Programa de cuidado de la fertilidad humana* promotes the integration of sexuality and human love (*www.procef.cl*).

37. *https://www.bioeticacs.org/?dst=ibcs*.

38. *https://www.ieb-eib.org/fr/*; *http://andoc.es/*; *https://www.bioethics.ch/sgbe/*.

39. Interview with Juan Francisco Vélez, March 12, 2021.

40. Interview with Verónica Valenzuela, March 15, 2021. *https://formando corazones.org/*. The prolife site Bioedge, from Australia, provides news on ethical issues related to euthanasia, abortion, and surrogacy (*https://www.bioedge.org/*). Also in Australia, Women's Forum Australia is a think tank that supports research, education, and public policy development on social, economic, health, and cultural issues affecting women. (*https://www.womensforumaustralia.org/*).

41. *https://winst.org/*.

42. *https://www.socialtrendsinstitute.org/*.

43. *http://thomasmoreinstitute.org.uk/*.

44. *https://www.lindenthal-institut.de/start.html*.

45. Interview with Salvador Bernal, November 25, 2020. *https://www.ace prensa.com/*.

46. *https://www.firstlife.de/*.

47. Interview with Lula Kiah, March 6, 2020. See *https://styleinnovators.com/*.

48. Interview with Elisa Álvarez Espejo y Paloma Díaz Soloaga, December 7, 2020.

49. Interview with Josefina Figueras, November 15, 2020. *https://asmoda.com/ home*. Other fashion websites set up by faithful of Opus Dei include, for example, *modaemodi* (Italia, 2004) and *notorious-mag* (Austria, 2012): *http://www. imore.it/rivista/; https://www.notorious-mag.com/*.

50. *https://www.fad.org.uk/*.

51. Interview with Enrique Concha, March 19, 2021.

52. Interview with Javier Muñoz, July 4, 2020.

53. Interview with José Gabriel López Antuñano, December 15, 2020.

54. *https://arsmagazine.com/*. Interview with Fernando Rayón, December 3, 2020.

55. *https://www.luxvide.it/en/; https://international.unicatt.it/ucscinternational-graduate-programs-master-in-international-screenwriting-and-production*.

56. Interview with Roberto Girault, March 13, 2020.

57. Interview with Alberto Fijo, November 24, 2020. *https://filasiete.com/*.

58. *https://decine21.com/; https://festivaleducacine.es/*. The Institute for Media and Entertainment specializes in training entrepreneurs in the media and entertainment industry. It began in 2004 in New York and three years later became a research center of IESE at its New York headquarters. *https://www.iese.edu/es/ claustro-investigacion/centros-investigacion/ime-institute-media-entertainment/*.

59. *https://www.romereports.com/*.

60. *https://www.goyaproducciones.com/; http://www.digitoidentidad.com/home/*.

61. *https://www.interaxiongroup.org/*.

62. *https://relevantradio.com/*.

63. *https://www.catholicvoices.org.uk/*.

EPILOGUE

On the Road
to the Hundredth Anniversary

As we have seen, the forty-seven years of the Work's founding period were followed by another forty-one years in which Opus Dei was led by two men who had worked closely with the Founder for many years and had been trained by him to head it. In this sense, the foundation and the immediate post-foundation period formed a single unit which closed with the death of Javier Echevarría on December 12, 2016. A new phase opened with new leaders who could not claim close, prolonged contact with the Founder. They would have to guide Opus Dei in a time of dramatic social, political, economic, and technological change in the world and of difficulties and hopes in the Church.

On January 23, 2017, the congress members and electors of Opus Dei chose Fernando Ocáriz as father and pastor in the Work. That same day, Pope Francis named him Prelate. Afterwards, with the approval of the congress, Msgr. Ocáriz appointed the members of the central government including Mariano Fazio, vicar general (who, in May 2019, became auxiliary vicar); Antoni Pujals, vicar central secretary (vicar general in May 2019); and Isabel Sanchez, central secretary.

The new Prelate summarized the conclusions of the General Congress in a pastoral letter published on opusdei.org. He began by stressing the centrality of Jesus Christ in the life of the Christian:

> What are the priorities that the Lord presents to us in this historical moment of the world, of the Church and of the Work? The answer is clear: in the first place, to take care of our union with God with the delicacy of lovers, starting from the contemplation of Jesus

Christ, the face of the Father's mercy. St. Josemaría's program will always be valid: 'May you seek Christ. May you find Christ. May you love Christ.' (*The Way*, n. 382).[1]

In the following years, Ocáriz wrote three other lengthy pastoral letters. Two touched on core themes of Christian life in the light of St. Josemaría's teachings: the gift of personal freedom (January 9, 2018), and the value of friendship, manifested in caring for others (November 1, 2019). The third reflects on the Christian vocation and its concrete manifestations in the different personal circumstances of the faithful of Opus Dei (October 28, 2020).[2]

The Prelate uses the phrase "dynamic fidelity" to refer to the development of the foundational charism of Opus Dei in the Church. He sees deepening the inheritance received as a source of creative impulse for the present task: "Fidelity to the Christian faith, which is fidelity to Jesus Christ, has always been dynamic, innovative and transformative." Given the great evolution of the Church and of society since the end of the foundational stage, he points out that "discernment is essential, above all to distinguish what is accidental from what is essential." "As St. Josemaría expressly affirmed: the ways of saying and doing things change, while the nucleus, the spirit, remains untouchable."[3]

Msgr. Ocáriz has stressed that Opus Dei is not about buildings but about people, especially its ninety-three thousand faithful and one hundred seventy-five thousand cooperators. These men and women live in Europe (57 percent Latin America (34 percent and the rest of the world (9 percent). Spain stands out with 43 percent of the total. As a reality that participates in the mission of the Church, Opus Dei seeks to spread Christian life both in the places where it has been working for decades and in Eastern Europe, the Arab world, India, and China, where it is still taking its first steps.

Within the Church, the Prelature of Opus Dei strives to be a serene and constructive presence. It maintains close relations with the Pope, the diocesan bishops, and the principal institutions of the Church. Both as an institution and through its individual members,

Opus Dei has tried to respond generously to Pope Francis's call to care for the most vulnerable and those living on the existential peripheries. The faithful of the Prelature and the members of the Priestly Society strive to give Christian witness in the particular churches to which they belong as well as in civil society. The 2018 beatification of a woman of the Work, Guadalupe Ortiz de Landázuri, has shown that the ideal of holiness is a goal to which ordinary people can aspire. According to Pope Francis,

> we are often tempted to think that holiness is reserved only for those who have the possibility of separating themselves from ordinary occupations, to devote much time to prayer. This is not so. We are all called to be saints by living with love and offering our witness in our daily occupations, wherever we find ourselves.[4]

Opus Dei's living message of secular holiness finds a response in the new generations of students and young people beginning their careers today. Whether single or married, many of them take up, as a personal mission, the challenge of being consistent Christians. In accordance with the teachings of St. Josemaría, they understand that incarnating the gospel and spreading it in the world of work, law, science, politics, culture, fashion, art, communications, and so on. is an adventure worth staking one's life on. This task requires freshness of approach rooted in the founding spirit and each person's innovative and creative capacity. Within the institution, young men and women are joining the central and regional governing bodies and taking on the tasks of spiritual direction and coordination in the local councils. They look to the Founder's message and the events of the past to discern the responses demanded by the present.

The people of the Work, of course, face many challenges: conveying a rational and permanent message in a context marked by relativism and volatility; evangelizing by "attraction" in a society immersed in digital technology; appreciating the modern world in a positive way and as a suitable space for the unfolding of Christian life; creating united and joyful family homes; transmitting the faith to their children; strengthening the Christian identity and professionalism of Opus Dei's apostolic activities; adapting corporate structures to the availability of personnel; and generally adapting to the circumstances of the times—including the coronavirus pandemic which accelerated contemporary social transformations and required creative responses to continue to provide formation and personal support in the midst of government lockdowns.

We would like to be able to say how many lay men and women and secular priests have been inspired by Opus Dei's message of sanctity in the world to seek holiness, to love God as Father, and to try to identify themselves with Christ through work and the other circumstances of their daily life. Although the answer to that numerical question lies hidden in the depths of individuals' hearts, it is clear that despite their limits and vulnerabilities, the members of the Work have brought their own dynamism to the social and ecclesial environments in which they live. Opus Dei as an institution, its individual members, and the many people inspired by its spirit are signs of the vitality of the Church—even in an increasingly secularized world.

Notes

1. Fernando Ocáriz, Pastoral Letter, February 14, 2017, n. 30. AGP Biblioteca, P17.

2. The full text of all of Ocáriz's pastoral letters, as well as of his shorter messages to the members of Opus Dei, can be found at www.opusdei.org.

3. Interview with Fernando Ocáriz, *Palabra* 649 (March, 2017), p.11.

4. Pope Francis, Apostolic Exhortation on the Call to Holiness in Today's World *Gaudete et Exsultate* (March 19, 2018), n. 14. *Vatican website: www.vatican.va.*

INDEX

This index does not contain entries for Josemaría Escrivá de Balaguer Albás, Álvaro Del Portillo y Diez de Sollano, or Javier Echevarría Rodríguez because of the frequency with which they appear.

Lightning Source UK Ltd.
Milton Keynes UK
UKHW021001221222
414275UK00009B/130